CHALLENGES OF THE MUSLIM WORLD: PRESENT, FUTURE AND PAST

International Symposia in Economic Theory and Econometrics

Series Editor: ***William A. Barnett***

Volume 14: *Economic Complexity*
Edited by W.A. Barnett, C. Deissenberg & G. Feichtinger

Volume 15: *Modelling Our Future: Population Ageing, Social Security and Taxation*
Edited by Ann Harding & Anil Gupta

Volume 16: *Modelling Our Future: Population Ageing, Health and Aged Care*
Edited by Anil Gupta & Ann Harding

Volume 17: *Topics in Analytical Political Economy*
Edited by Melvin Hinich & William A. Barnett

Volume 18: *Functional Structure Inference*
Edited by William A. Barnett & Apostolos Serletis

International Symposia in Economic Theory and Econometrics Volume 19

CHALLENGES OF THE MUSLIM WORLD: PRESENT, FUTURE AND PAST

William W. Cooper

The Red McCombs School of Business and
The IC^2 Institute in The University of Texas at Austin, USA

and

Piyu Yue

The IC^2 Institute in The University of Texas at Austin, USA

ELSEVIER

Amsterdam – Boston – Heidelberg – London – New York – Oxford – Paris –
San Diego – San Francisco – Singapore – Sydney – Tokyo

Elsevier
Radarweg 29, PO Box 211, 1000 AE Amsterdam, The Netherlands
Linacre House, Jordan Hill, Oxford OX2 8DP, UK

First edition 2008

Library of Congress Cataloging-in-Publication Data
A catalog record for this book is available from the Library of Congress

British Library Cataloguing in Publication Data
A catalogue record for this book is available from the British Library

ISBN: 978-0-444-53243-5
ISSN: 1571-0386

For information on all Elsevier publications visit our website at books.elsevier.com

Printed and bound in The Netherlands

08 09 10 11 12   10 9 8 7 6 5 4 3 2 1

Dedication

This book is one in the series of books produced by the IC2 Institute of the University of Texas at Austin.

It is dedicated to the late George Kozmetsky who inspired it and to his wife, Ronya, who supported it.

Introduction to the Series

The series *International Symposia in Economic Theory and Econometrics* publishes quality proceedings of conferences and symposia, collections of articles on a particular topic, and research monographs of high professional quality. Since all articles and books published in these volumes are refereed relative to the standards of the best journals, not all papers presented at the selected symposia are published in these proceedings volumes. Collections of papers and monographs on a topic must meet the same professional standards as the proceedings volumes included in the series and are refereed to the same high peer review standards. The topics chosen for these volumes are those of particular research importance at the time of the selection of the topic. Each volume has different co-editors, chosen to have expertise relevant to the focus of the volume.

Contents

Acknowledgments

We are grateful to the IC2 Institute for its support of the research underlying this book. Helpful comments were received from Robert Hardgrave in the Government Department of The University of Texas at Austin, Carl Woodring former chairman of the English Department in Columbia University and Leon Cooper, writer, inventor and retired president of Home Safeguard Industries. We are grateful William A. Barnett, Oswald Distinguished Professor of Macroeconomics in the Department of Economics at the University of Kansas who helped bring this book into existence and to Professor Mehmet Dalkir at the University of New Brunswick in Fredericton, Canada, for helping us on some of the subtleties and deeper aspects of Muslim life and religion.

Reader comments, corrections and criticisms are all welcome and will be appreciated. They may be directed to either author.

W.W. Cooper
The Red McCombs School of Business,
University of Texas at Austin
E-mail: cooperw@mail.utexase.edu

and

Piyu Yue
The IC2 Institute,
University of Texas at Austin
E-mail: piyuyue@sbcglobal.net

Austin, Texas, USA
November 2006

Preface

Introduction

This book deals with the 49 Muslim majority countries — their present, future and past. This order of development is intended to facilitate a first focus on topics of great current interest and importance. Hence the historical background, which is necessary to a full understanding, is presented in the last part, Part III, of this book. Part I deals with the oil and natural gas production and consumption of the Muslim world, and what can be expected in the future from the projections we use. Part II deals with demographic transitions that go far to explain what is happening and what is to be expected in the way of a turbulent world, now and in the future, as the demographic developments we describe in this part of the book continue into the future. Part III deals with the history of the Muslim countries, starting with the inception of Islam, continuing through the "golden age" and terminating with colonization of these Muslim countries by western countries in the 19th and early 20th centuries. The final chapter goes on to the current state of affairs including some of the radical Islamic thinking that is guiding the activities of organizations like al Qaeda. We leave other topics aside, such as the economic performances and social institutions of these Muslim countries, and reserve them for treatment in another book at a later date.

Part I: Consumption, Production and Location of Oil and Natural Gas

Part I of this book consists of three chapters that deal with oil and natural gas consumption, production and distribution. All of these topics are treated in a data dependent manner. That is, we try to let the "facts speak for themselves", which they do very forcefully, we think, in the tables and graphs we provide. We also accompany these tables and charts with verbal explanations and interpretations to help facilitate understanding, with readers free to draw their own conclusions, where and when they wish. Finally we also summarize what will be said, and what has been said, both in an introductory section at the beginning of each chapter, and in a concluding section at the end.

Chapter 1, in Part I of this book, deals with the demands for oil and natural gas after, first, briefly portraying the now dominant place of these two fuels in both the history and present state of energy uses as well as their present and future developments, as shown by the data and accompanying extrapolations. The situation in oil is one of the transitions during the periods covered. For instance, the US has remained at the top in terms of oil consumption over the period 1960–2006, as is portrayed in Figure 1.7 (Chapter 1, Figure 1.7). This figure also portrays a dramatic increase in demand for oil from the emerging economies (China, India, South Korea) that is about to displace the US, in 2006, and this projected growth will continue to put upward pressures on world oil prices. Turning to the supply side, the US has declined from producing 33.5% of world crude oil and, as shown in Table 2.1 (Chapter 2, Table 2.1), it has been replaced by Saudi Arabia, followed by the USA, Russia and Iran in terms of their respective production totals.

For perspective we start with Figure 1.1, in Chapter 1, which portrays world energy uses (oil, natural gas, coal, etc.) which has increased from 207 quadrillion Btu in 1970 to more than triple that amount, 645 quadrillion Btu, in 2025. The portrayal in Figure 1.2 shows that oil has been and will continue to be largest single source of primary energy fuel. However, the use of natural gas has nearly tripled in the last 30 years (1970–2000) from 36 to 95 quadrillion Btus and is now on a par with coal, with each projected to be 20%–25% of total world energy consumption by 2025.

The supply side is much more concentrated than is the case for demand. Tables 2.1 and 2.2 shows some 13 Muslim nations producing nearly 39% of oil output at 31 million barrels/day (Mb/day), with Saudi Arabia, the top producer, at 10 Mb/day in 2003 — which is nearly 13% of world oil output.

As graphed in Figure 2.3 the oil output of the Muslim countries fell dramatically, from a level of 42% to a level of 30% of world oil output between 1980–1985. This drop was due to the instability associated with the Iran–Iraq war. The Muslim countries subsequently recovered to their original 42% share by 2003 — but with part of this recovery due to the outputs from the six former Soviet Muslim nations, with Kazakhstan in the lead at better than 1 Mb/day in 2003 and Iran, but not Iraq, back to its prewar levels of production.

The situation for natural gas is dramatically different from oil. Here Russia, USA, Canada and UK are the top 4 producers in 2003, as shown in Table 2.2. These four countries are followed by Algeria and Iran as the two top producers for the Muslim countries.

World oil production began to shift into the Persian Gulf region with Saudi Arabia becoming the leading world producer of oil after discovery of the Al Ghawar field in 1948. Saudi Arabia now has about 80 oil and gas fields and over 1000 flowing wells that have been pumping out high grade crude oil at an average rate in excess of 9 Mb/day during the last 20 years. Saudi Arabia has also been the top oil exporter to the US, Japan, OECD Europe and other countries, too. Therefore, starting with Saudi Arabia, the location of these Middle East fields is exhibited in a series of maps and pinpointed by the discussions that accompany each map. These maps portray the location of the fields in each country. The next chapter, however, turns to the strategic location of Muslim countries on nearly all of the leading world oil transportation routes.

Chapter 3 portrays the net export and net import of oil by individual countries. This is followed by a series of maps which portray the strategic importance of

Muslim country locations. Examples are the Suez Canal, which is controlled by Egypt at one end of the Mediterranean, and by Morocco, which lies along the southern part of the Strait of Gibraltar at the other end. Similarly with the Strait of Bab Al Mandab, which lies at the other end of the Red Sea from Suez in between Yemen on the North and the Muslim countries of Djibouti and Eritrea on the south. Also to be considered is the Strait of Hormuz which lies between Iran and the United Arab Emirates at the entrance to the Persian Gulf. These and other "choke points" of world commerce are all totally or partially controlled by Muslim countries, including Indonesia's and Malaysia's location on the Strait of Malacca. Thus, these three chapters, which make up Part I of this book, cover the strategic importance of the Muslim countries in both the production and transportation of oil.

Part II: Demographic Changes and Social Instability

In Part II of this book we develop demographic features that help to explain present problems and foretell future prospects for relations between Muslim countries and the rest of the world. The first part, consisting of Chapters 4, 5 and 6, deals with population quantities such as size and demographic transitions in terms of age groups, etc., that are in process. Chapter 7 then deals with what can be termed population quality (intellectual quality) as measured by illiteracy rates and present and future education facilities and opportunities.

An example of the demographic changes that have occurred, and will occur, and their importance, is provided by the following quote from the Introduction to Part II: "Christians accounted for 30% of the total world population in 1980 while Muslims accounted for 16.5% (for a nearly 2 to 1 ratio). These percentages increased to 33% for Christians and 22% for Muslims in 2002. However, it is forecasted that by 2025 the percentage of Christians will probably reduce to 25% while Muslims increase to 30%. This means that in the next 20 years Islam will probably become the largest (i.e., most populous) religion in the world".

It is again to be noted that we deal only with the 49 countries that have a Muslim majority. For these 49 countries Figure 4.1 in Chapter 4 starts with a population of 384 million persons in 1950 compared to a current world total of 2.519 billion and projects to a total of 2.606 billion Muslims in 2050 compared to a world total of 8.919 billion. This is in contrast to countries like China and the US where China declines from 22% to 15.6% and the US declines from 6.3% to 4.6% of the world population over this same period (Figure 4.3).

For the 100 year period 1950–2050, as the graphs in Figure 4.4 show, the most rapid increase in Muslim population share will occur in sub-Sahara Africa with declines occurring in central and Southern Asia while the Middle East & North Africa proportions hold flat at 24%–25% of the total Muslim population.

Table 4.2 shows this by individual nations, with Pakistan going from 39.659 million in 1950 to 348.7 million in 2050. In the process, Pakistan will surpass Indonesia which has long been the most populous Muslim country. This is of special interest, as we shall find in Part III of this book, because Pakistan is the site of some of the most radical and violent forms of Muslim fundamentalism. Thus this kind of change is likely to be accompanied by world turbulence and serious social problems.

These broad aggregations of total population do not reveal some of the other, even more extreme, changes that are occurring. For this we turn to some of the demographic transitions. Starting at 15.2% of world population in 1950, the share of the 49 Muslim majority countries will increase to 29.2% in 2025, as shown in Figure 4.3. Both the world and the Muslim countries now have declining rates of growth, but the annual average growth rate of the Muslim countries exceeds the world rate of growth by a considerable margin, whereas this is not true for the western countries. See Figure 4.2.

Increases in world population, especially in western countries, have been accompanied by improved medical and health (e.g., sanitation) practices whereas in the Muslim world the population increase is due to high birth rates. The increases and decreases in life expectancy that result make the western countries a population of elders and the Muslim countries a population of younger people.

Of special interest is the cohort of male youngsters of ages 15 to 29. We have named this the "troublesome cohort" because of a long record of the involvement of this cohort in social turbulences. The troubles in the US in the 1960s and 1970s, for example, coincide with peaks in the proportion of the population in this cohort. The same is true for the Tian An Men square uprising in China in 1989. A process of relative social calm in both countries followed as the proportion of the population in this cohort declined. See Figure 5.9.

In this respect it is of interest to note from Figure 5.7 that this cohort is estimated to account for 15%–15.5% of the total population in the Middle East and North Africa countries for the period 2000–2010 and to peak in 2006. This cohort is a source of militants and "jihadists", which suggests a potential for social change and instability and other troubles, too. See the current peak of 17.6% for this cohort that is portrayed for Iran in Figure 5.10(A). Trouble is also likely to be brewing in the future from the Muslim countries of Sub-Sahara Africa where the overall proportion of these young Muslim males is expected to increase significantly in the next five decades. See Figure 5.8.

Chapter 6 discusses the rapid urbanization that Muslim countries are experiencing. This high rate of urbanization is likely to exacerbate the problems associated with social instability because Muslim young males migrate to cities where stagnant economies offer meager prospects for employment and lead to associated problems of crime and violence that also make for ease in recruiting militants.

Chapter 7 turns to population "qualities", as measured by illiteracy and educational opportunities. Illiteracy rates are falling in many Muslim countries, but the levels of female illiteracy reductions lag the reductions in male illiteracy, with a consequent widening of the gap — and both are far above the world averages. This lagging female illiteracy has serious implications for the future because females are generally in charge of educating the young in the very critical early years of life. For the importance of female illiteracy in Muslim countries and the difficulty of dealing with it, see the quotation in the first part of Chapter 7 from the insightful book, *What Went Wrong*, by Bernard Lewis.

Chapter 7 also deals with educational opportunities and problems in Muslim countries. With Muslim countries soon to be in charge of educating 1 in 3 of world children, it is hard to overemphasize the importance of this problem. The prospects are disquieting because the educational opportunities are badly wanting. In many Muslim countries the resources are inadequate. Even in those countries where this is not the case, the orientation is toward a religious education at the expense of the topics that are required to prepare students for careers in the modern world. In addition this religious teaching is often directed toward hatred or scorn for "infidels" — i.e., persons of different religions and beliefs, and even different Muslim sects and locations.

How did this all come about? That is the subject of Part III of this book which deals with historical developments from the 7th century start of Islam, with the teachings of Muhammad, and continues through the "Golden Age" when Muslim countries were in the vanguard of civilization and ended with colonization of most of the Muslim nations by Western countries in the 19th and early 20th century. See Table 9.1. This all enters into current attitudes and reactions from the Muslim world that are now affecting, and will continue to have effects elsewhere in the world.

Part III: History and the Contemporary Scene

Part III of this book presents a history starting with the birth of Muhammad (571–632) and the 3 Caliphates following his death. It next treats the "Golden Age" stretching for 400 years, from the mid 9th to the mid 13th century. We also treat the 9 crusades originating under Pope Urban II in the 11th century and lasting into the 13th and 14th century.

According to the *New Columbia Encyclopedia* the "Black Death", brought back by the crusaders in 1370, killed almost three fourth of the population of Europe in less than 20 years. The following cessation of crusading activities leads to a discussion of the Ottoman Empire, which began in the 14th century and lasted into the early part of the 20th century. We finally turn to the period of colonization of most of the Muslim countries by European powers during the 19th and early 20th century. We then provide an epilogue that suggests some ways of dealing with some of the problems we have described, such as an expanding Muslim population and its attendant consequences.

Chapter 8 describes the birth of Islam when Muhammad began to preach at age 40 after which he took over most of the Arabian Peninsula in 630 after a series of small regional battles with Mecca. Muhammad did not designate a successor when he died in 632. This led to a succession of 3 Caliphs, who were chosen by "consensus" and considered to be the leader of all Muslims. The 4th Caliph was Ali ibn Abi Talib, Muhammad's cousin and husband of his daughter Fatima. Starting in 656 this route of succession lasted in the form of a line of Imams until the 12th Imam.

This chapter then describes the split between the Shi'ites and the Sunnis. The former believe that Ali should have been the first Caliph. The latter (i.e., the Sunnis) reject this belief. They believe, instead, that the Caliph should be consensually selected. Although originally political in nature, this rift became the basis of theological differences and has led to many subsidiary sects.

Ali was assassinated in 661 C.E. (Common Era) after which his opponent Muawiyah declared himself Caliph, moved the capital to Damascus and established a Sunni dynasty. This lasted until it was overthrown in 750 after which the unity of the Arab world was terminated.

The Abbasid family took over the Caliphate as another Sunni dynasty in 786 C.E. This was the beginning of the "Golden Age of Islam" which evolved into a Muslim empire that extended from Spain and Moscow in the west to India in the east. Under the Abbasids this became a hybrid culture with elements of Arab, Latin, Greek and Jewish societies.

For 400 years, from the mid 9th to the mid 13th century, Islamic culture became preeminent in all of the fields of science, technology, theology, and literature. Highly innovative it replaced the Roman numeral system with the Hindu–Arabic system of decimals and introduced the concept of "zero". Europe, on the other hand, was still in its "dark ages" and was regarded as barbarian and lacking in culture in every way.

In 1258, the Mogul, Hulaga Khan, sacked Baghdad after which the Abbasid Caliph moved to Cairo where the dynasty finally disappeared. The Islamic empire then declined and scientific and technological progress came to a halt as the Golden Age of Islam reached its end.

Other topics treated in Chapter 8 include the Ottoman Empire and its defeat at Vienna followed by its withdrawal to the Balkans, after the treaty of Carlowitz in 1699, where this empire lasted until the termination of this empire after World War I in the early part of the 20th century. Also discussed are the nine crusades starting in the 11th and lasting through the 13th century. These were then succeeded by minor crusades in the 14th century that took place not only in Palestine but also in Spain and central Europe. Not confined to crusades against Muslims they also took the form of crusades against Christian "heretics" and "enemies" of the papacy that included the devastation of Constantinople in 1204.

Chapter 9 describes the expansion of Europe, starting in the 17th century and continuing into the period of colonization of Muslim countries in the 19th and early 20th century. See Table 9.1 of Section 9.2 in this chapter. It also describes the discovery of oil in Iran by Britain as a byproduct of attempts to eliminate piracy in the Persian Gulf. This discovery of oil in 1911 had little effect on activities in the region until after World War II. In the meantime, a US firm, Standard Oil of California (SOCAL), made discoveries in Bahrain in 1932 and in Saudi Arabia, 1938. Synoptic descriptions, country by country, then follow in this book along with descriptions of the often furious opposition to the following colonization.

This colonization led to cultural adaptations that took the form of distinctions between "modernization" and "westernization". This distinction made possible Muslim adoption of western technologies as distinguished from adoptions of western customs. It also led to fundamental responses such as the formation of the Muslim Brotherhood in 1928 and other organizations which rallied around statements like "God has not forsaken Muslims. Rather Muslims have forsaken God".

What is wanted by many of these creeds are Muslim states and, ultimately, a Caliphate that rules the entire world in the Muslim traditions. At present there are only two theological states: Iran and Saudi Arabia. Similar efforts in other states have, instead, witnessed one military dictatorship after another or endless civil wars like in Pakistan, Sudan and Algeria while Islamic fundamentalist movements envelop various loosely connected semi-secret "brotherhoods", which are dealt with in Chapter 10.

The Contemporary Scene and Its Challenges

Chapter 10 deals with the post-colonial and contemporary scenes and challenges. This has been a period of constant confrontation and conflict, much of it religiously motivated and rooted in the history we described in the preceding chapters. There have also been numerous conflicts between Muslim countries, with many of them motivated by access to oil and other sources of wealth.

We start with the conflict with Israel, which is near the center of Muslim land that includes 22 Muslim majority nations in the Middle East and North Africa. Except for Iran these countries belong to the Arab world and, in addition, three states in Sub-Sahara Africa (Somalia, Sudan and Mauritania) also belong to the Arab world. These locations have been a source of almost constant conflict.

We also cover the 8-year conflict between Iraq and Iran and the related revolution that led to the present theocratic state in Iran. The Iraq invasion of Kuwait that led to the first "GulfWar", in the form of "Operation Desert Storm" is also covered. We then go on to the 2 wars between Pakistan and India that led to the formation of Bangladesh as an independent Muslim state. Finally we come to the "War on Terrorism" that occupies the rest of this chapter.

Starting with the anti-Soviet "Jihad" in Afghanistan in 1979 (in which the US CIA invested about 2.1 billion US dollars and also supplied weapons and training) and then go on to subsequent developments.

This coverage includes al-Qaeda and its leader, Osama bin-Laden, whose terrorist activities led to the US invasion of Afghanistan with continuing military and other activities such as seizing or "freezing" financial and other assets that could be used to support terrorist activities.

Next we turn to some of ideologies that are used to motivate these activities. We start with "Wahhabism". This influential Islamic sect is based on the teaching of Muhammad ibn abd al-Wahhab, who believed that every idea added to Islam after the third century of the Muslim era (about 950 AD) was false and must be expunged. Adopted by the Saudi tribe these ideologies led the Saudi leader to believe that it was his duty to wage holy war to spread this doctrine and this took the form of a series of efforts that established the Saudi empire in 1811. This empire included all of the Arabian Peninsula except Yemen. Defeat by an Ottoman (Turkish) expedition from Egypt in 1818 led to a series of "ups and downs" until Ibn Saud who, with British support, established the modern state of Saudi Arabia.

Along with Iran, Saudi Arabia constitutes one of two Muslim nations with Islamic fundamentalism in power. Wahhabi advocacy of political activities in Saudi Arabia is directed "to cleanse the state". An accompanying endorsement of violent action exerts far reaching influence by holding that all non-Muslim elements must be eliminated. This has greatly influenced bin-Laden who has elevated extension of political activities to a global jihad with an emphasis on the United States. However, as noted by Haneef Oliver, in the source that we cite, bin-Laden subsequently dismissed Wahhabism and became a Qutbist.

Sayyid Qutb (1906–1966), the founder of Qutbism, was a leading fundamentalist and one of the key movers in the Egyptian "Muslim Brotherhood" movement that has spread throughout the Muslim world. Qutb was involved in an attempt to assassinate the Egyptian leader, Gamal Abdel Nasser, was charged with treason and hanged.

One of the core elements of Qutbism is that a secular government legislating behavior is illegitimate. It should therefore be eliminated in favor of an Islamic state ruled by Shariah law. Muhammad Qutb, the brother of Sayyid Qutb, moved from Egypt to Saudi Arabia where he became a professor of Islamic studies. One of his students, and an ardent follower, is Ayman al-Zawahiri who is second in command in al-Qaeda and the mentor of Osama bin-Laden.

Another highly influential person in the development of this line of belief was the Pakistani, Sayyid Mawdudi (1903–1979). His goal was to wage jihad until the whole natural universe is brought under the rule of Islam. The Qutbism from Egypt and the international terrorism led by bin-Laden have found ideological roots in Mawdudi's Islamism and jihad. This is all reflected in the current war on terrorism in Iraq which is directed to defeating the "Bush doctrine". The latter doctrine has the goal of establishing a free democratic society in Iraq as well as Afghanistan which we also discuss in this chapter.

Epilogue

The beliefs we have just described are very widely shared and very deeply felt in the Muslim world. They give direction to very powerful underlying forces that are now at work. These forces include the population increases which, as we noted, are now en route to making Islam the most populous religion in the world. This increase is accompanied by shifts in population composition that favor what we have referred to as the "troublesome cohort", consisting of the 15–29 year old males that constitutes a source for the supply of terrorists. Accentuating this tendency is the fact that these younger arrivals are confronted with the need for finding places in generally stagnant economies. These societies are also undergoing rapid urbanization, for which this cohort (and others in these Muslim societies) are ill prepared.

What is to be done in response to these developments? Military means alone are not up to the task. Under the "Bush doctrine", President Bush is seeking to democratize these societies, both in Iraq and Afghanistan, and he hopes that this will be accomplished by military activities and is thus reminiscent of the recent experience of these Muslim countries with colonization by Western powers.

One might suppose that the relatively recent history of colonization by these Muslim countries will militate against all attempts at change and modernization. The emerging economies of China, India and South Korea serve as shining counter examples. Malaysia, a Muslim country — see Table 9.1 — can also serve as a counter example. It is rapidly becoming a high tech economy with skyscrapers (including the tallest skyscraper in Asia). It is also modernizing in other ways that include building a high speed rail system that is equal to or better than others that have built elsewhere in the world.

Remark. Malaysia also shows its "forward looking" perspective even in the unusual manner of displaying its plans for the future, such as the building of a high speed rail system, on the recently issued Ringgit (the Malaysian unit of currency), which is part of a plan to make Malaysia a fully developed modern country by 2020. (This is in contrast to most currencies which display only historical figures and historical events.)

Other, non-military, approaches to deal with these, and potential future problems, should be possible. One such possibility could take the form of grants and contributions from non-governmental sources and hence are capable of avoiding suspicions of ulterior political motives. Such making of these kinds of grants has been followed in Malaysia and Thailand where substantial grants to institutions of higher learning have been welcomed with positive effects.

We would recommend that such grants and contributions not be confined to universities and like institutions of higher learning. Directing them to elementary education could have the advantage of dealing with the high illiteracy rates that we describe in this book. Ideally such grants could serve to deal with female as well as male illiteracy and thus help to break the vicious cycle associated with the fact that it is the females who are in charge of the early years of childhood education.

We believe that such efforts should be concentrated in one, or at most a few, Muslim countries, at least initially. A good choice would be Pakistan which, as described in Part II of this book, is slated to become the most populous Muslim country in the world by 2050. Pakistan has a deficient education system that focuses on religious training and neglects the subjects that are needed to prepare students for modern industrial (and citizen responsibility) careers. Furthermore, the Pakistani school systems, such as the Madrasa, have a long and well accepted tradition of private (nongovernmental) support and direction. We believe that this course of action by the western world would be welcomed by the present government, which has tried, but without success, to change and modernize the education system. This lack of success is partly because the schools in Pakistan are largely independent and privately financed. What we have in mind are "example schools" that could "show the way" and thereby help to accomplish what government edicts and like efforts have failed to accomplish in preparing young students to help in modernizing the country. See the conclusion to Part II of this book.

This recommendation is only one of the possible routes that might be followed to help redirect and modernize directions for the massive forces represented by the population changes that we have described. Other ideas and alternative approaches will also be needed. The present situation of jihads, if left unattended, is reminiscent of medieval Europe, when a rapidly increasing population led to the crusades that were initiated by a society under the domination of the Catholic Church in all aspects of living. See "Crusades" in the new *Columbia Encyclopedia* (Columbia University Press, 1975). This situation was pretty well terminated after the crusaders brought back the bubonic plague that killed some 75% of the European population. See "Plague" in the new *Columbia Encyclopedia*. New ideas and new approaches are needed to diminish the prospect of such crusading responses to the forces such as population increases and shifts, urbanization, stagnant economies and illiteracy, and ideologies such as "Qutbism" and "Mawdudism" that are presently providing guidance to the massive processes that are now at work in these Muslim countries.

Recommendations like the one we suggested above are directed toward dealing with the forces operating in the long-run, but which have already helped to bring current situations into being. They do not deal with the immediate present, such as the crisis in Iraq. For this case we suggest that a relatively easy and orderly withdrawal of US troops could occur if the Iraqi government asked the US government to withdraw them. To help bring this about, our enunciated policy needs to be changed to the following: "We will stay (1) until the job is done or (2) until the duly elected government asks us to leave. Taking the second rather than the first option would help to strengthen the Iraqi government by showing that it can be accomplish what violence and destructive activities on the part of the "insurgents" have been unable to do.

It is possible that the Iraqi government would be reluctant to ask the US to take the second of these two courses of action because of fear that this would result in a cessation of US economic aid. However a suitably phrased request for the US to leave could help to reduce this possibility. For instance the Iraqi government could first negotiate terms of withdrawal that would include conditions for continuing such aid for a specified period of time. This would make it possible for the US to threaten to withdraw the aid if continuation of insurgent activities began to offer a prospect of success. Needless to say, such economic aid in suitable amounts could also strengthen the Iraqi government and help to bring about the prosperous and free democracy that the present US administration has envisioned. This course of action could also demonstrate that our original intention was being carried out: to establish a fully functioning democracy in Iraq in place of the previously oppressive dictatorship. Finally, it could help to get the job done during the present administration — which was their original objective.

List of Tables

List of Figures

List of Maps

Unless otherwise noted, the maps in this book are in the public domain as taken from the collection maintained by the University of Texas Libraries: http://www.lib.utexas.edu/maps/fag.html#3.html.

Part I

Consumption, Production and Location of Oil and Natural Gas

Introduction

In the 20th century the world economy has been driven by an abundant supply of oil-based energy. Decades of cheap oil supported the growth of heavily energy-dependent industries in the developed world. This western modernization has raised living standards for nearly 903 million people (about 14.9% of world population[1]), but it has depended upon an abundant and reliable supplies of cheap fuel that comes from oil and natural gas, about 30%–40% of which are produced in Muslim countries.

Starting in the 1980s, a wave of oil-dependent modernization has swept through China and India, with more than 2.278 billion people (about 37.6% of world population[2]) trying to industrialize their economies and develop a modern life style. At present, the top 5%–10% of Chinese and Indians have begun to enjoy the western life style, such as living in single-family houses in suburbs, driving private cars, taking vacations on beautiful beaches in foreign lands, and using the Internet and mobile phones as well as a variety of novel electronic gadgets. These emerging rich classes are also found in transitional economies in Eastern Europe, Russia and South America. All together they may add an additional 100–200 million people to the 900-million population pool of high-income countries which depend on oil-based energy. Thus, economies around the globe — maturely industrialized economies or newly industrialized and emerging market economies — all rely upon the Muslim world for supplying abundant oil and natural gas as their main sources of energy.

Part I of this book provides a synoptic portrayal of how and why the world has come to depend on Muslim countries for their energy and how the Muslim world has been linked with the West through global oil markets. In this part of the book we examine major players in global oil markets in terms of consumption, production, reserves and international trade as well as in terms of the control of oil flows around the globe. It will be seen that Muslim countries have played a crucial role and will continue to do so in every aspect of the global oil and natural gas markets. Hence, it needs to be understood that Muslim countries must be incorporated into the world economic system with accompanying respect and benefits.

This, Part I of the book, includes three chapters: Chapter 1 discusses world energy use and the demand side of global markets for oil and natural gas. Chapter 2

---

[1] In 2000 the total population of high-income countries — or the high income group of countries that we refer to in later discussion — was 902.854 million, accounting for 14.9% of the world population of 6057.261 million.

[2] In 2000 China's population was 1.2625 billion and India's population was 1.0159 billion.

analyzes the supply side of oil and natural gas markets, including oil and natural gas production and reserves, and demonstrates the critical role played by Muslim countries in the global economic arena. Chapter 3 further illustrates world dependency on the Muslim world through international trade in oil and natural gas, as well as the strategic geography of the Muslim world which enables them to control flows of energy into countries around the globe.

Chapter 1

World Demand for Oil and Natural Gas

This chapter will provide an analysis of the demand side of global oil markets. It will examine (1) why oil and natural gas have become the most important energy source for the entire world, (2) how demand for oil and natural gas expanded over the last four decades, (3) which groups of countries have been major driving forces in oil consumption, and (4) how locations of the demand side of global oil markets have shifted over time.

This chapter contains three sections. In Section 1.1 we examine technology changes and the industrial revolutions, along with their usage of different energy sources, that have transformed economies and societies. This evolution continues into the present situation of heavy dependency on fossil fuel,[1] particularly oil and natural gas. In Section 1.2 we describe the changing energy consumption patterns by classifying them into three groups that have characterized the economy of the world over the last fifty years. These changing oil consumption patterns are displayed by major regions and countries in Section 1.3.

This and the next chapter, which deals with energy supply, will then serve as underpinning for understanding why the Muslim world has become so important to the entire world.

1.1. Industrial Revolutions Change Energy Consumption

Human life on earth is driven by the use of energy. The most important of the earliest human innovations were the use of fire[2] and the exploitation of animal power, which made possible the early beginnings of human civilization.

For hundreds of thousands of years, human beings used dry grass and wood to make fire until the development of charcoal which improved the efficiency of energy use and made a substantial contribution to metallurgy and to the emerging metal tools and weapons production that allowed human beings to survive through hostile environmental changes and into higher stages of human development.

---

[1] Coal, Oil and Gas are called "fossil fuels" because they have been formed from the fossilized remains of prehistoric plants and animals.

[2] Fire was used in northern China more than 400 000 years ago, and there is evidence suggesting that it may have been used long before that. (Gowlett, John A., *Mental Abilities of Early Man: A Look at Some Hard Evidence*, in: R. Foley (Ed.), *Hominid Evolution and Community Ecology*, London: Academic Press, pp. 167–192.)

International Symposia in Economic Theory and Econometrics, Vol. 19
William W. Cooper and Piyu Yue

ISSN: 1571-0386/DOI: 10.1016/S1571-0386(07)00010-5

A few millennia later the English found that coal could provide a fuel that burned cleaner and hotter than charcoal and so coal has been used to heat living space in England since the Norman Conquest.[3] The development of coke and its suitability for steelmaking helped to initiate the First Industrial Revolution in the late 18th and early 19th century. A steam engine invented by James Watt was fueled by coal and was one of the main drivers of major technological, socioeconomic and cultural changes. Economies in Britain and continental Europe were transformed from manual-labor based technologies to ones that used new textile machinery and new iron and steel factories, in which coal was burned to make the steam that drove the machinery. The First Industrial Revolution made coal a valuable commodity that was sometimes referred to as black gold.

Starting in the 1830s, the Second Industrial Revolution was marked by railroad construction.[4] Railroads lowered transportation costs, brought new products and areas into commercial markets and also made possible a rapid expansion of export sectors. Constructing and maintaining substantial railroad systems also led to development of modern coal, iron, steel and engineering industries. Expanding sectors during this age included cotton textiles, heavy-industry complexes based on railroads, and industries for military end-products as well as a wide variety of consumer goods. Coal and coke were the primary sources of energy to power these industries for economic growth.

The Third Industrial Revolution started with breakthroughs in the internal combustion engine, electricity, and modern chemicals around the turn of the 20th century. A spectrum of new industries was created with technological inventions and innovations, including automobiles, chemicals, petroleum, rubber, aeronautics and space industries. The mass-produced automobiles of the 1920s led to their widespread use and a vast internal migration into newly constructed single-family houses in suburbs that also created mass markets for household appliances and consumer durables.[5] Economic and social life of advanced industrial countries have been changed by gasoline fueled automobiles, expanding highways and mushrooming suburbs, commercial fertilizers and pesticides, farming implements of tractors and trailers, as well as new food processes and storage abilities, clothing and appliances.

Manufacturing, construction, transportation, agriculture, water distribution, modern medicine, and high-tech industries, as well as national defense and related industries are powered mainly by oil-based energy and supplied by chemicals derived from petroleum. Over the years, engineers developed a variety of new and

[3] The Norman Conquest was the conquest of the Kingdom of England by William the Conqueror (Duke of Normandy) in 1066 and the subsequent Norman control of England.
[4] W.W. Rostow, *Theorists of Economic Growth from David Hume to the Present*, Oxford University Press, 1990, pp. 456.
[5] George Kozmetsky and Piyu Yue, *The Economic Transformation of the United States, 1950–2000*, Purdue University Press, 2005, pp. 55.

more efficient fuels for industrial, commercial and household usage, such as liquefied petroleum gas, aviation jet fuel, gasoline, kerosene, diesel engine and other road vehicle fuels, as well as gas oil and fuel oil, which are used in boilers — all of which are derived from crude oil and natural gas. Hence crude oil is both a valuable commodity and a strategic resource that constitutes the lifeblood of modern industries and civilizations.

1.2. Energy Consumption by Nation Groups and Energy Types

In this section we provide two graphs with total consumption (or use) on the left vertical axis and percentage of world energy use on the right vertical axis to show that (1) energy consumption worldwide has increased rapidly and much of the future growth in energy use is expected to occur in emerging economies like China and India, and (2) oil and natural gas has been and will continue to be the most important source of world energy consumption.

Figure 1.1 exhibits the total energy consumption and its distribution over three groups of economies: mature market economies, transitional economies and emerging economies. This tri-partite grouping of world countries was recently introduced by International Energy Outlook (2005), a publication of the Energy Information Administration (EIA).[6] Figure 1.2, displays world energy consumption by energy types, including oil, natural gas, coal, renewable energy and nuclear energy.

The group of mature market economies consists of the following countries: (1) North America (the United States, Canada, and Mexico), (2) Western Europe, (3) Japan, (4) Australia and New Zealand. The transitional economies include nations that are transitioning away from the centrally planned economies such as in the Soviet Union to free market economies. This group includes Eastern Europe (EE), and the former Soviet Union (FSU), and is identical to the previous group EE/FSU. Excluding the first and second groups, the rest of the world belongs to the third group of emerging economies, which used to be called the developing world. It includes some countries with currently less developed economies but expected to grow rapidly over the next two decades. These countries have fairly energy-intensive industrial sectors and are projected to develop energy use patterns resembling those of the first group of countries in their industrializing age.

[6] The Energy Information Administration (EIA) was created by Congress in 1977 as a statistical agency of the US Department of Energy. International Energy Outlook 2005 has changed its country groupings of the previous three — Industrialized, EE/FSU (Eastern Europe and the Former Soviet Union), and Developing. It now uses the following three new groupings — Mature market economies, Transitional economies, and Emerging economies — to allow for the fact that some countries such as China, India and South Korea could today be fairly called "industrialized".

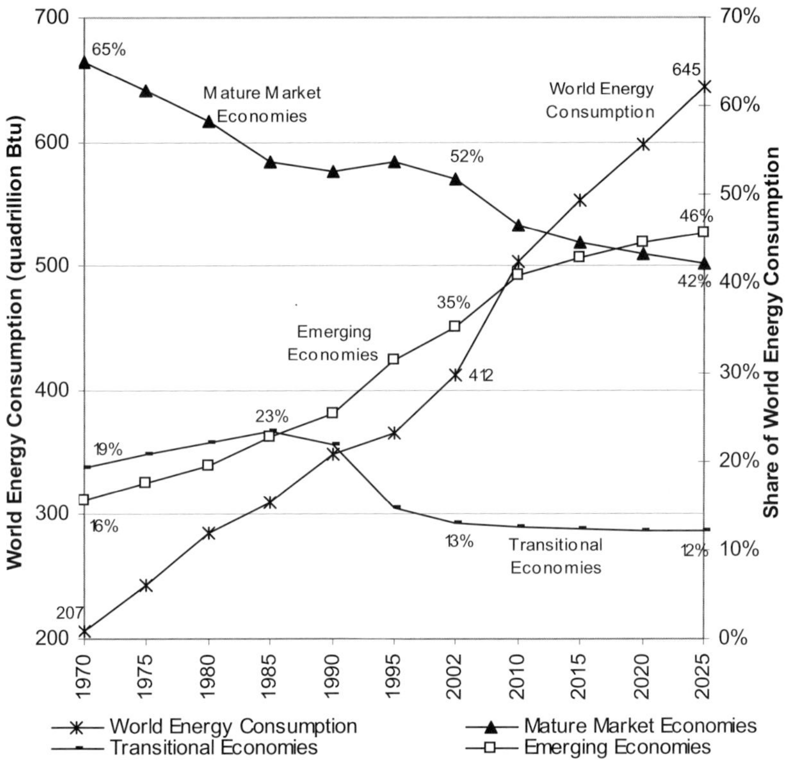

Figure 1.1: World Energy Consumption by Economies (1970–2025).

China, India, countries in the Middle East, Africa and Central and South America are all included in this group of emerging economies. Thus, all Muslim-majority countries, except for six former Soviet republics in Central Asia (which belong to the EE/FSU group), are categorized in the group of emerging economies.

The curve of total world energy consumption in Figure 1.1 displays a rapid increase in worldwide energy use. This use rose from 207 quadrillion Btus[7] in 1970 to 412 quadrillion Btus in 2002 and is projected to be 645 quadrillion Btus in 2025, as represented on the vertical axis on the left of Figure 1.1. Energy consumption shares of the three groups have changed over time and exhibited different patterns, which are shown in terms of percentage of world consumption on the right vertical axis (energy consumption quantities of the three groups do not appear in Figure 1.1).

[7] Btu means British thermal unit and is defined as the quantity of heat needed to raise the temperature of 1 pound of water by 1 °F at or near a temperature of 39.2 °F.

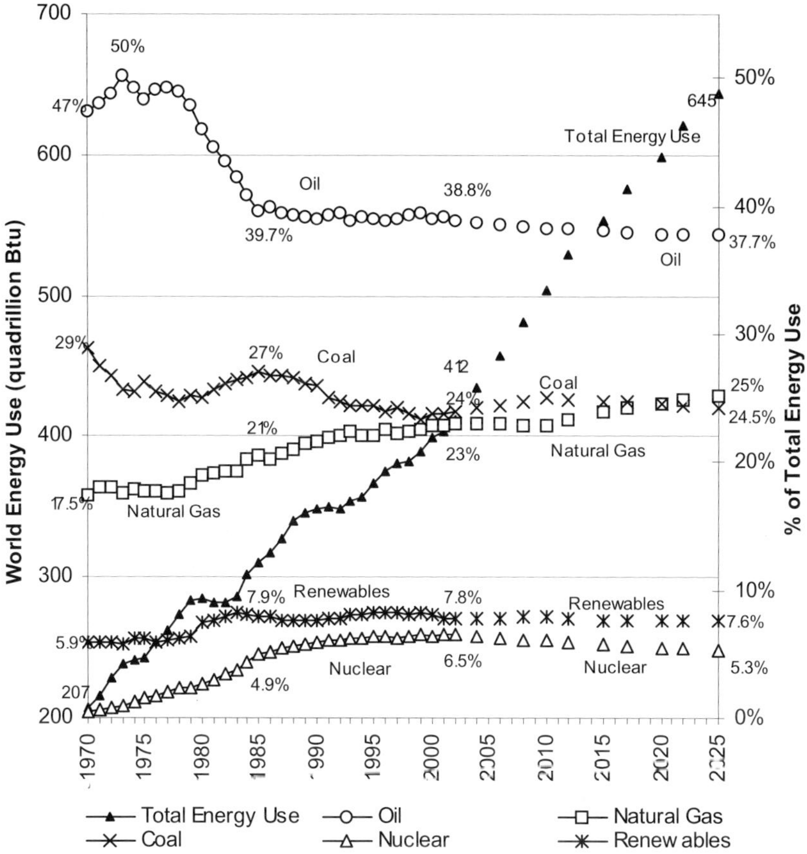

Figure 1.2: World Energy Use by Energy Type (1970–2025).

Many mature market economics have been transformed from energy-intensive industries to knowledge-intensive service industries. In addition their rate of economic growth has reduced to below 4% per year since the first oil crisis in 1973. Thus the growth of energy consumption in this mature-market-economy group has slowed substantially and this has led to the continuous decline in its share of energy consumption that is exhibited by the curve starting on the left at the top of Figure 1.1.

In 1970 energy use of mature market economies was about 135 quadrillion Btus and accounted for 65% of total world energy use. In 2002, it increased to 214 quadrillion Btus, but accounted for only 52% of worldwide energy use because world energy use increased much faster than in the group of countries with mature market economies. The forecast of energy use for this group is about 272 quadrillion Btus by 2025 and results in a decline to the 42% of total world energy consumption that is represented by its intersection with the vertical axis on the right. This result reflects an expectation of continuous structural changes in general production and consumption of mature market economies as well as lower rates of economic growth in the next two decades.[8]

Energy consumption of transitional economies rose from 39.7 quadrillion Btus (about 16% of total energy use worldwide) in 1970 to 72.7 quadrillion Btus (23%) in 1985. In the 1990s most transitional countries suffered from political, economic, and social turbulence. This resulted in drastic declines in economic performance. For instance, Russia's GDP declined by 20% in the single year of 1992, and its inflation rate reached 900% in 1993. Russia's currency, the ruble, was devalued by more than 90%, from $4.5 per ruble in 1991 to $0.041 per ruble in 1998. Russia's population was also reduced by 3 million persons in ten years from 148 million in 1990 to 145 million in 2000, and it is projected to continue declining, reaching 125 million by 2025. These economic and social factors are reflected in changing patterns of energy consumption for the transitional economies. The energy use of this group was reduced by nearly 30%, from 76.2 quadrillion Btus in 1990 to 54 quadrillion Btus in 2002, and its energy share declined from 23% in 1985 to 13% in 2002. The future energy consumption for this transitional-economy group is projected to be about 77.7 quadrillion Btus (or 12% of total world use) by 2025.

The group of emerging economies is a complex of countries at various stages of economic development. The total population of this group was approximately 4.6 billion in 2000 and accounted for 76% of world population. China and India, as members of this group, both experienced phenomenal economic growth in the last two decades. According to statistical data from the World Bank,[9] China's real GDP growth rate was on average 9.5% per year during 1978–2000. A double-digit growth rate followed: 1984 (15%), 1985 (12%), 1992 (14%), 1993 (13.5%), 1994 (12.8%) and 1995 (10%). India's GDP grew on average at 5.8% per year during 1985–2000. Muslim countries in this group like Malaysia and Indonesia also showed tremendous economic growth in the last three decades, which we will discuss in Part III of this book.

As was true for western countries in their industrializing age, rapid economic growth in these emerging economies drives a high demand for energy use. As Figure 1.1 shows, emerging economies dramatically increased their energy consumption over the period 1970–2002 and the projection in Figure 1.1 points to continuation of this increased energy consumption over the next two decades. Total energy use of emerging economies accounted for only 16% of world energy use in 1970 (about 32.5 quadrillion Btus). The consumption share of emerg-

[8] See George Kozmetsky and Piyu Yue, *The Economic Transformation of the United States, 1950–2000*, Purdue University Press, 2005.

[9] "*The World Development Indicators*" database of the World Bank, 2003.

ing economies rose to 35% and consumption quantity increased fourfold to 144 quadrillion Btus by 2002. Forecasted rates of higher economic growth in emerging economies lead to a large projected increase in their future demands for energy. Thus, it is projected that the energy consumption of this group will be 266.6 quadrillion Btus by 2020, exceeding the 258.7 quadrillion Btus of mature market economies. As shown in Figure 1.1, the energy use gap between the former and the latter groups is expected to become even wider, with 271.8 quadrillion Btus (42% of the total energy use worldwide) for mature market economies versus 295.1 quadrillion Btus (46%) for emerging economies.

To compare world consumption of oil and natural gas with other types of energy sources, we used the latest available data[10] to calculate the energy use by energy type as a percentage of total world energy consumption. Figure 1.2 presents the results of these estimates for 1970–2002 and of projections up to 2025.

The curve of total energy use in Figure 1.2 is the same as the curve for world energy consumption in Figure 1.1. World consumption of all energy sources increased from 207 quadrillion Btus in 1970 to 411 quadrillion Btus in 2002, and it is projected to increase to 644 quadrillion Btus in 2025. World energy consumption increased by 2.2% per year on average from 1970 to 2002 and is projected to grow by 2.0% per year, on average, from 2003 to 2025.

As Figure 1.2 shows, oil has been and will continue to be the single largest primary energy fuel used in the world with its share increasing from 47% in 1970 to the all time high of 50%, right before the first oil crisis in 1973, and then falling back to 39.7% in 1985. This drop in oil consumption was caused by the first and second oil crises that we will discuss in Chapter 2, and in Part III of this book. Since 1985, the oil share of total energy consumption has stabilized around 38.5% and is projected to be 37.7% by 2025. Hence, oil will remain the largest type of fuel used worldwide for the next twenty years.

As Figure 1.2 shows, other components of world primary energy use, such as natural gas, coal, nuclear energy and renewable energy (hydroelectricity, wind, solar, geothermal, and biomass energy), have used much smaller shares and none of them will be able to replace oil as the largest component in the worldwide energy consumption mix in the next twenty years.

The amount of world consumption of natural gas almost tripled in the last thirty years. It rose from 36 quadrillion Btus in 1970 to 95 quadrillion Btus in 2002. The natural gas percentage share of world energy use increased from 17.5% in 1970 to 23% in 2002, and is projected to reach 25% by 2025. This increasing share of natural gas indicates faster growing demand for natural gas than for any other form of energy. The International Energy Agency[11] has projected that demand for

---

[10] International Energy Outlook, 2005, Energy Information Administration, the US Department of Energy, July 2005.

[11] International Energy Agency (IEA) is an intergovernmental body committed to advancing the security of energy supply, economic growth and environmental sustainability

natural gas will grow at an annual rate of 2.4%, which is faster than that of any of the other primary fuels such as oil, coal, hydro or nuclear energy.[12] Natural gas is regarded as a desirable fuel for the electricity generation industry because it burns more cleanly than either oil or coal and thus is more attractive for reducing greenhouse gas emissions. Natural gas consumption worldwide is projected to increase by 76% from 95 quadrillion Btus in 2002 to 167 quadrillion Btus in 2025, and is expected to replace coal as the second largest component of world energy use by 2020 (see the right-hand side of Figure 1.2).

The combined share of oil and natural gas consumption has not changed much over the last three decades, falling from 64.5% in 1970 to 61.8% in 2002, and is expected to reach 62.7% in 2025. The combined share of oil, natural gas and coal was 93.5% in 1970 and 85.8% in 2002, and is projected to be 87% by 2025. This means that the entire world has depended on fossil fuel and will continue to do so in the next two decades. It therefore seems unrealistic to think about finding easy solutions to reduce this heavy dependency on oil and natural gas, e.g., by using market mechanisms such as price increases to stimulate energy conservation and substitution. To take over from oil and natural gas as the major source of energy use, such an alternative energy source would have to be cheap and abundant, and the technology to exploit it would have to be capable of being utilized all over the world. In the rather short time of several decades, it is unlikely that any known energy source is likely to meet these requirements.

Coal is the most plentiful fuel in the fossil family and, as described in the previous Section 1.1, it has the longest history. The energy generated by coal has been the second largest next to that of oil, and accounted for 29% of world energy use in 1970 and 24% in 2002. Coal's share is projected to be 24.3% by 2025, but coal's position as second in world energy use will, as previously noted, be taken over by natural gas around 2020.

Coal is the most abundant fossil fuel on earth, but it is far from a perfect fuel. Impurities like sulfur and nitrogen trapped inside coal are released into the air when it burns. These substances can combine with water vapor in clouds and form droplets that fall to earth as "acid rain". The smoke that comes out of a coal smokestack contains millions of tiny particles in the form of minerals and ash that become major sources of air pollution.

Coal, like all fossil fuels, is formed from carbon. When coal burns, its carbon combines with oxygen in the air and forms carbon dioxide, which is one of several gases that can trap the earth's heat. This causes the earth's temperature to rise and

through energy policy cooperation. It was founded during the oil crisis of 1973–1974 and now works as an energy policy advisor for its 26 member countries on broader energy issues, including climate change policies, market reform, energy technology collaboration and outreach to the rest of the world.

[12] World Energy Outlook 2002, OECD/IEA, 2002.

generates what is called the "greenhouse effect" and thereby contributes to climate changes. In the last two decades, scientists and engineers have been working on "clean coal technologies" that promise to filter out 99% of the particles and to remove more than 95% of the acid rain pollutants in coal. But the cost is very high.[13] In the next several decades, coal is therefore unlikely to take over from oil and natural gas as a top component in the world energy mix.

Renewable energy sources include several types such as biomass, hydropower, solar, wind and geothermal energy. The energy use share of all the renewable sources accounted for only 7.8% of total energy use worldwide in 2002 and it is expected to reach 7.6% by 2025. Thus, none of renewable energy sources so far discovered is able to provide more than 10% of world demand for energy use. For example, biomass is an important source of energy in many countries of the world. But all the world wood fires and grain alcohol added to gasoline and agricultural wastes cannot produce large enough quantities of energy for industrial usage. Biomass conversion has little growth potential, and it also competes for fertile land with food crops and timber. Hydropower potential may be much larger than biomass, but it is not sufficient to take over from oil and natural gas, and huge dams would submerge rich agricultural soils and create environmental hazards — as was the case for the Egyptian experience with the Aswan Dam that is described in Chapter 3.

The potential of solar, wind, waves, tides, ocean thermal energy conversion, and geothermal sources is also limited and unable to produce the quantity needed for present and future worldwide energy uses. Solar thermal collection devices are only operational when it is hot and sunny, and these devices are too expansive and too inefficient to supplant the energy available from oil and natural gas.

The production of electricity from nuclear fission has been increasing. Although it increased dramatically from 0.44% in 1970 (see Figure 1.2), nuclear sources supplied only about 6.5% of the total world energy use in 2002. Fission reactors could produce a great deal more energy if fast-breeder reactor[14] (FBR) technologies were used. It is generally agreed, however, that the FBR poses a greater risk of proliferation of nuclear weapons than other types of nuclear reactors. This is true because FBRs can produce weapons grade nuclear material and

---

[13] Since the mid-1980s, as estimated by the Office of Fossil Energy, the US Department of Energy, the US Government has invested more than $2 billion in developing and testing clean coal technology processes in power plants and factories around the country. Private companies and State governments have contributed more than $4 billion to these projects with results that are not very impressive compared to the need.

[14] The fast breeder reactor (FBR) is a type of fast neutron reactor that produces more fissile material than it consumes. It relies on fast neutrons to sustain its chain reaction and requires high-grade fuel. But once this has been provided for the initial startup the reactor produces its own fuel and a surplus that can then be used to start other FBRs, hence acting as a breeder.

there is considerable political pressure to prevent nuclear weapons proliferation as well as increasing public concerns about nuclear wastes from nuclear power stations. Hence public confidence in all types of reactors is low, and the cost of their construction is high. This leads to low expectations for future use of nuclear energy. As Figure 1.2 shows, the energy share from use of nuclear energy is projected to be only 5.3% by 2025.

An alluring long term potential to replace fossil fuel might result from the use of so-called "controlled thermonuclear fusion". In a process of nuclear fusion — the nuclei of lighter elements such as hydrogen are fused together at extremely high temperatures and pressures to form heavier elements such as helium — enormous amounts of energy are released. This is the energy source of stars in the sky, including the sun. In response scientists have been working for the last four decades to develop practical methods for fusion reactions with the hope of realizing this potential source of energy. However, this has proved to be a difficult, long-term challenge. Current research is still experimental and oriented to demonstrating the scientific and technological feasibility of fusion energy. The technology for its commercialization has not been developed so it is unrealistic to hope that the world's energy problems and the world's dependency on fossil fuel could be resolved in the next several decades by development of commercially available "controlled thermonuclear fusion" energy sources.

We can conclude that no single energy source is ready to replace fossil fuels, particularly oil and natural gas. Energy conservation and a combination of alternative energy sources may help a little but will not resolve world energy dependency problems. Oil and natural gas have been and will continue to be the largest energy source which is sufficiently abundant and available to human beings now and in the next twenty five years. Thus, demand for oil and natural gas will be the focus of our analyses in the following two sections.

More than 40% of world oil is produced in Muslim countries. These Muslim countries are also major exporters of oil and natural gas to the rest of the world. To sustain economic growth and social prosperity created by mature market economies in the 20th century and to continue the present growth trend initiated in the last two decades for emerging economies, the world greatly needs the oil and natural gas produced in Muslim countries and exported around the globe. On the other hand, the wealth generated from oil and natural gas for Muslim nations depends on the demand side of global markets. To view global oil markets from the demand side we will provide, in the next section, an analysis of the world demand for oil and natural gas by using historical data from 1960 through 2004 and short-term forecasts up to 2006.[15]

[15] These data are published in International Petroleum Information database and in International Energy Outlook 2005 by the US Energy Information Administration (EIA) of the US Department of Energy.

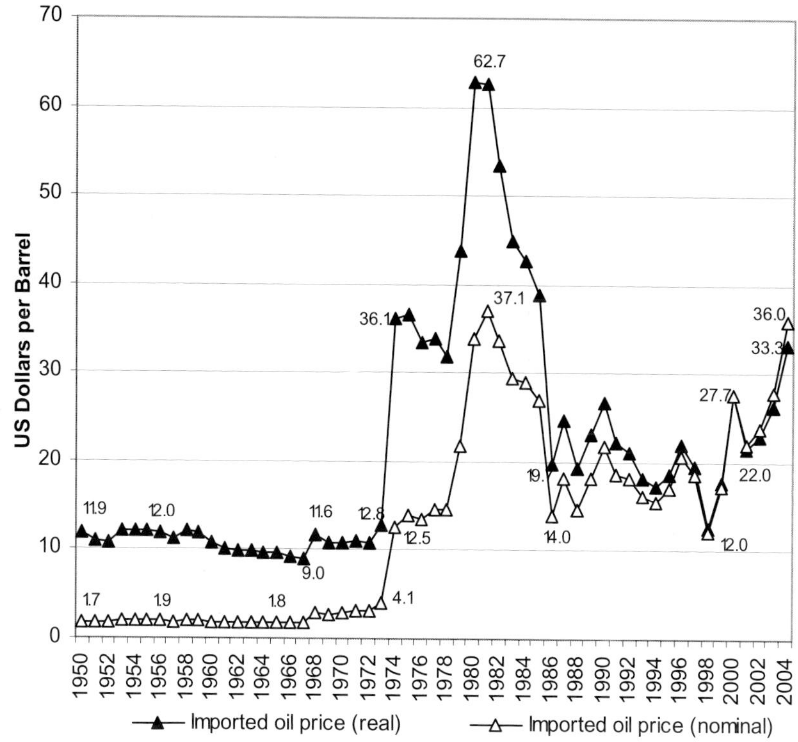

Figure 1.3: World Crude Oil Price (1968–2004).

1.3. World Demand for Oil and Natural Gas

World demand for oil and natural gas is generally driven by economic growth and social development across the globe, but geo-political struggles in the Muslim world have significantly affected demand for oil and natural gas with effects on oil prices in global markets and through manipulations from the supply side. Thus, demand, supply and oil prices and political turmoil and other considerations are all closely connected in global markets.

The world oil price exhibited in Figure 1.3 is defined as the US refinery acquisition cost of imported crude oil[16] and, as shown at the bottom of this figure, is represented with two measures: nominal and real. The nominal price is the current price of oil or the value of one barrel of oil measured by the current US dollar. The

---

[16] The oil price of 1968–2004 in Figure 2.3 is the cost of US refiner acquisition of imported crude oil in that time period, and the oil price of 1950–1967 is the price of Arabian Light posted at the Port of Ras Tanura where a Saudi Aramco terminal is located.

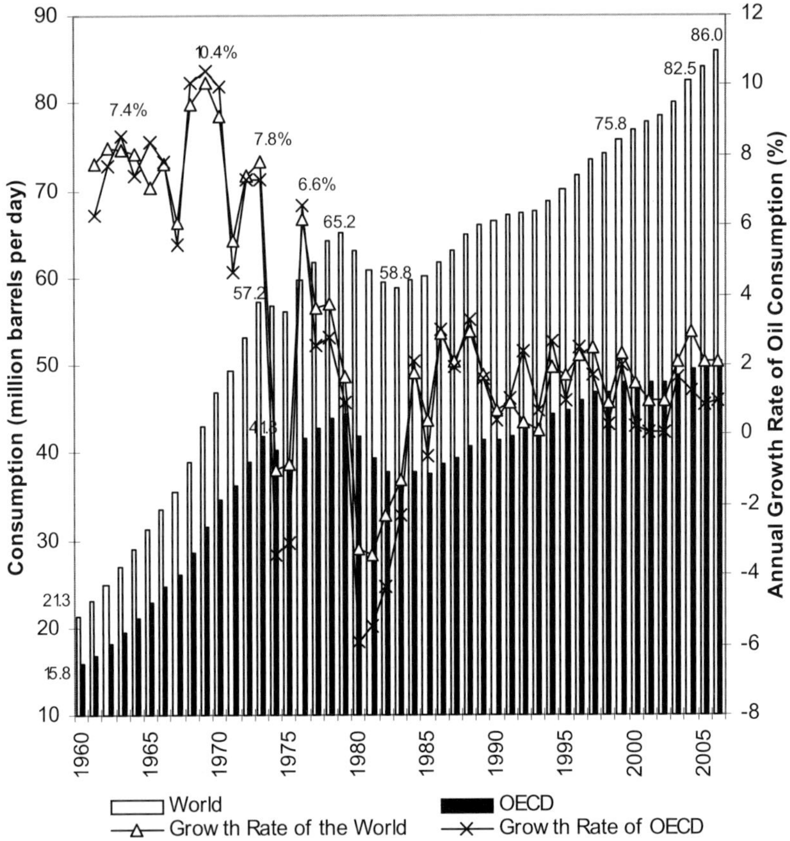

Figure 1.4: World Consumption of Oil (1960–2006).

real price is the value of one barrel of oil measured by the constant US dollar of a given year, here the year 2000 in Figure 1.3, and is calculated by using GDP implicit price deflaters. Thus the effect on oil prices of different inflation rates over time and the time value of money has been taken into account in real oil prices. This allows us to make comparisons of oil prices in different years. Figure 1.4 displays oil consumption both worldwide and by OECD countries.

Figures 1.3 and 1.4 suggest a close link between world oil prices and oil consumption and, in general, a negative correlation between oil prices and the growth rate of oil consumption as predicted by economic theory. This negative relation would be shown by the corresponding curves that move in opposite directions. For instance, Figure 1.3 shows a marked increase in oil prices during the 1970s while Figure 1.4 shows a notable decrease in the growth rate of oil demand during that period. In the early 1980s, however, the oil price decreased substantially while the

Table 1.1: GDP Growth Rate of Countries during the Oil Crises

Year	GDP Growth Rate (% per year)								
	USA	Canada	Japan	UK	Germany	France	Italy	South Korea	China
1965	5.60	NA	5.82	2.79	NA	4.78	3.27	5.19	16.36
1969	2.67	5.26	12.48	2.05	NA	6.99	6.10	14.10	10.14
1973	5.90	7.16	8.03	7.31	4.77	5.44	6.55	12.34	7.98
1974	**−0.56**	4.09	**−1.23**	**−1.68**	0.19	3.11	5.27	7.39	2.69
1975	**−0.34**	2.25	3.09	**−0.68**	**−1.25**	**−0.28**	**−2.05**	6.53	6.94
1979	3.21	4.16	5.48	2.75	4.22	3.31	5.53	7.06	7.28
1980	**−0.24**	1.34	2.82	**−2.18**	0.98	1.61	3.48	**−2.09**	5.96
1981	2.45	3.11	2.85	**−1.27**	0.49	1.22	0.78	6.47	5.75
1982	**−2.10**	**−3.04**	3.14	1.80	**−0.55**	2.63	0.63	7.25	9.57
1983	4.33	2.90	2.27	3.75	2.05	1.49	1.24	10.70	10.85
1985	3.81	5.41	4.36	3.78	2.35	1.45	2.97	6.47	12.59
1990	1.74	0.24	5.33	0.66	3.23	2.61	1.97	8.98	3.98
1991	**−0.50**	**−1.91**	3.11	**−1.47**	2.84	0.99	1.39	9.23	9.19
1992	3.06	0.91	0.93	0.07	2.24	1.49	0.76	5.44	14.27
1993	2.67	2.30	0.42	2.33	**−1.09**	**−0.89**	**−0.88**	5.49	13.54
1997	4.48	4.39	1.80	3.51	1.39	1.90	2.03	5.01	8.84
1998	4.40	3.30	**−1.10**	2.64	2.05	3.40	1.81	**−6.69**	7.80
1999	4.26	4.59	0.76	2.29	1.56	2.92	1.61	10.89	7.05
2000	4.20	4.50	2.40	3.07	2.95	3.10	2.91	8.81	7.94

oil demand also declined from 65.2 million barrels per day in 1979 to 58.8 million barrels per day in 1983. This is unusual and would not be so in competitive markets. However, it needs to be remembered that this price change was controlled by the OPEC countries so the marked decrease in oil prices in the early 1980s resulted in the decrease, partly in response to OPEC rather than the increase in oil consumption that would be expected within competitive markets (see also the discussion of the Yom Kippur War in Section 2.1.2 of the next chapter).

Table 1.1 displays real GDP growth rate for the G7[17] nations and two emerging-economy countries — South Korea and China — in selected years from 1965 to 2000. G7 nations represent a group of mature market economies and China and South Korea represent a group of emerging economies. These nine countries are all large consumers in world oil markets.

In the following discussion Figures 1.3 and 1.4 and Table 1.1 will be referenced to each other in order to identify sources and consequences of changes in oil prices and worldwide oil demand. Impacts of oil-price changes on these economies are illustrated by changes in the growth rates of GDP in Table 1.1.

[17] G7 is a group of the world's leading powers — United States, Canada, Great Britain, France, Germany, Italy and Japan — that meets regularly to discuss common policy issues.

As shown by the bar charts in Figure 1.4, world consumption of oil was 21.3 mb/day[18] in 1960, rose to 57.2 mb/day in 1973, fell and then rebounded to 65.2 mb/day in 1979. Since 1985 it has continuously increased, reaching 82.5 mb/day in 2004 and is projected to be 86 mb/day by 2006. In the same manner as world consumption, the oil consumption by OECD rose from 15.8 mb/day in 1960 to 41.8 mb/day in 1973, reached 49.5 mb/day in 2004, and is projected to be 50.4 mb/day by 2006.

Now we turn to why oil prices changed so dramatically in the 1970s and 1980s. As Figure 1.3 shows, nominal oil price was only $1.7 per barrel in 1950 and $4.1 per barrel in 1973, while the corresponding real oil price was only slightly above $10 before 1974. In 1950–1973 both nominal and real oil prices were at their lowest levels in the last 50 years. This stimulated oil usage in rebuilding Europe and Japan after the World War II, and fueled economic expansion in North America, Western Europe, and Eastern Asia. As Figure 1.4 shows, world oil consumption rose from 21.34 mb/day in 1960 to 57.24 mb/day in 1973, and oil used by OECD[19] countries increased from 15.78 to 41.8 mb/day in the same time period. Growth rates of both oil consumptions were 8.5% per year on average in the 1960s, and exceeded 10% in 1968, 1969 and 1970. The economic growth of the G7 nations in Table 1.1 also shows high positive rates in 1965, 1969 and 1973.

In 1974 world oil price (nominal) jumped threefold — from $4.1 to $12.5 per barrel. This was caused by OPEC's oil embargo, and is referred to as the "first oil crisis". This embargo was trigged by a war by Egypt and Syria against Israel in 1973, which we will discuss in Chapter 2 and in Part III of this book. After 1973, nominal oil prices stayed around $13 per barrel for four more years and then jumped to $37.1 per barrel by 1981 and remained well above $20 per barrel until 1986. This large increase in world oil price was caused by a revolution taking place in a large oil-producing country, Iran, and it was also intensified and prolonged by a war between two large oil-producing countries, Iran and Iraq (see Part III of this book). This surge of world oil prices depressed oil demand in OECD countries as well as worldwide. In 1974–1975 and in 1980–1983 oil consumption declined at 3–5% per year on average (see Figure 1.4).

GDP growth rates in Table 1.1 show that on the eve of the first oil crisis G7 national growth rates of GDP were in the range of 4.77%–8.03% per year in 1973.

---

[18] From now on we use the notation — mb/day — to represent "million barrels per day".

[19] OECD refers to the Organization for Economic Co-operation and Development. It was formed in 1961 from the Organization for European Economic Co-operation (OEEC), which administered American and Canadian aid under the Marshall Plan for the reconstruction of Europe after World War II. The primary goal of the OECD is to promote policies to secure the highest sustainable economic growth and employment, and thereby produce a rising standard of living in member countries. It has 20 original member countries, including Canada, US, France, Germany, Italy, UK. A further 10 countries have become members of OECD, including Japan, South Korea, Mexico, Australia, Hungary, Poland and the Slovak Republic.

In 1974 and 1975 G7 national GDP growth rates fell into negative values, except for energy-rich Canada. However, G7 economies recovered, with GDP growth rates rising into the range of 2.75%–5.53% per year in 1979. However, in 1980–1982 an economic recession occurred in the USA, Canada, UK and Germany. Although Japan, France and Italy did not have economic recessions during this time, their GDP growth rates were substantially reduced.

High oil prices also led to high inflation. This is not shown directly in Figures 1.3 and 1.4, but it can be viewed indirectly via the gap between real and nominal oil prices — for instance, the $62.7 per barrel real price versus the $37.1 per barrel nominal price in 1981 shown in Figure 1.3. In 1983 the G7 economies began a slow recovery and in 1984 the world demand for oil started to pick up. The nominal world oil price stabilized in a range of $15–$20 per barrel in 1986–1997. This occurred even though Iraq's invasion of Kuwait stressed global oil markets from the supply side and induced a brief hike in oil price in 1990. In 1991 a short economic recession occurred in the United States, Canada and UK, as well as in Germany, France and Italy. Since then, slow economic growth (below 3%) has predominated in the G7 nations in Europe and Japan, while the US and Canada maintained a growth rate of 4.0%–4.5%. Thus oil consumption both worldwide and by OECD nations slowly increased at a rate of 0%–2.5% per year.

A currency crisis started in Thailand in 1997 and rampaged across other East Asian countries like South Korea, Malaysia, Indonesia and Singapore in 1998. This financial crisis also contributed to Russian and Brazilian economic crises and thrust the Japanese economy into a recession in 1998. The possibility of a potential worldwide recession led to a fall of both nominal and real world oil prices to $12 per barrel in 1998. This decline in oil prices was short-lived, however, thanks to international cooperative efforts in which the US played a critical role in stimulating the world economy.

In spite of this drag from external forces during this time, the US economy continued to grow at 4.4% per year. See Table 1.1. The US also lent a powerful hand to many troubled nations around the globe by opening its huge domestic market to foreign goods and services. Exporting to the United States became an important source for many troubled nations to help pull their economies out of recession.

At this time China had also become an important player in the world economic arena. China not only successfully avoided the 1997–1998 Asian financial crises but also managed to expand its economy at the highest rate in the world, 8.84% in 1997 and 7.80% in 1998. Consequently a worldwide recession did not occur even though Western European economies were still unable to restore their previous growth pace. World demand for oil continued to grow and oil prices rebounded quickly.

From Figure 1.4 one can observe that before 1996, the growth-rate curve of oil consumption by OECD was revolving around the growth-rate curve of oil consumption worldwide but was more volatile than the latter. This implies that OECD nations dominated the demand side of world oil markets. After 1996, however, these two growth-rate curves began to separate and the growth-rate curve for the world stayed above the OECD growth-rate curve. This indicates that significant new demand forces entered world oil markets and began to change the slope of world oil consumption curve after 1996. This effect from new demand forces can also be seen in world oil prices, which rose from $12 in 1998 to $27.7 in 2000, and then from $22.0 in 2001 to $36.0 in 2004.[20] This occurred even though oil demand from the OECD was flat in 2000–2002 and expanded at less than 2% in 2003–2005.

South Korea and China are among the new emerging economies that have become new forces in pushing up oil demand in recent years. Table 1.1 provides the Korean and Chinese GDP growth rates, which were double or triple their G7 counterparts in many years. These Korean and Chinese growth rates were also less severely affected than the G7 nations by these oil price changes. Thus we need to study oil consumption by individual nations as we do in Section 1.4 in order to see more of the dynamics from the demand side of world oil markets. Before moving in that direction, however, we turn to Figure 1.5 for a brief discussion of world demand for natural gas.

Figure 1.5 exhibits world natural gas consumption over 1970–2003 and the price of natural gas over 1950–2004. The price over 1950–1983 was the US natural gas wellhead price[21] and the price over 1984–2004 was US imported natural gas price, both stated in real and nominal terms. World consumption data for natural gas are the same as were used to calculate the natural gas share depicted in Figure 1.2. Comparisons of Figure 1.5 with Figures 1.3 and 1.4 show that world natural gas consumption and the price of natural gas follow world oil consumption and price fairly closely.

The following Figure 1.6 displays annual growth rates of world consumptions of oil and natural gas. Except for a few years, the growth rate of natural gas was greater than the growth rate of oil and has also become more volatile than the growth rate of oil since 1984. Figures 1.5 and 1.6 show that the world demand for natural gas has increased at a faster pace than that of oil since 1984, and this trend is expected to continue. Because both demand and the price for oil and natural gas exhibit similar patterns we will concentrate our attention on oil.

---

[20] World oil prices continued rising in 2005 and hit nearly $70 per barrel in early September 2005. Traders were speculating on large interruptions of oil supplies due to huge damages in New Orleans made by Hurricane Katrina and damages in Louisiana and Texas Gulf of Mexico coastlines by Hurricane Rita later. Figure 1.3 does not reflect the oil price surge in 2005. The outbreak of war between Lebanon and Israel on July 12, 2006 helped send oil price to a record high of $78.40 a barrel on July 14, 2006.

[21] The term "wellhead" refers to the production site or lease property. The wellhead price is considered to be the sales price obtainable by a third party in an arm's length transaction.

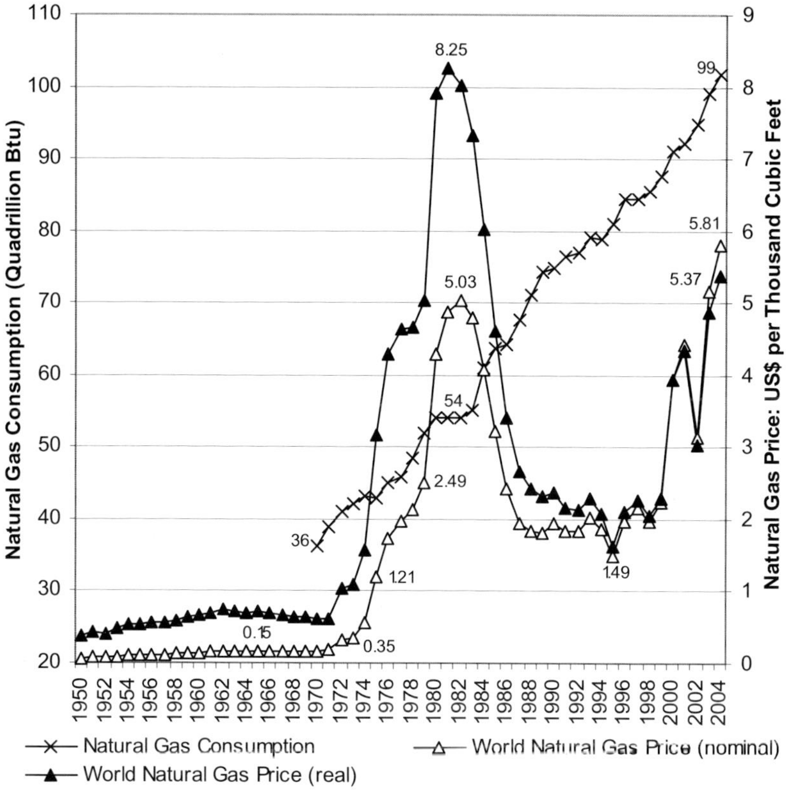

Figure 1.5: World Natural Gas Consumption and Price (1950–2004).

1.4. Oil Consumption by Countries

In global oil markets the United States, China and Japan were the top three largest consumers by 2003. See Table 1.2. In Figure 1.7 we present oil consumption curves for these top three countries along with oil consumption curves for European nations in OECD (or OECD Europe), Russia, and a group of emerging-economy nations as well as for the 48 Muslim-majority countries. The group of emerging-economy nations consists of China, South Korea, India, Brazil and five Muslim majority nations, Saudi Arabia, Egypt, Iran, Indonesia, and Turkey. These countries are selected because they have shown relatively rapid economic growth and increasing oil consumption for last two decades.

The United States is and remains the largest consumer in global oil markets with oil consumption rising rapidly from 9.8 mb/day in 1960 to 17.3 mb/day in 1973. The oil crises substantially curbed their increasing momentum in oil use

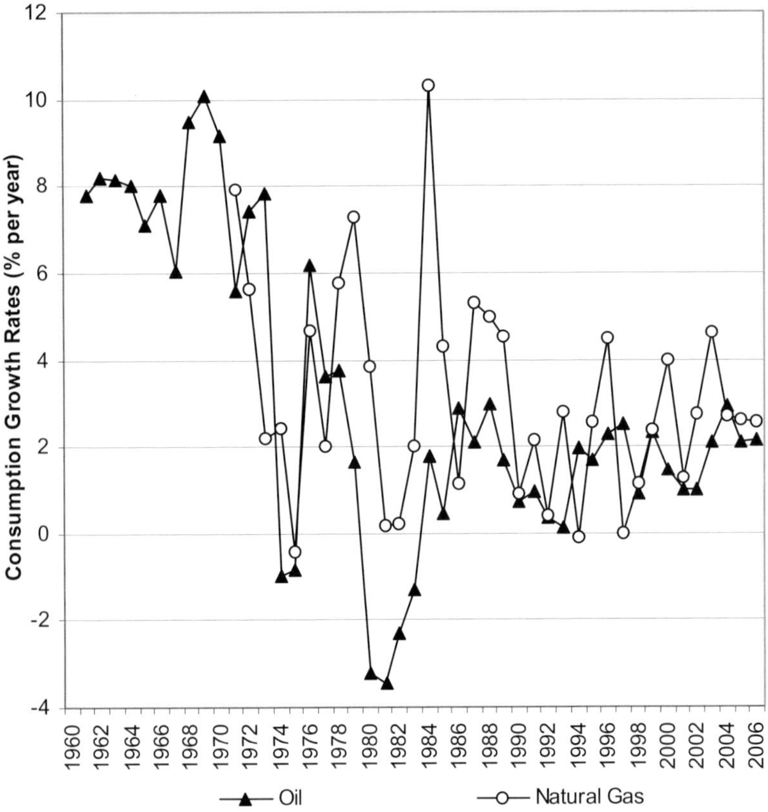

Figure 1.6: World Consumption Growth Rates of Natural Gas vs. Oil (1960–2004).

and eventually led to declines in US consumption of oil in 1978–1983. Since then US consumption resumed its ascending trend rising to 20.7 mb/day in 2004 and is projected to be 21.2 mb/day by 2006. OECD Europe increased its oil consumption much more rapidly than the US in the 1960s and reached the same consumption level as that of US in 1973. The oil crisis of 1974 had a larger impact on OECD oil consumption and led to a continuous decline in oil use until 1986 after which a slow recovery from 13.3 mb/day occurred in 1986 to 15.6 mb/day in 2004. It is projected to be 15.7 mb/day by 2006.

Like OECD Europe, Japan experienced a rapid increase in oil consumption during the 1960s and the oil crises did little to reduce its consumption, which stayed above 4.4 mb/day and remained virtually flat for the last three decades. It is expected to be 5.4 mb/day by 2006. Russia's oil consumption reduced from 4.4 mb/day in 1992 to 2.7 mb/day in 1996 and has stayed at almost the same

Table 1.2(A): Top 25 Largest Oil Consumer Countries (Oil Use in 1 000 Barrels per Day)

Rank	1980		1985	
	Country	Oil Use	Country	Oil Use
1	USA	17 056 (27%)	USA	15 726 (26%)
2	F-USSR	8 995 (14.3%)	F-USSR	8 950 (14.9%)
3	Japan	4 960 (7.86%)	Japan	4 436 (7.38%)
4	W Germany	2 707 (4.29%)	W Germany	2 338 (3.89%)
5	France	2 256 (3.57%)	China	1 885 (3.14%)
6	Italy	1 934 (3.06%)	France	1 753 (2.92%)
7	Canada	1 873 (2.97%)	Italy	1 705 (2.84%)
8	China	1 765 (2.80%)	UK	1 617 (2.69%)
9	UK	1 725 (2.73%)	Canada	1 526 (2.54%)
10	Mexico	1 270 (2.01%)	Mexico	1 476 (2.46%)
11	Brazil	1 148 (1.82%)	Brazil	1 079 (1.80%)
12	Spain	990 (1.57%)	Saudi Arabia	939 (1.56%)
13	Netherlands	792 (1.26%)	India	895 (1.49%)
14	India	643 (1.02%)	Spain	858 (1.43%)
15	Saudi Arabia	610 (0.97%)	Iran	790 (1.31%)
16	Australia	594 (0.94%)	Australia	639 (1.06%)
17	Iran	590 (0.93%)	Netherlands	610 (1.02%)
18	Korea South	537 (0.85%)	Korea South	552 (0.92%)
19	Sweden	527 (0.84%)	Indonesia	465 (0.77%)
20	Belgium	522 (0.83%)	Egypt	430 (0.72%)
21	Argentina	499 (0.79%)	Argentina	415 (0.69%)
22	Indonesia	408 (0.65%)	Belgium	405 (0.67%)
23	Venezuela	400 (0.63%)	Venezuela	383 (0.64%)
24	Poland	387 (0.61%)	Taiwan	378 (0.63%)
25	Taiwan	380 (0.60%)	Turkey	359 (0.60%)
Sum of 25		**53 568 (84.9%)**	**Sum of 25**	**50 610 (84.2%)**
3	Muslim Nations	1 608 (2.55%)	5 Muslim Nations	2 983 (4.96%)
10	Emerging-Economy Nations	6 980 (11.1%)	12 Emerging-Economy Nations	8 571 (14.3%)
15	Mature-Market Nations	46 588 (73.8%)	13 Mature-Market Nations	42 039 (69.9%)

level until 2003. The former Soviet republics that became independent states in the early 1990s are excluded from the new state of Russia and their oil data were separated from Russia's after 1992. We do not use the former Soviet data over 1960–1991 to represent Russia. Thus Russia's data start with 1992.

A significant new factor from the demand side of global oil markets has been established from the following three significant developments: (1) China has overtaken Japan in 2003. China's oil consumption was 5.55 mb/day in 2003 and 6.52 mb/day in 2004 versus Japan's 5.50 and 5.35 mb/day in the correspond-

Table 1.2(B): Top 25 Largest Oil Consumer Countries (Oil Use in 1 000 Barrels per Day)

Rank	1992		2003		
	Country	Oil Use	Country		Oil Use
1	USA	17 033 (25%)	USA		20 034 (25%)
2	Japan	5 493 (8.14%)	China		5 550 (6.93%)
3	Russia	4 423 (6.56%)	Japan		5 501 (6.87%)
4	Germany	2 841 (4.21%)	Germany		2 677 (3.34%)
5	China	2 662 (3.95%)	Russia		2 675 (3.33%)
6	France	1 933 (2.87%)	India		2 320 (2.90%)
7	Italy	1 894 (2.81%)	Canada		2 193 (2.7%)
8	Mexico	1 855 (2.75%)	Korea South		2 168 (2.71%)
9	UK	1 815 (2.69%)	Brazil		2 100 (2.62%)
10	Canada	1 722 (2.55%)	France		2 060 (2.57%)
11	Korea South	1 527 (2.26%)	Mexico		2 015 (2.52%)
12	Brazil	1 521 (2.25%)	Italy		1 874 (2.34%)
13	India	1 275 (1.89%)	Saudi Arabia		1 775 (2.22%)
14	Saudi Arabia	1 219 (1.81%)	UK		1 722 (2.15%)
15	Spain	1 104 (1.64%)	Spain		1 544 (1.93%)
16	Iran	1 083 (1.61%)	Iran		1 425 (1.78%)
17	Ukraine	813 (1.20%)	Indonesia		1 155 (1.44%)
18	Netherlands	769 (1.14%)	Netherlands		920 (1.15%)
19	Australia	729 (1.08%)	Taiwan		915 (1.14%)
20	Indonesia	707 (1.05%)	Australia		876 (1.09%)
21	Taiwan	557 (0.83%)	Thailand		810 (1.01%)
22	Belgium	509 (0.75%)	Singapore		705 (0.88%)
23	Turkey	492 (0.73%)	Turkey		653 (0.82%)
24	Thailand	476 (0.71%)	Belgium		624 (0.78%)
25	Argentina	445 (0.66%)	Egypt		566 (0.71%)
Sum of 25		**54 895 (81.4%)**	**Sum of 25**		**64 936 (81.1%)**
4	Muslim Nations	3 501 (5.19%)	5	Muslim Nations	5 574 (6.96%)
11	Emerging-Economy Nations	11 962 (17.7%)	12	Emerging-Economy Countries	20 142 (25.2%)
14	Mature-Market Nations	42 933 (63.7%)	13	Mature-Market Nations	44 794 (55.9%)

ing years. (2) The oil consumption of the group of emerging-economy consisting of many nations (China, South Korea, India, Brazil, Saudi Arabia, Egypt, Iran, Indonesia, and Turkey) has exceeded the oil consumption of OECD Europe since 1999. Their combined oil consumption was 15.42 mb/day in 1999 versus 15.29 mb/day for OECD Europe. (3) The 48 Muslim-majority countries as a whole have become a significant consumer in global oil markets. The combined oil consumption of these Muslim nations increased from 3.9 mb/day in 1980 to

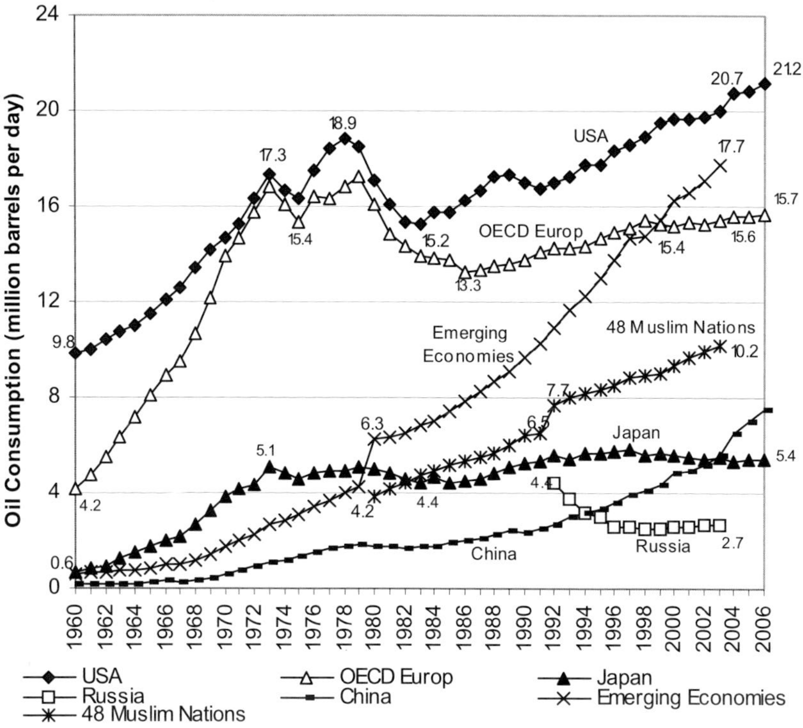

Figure 1.7: Oil Consumption by Countries (1960–2006).

6.5 mb/day in 1991 and rose from 7.7 mb/day in 1992 to 10.2 mb/day in 2003. One can notice a jump in the Muslim group's oil use in 1991 to 1992, due to the addition of six former Soviet republics into this Muslim group.

Muslim countries are conventionally considered to be oil producers but not oil consumers. However, their combined oil consumption of more than 10 mb/day in 2003, for instance, was almost two times as large as Japan's. The Muslim world must now be considered not only major oil producers but also, collectively, a major oil consumer.

Since the early 1980s emerging economies have also become a new force to be reckoned with on the demand side of global oil markets. The group of the above nine "representative" countries has increased their oil demand from 6.3 mb/day in 1980 to 17.7 mb/day in 2003. This placed them second to the US. One can also notice the large increase from 4.2 to 6.3 mb/day in 1980 that is exhibited for emerging economies in Figure 1.7. This was due to an addition into this group of five Muslim nations which do not have oil use data over 1960–1979. Many countries in this group have experienced rapid economic expansion and are expected to continue their upward trend and thus lead to further increases in their oil consumption in the near nature.

We use Tables 1.2(A) and 1.2(B) to show the top largest 25 consumer countries in global oil markets for the four years, 1980, 1985, 1992 and 2003. These countries are selected in terms of their oil consumption level from among 220 countries that have records of oil consumption in the EIA database. From this table one can observe how the demand side has gradually shifted from Western-nation domination to an increasing weight of emerging-economy nations, including some Muslim-majority countries.

Numbers in the first column of Tables 1.2(A) and 1.2(B) denote country ranks in terms of their oil consumption levels and the numbers in parentheses denote country shares (as percentages) of total world oil consumption. Before turning to individual country results we first look at the aggregates in the bottom four rows. The combined oil consumption of the 25 top consumer countries was 53.568 mb/day in 1980 and accounted for 84.9% of overall oil consumption worldwide. See the "Sum of 25" in the fourth row from the bottom of Tables 1.2(A) and 1.2(B). As shown in this row these numbers became 50.61, 54.985, and 64.936 mb/day and represent 84.2%, 81.4%, and 81.1% of total world consumption in 1985, 1992 and 2003, respectively. This means that the top 25 consumer nations dominated the demand side of world oil market with their combined consumption share remaining at greater than 80% over the period of 1980–2003 as shown in these tables.

There were 3 Muslim-majority countries in the 25-top list for 1980 — Iran, Saudi Arabia and Indonesia — with an oil consumption share of 2.55%. The Muslim country position substantially increased over time. As of 2003 there were 5 Muslim nations in the top 25 — Iran, Saudi Arabia, Indonesia, Turkey and Egypt — with an oil consumption share of 6.96%, which more than doubled their 1980 share. In 1980 ten countries of the emerging economy group entered the top-25 list with a combined share of 11.1%. In 2003 twelve countries in this group were in the top 25 and their share was 25.2%, which slightly exceeded the US share of 25%. This more than doubled their 1980 share. The last row in Tables 1.2(A) and 1.2(B) shows both oil consumption and shares by countries in the top 25 list that belonged to the mature market group and the former Soviet group. Their combined oil consumption reduced from 46.588 mb/day (about 73.8% of oil use worldwide) in 1980 to 44.794 mb/day (55.9%) in 2003. The summary rows in Tables 1.2(A) and 1.2(B) thus clearly show the shifting character of the demand side in global oil markets.

One can also use Table 1.2 to track changes in oil consumption for each individual country. Some significant developments over 1980–2003 are the following.

(1) The United States and Germany retained number 1 and number 4 positions, respectively, over 1980–2003. US oil consumption increased from 17 to 20 mb/day from 1980 to 2003, but its share reduced from 27% to 25%. Ger-

many's oil consumption was in a narrow range of 2.3–2.8 mb/day and its share declined from 4.29% to 3.34% over 1980–2003.

(2) The rank of China rose from number 8 in 1980 to number 2 in 2003 when it exceeded Japan and became next to the US. India moved up from number 14 to number 6 and South Korea moved up from number 18 to number 8 over 1980–2003.

(3) The rank of Saudi Arabia rose from number 15 to number 13 and surpassed the United Kingdom in 2003. Indonesia moved in rank from number 22 to number 17 in 2003 and exceeded the Netherlands — which had colonized Indonesia in the early 17th century (see Part III of this book). Iran retained its rank as number 17, 16, and 15 over 1980–2003. Turkey entered the top-25 list in 1985 and ranked number 23 in 1992 and 2003. Egypt made a first appearance in the top 25 list in 2003.

(4) As of 2003, Sweden, Argentina, Venezuela and Poland moved out of the list and Thailand, Singapore, Turkey and Egypt moved in.

(5) The ranks of Russia, France, Italy, United Kingdom, Spain, Netherlands and Australia moved down substantially and the last two (Netherlands and Australia) may move out of the list in the near future because their oil use was less than one mb/day compared to oil consumption which ran up very fast in some emerging economies.

Summary of Chapter 1

In summary, this chapter provides an analysis of the demand side of global oil markets. It shows that the entire world has become heavily dependent upon oil and natural gas as the major energy source that drives economic growth and improves living standards. Advanced nations have managed their mature market economies and retained high standards of living with high levels of oil consumption. The United States is and remains the largest consumer of oil, but Japan as well as Western European countries have reduced their collective position.

This situation is not likely to be improved as witness the increase in demand from emerging economies portrayed in Figure 1.7. As shown in Table 1.2(B), by 2003 China overtook Japan as the second largest oil consumer next to the USA. India moved up from number 14 to number 6 and South Korea moved up from number 18 to number 8 in the rank of oil consumption over the last two decades. These emerging-economy countries have become a major driving force on the demand side of global oil markets and will continue to do so. However, the world spare capacity of oil production is estimated to fall below 1.0 mb/day in 2006, which is barely 1.2% of world oil demand. This is not nearly enough to cover a significant disruption of oil flows from Iraq, Nigeria or Venezuela. To balance out the rapidly increasing demand the oil price rose to $75 per barrel in the summer of 2006, which was an all time high, to that point in time, in both real and nominal term. Accelerating oil demand by these emerging-economy countries will continue to keep world oil prices at high levels.

The Muslim world has also become a significant collective consumer of oil and five Muslim-majority countries — Saudi Arabia, Iran, Indonesia, Turkey and Egypt — were ranked among the top 25 of the world's largest oil consumers in 2003. More importantly, the Muslim world has been and continues to be a leading force on the supply side of oil markets as we will see in the next chapter.

Chapter 2

World Production and Reserves of Oil and Natural Gas

This chapter provides an analysis of the supply side for global oil markets. It consists of three sections. Section 2.1 describes the evolution of world crude oil production and the shifting positions of major oil producers over the last four decades. Section 2.2 provides a similar analysis for world production and the leading producers of natural gas. Section 2.3 focuses on the leading oil producers of OPEC and the emerging new Muslim country producers in the Caspian Sea region. Section 2.3.4 discusses world reserves of oil and natural gas and the potential outlook for the near future.

We focus on the dynamics of the supply side of global oil and natural gas markets because this will make it possible to understand how the Muslim world has been involved in the development of global oil and natural gas markets. The Muslim world is the dominant force. It controls about 42% of world crude oil production and about 26% of world natural gas output and it holds 55%–64% of world oil reserves and 45%–51% of world natural gas reserves. These developments have positioned the Muslim world to play a critical role in the global economic arena, both at present and in the foreseeable future, in a manner that is summarized with the aid of Table 2.3 at the end of this chapter.

2.1. World Production of Oil

The United States and the former USSR were the top two oil producers of the world in the 1960s and the early 1970s. However, US oil production peaked at 9.6 mb/day in 1970 and then began to decline, so its occupation of the top spot proved to be short-lived. Besides Russia, a new leader, Saudi Arabia, has since emerged and risen to the top as we shall see.

Following the fall of the Soviet Union in 1991 Russia's oil production fell precipitously. However, Russia's oil production rebounded after 1998 and expanded swiftly. This allowed Russia to become the world's second largest producer of crude oil behind only Saudi Arabia. Dynamic changes in top oil producers have shifted the supply side and opened the door for many emerging oil producers, in general, and for Muslim country producers in particular.

International Symposia in Economic Theory and Econometrics, Vol. 19
William W. Cooper and Piyu Yue

ISSN: 1571-0386/DOI: 10.1016/S1571-0386(07)00011-7

2.1.1. Crude Oil Production by the United States and Russia

We start with a review of what happened to the US and Russia. Figure 2.1 displays US, former USSR and Russian crude oil production and the corresponding shares of these producers that accounted for total world crude oil production (or their production shares) over the period from 1960 to 2004.

The United States discovered its first oilfields in Eastern Pennsylvania in 1859, and then in East Texas in 1930. Large reserves of oil were also found in the Gulf of Mexico, Alaska, California, Louisiana, Oklahoma and Wyoming. Six major oil producing corporations were formed in the United States and this led to US domination in the petroleum industry as both the largest oil producer and the largest oil consumer in the world.

As shown in Figure 2.1, in 1960 US crude oil production was around 7.0 mb/day and accounted for 33.5% of world crude oil production. At its peak, US crude oil production reached 9.64 mb/day in 1970, but, at the same time, the US share was reduced to 21%. This was due to the fact that other producers, like

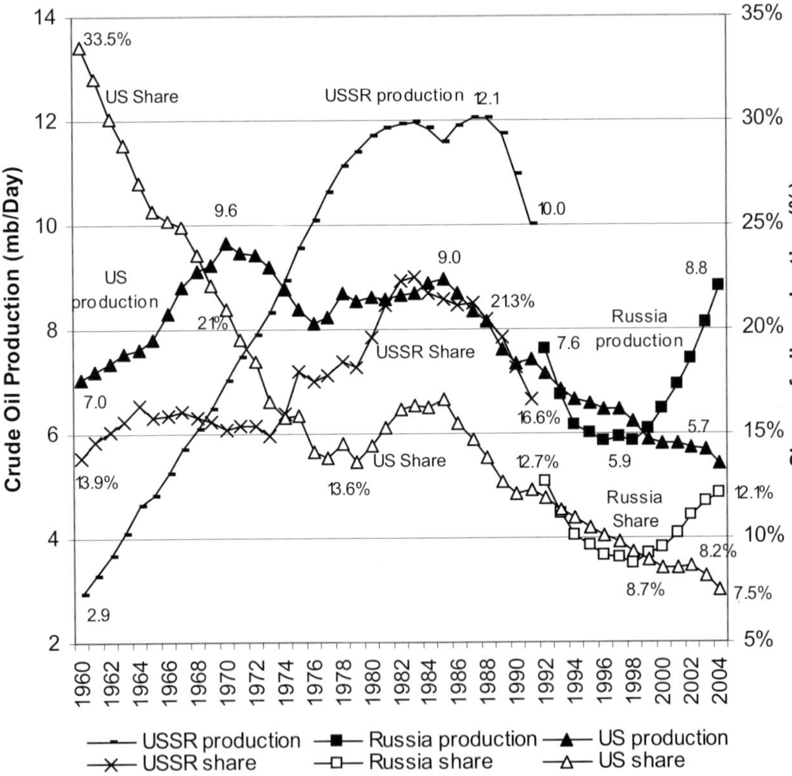

Figure 2.1: Crude Oil Production and World Share for USA and Russia.

the former USSR, expanded their oil production at a faster rate than the US and thus reduced the US share.

In 1974 the former USSR took the place of the United States as the largest oil producer in the world when US crude oil production began to decline after peaking at 9.6 mb/day in 1970, and only partially recovered in the early 1980s after again peaking at 9.0 mb/day in 1985. Following the oil price collapse of 1985 and 1986 (see Figure 1.3 in Chapter 1), US crude oil production resumed its declining trend. The sharp decline in oil prices in late 1997 and 1998 — see Figure 1.3 — led to a continuous decline in US crude oil production, which has stayed below 6 mb/day since 1999. During 2003, the United States produced crude oil at an average rate of 5.7 million barrels per day, thus accounting for only 8.2% of the world total. Adding natural gas plant liquids, other liquids, and refinery processing gains, US oil production was around 8.7 mb/day in 2003 (not shown in Figure 2.1), and this was a 50-year low.

In the meantime US oil consumption has continued to accelerate. As Table 1.2 in Chapter 1 showed, US oil consumption reached 20 mb/day in 2003. This huge gap between oil consumption and production has made the United States one of the largest oil-importing countries. Consequently the US economy and the American life style are now heavily dependent upon oil supplies from the rest of the world.

As shown in Figure 2.1, crude oil production in the former USSR was about 2.9 mb/day in 1960 and its production share was only 13.9% — less than half the US share. However, rapid expansion in the two decades of 1960–1980 brought USSR crude oil production to a peak of 12.1 mb/day in 1988. This compares to US production which fell to 8 mb/day in the same year. Most of this peak production in the former Soviet Union came mainly from the Western Siberian region — also known as the "Russian Core". As a result, the former USSR became the world's largest producer of crude oil during the 1980s with the United States second.

On the eve of the fall of the USSR, its crude oil production had already declined by 20%, from 12.1 to 10.0 mb/day from 1988 to 1991, and its world share of production declined from 21.3% to 16.6%. The collapse of the Soviet system and depletion of its largest oil fields led to a further decline in Russia's crude oil production from 7.6 to 5.9 mb/day over 1992–1998 — an output that was merely one-half the Soviet-era peak (see Figure 2.1). A turnaround in Russian oil output began in 1999 after privatization provided incentives that led to increased production. High oil prices in 1999 and 2000 (see Figure 1.3 in Chapter 1) and devaluation of Russia's currency (the ruble) after the 1998 financial crisis also contributed to rejuvenation of Russian oil production.

By 2004, Russia's crude oil production reached 8.8 mb/day resulting in a world production share of 12.1% versus US crude oil output of 5.4 mb/day and a US production share of 7.5% in the same year (see Figure 2.1). As of 2004, the United States was the world's third largest crude oil producer, Russia was the second, and a Muslim majority-country — Saudi Arabia — was the first. The crude oil production of Saudi Arabia in 2004 was 9.1 mb/day. In terms of total oil production (crude oil plus natural gas plant liquids, other liquids, and refinery processing gains) Russia was number 3, the United States was number 2 and Saudi Arabia was number one in 2003 (see Table 2.1, in Section 2.1.3).

These changes in oil production of the previous top two producers (the United States and Russia) and the sustained high oil prices (see Figure 1.3 in Chapter 1) created incentives for oil-rich countries to accelerate their oil production over the last three decades. Other countries have either become leading oil producers or emerging oil suppliers to the world with many of them belonging to OPEC (Organization of Petroleum Exporting Countries). Like the demand side of the global oil market, where a group of OECD countries drives overall demand, the supply side of the global oil market is also controlled by another group of countries called OPEC. Hence, in the next sub-section we will examine ways in which OPEC affects global oil markets.

2.1.2. Oil Production of OPEC and the Muslim World

OPEC (Organization of Petroleum Exporting Countries) was created as a permanent, intergovernmental organization at the Baghdad Conference on September 10–14, 1960 by five founding members: Iran, Iraq, Kuwait, Saudi Arabia and Venezuela.[1] It was later joined by others. OPEC is now made up of Algeria, Indonesia, Iran, Iraq, Kuwait, Libya, Nigeria, Qatar, Saudi Arabia, the United Arab Emirates and Venezuela. Ten of its eleven members are Muslim-majority countries, and only one, Venezuela, is a non-Muslim country. OPEC has its headquarters in Vienna, Austria, and functions as a cartel. The objective of OPEC is to coordinate petroleum policies among member countries in order to control oil prices, primarily by setting quotas for its members. The Oil and Energy Ministers of OPEC members meet regularly to discuss oil prices and to decide on the Organization's output level, as well as to set crude oil production quotas for member countries. Large non-OPEC producers such as Mexico, Norway, and Russia, sometimes go along with cartel positions.

Before the days of OPEC, the great oil companies in the West, owned mostly by US, British, and Dutch nationals, often retained 65% or more of the oil revenues obtained from oil producing countries. Partly in response, the oil producing nations from the Muslim world formed the OPEC cartel in 1960 to protect their interests. OPEC, however, had little impact from its founding in 1960 until 1973,

[1] Juan Pablo Perez Alfonzo (1903–1979), a brilliant Venezuelan lawyer, was the Minister of Mines and Hydrocarbons of Venezuela during 1959–1963. He led the Venezuelan delegation that devised the Organization of Exporting Petroleum Countries (OPEC) in the first Arab Oil Congress. He is therefore considered to be the "Father of OPEC".

when OPEC struck against the West during the midst of the Yom Kippur War[2] by imposing an oil embargo on the US and America's Western European allies that supported Israel. This embargo led to a quadrupling of oil prices, which lasted from October 1973 to early 1975 (see Figure 1.3 in Chapter 1).

The effects of this oil price increase were immediate and devastating. The West and much of the world experienced inflation and economic recession (see Table 1.1 in Chapter 1). During that time, many oil-producing countries nationalized their oil industries. Acting as a coalition of primary oil producers in the world, OPEC demanded "stable" and "just' oil prices and called for an international food and agriculture program as well as a technology transfer from the West to developing countries. These efforts by OPEC were aimed at establishing a new international economic order. The 1973 oil crisis provided dramatic evidence of the potential power of Muslim nations as strategic energy suppliers and their vast reserves of oil and natural gas have guaranteed the Muslim world continuing strategic importance in world affairs.

The "second oil crisis" in 1979 followed the overthrow of the Shah of Iran that resulted in the "Iranian Islamic Revolution" and the outbreak of war between two major OPEC members, Iraq and Iran. The war began officially in September, 1980, and resulted in protracted military conflicts for eight years (see Part III in this book). The war was disastrous for Iran and Iraq, stalling economic development and disrupting oil production and exports, and costing an estimated 1.5 million lives for Iran alone.

As Figure 2.2, below, shows OPEC cartel crude oil production was merely 8.7 mb/day in 1960 and accounted for about 41.5% of world crude oil production. During the 1960s OPEC output grew at 12% per year, a rate which was 50% greater than the world market growth rate of around 8% per year. This continuing growth boosted OPEC production to 30.6 mb/day in 1973 and raised the OPEC production share to 55%.

In the first (1973) oil crisis OPEC reduced output to 26.8 mb/day in 1975 (a 12.4% fall from its 1973 output). This did not affect the world supply of crude oil too greatly as world supply dropped to 52.83 mb/day in 1975 (a 5% fall from world crude oil production in 1973). World production soon reached a new high — 62.7 mb/day — in 1979. However, the OPEC decision to invoke an embargo pushed oil prices to a level the world had never before seen (see Figure 1.3 in Chapter 1). High oil prices created strong economic incentives for oil producers to expand so the embargo led to only a small reduction in world oil supply in 1975 (from 55.7 mb/day in 1974 to 52.8 mb/day in 1975) followed by a rapid rebound

[2] The Yom Kippur War is also called the "Ramadan War". It refers to an attack on Israel by Egypt and Syria on the Jewish holy day of Yom Kippur in October, 1973, which led to a war between Israel and the Arab world. See Part III in this book: Retrospection — Heritage of the Muslim Nations.

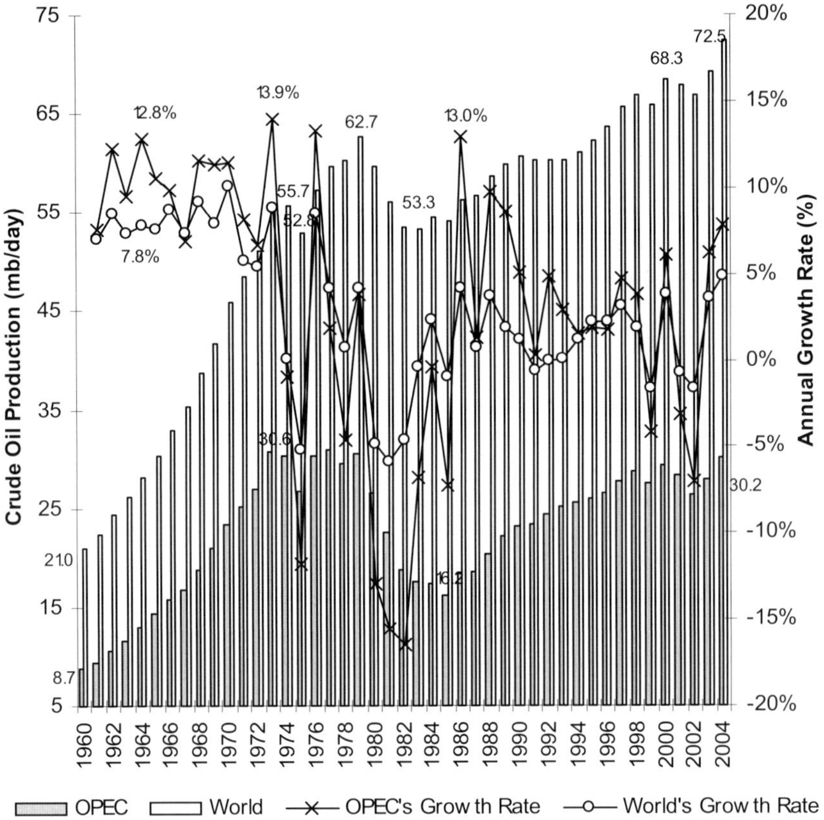

Figure 2.2: Crude Oil Production and Growth Rate (1960–2004).

in 1976 along with a subsequent ascension to the record high of 62.7 mb/day in 1979 exhibited in Figure 2.2.

However, the second oil crisis precipitated by the Iran–Iraq War in 1979 impacted world oil supply so hard that OPEC output fell to 16.2 mb/day in 1985, compared to its 1973 peak production of 30.6 mb/day as shown in Figure 2.2. This decline in OPEC production followed in the wake of the Iranian Revolution in 1979 which transformed Iran from an autocratic pro-west monarchy under Shah Pahlavi to an Islamic theocracy under the rule of Ayatollah Khomeini. Iranian protestors shuttered the oil sector of the country and the new regime resumed oil production and exports at a lower volume, driving up prices. In the next eight years Iran and Iraq engaged in a prolonged war and problems in Middle East oil escalated. In 1980, Iraq crude oil production fell by 2.7 million per day and production by Iran fell by 0.6 million barrels per day. The combination of these two events resulted in crude oil prices more than doubling from \$14 in 1978 to \$36 per barrel in 1981. This reduction in OPEC oil production also led to a worldwide crude oil output fall to 53.3 mb/day in 1983 — a 15% drop from the 1979-output level.

The effect of Iraq's subsequent invasion of Kuwait in 1990–1991 on oil production of OPEC (and worldwide) was fairly mild, thanks to the "Desert Storm" response led by the US that quickly restored order in the Persian Gulf region. OPEC crude oil output was flat at about 23.2 mb/day in 1990 and 1991, and world output was reduced slightly, from 60.57 to 60.21 mb/day in 1990–1991.

From the growth rates exhibited in Figure 2.2 it can be seen that OPEC output became volatile after 1998, but closely followed world output. It fell in 1999, rebounded in 2000, fell again in 2001 and 2002, and again rebounded in 2003 and 2004. As was discussed in Section 1.3 of Chapter 1, the demand shifts in world oil markets resulted in changing patterns of oil consumption. Oil demand declined in 1999 due to financial crises in Asia and other parts of the world that led to a decrease in oil supply, but the following economic recovery and the expansion of emerging economies drove up both demand and supply.

According to recent data world crude oil output reached 72.48 mb/day in 2004 with OPEC at 30.16 mb/day — which was slightly below its record high of 30.89 mb/day reached in 1977. The production share of OPEC was 41.6% in 2004, constituting essentially the same share as in 1960. It is now projected that OPEC oil production could reach 54.9 mb/day by 2025 and account for about 47.5% of total world oil production. OPEC achieved its largest production share of 55.0% in 1973. Since then the OPEC share has become significantly smaller and is not expected to return to this previous high in the next thirty years. Hence, OPEC still possesses substantial market power but the day of world oil production changing in accordance with OPEC's will seems to be diminishing. OPEC countries — most of which are Muslim-majority — have now been incorporated in the world economic system through global oil markets. Their oil production and wealth generated from oil have increasingly been affected by world oil consumption in other economies and societies around the globe.

Saudi Arabia has played a dominating role among the eleven members of OPEC. Indeed, much of OPEC's success in controlling oil prices can be attributed to Saudi Arabia. With most members at full production and some members often cheating and going beyond their quotas, Saudi Arabia is the only member with spare capacity that can be used to increase supply if needed. It can also cut its own production to compensate for other members having exceeded their production quotas. (We will continue our discussion of this most important oil producer in the following Section 2.3.)

By aggregating individual country oil production from data supplied by the Energy Information Administration we have calculated the total oil production for these 48 Muslim countries and their corresponding production share in the world total. Figure 2.3 displays the results for the time period from 1980 through 2003. Oil production here represents the total output of hydrocarbon liquids, includ-

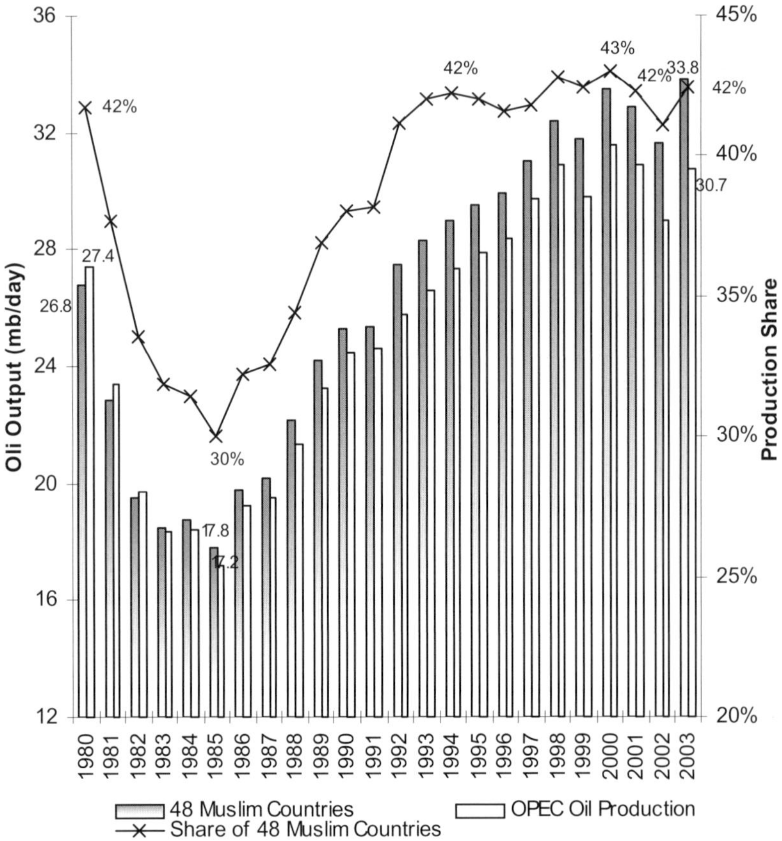

Figure 2.3: Oil Output of OPEC and Muslim Countries (1980–2003).

ing crude oil, natural gas plant liquids and other liquids, and refinery processing gains.[3] For comparison purposes, oil production of OPEC is also exhibited in Figure 2.3.

As Figure 2.3 shows, oil production of the 48 Muslim nations was 26.8 mb/day in 1980 and less than OPEC production (27.4 mb/day). But this situation began to change in 1985 when production of both OPEC and the Muslim world reached a trough with OPEC output less than that of the 48 Muslim nations (17.2 versus 17.8 mb/day). This fall in oil production and the reduced share of OPEC and the Muslim world over 1980–1985 occurred during the second oil crisis, occasioned

[3] Individual country data are provided in International Energy Annual 2003 by the Energy Information Administration.

by the Iran–Iraq War. After 1985, Muslim world oil production began to recover and rose to a high of 33.8 mb/day in 2003 when it accounted for about 42% of world oil production.

A large increase in Muslim world oil production from 1991 to 1992 was due to output from the six former Soviet Muslim countries in Central Asia. It was the first time that their data were included in outputs of the Muslim world. This is in contrast to the way they were treated (as nil) for the period 1980–1991 because of lack of separate oil production data from the former Soviet Union. The Muslim countries in Central Asia do not belong to OPEC, however, and this has made a difference between oil output of OPEC and the Muslim world as shown in Figure 2.3. In 2003, oil output of OPEC was 30.7 million barrels per day and was less than total output of the Muslim world at 33.8 million barrels per day. Kazakhstan, for instance, is one such Muslim country and its oil output exceeded 1 mb/day in 2003 as we will see in the next subsection.

2.1.3. Oil Production by Countries

Table 2.1, lists the top 25 oil producing countries along with their production and world share percentage in four selected years, 1980, 1985, 1992 and 2003. Data for production used in this section refer to the world total supply of oil and include crude oil output plus natural gas plant liquids, other liquids, and refinery processing gains, in which crude oil forms the lion's share.

The countries in Table 2.1 are selected from 220 countries in the world in terms of oil production rank for each of the four years. The bottom three rows of Table 2.1 provide summaries. As shown in the first of these three rows combined oil production of the top 25 countries declined from 61.2 mb/day (or 95.5% of world total oil production) in 1980 to 55.6 mb/day (or 93.9% of world total) in 1985 and then rebounded in 1992. Production of the top 25 reached 71.2 mb/day in 2003, but their share was reduced to 89.4%. This shows that world oil production is dominated by the top 25 producing countries even though their percentage reduced a little in 2003. The top three produced 51.6% of world oil production in 1980, but their share has continued falling to reducing to 45.4%, 39.9% and 34.5% in 1985, 1992 and 2003, respectively. Oil output of the top three also fell from 33 mb/day in 1980 to 27.5 mb/day, mainly due to reductions in US and Russian oil outputs. 13 Muslim countries entered the top 25 list in 1980, 1985 and 2003, and 12 of them in 1992. This group of Muslim countries increased their oil production from 26.4 to 30.8 mb/day in 1980–2003, but their production share decreased from 41.1% in 1980 to 38.7% in 2003.

In terms of individual countries, Saudi Arabia moved from number 3 in 1980 to number 1 in 2003, but its oil output and production share declined from 16.0% in 1980 to 12.7% in 2003. Iraq was number 4 in 1980 with output of 2.5 mb/day and a production share of nearly 4%. Iraq then declined to number 11 in 1985 and was removed from the top 25 list in 1992, to number 29, and returned as number

Table 2.1: Top 25 Largest Oil Producers (Oil Output in 1 000 Barrels per Day)

R	1980		1985		1992		2003	
	Country	Oil Output	Country	Oil Output	Country	Oil Output	Country	Oil Output
1	Former USSR	11 991 (18.7%)	Former USSR	11 935 (20.2%)	USA	9 768 (14.6%)	Saudi Arabia	10 133 (12.7%)
2	USA	10 811 (16.9%)	USA	11 192 (18.9%)	Saudi Arabia	9 036 (13.5%)	USA	8 797 (11.0%)
3	Saudi Arabia	10 285 (16.0%)	Saudi Arabia	3 778 (6.38%)	Russia	7 819 (11.7%)	Russia	8 527 (10.7%)
4	Iraq	2 526 (3.94%)	Mexico	3 044 (5.14%)	Iran	3 476 (5.20%)	Iran	3 831 (4.81%)
5	Venezuela	2 246 (3.50%)	UK	2 728 (4.60%)	Mexico	3 134 (4.69%)	Mexico	3 797 (4.77%)
6	Mexico	2 153 (3.36%)	China	2 505 (4.23%)	China	2 852 (4.27%)	China	3 549 (4.46%)
7	China	2 114 (3.30%)	Iran	2 272 (3.83%)	Venezuela	2 520 (3.77%)	Norway	3 266 (4.10%)
8	Nigeria	2 060 (3.21%)	Canada	1 848 (3.12%)	UAE	2 410 (3.61%)	Canada	3 110 (3.91%)
9	Libya	1 827 (2.85%)	Venezuela	1 757 (2.97%)	Norway	2 332 (3.49%)	UAE	2 681 (3.37%)
10	Canada	1 816 (2.83%)	Nigeria	1 500 (2.53%)	Canada	2 127 (3.19%)	Venezuela	2 582 (3.24%)
11	Kuwait	1 760 (2.74%)	Iraq	1 447 (2.44%)	UK	2 045 (3.06%)	UK	2 393 (3.01%)
12	UAE	1 747 (2.72%)	Indonesia	1 380 (2.33%)	Nigeria	1 951 (2.92%)	Kuwait	2 318 (2.91%)
13	UK	1 709 (2.66%)	UAE	1 356 (2.29%)	Indonesia	1 577 (2.36%)	Nigeria	2 246 (2.82%)
14	Iran	1 683 (2.62%)	Algeria	1 158 (1.95%)	Libya	1 470 (2.20%)	Algeria	1 890 (2.37%)
15	Indonesia	1 659 (2.59%)	Kuwait	1 086 (1.83%)	Algeria	1 354 (2.03%)	Brazil	1 842 (2.31%)
16	Algeria	1 143 (1.78%)	Libya	1 085 (1.83%)	Kuwait	1 084 (1.62%)	Libya	1 485 (1.86%)
17	Egypt	613 (0.96%)	Egypt	915 (1.54%)	Egypt	914 (1.37%)	Iraq	1 318 (1.65%)
18	Norway	569 (0.89%)	Norway	832 (1.40%)	Brazil	824 (1.23%)	Indonesia	1 240 (1.56%)
19	Argentina	508 (0.79%)	Brazil	734 (1.24%)	Oman	744 (1.11%)	Kazakhs-tan	1 036 (1.30%)
20	Qatar	483 (0.75%)	Australia	653 (1.10%)	Malaysia	667 (1.00%)	Qatar	1 000 (1.26%)
21	Australia	453 (0.71%)	India	626 (1.06%)	Australia	620 (0.93%)	Angola	902 (1.13%)

(continued on next page)

Table 2.1: (*continued*)

R	1980 Country	Oil Output	1985 Country	Oil Output	1992 Country	Oil Output	2003 Country	Oil Output
22	Malaysia	284 (0.44%)	Oman	502 (0.85%)	India	602 (0.90%)	Malaysia	840 (1.06%)
23	Oman	284 (0.44%)	Argentina	485 (0.82%)	Argentina	597 (0.89%)	Oman	823 (1.03%)
24	Brunei	270 (0.42%)	Malaysia	451 (0.76%)	Kazakhs-tan	529 (0.79%)	India	815 (1.02%)
25	Romania	252 (0.39%)	Qatar	332 (0.56%)	Angola	526 (0.79%)	Argentina	809 (1.02%)
	Sum of 25	61 246 (95.5%)	Sum of 25	55 602 (93.9%)	Sum of 25	60 978 (91.3%)	Sum of 25	71 232 (89.4%)
	Top 3	33 087 (51.6%)	Top 3	26 905 (45.4%)	Top 3	26 623 (39.9%)	Top 3	27 458 (34.5%)
	13 Muslim Nations	26 354 (41.1%)	13 Muslim Nations	17 262 (29.1%)	12 Muslim Nations	25 212 (37.8	13 Muslim Nations	30 842 (38.7%)

17 in 2003 with oil output at 1.3 mb/day and 1.65% of production share. Among the top 25 oil producers, countries that experienced a declining rank because of reductions in oil output or production share over 1980–2003 include Venezuela (from number 5 to 10), Nigeria (from number 8 to 13), Libya (from number 9 to 16) Indonesia (from number 15 to 18) and Argentina (from number 19 to 25). Countries that fell from the top 25 list during 1980–2003 were Egypt (number 26 in 2003), Australia (number 27 in 2003), Brunei (number 42 in 2003) and Romania (number 47 in 2003).

In 1985 and 1992, when OPEC countries reduced their oil production, countries like China, Mexico and Canada increased their oil output and thus increased their production percentages. Their ranks also improved with movement into the top 8 by 2003. Unlike Iraq, Iran has managed to raise its oil output and gain production share. It was number 14 in 1980 with oil output at about 1.68 mb/day and a production share of 2.62%. By 2003, Iran's rank rose to number 4, next only to Russia, and it produced oil at 3.83 mb/day with a production share of 4.81%. In 2003 Iran replaced Iraq as number 4 — the position held by Iraq in 1980. Other oil producers with a significant rise in rank in 2003 include Norway (7), Brazil (15), United Arab Emirates (9), Kuwait (12) and the United Kingdom (11).

Two rising oil producers emerging in the 1990s were Kazakhstan and Angola. Both entered the top 25 list (at number 24 and 25) in 1992 with oil output about 0.5 mb/day and production share less than 0.8%. By 2003, their oil output rose to 1.04 and 0.9 mb/day, their production share exceeded 1.0%, and their rank rose to numbers 19 and 21, respectively.

Finally, we observe that among top 25 oil producers in 2003, only 6 countries — United States, Russia, Mexico, Norway, Canada and the United Kingdom — belong to the mature-market group. The other 19 countries are all emerging-economy countries and 13 of them are Muslim-majority countries. In the next section, Section 2.3, we therefore describe the petroleum resources of these major oil producing Muslim countries. Before doing so, however, it is desirable to examine the general picture of world production of natural gas and the importance of Muslim countries in global natural gas markets.

2.2. World Production of Natural Gas

As described in Section 1.3 of Chapter 1 in this book, world demand for natural gas has accelerated for the last twenty five years and natural gas prices have substantially increased over time. These two factors have provided economic incentives to expand worldwide production of natural gas.

Figure 2.4, below, exhibits the growing total world output of natural gas along with the combined output of 48 Muslin countries and the outputs of two other major natural gas producers — the United States and Russia. The total world output is expressed in the production volume of trillion cubic feet, while production for USA, Russia, and the 48 Muslim countries is expressed in the percentage of their production relative to the total world output. Figure 2.4 shows that the total world output increased from 53 trillion cubic feet in 1980 to 95 trillion cubic feet in 2003. In 1982–1985 when world oil output was substantially reduced (see Figure 2.2), world production of natural gas began to rise, reaching 62 trillion cubic feet in 1985. Since then it has grown without interruption except for two brief periods, when it was flat, 1991–1992 and 1996–1997.

US natural gas production percentage declined in 1980–1986, rebounded slightly in 1994, and then continued to decline. US percentage share was reduced from 36.4% in 1980 to 20.0% in 2003 due to the rapid growth of total world output of natural gas and declining US natural gas production over 1980–2003. The situation of Russia in natural gas is similar to what was discussed for Russian oil in Section 2.1.1 (see Figure 2.1). Unlike the situation in oil, however, Russia's share of natural gas did not rebound after the huge decline from the former USSR in 1992.

Figure 2.4 also shows the acceleration of natural gas production in the Muslim world, which rose from 6% of the total world output (about 3.2 trillion cubic feet) in 1980 to 25.8% of the total world output (24.6 trillion cubic feet) in 2003. As shown earlier in Figure 2.3, the oil output of these Muslim countries accounted for 42.5% of the world total in 2003. This compares to their output of natural gas, as shown in Figure 2.4, which accounted for 25.8% of the world total in the same year. These numbers suggest that Muslim world domination in global energy markets is thus far focused mainly on oil rather than natural gas. With the swift

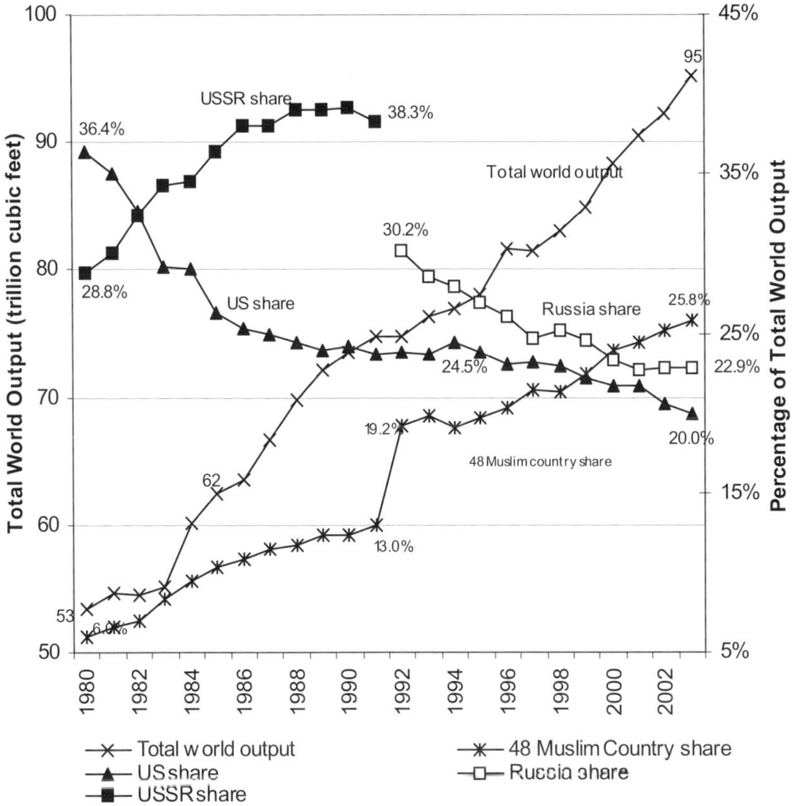

Figure 2.4: Production of Natural Gas (1980–2003).

growth of the last twenty five years, however, and huge underexploited natural gas reserves, production of natural gas by the Muslim world may soon gain a much larger share than today's production.

We next examine significant individual natural gas producing countries for four years — 1980, 1985, 1992 and 2003 — for which we use Table 2.2. In a manner similar to Table 2.1, Table 2.2 consists of 25 countries from among 220 countries of the world for each of the selected years, ranked according to their production of natural gas. Listed numbers are output and production share (in parentheses) for each country along with its rank indicated by the order (top to bottom) in which it appears.

The bottom row in Table 2.2 shows that these 25 countries accounted for more than 90% of the world production of natural gas in each period. This group of 25 countries thus contains all of the significant producers in the global natural gas market. Russia and the United States have been the world's top two producers but

Table 2.2: Top 25 Largest Producers of Natural Gas (in Trillion Cubic Feet)

R	1980		1985		1992		2003	
	Country	Natural gas	Country	Natural gas	Country	Natural gas	Country	Natural gas
1	USA	19.4 (36.4%)	Former USSR	22.71 (36.4%)	Russia	21.81 (28.6%)	Russia	21.77 (22.9%)
2	Former USSR	15.37 (28.8%)	USA	16.45 (26.4%)	USA	18.1 (23.7%)	USA	19.04 (20.0%)
3	Netherlands	3.4 (6.37%)	Canada	3.04 (4.87%)	Canada	4.91 (6.43%)	Canada	6.45 (6.78%)
4	Canada	2.76 (5.17%)	Netherlands	3.01 (4.82%)	Netherlands	3.11 (4.07%)	UK	3.63 (3.81%)
5	UK	1.32 (2.47%)	UK	1.52 (2.44%)	UK	2.31 (3.03%)	Algeria	2.91 (3.06%)
6	Romania	1.2 (2.25%)	Algeria	1.36 (2.18%)	Turkmenistan	2.29 (3.00%)	Iran	2.79 (2.93%)
7	Norway	0.92 (1.72%)	Romania	1.27 (2.04%)	Indonesia	1.97 (2.58%)	Indonesia	2.62 (2.75%)
8	Mexico	0.9 (1.69%)	Indonesia	1.23 (1.97%)	Algeria	1.90 (2.49%)	Norway	2.59 (2.72%)
9	Germany West	0.68 (1.27%)	Mexico	1.00 (1.60%)	Uzbekistan	1.59 (2.08%)	Netherlands	2.58 (2.71%)
10	Indonesia	0.63 (1.18%)	Norway	0.94 (1.51%)	Saudi Arabia	1.27 (1.66%)	Saudi Arabia	2.12 (2.23%)
11	Venezuela	0.52 (0.97%)	Saudi Arabia	0.72 (1.15%)	Norway	0.97 (1.27%)	Turkmenistan	2.08 (2.19%)
12	China	0.51 (0.96%)	Venezuela	0.62 (0.99%)	Iran	0.96 (1.26%)	Uzbekistan	2.03 (2.13%)
13	Italy	0.44 (0.82%)	Iran	0.6 (0.96%)	Mexico	0.95 (1.24%)	Malaysia	1.89 (1.99%)
14	Algeria	0.41 (0.77%)	Germany West	0.6 (0.96%)	UAE	0.94 (1.23%)	UAE	1.58 (1.66%)
15	Saudi Arabia	0.33 (0.62%)	Italy	0.5 (0.80%)	Malaysia	0.88 (1.15%)	Mexico	1.49 (1.57%)
16	Brunei	0.32 (0.60%)	Argentina	0.5 (0.80%)	Australia	0.86 (1.13%)	Argentina	1.45 (1.52%)
17	Australia	0.31 (0.58%)	UAE	0.48 (0.77%)	Venezuela	0.82 (1.07%)	Australia	1.26 (1.32%)
18	Pakistan	0.29 (0.54%)	China	0.46 (0.74%)	Argentina	0.76 (1.00%)	China	1.21 (1.27%)
19	Argentina	0.28 (0.52%)	Australia	0.46 (0.74%)	Romania	0.75 (0.98%)	Qatar	1.09 (1.15%)
20	France	0.28 (0.52%)	Malaysia	0.44 (0.71%)	Italy	0.69 (0.90%)	Venezuela	1.05 (1.10%)
21	Germany East	0.25 (0.47%)	Pakistan	0.37 (0.59%)	Ukraine	0.68 (0.89%)	India	0.96 (1.01%)

(continued on next page)

Table 2.2: (*continued*)

R	1980		1985		1992		2003	
	Country	Natural gas	Country	Natural gas	Country	Natural gas	Country	Natural gas
22	Iran	0.25 (0.47%)	Germany East	0.33 (0.53%)	Germany	0.68 (0.89%)	Egypt	0.95 (1.00%)
23	Kuwait	0.24 (0.45%)	Brunei	0.3 (0.48%)	Pakistan	0.58 (0.76%)	Trinidad Tobago	0.87 (0.91%)
24	Poland	0.24 (0.45%)	Hungary	0.26 (0.42%)	China	0.56 (0.73%)	Pakistan	0.84 (0.88%)
25	Hungary	0.22 (0.41%)	Poland	0.24 (0.38%)	India	0.53 (0.69%)	Thailand	0.79 (0.83%)
	Top 2	34.77 (65.17%)	Top 2	39.16 (62.77%)	Top 2	39.91 (52.27%)	Top 2	40.81 (42.88%)
	6 Muslim Nations	2.15 (4.03%)	7 Muslim Nations	5.2 (8.33%)	9 Muslim Nations	12.38 (16.21%)	9 Muslim Nations	17.92 (18.83%)
	Sum 25	51.47 (96.48%)	Sum 25	59.41 (95.22%)	Sum 25	70.87 (92.81%)	Sum 25	86.04 (90.40%)

their combined share decreased from 65.17% in 1980 to 42.88% in 2003 while their output rose from 34.77 to 40.81 trillion cubic feet in 2003. Their loss in production share was accounted for by gains in other countries. Six Muslim countries were in the top 25 in 1980, seven in 1985 and nine in 1992 and 2003, with their combined share rising from 4.03% to 18.83% during this period.

Netherlands lost its number 3 rank in 1980 and became number 9 in 2003. Canada, United Kingdom and Norway retained their relative rank of number 3 to number 8 over 1980–2003. Venezuela experienced a reduction in rank from number 11 in 1980 to number 20 in 2003 while Mexico dropped from number 8 to number 15 and China fell from number 12 to number 18. Many European countries that were ranked in the top 25 for 1980 dropped out from the list of top 25 in 2003. Examples with their ranks in 1980 are Romania (number 6), West Germany (number 9), Italy (number 13), France (number 20), East Germany (number 21), Poland (number 24) and Hungary (number 25). This was caused by reduced production. Brunei (number 16 in 1980) also moved out of the top 25 list.

The positions occupied by these European countries in 1980 were taken over by Muslim countries with swiftly rising production shares. This includes Indonesia, which moved from number 10 in 1980 to number 7 in 2003, Saudi Arabia (from number 15 to number 10), Algeria (from number 14 to number 5), Iran (from number 22 to number 6) and Malaysia (from below 25 in 1980 to number 13 in 2003), UAE (from below 25 in 1980 to number 14 in 2003), Qatar (from below 25 in 1992 to number 19 in 2003), and Egypt and Pakistan (both from below 25 to numbers 22 and 24 respectively). Newcomers in the 2003 list include India (number 21) and Thailand (number 25).

Increasing worldwide natural gas production for the last twenty five years has come from many Muslim countries, in general, and Algeria, Iran, Indonesia, Saudi Arabia, Turkmenistan, Uzbekistan, Malaysia and United Arab Emirates in particular. Many European producing countries have become insignificant players in the supply of world natural gas. This increases the advantage of the Muslim world relative to the Western world. With accelerating demand for natural gas and increasing usage of natural gas to replace oil for heating homes and generating electricity, production of natural gas is likely to continue to expand rapidly in the foreseeable future. This trend will allow the Muslim world to assume an increasingly strategic role in global natural gas markets in a manner similar to its role in global oil markets. As we will see, in Section 2.3.4, some 45–51% of world reserves of natural gas are concentrated in a handful of Muslim countries.

2.3. Oil and Natural Gas Resources in Muslim Countries

In this section we briefly describe oil and natural gas production and the location of reserves in Muslim countries that have played important roles in the global market. Countries in the Persian Gulf region are first introduced followed by Algeria, Libya, Nigeria, and Indonesia (Muslim countries that are OPEC members). We then provide an overview of emerging oil producers in the Caspian Sea Region.

2.3.1. Persian Gulf Region

In the Persian Gulf Region there are eight countries — Saudi Arabia, Bahrain, Kuwait, Qatar, United Arab Emirates, Iran, Iraq and Oman. All are Muslim-majority countries. Except for Bahrain and Oman these Persian Gulf countries are OPEC members.

Saudi Arabia

As previously discussed, Saudi Arabia became the world's largest oil producer in 2003 with a crude oil output of 9.1 mb/day or 12.6% of the world total. This contrasts with 1960 when Saudi Arabia's crude oil output was only 1.3 mb/day or 6.2% of world production versus US crude oil production of 7 mb/day or 33.5% of the world total.

World oil production began to shift into the Persian Gulf region after discovery of the Al Ghawar Field in Saudi Arabia in 1948. The Al Ghawar Field is the largest and most productive oil field in the world. It began producing in 1951 and expanded rapidly with 219 flowing wells by 1990. The world's largest offshore field is As Safaniya. Located off the eastern coast of Saudi Arabia near Kuwait, As

Safaniya was discovered in 1951, and began production in 1957. By 1990 it had 223 flowing wells. During the 1960s and 1970s, many other major oil producing fields were found in the Eastern provinces and offshore of Saudi Arabia that we will identify with the aid of the map that follows.

The article "*Basement tectonics of Saudi Arabia as related to oil field structures*" (Saudi Ministry of Petroleum 1984) states the present situation succinctly: "Anticlinal or domal structures in the sedimentary sequence of the northeastern Arabian Platform and its offshore extension contain all the known oil and gas fields of Saudi Arabia. These currently comprise some fifty six oil fields and four gas fields as shown in the following map, all of which owe their origin to deep-seated tectonic movements in the Precambrian crystalline basement. The thickness of the sedimentary sequence varies in 4500–13 700 m by gradual thickening towards the northeast".

According to the Energy Information Administration (EIA), Saudi Arabia has about eighty oil and gas fields and over 1000 flowing wells, pumping crude oil out at an average rate of nine mb/day during the last twenty years. The crude oil flowing from these wells is generally the more desirable light oil with refinery yields of more high-value products such as gasoline and jet fuel and, hence, commands a higher price in global oil markets. Saudi Arabia is not only the world's leading oil producer, with more than one–fourth of the world total proven oil reserves, it also ranks fourth in natural gas production, with proven reserves estimated at 224.7 trillion cubit feet (Tcf). Saudi Arabia's current natural gas reserves consist of associated gas from its major oil fields as well as non-associated gas reserves located in deep reservoirs underlying the Ghawar oil field and in northwest sections of the country. Saudi Arabia has been the top oil exporting country to the United States, Japan, OECD Europe, and Asian countries. Both oil and mineral deposits as well as natural gas in Saudi Arabia are exhibited in Maps 2.1–2.2.

The coastal states in the Arabian Peninsula include Kuwait, Bahrain, Qatar, Iraq, and the United Arab Emirates (a federation of seven emirates). All of them have huge oil reserves and numerous flowing wells that produce and export large quantities of crude oil and natural gas. The following four maps show major oil and natural gas fields and pipelines in Bahrain, Kuwait, Qatar and the United Arab Emirates.

Bahrain

The Awali field of Bahrain was discovered in 1932 and developed into the first oil field in the Persian Gulf region. Awali's crude oil production peaked in the 1970s, and has since declined. As Map 2.3 of Bahrain shows that Bahrain also has potential offshore oil reserves in the Gulf of Bahrain and natural gas reserves of about 3.25 trillion cubic feet (Tcf).

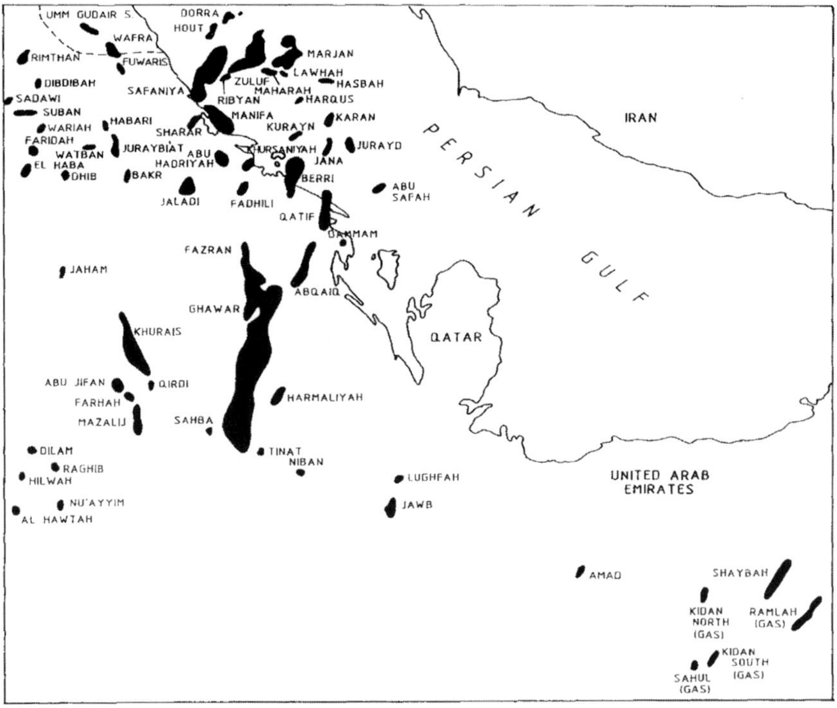

Map 2.1: Map of the Oil and Gas Fields of Saudi Arabia. From *Basement Tectonics of Saudi Arabia as Related to Oil Field Structures* Saudi Ministry of Petroleum, 1984.

Kuwait

According to the Energy Information Administration (EIA), Kuwait contains an estimated 99 billion barrels of proven oil reserves, with 2.5 billion barrels located in what is called the "Divided Zone," or the Saudi-Kuwait Neutral Zone. See Map 2.4. Most of Kuwait's oil is concentrated in the Great Al Burqan area, which is considered to be the world's second largest oil field behind Saudi Arabia's Ghawar field.

Kuwait's oil fields have been producing since the 1950s with a capacity of about 1.5–2.0 mb/day of medium and light crude oil. In 1984 and 2003, Kuwait announced new discoveries of light crude oil reserves. Kuwait exports the majority of its crude oil to Asian countries such as Japan, China, India, South Korea and Singapore, as well as to the United States and Europe. Natural gas has also been found and produced in Kuwait in conjunction with oil (so-called "associated gas"). Kuwait's natural gas production is relatively modest, being 293 billion cubic feet in volume in 2002.

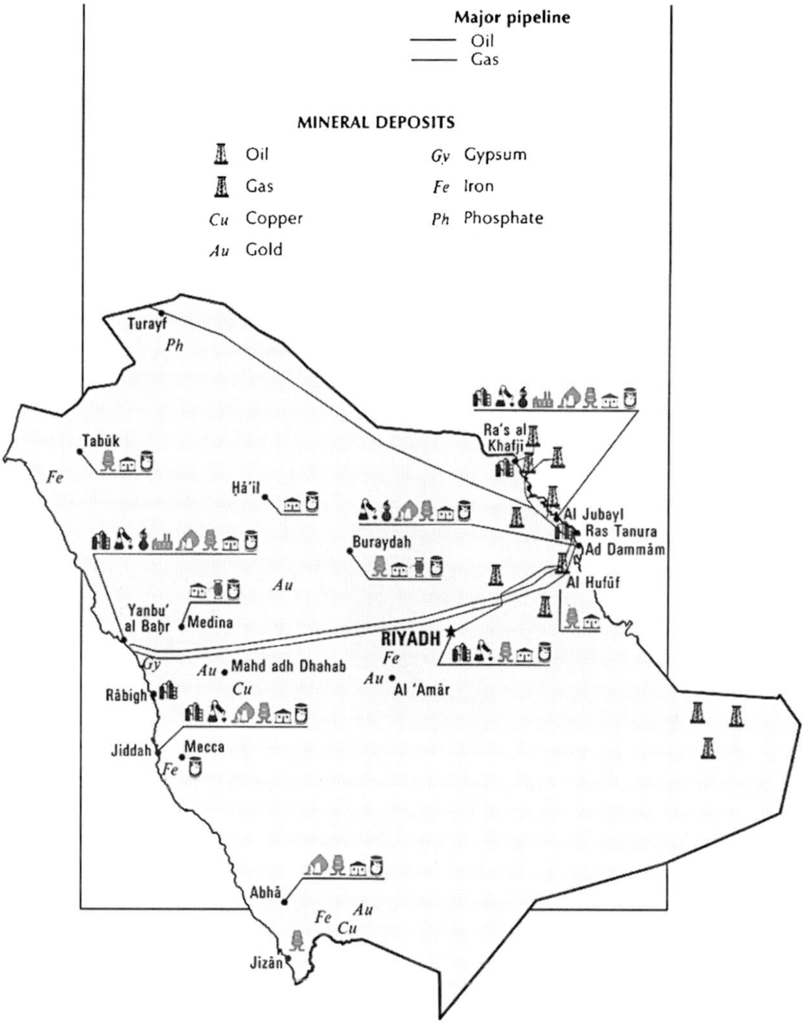

Map 2.2: Map of Saudi Arabia.

Qatar

Qatar is a very small Muslim country with only 11-thousand square kilometers of land (see Map 2.5), but its natural gas reserves rank third in size behind Russia and Iran at 509 trillion cubic feet (Tcf).

Most of Qatar's natural gas is located in the offshore North Dome. This is the largest known non-associated natural gas field in the world. This vast natural gas potential will allow Qatar to play an important role in the global energy mar-

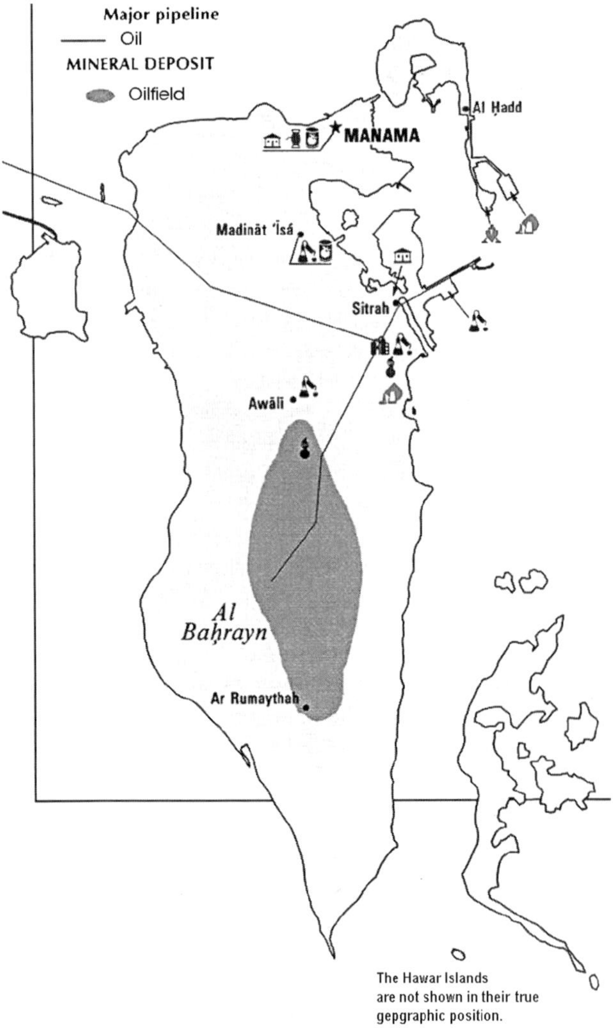

Map 2.3: Map of Bahrain.

ket. Qatar also has proven oil reserves of about 15.2 billion barrels in its onshore Dukhan field and six offshore fields. It exports almost all of its oil to Asia, particularly to Japan.

The United Arab Emirates (UAE)

We turn now to the United Arab Emirates (UAE) which is a federation of seven emirates, in which two large emirates, Abu Dhabi and Dubai (see Map 2.6), con-

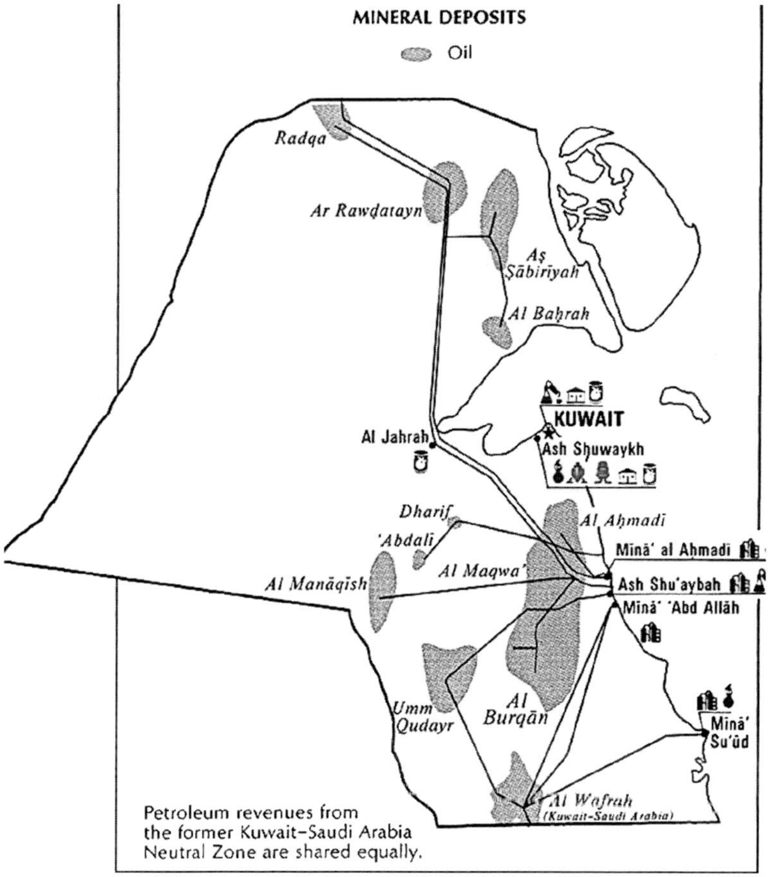

Map 2.4: Map of Kuwait.

tain a dominant share of the UAE's proven oil reserves of 97.8-billion barrels. Most of the UAE oil fields began to produce in the 1960s and 1970s and continue to do so. During the last decade, Abu Dhabi, holding 94% of these oil reserves, has identified new reserves or discovered new oil-rich geological structures in existing fields.

The UAE also has about 212-trillion cubic feet (Tcf) of natural gas reserves, the world's fifth largest — after Russia, Iran, Qatar and Saudi Arabia — and these reserves are projected to last for some 150–170 years.

Iran

The British discovered oil in Iran as early as 1908 (see Map 2.7). This led to formation of the Anglo Persian Oil Company to develop oil fields in the Persian

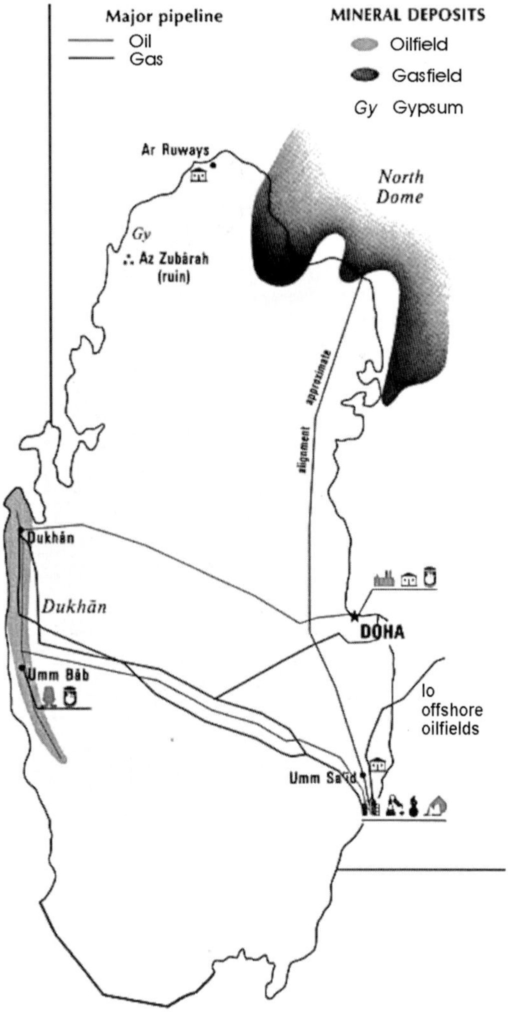

Map 2.5: Map of Qatar.

Gulf region. Today, as British Petroleum Company (BP), it is one of Britain's biggest companies and one of the world's largest oil and petrochemical producers. Iran is OPEC's second largest oil producer — next to Saudi Arabia — with a sustainable crude oil production capacity around 3.75 million barrels per day. It exports nearly 2.6 mb/day of crude oil to Japan, China, South Korea, and some European countries. Iran contains around 90 billion barrels of proven oil reserves in 25 onshore and 7 offshore fields. The giant onshore fields are located in the southwestern region near the Iraqi border and the Persian Gulf.

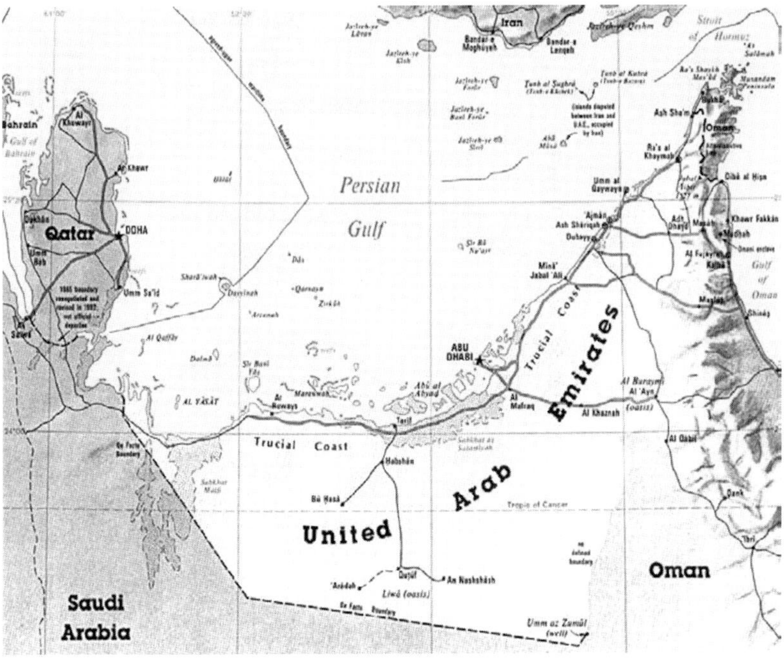

Map 2.6: Map of the United Arab Emirates.

In 1999, Iran announced the biggest oil discovery in 30 years. A new giant onshore field, Azadegan (not shown on this map), contains oil reserves of 26–70 billion barrels, with potential production at 0.3–0.4 mb/day lasting over a 20-year period. Japanese, French, Dutch, Norwegian, Chinese and Indian companies have been invited to bid for developing the giant untapped Azadegan oilfield which is located in western Iran close to Iraq and Kuwait. In February 2004, Inpex, a Japanese government-linked oil developer, signed a contract with the Iranian side on the development of the Azadegan oil field. Iran also has potentially significant oil reserves in the Caspian area of up to 15 billion barrels where it also has natural gas reserves of 11 trillion cubic feet. Iran's total proven natural gas reserves are estimated to be 812 trillion cubic feet. This is the world's second largest reserve, next to Russia. Most Iranian natural gas reserves are located in non-associated fields and have not been developed. This implies a huge potential for nature gas production with potentially enormous effects on future global energy markets.

Iraq

For the last two decades Iraq has been a point of interest to the entire world on issues related to regional and global security as well as its huge reserves of oil

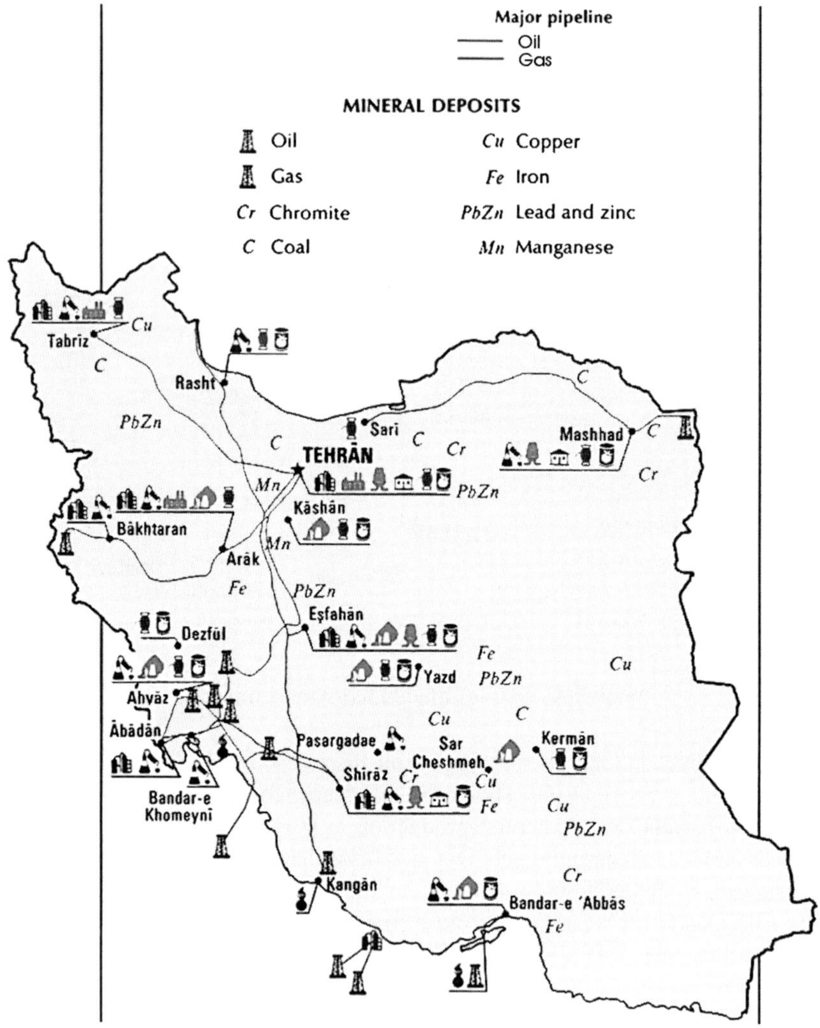

Map 2.7: Map of Iran.

and natural gas. Iraq's proven oil reserves are estimated to be 115 billion barrels. This is third largest in the world behind Saudi Arabia and Canada. Many more oil reserves could also be discovered in unexplored areas of the country because only 10% or so of the country has been explored.

Britain was the first to obtain a concession to exploit oil in Iraq. In 1909 the Anglo–Persian Oil Company (later the Anglo–Iranian Oil Company) was formed to develop this then new industry in this region. In 1931, oil exploitation was made official when the Iraqi government signed a deal with the Iraq Petroleum Company, which represented Royal-Dutch Shell, the Anglo–Persian Oil Company, some French companies, and the Standard Oil[4] of America. The Iraq National Oil Company (INOC) took over the country's oil industry after nationalization of Iraqi oil during 1972–1975.

Iraq's main northern oilfield, the Kirkuk oilfield, was discovered in northern Kirkuk in 1972 with an estimated 8.7 billion barrels of proven reserves. The centrally-located oil field is the East Baghdad field with about 11-billion barrels of proven oil reserves. The largest oil fields of Iraq are located in Rumaila, the southern part of the country, which extends a short distance into Kuwaiti territory. See Map 2.8. Historically, Iraqi oil production peaked in 1979 at the rate of 3.7 million barrels per day, and was reduced to 3.5 mb/day just prior to the invasion of Kuwait by Iraq in 1990.

Under UN economic sanctions and the "oil-for-food" program, Iraq's crude oil production recovered to 1.2 mb/day in 1997, and rose to 2.5 mb/day during 1999–2001. Under the UN oil for food program some 3.4 billion barrels of Iraqi oil were exported in exchange for food and other supplies. Prior to the present US invasion in 2003, experts generally assessed Iraq's sustainable oil production capacity at about 2.8–3.0 million barrels per day. Approximately 2.0 mb/day prewar capacity came from oil fields in the Rumaila area and the remaining pre-war capacity was located in the northern and central fields.

During the 2003 US led war, 7 Iraqi oil wells were set on fire. This is a small number from about 1600 flowing wells in Iraq. Thus, little damage was done to Iraq's oil fields during the war. However, sabotage, looting, and terrorist attacks after the war have been highly destructive to the oil infrastructure, including the country's 4350-mile pipeline system and 11 000-mile-long power grid.

Iraq has estimated natural gas reserves of around 110 trillion cubic feet (Tcf), and natural gas that could be produced in conjunction with oil accounts for about 70% of Iraq's natural gas reserves. Since most of Iraq's natural gas production is from associated oil fields, the country's changing oil output directly affects the gas production. In 2002, Iraq produced 83 billion cubic feet of natural gas, which was down dramatically from its peak of 700 billion cubic feet in 1979. Despite the challenges facing oil and gas production and exports in Iraq, the huge potential

[4] Standard Oil was a large integrated, oil producing, transporting, refining, and marketing organization. It began as an Ohio partnership formed by the well-known industrialist John D. Rockefeller. In 1911, Standard Oil was forced to separate into 34 companies under terms of an anti-trade court order. It then formed the core of today's US oil industry, including Exxon Mobil (formerly Standard of New Jersey and Standard of New York), Conoco Phillips (the Conoco side, which was Standard's company in the Rocky Mountain states), Chevron (Standard of California), Amoco and Sohio (Standard of Indiana and Standard of Ohio) and many other smaller companies.

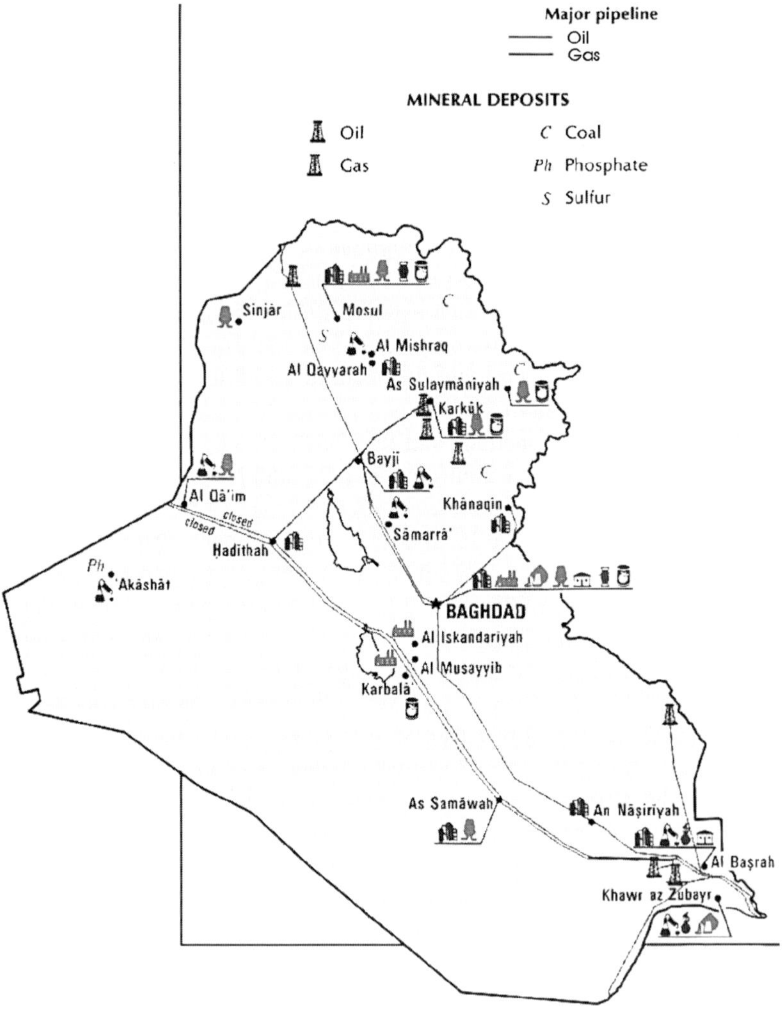

Map 2.8: Map of Iraq.

for development of oil and gas makes Iraq a major player in global oil and natural gas markets.

Oman

Oman is a Muslim country located on the coasts of the Gulf of Oman and the Arabian Sea. Its location overlooks the strategically important Strait of Hormuz (located in Map 2.9), so Oman is also important to world oil markets for this reason. Compared with neighboring Persian Gulf states, Oman's oil fields were

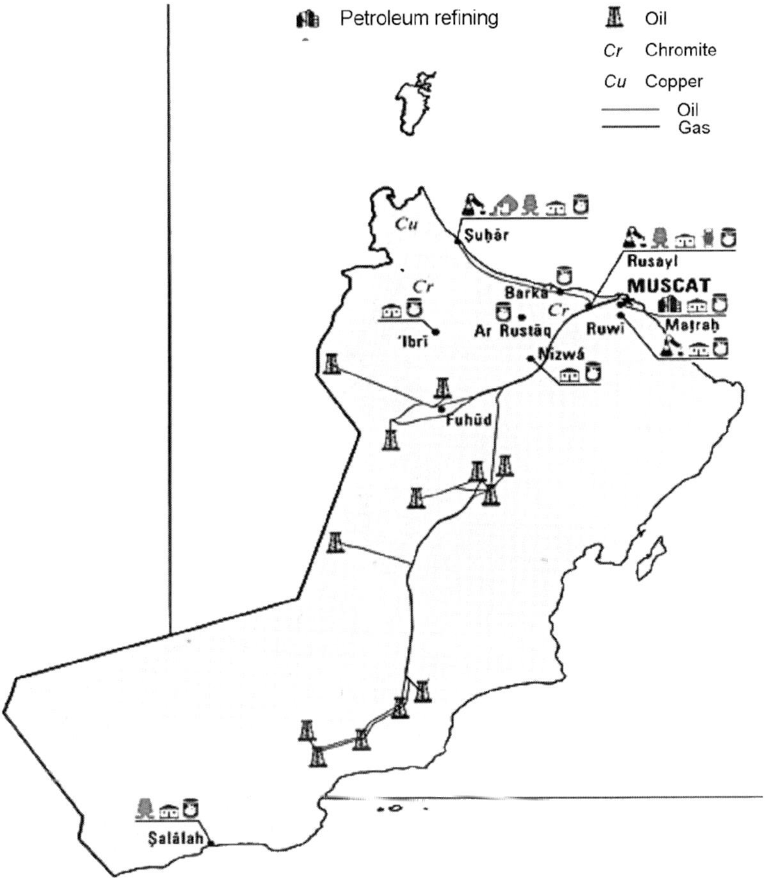

Map 2.9: Map of Oman.

discovered decades later and are generally smaller, less concentrated, more costly to produce and less productive. Its proven oil reserves of 5.5 billion barrels are modest by Persian Gulf standards. Oman's chief focus has been on natural gas development with intense exploration that has increased the proven natural gas reserves from 12.3 trillion cubic feet to nearly 30 trillion cubic feet in the last ten years (1992–2003).

Overall Picture of the Persian Gulf Countries

To summarize the above discussion of Muslim nations in the Persian Gulf region, we use statistical data to present an overall picture of crude oil for the region. In world energy databases, such as those of the Energy Information Administration

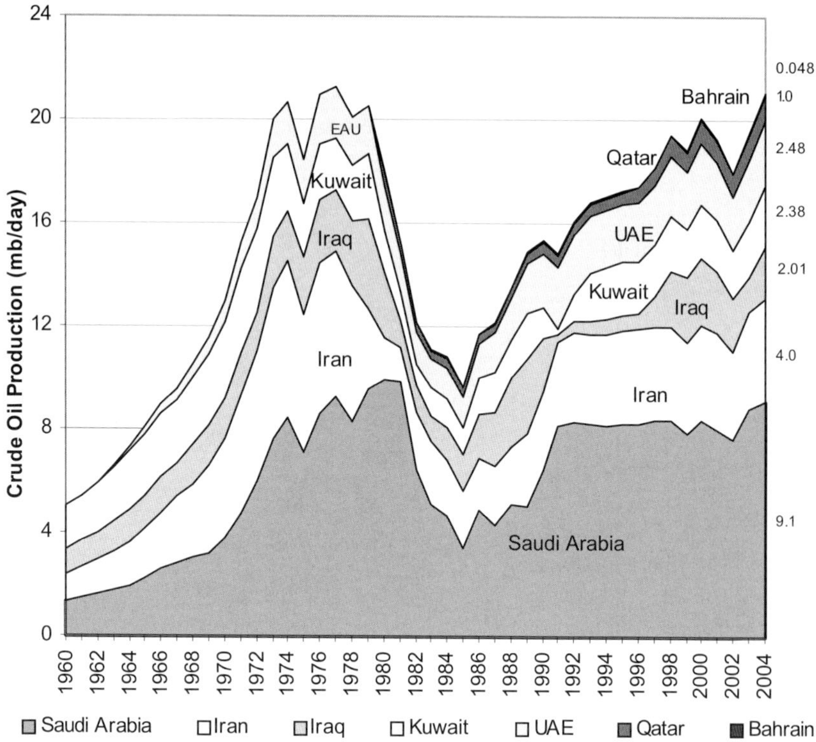

Figure 2.5: Crude Oil Produced by Persian Gulf Nations (1960–2004).

(EIA),[5] Oman is usually not included in the group of Persian Gulf oil producing nations, so we follow this convention in our data demonstration.

The crude oil production curves presented in Figure 2.5, present crude oil production over the period 1960 through 2004, for seven Persian Gulf nations: Saudi Arabia, Iran, Iraq, Kuwait, United Arab Emirates (UAE), Qatar and Bahrain.

The numbers on the right vertical axis of this figure show that these seven Muslim countries produced crude oil, each at rate of 9.1, 4.0, 2.01, 2.38, 2.48, 1.0 and 0.048 mb/day, respectively, in 2004. Thus, as shown on the left vertical axis, the combined crude oil production in the Persian Gulf region reached nearly 21.02 mb/day in 2004 and accounted for 29% of world crude oil production. In 1960, Persian Gulf region crude oil output was only 5.04 mb/day and accounted for but 24% of the world total. The increasing production share, from 24% to 29%, shows that crude oil output in the Persian Gulf region grew faster than the

[5] See note 6 in Chapter 1.

world total. Recalling our analysis in Section 2.1.2 of this chapter, OPEC's crude oil output was 8.7 and 30.2 mb/day in 1960 and 2004, respectively. Thus, Persian Gulf region crude oil output accounted for 58% of OPEC's crude oil production in 1960 and 69.6% in 2004. This increasing percentage share underlies the increasing power of Persian Gulf countries in the international OPEC cartel.

Kuwait and Saudi Arabia were the top oil producers of this region in 1960 with crude oil output of 1.69 and 1.31 million barrels per day, respectively. Crude oil outputs of both Iran and Iraq were around 1.0 mb/day and the other three countries (UAE, Qatar and Bahrain) had negligible outputs in 1960. Rapid development of the petroleum industry in this region led to "take offs" for oil production in these countries, particularly in Saudi Arabia, Iran, UAE, Kuwait and Qatar. Iraq's huge oil reserve has not been successfully turned into crude oil due to continuous political and social upheaval and the wars we will discuss in Part III of this book.

During the "second oil crisis" of 1979 all Persian Gulf countries cut back their oil production so their crude oil output in 1985 was less than half the level of 1976. By 2004 their production (21.02 million barrels per day) was just slightly above the previous high of 20.97 million barrels per day, which was reached in 1976. The production share was 29% in 2004 which is much smaller than the 1974-production share 37.2%. These declines in crude oil output and production share have not been due to limitations in oil reserves or production capacity. Rather, they are due to almost continuous social and geopolitical conflicts such as the Arab–Israeli war, the Iranian revolution, the Iran–Iraq war, Iraq's invasion of Kuwait, and the US led invasion of Iraq, along with Islamic extremist movements and terrorist attacks. In this respect oil production and exports have also served as weapons to fight the West. Nevertheless, *International Energy Oulook 2004* by the Energy Information Administration projects an increase in oil output from Persian Gulf nations that is expected to reach 40.19 mb/day by 2025 and account for 34.8% of total world oil production. Hence, the importance of Persian Gulf nations in global oil markets is expected to increase substantially.

2.3.2. Other OPEC Muslim Countries

We move next to OPEC countries other than these Persian Gulf states. Muslim-majority countries like Algeria, Libya, Nigeria and Indonesia are OPEC members and have also been significant oil producers, so we cover them in the following section starting with Algeria in North Africa.

Algeria

Algeria is presently under-explored although its largest oil field, the Hassi Messaoud (located in the center of the country), was discovered in 1956. See Map 2.10 of Algeria, below. Algeria's proven oil reserves are estimated at 11.3 billion barrels. However, according to some industry experts, undiscovered oil reserves in Algeria could be as high as 43 billion barrels.

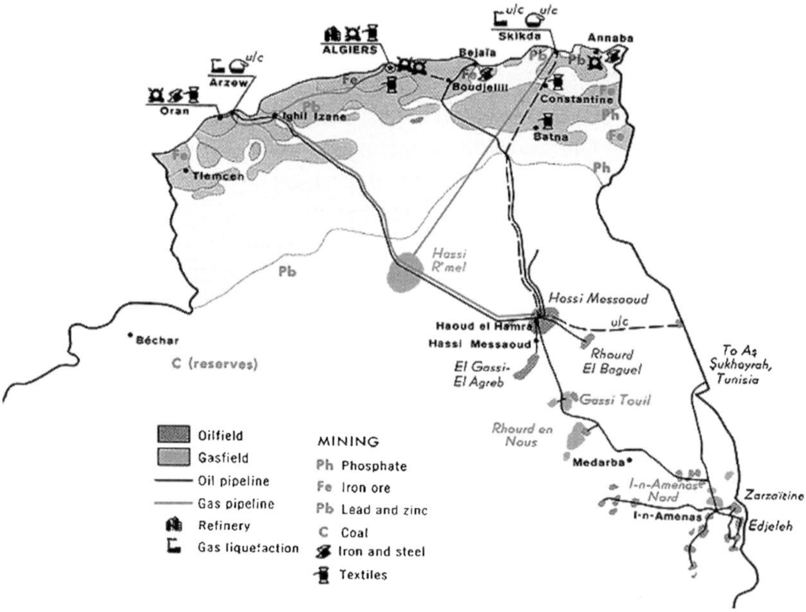

Map 2.10: Map of Algeria.

Total oil production (conventional oil, lease condensate and natural gas liquids) of Algeria reached about 1.86 mb/day during 2003, up from 1.57 mb/day in 2002. The country has attracted billions of dollars of foreign investment into oil exploration and development efforts, so Algeria's oil production capacity should increase rapidly in coming years. Hassi Messaoud is the largest and most prominent oil field with an estimated 6.4 billion barrels of oil reserves, that account for nearly 60% of the country's proven oil reserves. An expanding oil refinery is also located in Hassi Messaoud and many pipelines carry crude from the oil fields to the coastal cities of Skikda, Algiers, Bejaïa, and Arzew in the north, where oil is then exported to Europe. Rhourd El Baguel, located to the southeast of Hassi Messaoud, is Algeria's second largest oilfield with about three billion barrels of oil, of which less than 450 million barrels has been produced since 1963. Algeria has been a net oil exporting country with most of its oil going to Italy, Germany, France, the Netherlands and Spain.

Algeria also has 160 trillion cubic feet of proven natural gas reserves and ranks in the top ten, worldwide. Its potential for recoverable natural gas is estimated at as high as 282 trillion cubic feet. In 2000, natural gas and natural gas liquids accounted for about 60% of Algeria's total hydrocarbons production and its exports of natural gas accounted for 20% of natural gas imports of the countries in the European Union. Its largest gas field is located in Hassi R'mel, northwest of its largest oilfield, Hassi Messaoud, and directly south of the capital city Algiers.

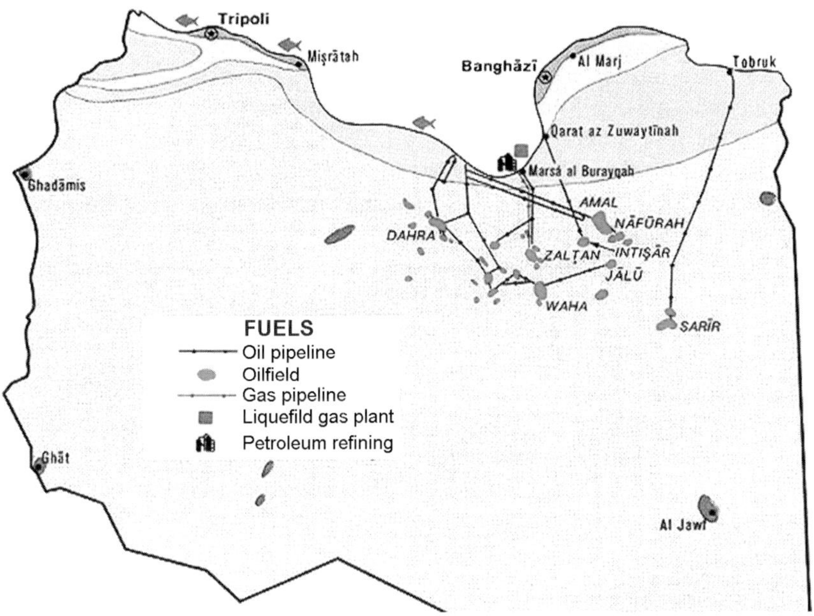

Map 2.11: Map of Libya.

Libya

Libya is a current member of OPEC and a major oil exporter, particularly to Europe. Oil exploration began in 1955 with the first oil fields being discovered in 1959 at Amal and Zaltan, after which oil exports began in 1961. Currently, Libya's proven oil reserves are estimated to be 36 billion barrels mainly located in 14 large oil fields shown on Map 2.11. The country is, however, largely unexplored with great potential for more oil discoveries.

UN sanctions were imposed in 1992 for Libya's involvement in bombing Pan Am flight 103 over Lockerbie, Scotland, in 1988. This led to political and economic isolation of Libya for most of the 1990s. Sanctions caused delays in oil field development, eroded refining capacity, and deterred capital investment and oil exploration. Oil production declined from 3.3 mb/day in 1970 to 1.5 mb/day in 1975 and has stayed at about 1.4 mb/day in the 1990s. Libya also has vast natural gas resources. Proven natural gas reserves are estimated at 46.4 trillion cubic feet. Gas reserves are largely unexplored, however, and may be much larger — as much as 70–100 trillion cubic feet.

UN sanctions were lifted in September 2003, and this could help to boost the country's oil industry. Great potential therefore exists for large increases in Libya's oil and gas exports to Europe.

Nigeria

Nigeria, a Muslim-majority country on the Western Coast of Africa, is an OPEC member and a major oil supplier to Western Europe and the United States. Nigeria's estimated proven oil reserves, in a range of 24 to 31.5 billion barrels, are located along the country's coastal Niger River Delta and in deep offshore waters. See the Gas and Oil map (Map 2.13) which is positioned below the map of the country of Nigeria (Map 2.12).

Crude oil production in Nigeria averaged 2.25 mb/day in 2003. A major portion of this oil output is exported to the United States and Western Europe, and, increasingly, to Asia. Nigeria also has an estimated 124 trillion cubic feet of proven natural gas, which ranks it as ninth largest in the world.

Due to lack of facilities and investment in oil and gas production, about 75% of the natural gas produced in conjunction with oil production was flared and 12% was re-injected to enhance production of oil reserves. This huge potential for gas production and liquefied natural gas has begun to attract global petroleum companies so the present deficiencies should be corrected in the foreseeable future.

Indonesia

Indonesia (see Map 2.14), with about 5 billion barrels of proven oil reserves, is a member of OPEC. Much of Indonesia's proven reserves are located in the central and western sections of the country. The island of Sumatra is the country's largest oil producing province and the location of its largest oil fields. Indonesia's crude oil production has been declining mainly due to aging oil fields and new discoveries have been too small to offset this decline. Oil production averaged about 1.24 mb/day during 2003 and this includes natural gas liquids and lease condensate[6] of about 0.23 million barrels per day.

Indonesia has proven natural gas reserves of 92.5 trillion cubic feet that are located near the oil fields in Northern Sumatra and around oil fields in East Kalimantan, as well as some small fields in offshore Java. Indonesia is the world's largest exporter of liquefied natural gas (LNG). Nearly 70% of its LNG exports go to Japan and the remainder to South Korea and Taiwan. As the only OPEC member in Asia and one of the leading oil exporters to Asian countries, Indonesia is very important and needs help to develop its rich petroleum and natural gas resources in order to fuel rapidly growing Asian economies.

From the above brief description and from present assessments one can see that huge oil and natural gas reserves on our planet are located in many Muslim countries. These countries do not act alone or individually in the world economic and political arena. Rather, they collaborate closely through the OPEC cartel in

[6] Lease condensate is a mixture consisting primarily of pentanes and heavier hydrocarbons and is recovered as a liquid from natural gas in lease separation facilities.

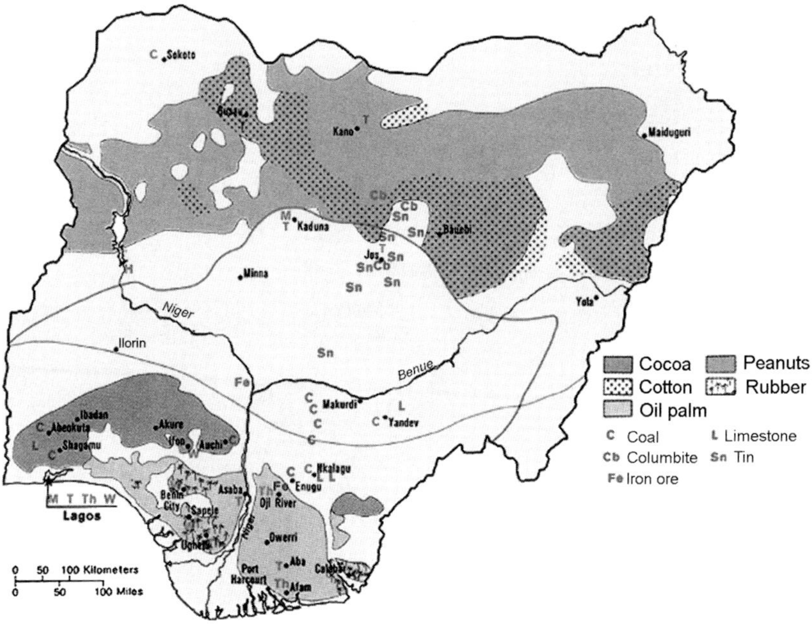

Map 2.12: Map of Nigeria.

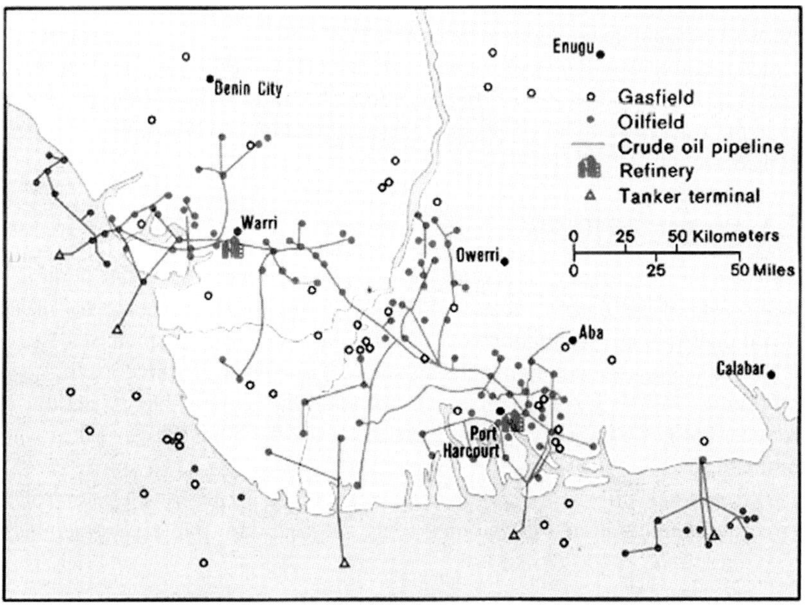

Map 2.13: Oil and Gas of Nigeria.

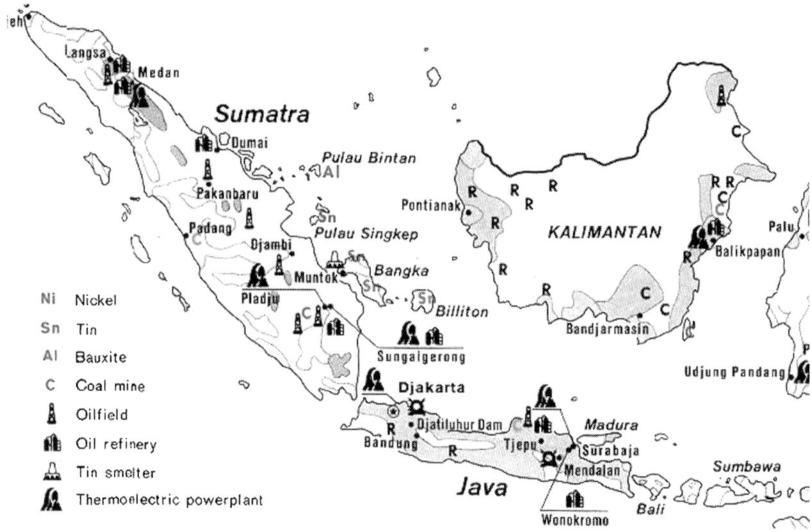

Map 2.14: Map of Indonesia.

order to try to maximize their collective benefit and to exercise influence in the world by controlling strategic resources in oil and natural gas.[7]

The strategic position of the Muslim world, in terms of production and proven reserves of oil and natural gas, is determined not only by the OPEC cartel but also by the emerging economies of the former Soviet republics in Central Asia. These nations hold great potential for future production and exports of oil and natural gas in the world. We therefore discuss these nations in the Caspian Sea Region in the next section.

2.3.3. Caspian Sea Region

The Caspian Sea Region is another place of interest because it has significant oil and natural gas reserves that could make the region a major base for oil and gas production and exportation over coming decades. The Caspian Sea Region includes the five littoral nations of Azerbaijan, Kazakhstan, Turkmenistan, Russia and Iran, as well as Uzbekistan, a sixth member, the region's largest natural gas producer but not a littoral state. Except for Russia, the other five are all Muslim-dominated.

With its huge oil and natural gas reserves and its earlier development of the petroleum industry, Iran is already a leading oil production and export member of

[7] In Section 2.1.2 we described the evolution of OPEC's crude oil production over 1960–2004 as well as OPEC's power in global oil markets.

Map 2.15: Map of the Caspian Sea Region.

OPEC. Azerbaijan and Kazakhstan have the Caspian Region's biggest known oil fields such as the Baku field and the Tengiz field. They are generally considered to be relatively minor oil and gas producers in the present world picture, however, and are struggling with difficult economic and political transitions after achieving independence from the former Soviet Union. The geographic location of the Caspian region is depicted in Map 2.15.

Estimates of Kazakhstan's oil reserves range between 9.0 and 17.6 billion barrels. Most are located in three big oil fields: the Tengiz field along the northeastern shore of the Caspian Sea, the Kashagan field off the northern shore of the Sea, and an onshore field in the country's northern border with Russia. In 2003, Kazakhstan produced oil at a rate of 1.04 mb/day and entered the top 25 oil producer list of the world (see Table 2.1). It exported most of its crude oil in the following three directions, northward via Russian pipelines, westward via Caspian pipelines, and southward via swaps with Iran. Kazakhstan also has sizeable proven natural gas reserves of 65 trillion cubic feet, but these resources have not been exploited. The country's rich hydrocarbon reserves have, however, attracted significant foreign investment to finance several large international projects that could boost oil production to 2.4 mb/day by 2010, and 3.6 mb/day by 2015 — and this would exceed Iran's oil production at 3.53 mb/day in 2002.

Azerbaijan is a Caspian littoral nation with sizeable hydrocarbon resources. Estimates of Azerbaijan's proven crude oil reserves are between 7 and 13 billion

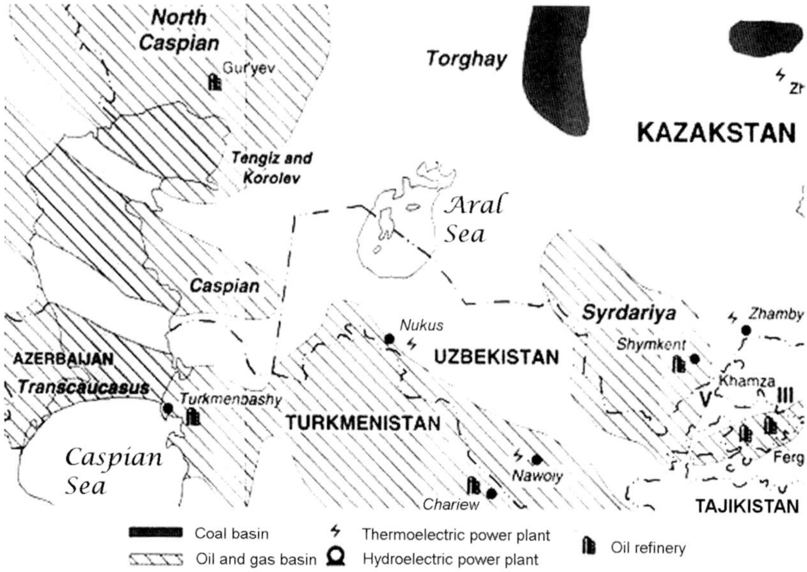

Map 2.16: Map of Fuel and Energy Centers.

barrels, and its proven natural gas reserves are around 30 trillion cubic feet. There is also a potential for identifying even greater oil and gas reserves. The country's largest hydrocarbon structures are located offshore in the Caspian Sea and are the source of the majority of its oil output. During 2003, Azerbaijan produced oil at 0.328 million barrels per day, and exported 0.178 million barrels per day. The country's Soviet-era fields are in decline, but an inflow of foreign investment in recent years is revitalizing its petroleum industry. If the construction of new pipelines from the Caspian Sea Region materializes Azerbaijan is expected to export approximately 1 mb/day by 2010. Insufficient infrastructure to deliver the country's natural gas from offshore fields has led to its natural gas being flared off. Great potential for exploiting and capitalizing the country's rich natural gas reserves could therefore turn Azerbaijan from a natural-gas importer, as at present, into a significant exporter in the coming decade.

Proven oil and natural gas reserves in Turkmenistan and Uzbekistan are considerably smaller than those of other states in the Caspian Sea Region. Hence development of their oil industry has been slower than their neighboring nations. The potential for the Caspian Sea Region to create wealth from its hydrocarbon reserves has been delayed and complicated by social, political and economic factors that include disagreement over Caspian Sea demarcations, border disputes between the littoral states, and clashes over new export routes and pipelines, as well as a lack of adequate oil production and export infrastructures.

2.3.4. Oil and Natural Gas Reserves

Existing petroleum resources are measured by proven reserves of oil and natural gas, which can somehow be estimated. There is a heated debate in the oil industry and the news media over how to estimate oil reserves. Many questions arise, such as what kind of oil resources should be included in the reserve estimate, conventional oil or unconventional oil? Should geological considerations determine how much oil resources exist or should investment and economic factors, including oil field technology revolutions, affect the reserve estimates? Thus estimating reserves is a scientific guesswork with a fuzzy nature.

We use two different kinds of estimates to provide a general picture of possible petroleum resources existing in the world and in some major Muslim nations. One kind of estimate comes from issues of the *Oil & Gas Journal* with reserve

Table 2.3: Crude Oil and Natural Gas Reserves

Region/Country	Crude Oil (billion barrels)		Natural Gas (trillion cubic feet)	
	Journal (2005)	USGS (2000)	Journal (2005)	USGS (2000)
World total	1277.7	1617.8	6040.2	9941.4
Muslim World	845.8	893.7	3414.9	4503.1
OPEC (excluding Venezuela)	808.0	804.4	2941.4	3483.5
7 Persian Gulf States	717.3	685.2	2465.9	2788.1
Saudi Arabia	261.9	297.8	235.0	968.9
Iran	125.8	124.4	940.0	935.8
Iraq	115.0	122.8	110.0	189.4
Kuwait	101.5	58.1	55.5	64.6
United Arab Emirates	97.8	64.9	212.1	184.2
Libya	39.0	33.0	52.0	72.3
Nigeria	35.3	55.0	176.0	206.7
Algeria	11.8	16.9	160.5	221.9
Kazakhstan	9.0	35.7	65.0	141.4
% of the World total	%	%	%	%
Muslim World	66.2	55.2	56.5	45.3
OPEC (excluding Venezuela)	63.3	49.7	48.7	35.0
7 Persian Gulf States	56.1	42.4	40.8	28.0
Saudi Arabia	20.5	18.4	3.9	9.7
Iran	9.9	7.7	15.6	9.4
Iraq	9.0	7.6	1.8	1.9
Kuwait	7.9	3.9	0.9	0.7
United Arab Emirates	7.7	4.0	3.5	1.9
Libya	3.1	2.0	0.9	0.7
Nigeria	2.8	3.4	2.9	2.1
Algeria	0.9	1.0	2.7	2.2
Kazakhstan	0.7	2.2	1.1	1.4

estimates provided up to January 1, 2005. Our other estimate comes from the US Geological Survey World Petroleum Assessment 2000 (USGS 2000), in which the estimates are defined as remaining reserves plus the mean of undiscovered conventional oil (or natural gas). Both kinds of estimates are published by the Energy Information Administration and Table 2.3 summarizes the oil reserve and natural gas reserve estimates from these two sources.

As can be observed in Table 2.3, the two kinds of estimates do not agree on specific numbers. The USGS estimates show greater volumes of oil and natural gas reserves than the Oil & Gas Journal for the entire world, as well as regions and individual countries. Also, the relative shares of the Muslim world, the seven Persian Gulf states and OPEC are smaller for the USGS estimates than for the Oil & Gas Journal. No matter which estimates are used for evaluating future petroleum resources, however, the Muslim world maintains its dominance with its oil reserves accounting for (55–66)% of total world oil reserves and natural gas reserves accounting for (45–56)% of the world total. The seven Persian Gulf states in particular are projected to have (42–56)% of world oil reserves, and (35–48)% of world natural gas reserves.

Summary of Chapter 2

This chapter has provided an analysis of the world oil and natural gas production over the last four decades, showing the declining oil production of leading oil producers of USA and former USSR, and the increasing oil production of new leading oil producers of the Muslim countries like Saudi Arabia, Iran, Iraq and other Persian Gulf countries.

This chapter also examined the crucial role of OPEC in the world oil crises in 1973 and 1979 through its manipulation of oil production that largely affected world oil prices. The increasing importance of Muslim countries in global oil and natural gas markets is exhibited by the rising oil production share of the 48 Muslim countries from 30% of the total world oil output in 1985 to 42.5% of the world total in 2003 and by the increasing natural gas production share from 6.0% in 1980 to 25.8% in 2003. Therefore, this chapter provides a brief description of oil and natural gas resources for the Muslim countries that are OPEC members and for the Muslim countries in the Caspian Sea region, which is expected to become a world's new center for fuel and energy.

As this chapter makes clear, the world will continue to be dependent on the Muslim countries and especially the Persian Gulf countries for both oil and natural gas. Large additional petroleum reserves are fore casted to be found in Saudi Arabia, Iran, Iraq, UAE, Kuwait, Nigeria, Libya, and Algeria. These estimates of future petroleum resources and relative shares in total world reserves are also represented in Table 2.3, above. According to these estimates, about (18–20)% of world oil reserves will be located in Saudi Arabia, (7–10)% in Iran, (7–9)%

in Iraq, and (4–8)% in each of the UAE and Kuwait. Thus the Muslim world in general and the Persian Gulf states in particular will continue to be strategically important to the security and prosperity of the entire world because of the world's increasing dependency upon them for their huge petroleum resources.

As discussed in Chapter 1 of this book, the world has been increasingly in need of oil and natural gas as major energy sources. As long as advanced mature-market-economy countries in the world continue to use oil to fuel their economies and the emerging-economy countries, like China and India, continue to move toward the advanced group, the dominating position of the Muslim world in the current and future global oil markets will continue to assure the strategic importance of the Muslim world.

We will carry the topic of strategic importance further by reference to the geographic location of these Muslim countries relative to important "choke points" for oversea traffic, especially in oil and gas, in the next chapter of this, Part I, of the book. This is done after first briefly surveying international trade in oil with special reference to individual countries that are not importers and not exporters as well as how these individual countries relate to each other.

Chapter 3

Global Oil Flow and Strategic Geography of the Muslim World

Chapter 1 provided a general picture of the demand side of global oil and natural gas markets as well as specific groups of countries and the significant countries that have contributed to expanding worldwide demand. Chapter 2 provided an analysis of the supply side of markets. From these two chapters one can see that, except for the United States and a few other countries, significant suppliers are not significant consumers and vice versa. Countries with excess demand for oil and natural gas must import from abroad to meet domestic demand and countries with excess production of oil and natural gas must export to other countries in order to generate wealth and economic activity. International trade links producers to consumers and forms global markets that allow oil and natural gas to flow across borders between regions and countries.

This chapter therefore provides an analysis of international trade in oil in order to help in understanding relations between countries, in general, and relationships between the West and the Muslim world in particular. In terms of quality and location there are many different kinds of oil that are traded in global markets so it would be very difficult to use these detailed trading data without losing more important facets of the big picture. Our analysis is therefore based on aggregate consumption and production data of individual countries. Net imports are defined as a country's consumption minus its production of oil and, similarly, net exports are defined as a country's production minus its consumption of oil. Therefore a country could export and import various kinds of oil at the same time, but only the net exports or net imports are considered here.

This chapter consists of two sections. Section 3.1 identifies leading net importers and net exporters in global oil markets and analyzes the link between advanced and Muslim countries. These importer and exporter countries have been subject to dynamic changes that are summarized in Tables 3.3 and 3.4. Section 3.2 provides a geographic overview of the Muslim world that is crucial to understanding the strategic control of oil and natural gas flows from production locations to consumption destinations.

3.1. International Trade on Oil

3.1.1. Net Importer and Net Exporter of Oil

The net exports and net imports of oil, as defined above, can be calculated by using data for consumption and production of oil by individual countries. There

International Symposia in Economic Theory and Econometrics, Vol. 19
William W. Cooper and Piyu Yue

ISSN: 1571-0386/DOI: 10.1016/S1571-0386(07)00012-9

are 220 countries in the Energy Information Administration (EIA) database that are used to conduct these calculations. Countries are then ranked according to their net import (export) quantities in each year and the net imports (exports) of countries are added together to yield world net imports (exports) of oil. In principle, world net imports must equal world net exports if the international trade is to be balanced. In practice, however, this balance is reached only approximately each year. In our calculations the largest discrepancy between world net imports and net exports over 1980–2003, the period we cover, was about 5% in one year and for most years it was less than 2%. Hence we consider world net oil imports to be equal to world net oil exports and use one or the other as a denominator to calculate approximately market share for net importer and net exporter countries.

Figure 3.1 displays world net exports (or imports) of oil along with the net-export shares of the 7 Persian Gulf countries and the 48 Muslim countries. As calibrated on the left vertical axis, world net exports of oil were about 30.1 mb/day in 1980, but reduced to 24.2 mb/day in 1985 due to the "second oil crisis". Since 1985, as the graph shows, world exports (imports) have been continuously increasing, reaching 43.1 mb/day in 2003. This behavior is consistent with our analysis of accelerating worldwide demand for oil that we discussed in Sections 1.3 and 1.4 of Chapter 1.

Turning to the percentages calibrated on the right vertical axis, the Muslim world total net exports of oil accounted for 73.7% of world total net oil exports

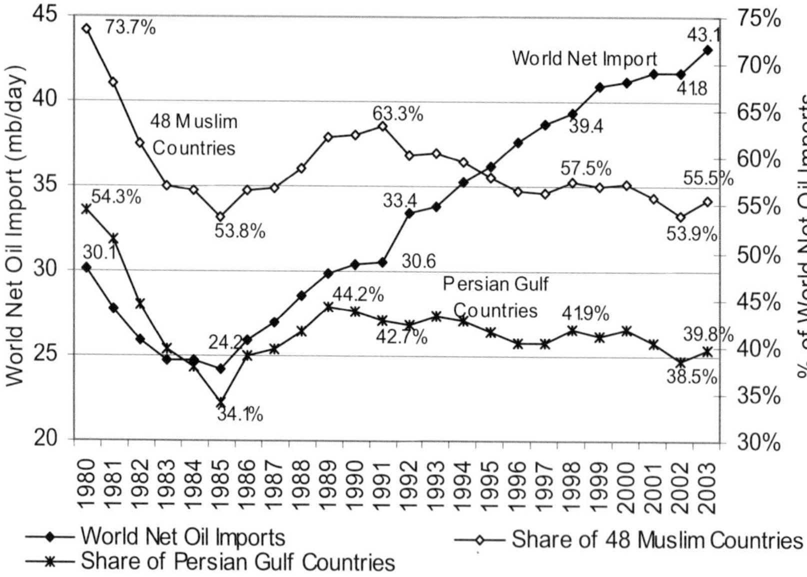

Figure 3.1: World Net Oil Imports and Muslim Country Shares.

in 1980. As shown in Figure 3.1, this share was reduced to 53.8% in 1985 but rebounded to 63.3% in 1991 and reached 55.5% in 2003. Comparing the curve of net oil export share for Muslim countries with the curve for Persian Gulf countries in Figure 3.1 one can see that the movement of net oil exports of the Muslim world was greatly influenced by Persian Gulf countries, whose net export share declined from 54.3% in 1980 to 34.1% in 1985, rebounded to 44.2% in 1989 and reached 39.8% in 2003. The declining market share of the Muslim world portrayed in Figure 3.1 indicates that new exporters entered global oil markets and took over part of the market share of Muslim countries. Nevertheless, the Muslim world still controls more than 50% of world net exports of oil and the group of 7 Persian Gulf Muslim countries controls nearly 40% of the world total.

Figure 3.2, shows net oil imports by the world's six largest net oil importers and the accompanying Figure 3.3 shows net oil exports by the world's largest six net exporters over the period of 1980–2003.

As shown in Figure 3.2, the United States has been the largest net importer in global oil markets. US net imports were about 6.2 mb/day in 1980, temporarily reduced in 1981–1985, exceeded its previous high in 1988, and has continuously increased without major interruption, reaching an all time high at 11.2 mb/day in 2003. This curve clearly shows a US dependency on imported oil that has greatly intensified over 1985–2003. This is a result of both accelerating consumption and the declining US production of oil that was previously exhibited in Figures 1.7 and 2.1.

Japan and Germany are the world's second and third largest net importers of oil, but neither of them expanded their dependency on imported oil as was the case for the US Japan's net imports rose from 4.9 to 5.5 mb/day in 1980–2003, and its highest net import of 5.7 million barrels per day occurred in only two years, 1996 and 1997. Germany's net oil imports actually declined from 3.0 to 2.5 mb/day in 1980–2003.

South Korea, China and India raised their net oil imports substantially, particularly in the 1990s. Before 1993, China was a net exporter in global oil markets, but in 1993 China jumped to the other side and became a net oil importer. Since 1994 China's net oil imports have greatly increased, reaching about 2.0 mb/day in 2003. (As discussed in Chapter 1, these three countries have rapidly growing economies and need increasingly large quantities of oil to sustain their high rates of development.)

Figure 3.3 depicts three Muslim countries (Saudi Arabia, Iran and UAE) along with three non-Muslim countries (Russia, Norway and Venezuela) all of which are significant net oil exporters. Saudi Arabia has been and continues to be the largest net exporter of oil. Its net exports were 9.7 mb/day in 1980, reduced to 2.8 mb/day in 1985, during the second oil crisis, and has been gradually restored. By 2003, Saudi net exports were about 8.4 million barrels per day, which were still less than its 1980 net export of 9.7 mb/day.

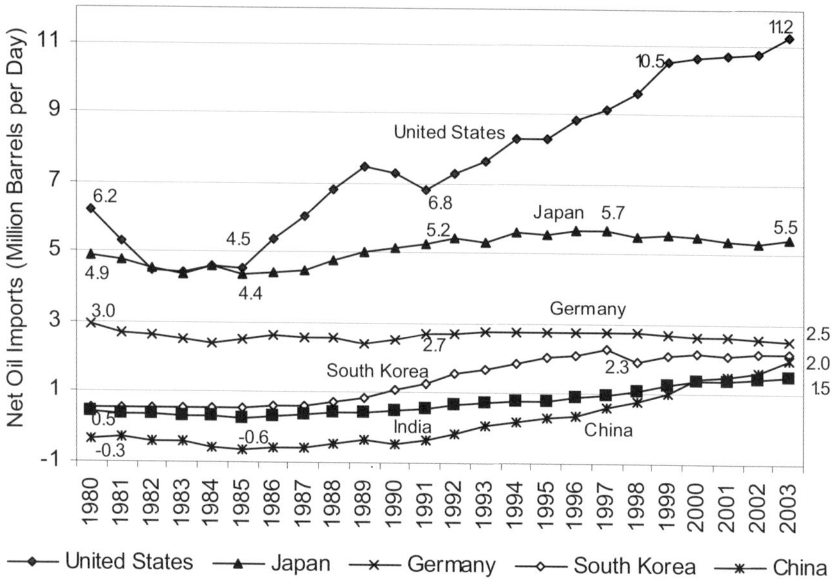

Figure 3.2: Top Oil Importer Countries (1980–2003).

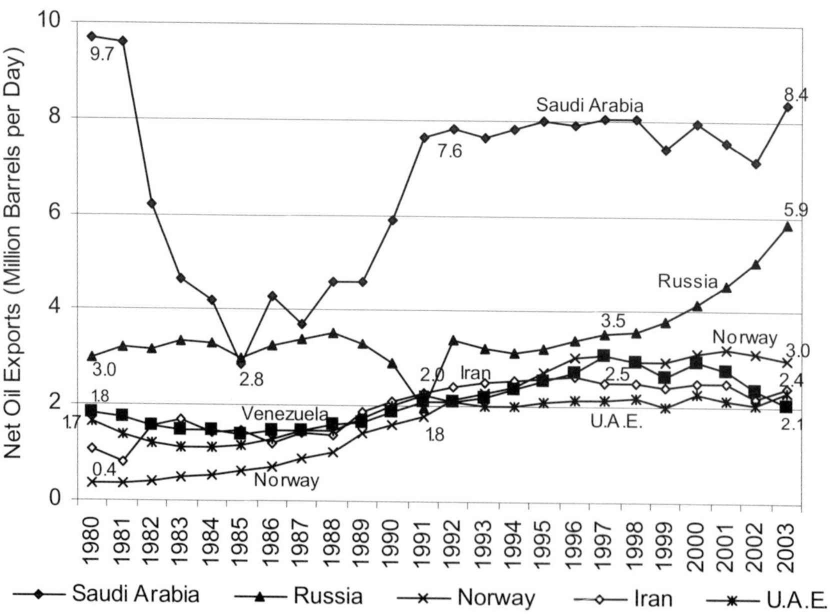

Figure 3.3: Top Net Oil Export Countries (1980–2003).

Russia has been the second largest net oil exporter for the last twenty five years. Here, the net export data over 1980–1991 is also for the former USSR. As a new state, Russia, a drop in net export to 2 mb/day in 1991 followed by a rise 3.4 mb/day in 1992, has quickly raised its net exports after 1994. In 2003, Russia's net export of oil reached 5.9 million barrels per day and continues to rise along this upward trend. The other four exporters exhibited in Figure 3.3 have been far behind these top two exporters. Their net exports of oil have, however, gradually increased except for Venezuela, where net exports of oil declined from about 3 mb/day in 2000 to 2.1 mb/day in 2003.

For detailed individual country information we provide the following Tables 3.1 and 3.2. Table 3.1 lists the largest 25 net importers and Table 3.2 lists the largest 20 net exporters in global oil markets for 1980, 1985, 1992 and 2003. It is worth notice that: (1) West Bank and Gaza is excluded from our analysis due to lack of data. (2) As shown in the next to last row of Table 3.2, the 12 to 13 Muslim countries at the top of this list of 20 countries showed the following percentages: 75.1% in 1980, 56.9% in 1985, 62.8% in 1992 and 55.7% in 2003. These percentages are all greater than the 48 Muslim country shares in the same years, as shown by the 48-Muslim-country curve in Figure 3.1, above. This is because Turkey and Pakistan are larger net importers of oil and other, smaller net importers are included such as Jordan, Lebanon and Morocco. As Table 3.1 shows Turkey was in the top 25 list of largest net importers of oil in all four of the described years and Pakistan was in this list as number 22 in 2003. Hence these net importer Muslim countries have contributed negatively to the 48 Muslim country aggregate share of net exports of oil as shown in Figure 3.1.

The bottom row in Table 3.1 shows that the top 25 net importers (Sum 25) accounted for nearly 87% of world total net imports of oil, and the bottom row of Table 3.2 shows that the top 20 net exporters supplied more than 92% of the world total exports of oil in 1980–2003. Thus the supply side of global oil markets is more concentrated than the demand side. More countries need to import oil and fewer countries export it. In 2003, the top three importers, United States, Japan and Germany, took nearly 45% of total world net imports of oil, while the top two exporters, Saudi Arabia and Russia, supplied one third of total world net exports. Twelve Muslim countries in the 2003 list controlled about 56% of world total net exports. Significant non-Muslim competitors on the supply side are Russia, Norway, Venezuela and Mexico. New emerging countries are Angola and Argentina. Both did not appear in the 1980 and 1985 lists.

Of interest is the fact that China was a significant net exporter of oil and ranked as number 16 in 1980 and number 15 in 1985 in Table 3.2. In 1992, however, China's net exports of oil declined to 0.190 mb/day and then dropped entirely off the list of net exporters in Table 3.2. China began to import oil in 1993. As of 2003, China became the fifth largest net importer of oil in the world, with net imports of 2.0 mb/day shown in Table 3.1.

Table 3.1: Top 25 Largest Net Importers of Oil (in 1 000 Barrels per Day)

R	1980		1985		1992		2003	
	Country	Net Oil Imports	Country	Net Oil Imports	Country	Net Oil Imports	Country	Net Oil Imports
1	USA	6 245 (20.8%)	USA	4 534 (18.7%)	USA	7 265 (21.7%)	USA	11 236 (26.1%)
2	Japan	4 921 (16.4%)	Japan	4 385 (18.1%)	Japan	5 412 (16.2%)	Japan	5 458 (12.7%)
3	Germany West	2 582 (8.58%)	Germany West	2 190 (9.03%)	Germany	2 704 (8.09%)	Germany	2 519 (5.84%)
4	France	2 173 (7.22%)	France	1 647 (6.79%)	France	1 818 (5.44%)	Korea South	2 165 (5.02%)
5	Italy	1 866 (6.20%)	Italy	1 621 (6.69%)	Italy	1 782 (5.33%)	China	2 001 (4.64%)
6	Spain	946 (3.14%)	Spain	801 (3.30%)	Korea South	1 550 (4.64%)	France	1 984 (4.60%)
7	Brazil	904 (3.00%)	Korea South	562 (2.32%)	Spain	1 064 (3.18%)	Italy	1 738 (4.03%)
8	Nether-lands	736 (2.45%)	Nether-lands	490 (2.02%)	Ukraine	732 (2.19%)	Spain	1 520 (3.53%)
9	Korea South	554 (1.84%)	Belgium	394 (1.63%)	Brazil	697 (2.08%)	India	1 505 (3.49%)
10	Sweden	524 (1.74%)	Taiwan	372 (1.53%)	Nether-lands	682 (2.04%)	Taiwan	907 (2.10%)
11	Belgium	514 (1.71%)	Sweden	353 (1.46%)	India	673 (2.01%)	Nether-lands	825 (1.91%)
12	India	458 (1.52%)	Brazil	345 (1.42%)	Taiwan	562 (1.68%)	Singa-pore	697 (1.62%)
13	Germany East	381 (1.27%)	Germany East	319 (1.32%)	Belgium	499 (1.49%)	Belgium	611 (1.42%)
14	Poland	379 (1.26%)	Turkey	314 (1.30%)	Singa-pore	424 (1.27%)	Turkey	607 (1.41%)
15	Taiwan	371 (1.23%)	Poland	312 (1.29%)	Turkey	411 (1.23%)	Thailand	555 (1.29%)
16	Czecho-slovakia	353 (1.17%)	Czecho-slovakia	298 (1.23%)	Thailand	409 (1.22%)	Poland	452 (1.05%)
17	South Africa	312 (1.04%)	South Africa	290 (1.20%)	Sweden	336 (1.01%)	Greece	423 (0.98%)
18	Switzer-land	306 (1.02%)	Bulgaria	284 (1.17%)	Belarus	333 (1.00%)	Sweden	344 (0.80%)
19	Bulgaria	303 (1.01%)	Switzer-land	270 (1.11%)	Greece	306 (0.92%)	Portugal	323 (0.75%)
20	Denmark	281 (0.92%)	India	269 (1.11%)	Switzer-land	280 (0.84%)	Philip-pines	321 (0.74%)
21	Finland	271 (0.90%)	Yugo-slavia	241 (0.99%)	Portugal	280 (0.84%)	Ukraine	314 (0.73%)
22	Turkey	265 (0.88%)	Singa-pore	223 (0.92%)	Poland	273 (0.82%)	Pakistan	276 (0.64%)

(*continued on next page*)

Table 3.1: (*continued*)

R	1980		1985		1992		2003	
	Country	Net Oil Imports	Country	Net Oil Imports	Country	Net Oil Imports	Country	Net Oil Imports
23	Greece	261 (0.87%)	Greece	212 (0.87%)	South Africa	271 (0.81%)	Israel	267 (0.62%)
24	Thailand	222 (0.74%)	Finland	205 (0.85%)	Philip-pines	252 (0.75%)	South Africa	267 (0.62%)
25	Yugo-slavia	213 (0.71%)	Cuba	198 (0.82%)	Czecho-slovakia	242 (0.72%)	Austria	261 (0.60%)
	Top 3	13 748 (45.7%)	Top 3	11 109 (45.8%)	Top 3	15 381 (46.0%)	Top 3	19 213 (44.6%)
	Sum 25	26 340 (87.6%)	Sum 25	21 129 (87.2%)	Sum 25	29 259 (87.5%)	Sum 25	37 574 (87.2%)

Table 3.2: Top 20 Largest Net Exporters of Oil (in 1 000 Barrels per Day)

R	1980		1985		1992		2003	
	Country	Net Oil Exports	Country	Net Oil Exports	Country	Net Oil Exports	Country	Net Oil Exports
1	Saudi Arabia	9 675 (31.1%)	USSR	2 985 (12.8%)	Saudi Arabia	7 817 (23.9%)	Saudi Arabia	8 358 (19.6%)
2	USSR	2 996 (9.63%)	Saudi Arabia	2 839 (12.1%)	Russia	3 396 (10.4%)	Russia	5 852 (13.7%)
3	Iraq	2 309 (7.42%)	Mexico	1 568 (6.70%)	Iran	2 394 (7.30%)	Norway	3 009 (7.05%)
4	Nigeria	1 890 (6.07%)	Iran	1 482 (6.33%)	Norway	2 144 (6.54%)	Iran	2 406 (5.64%)
5	Vene-zuela	1 846 (5.93%)	Vene-zuela	1 374 (5.87%)	Vene-zuela	2 106 (6.42%)	UAE	2 326 (5.45%)
6	Libya	1 727 (5.55%)	Nigeria	1 278 (5.46%)	UAE	2,105 (6.42%)	Vene-zuela	2 052 (4.81%)
7	UAE	1 672 (5.37%)	Iraq	1 189 (5.08%)	Nigeria	1 686 (5.14%)	Kuwait	2 013 (4.72%)
8	Kuwait	1 654 (5.31%)	UAE	1 171 (5.00%)	Libya	1 321 (4.03%)	Nigeria	1 936 (4.54%)
9	Indonesia	1 251 (4.02%)	UK	1 111 (4.75%)	Mexico	1 279 (3.90%)	Mexico	1 782 (4.18%)
10	Iran	1 093 (3.51%)	Algeria	993 (4.24%)	Algeria	1 143 (3.49%)	Algeria	1 658 (3.89%)
11	Algeria	1 022 (3.28%)	Kuwait	965 (4.13%)	Kuwait	964 (2.94%)	Libya	1 249 (2.93%)
12	Mexico	883 (2.84%)	Libya	957 (4.09%)	Indonesia	870 (2.65%)	Qatar	967 (2.27%)

(*continued on next page*)

Table 3.2: (*continued*)

R	1980		1985		1992		2003	
	Country	Net Oil Exports	Country	Net Oil Exports	Country	Net Oil Exports	Country	Net Oil Exports
13	Qatar	472 (1.52%)	Indonesia	915 (3.91%)	Oman	705 (2.15%)	Canada	917 (2.15%)
14	Norway	369 (1.19%)	Norway	635 (2.71%)	Angola	500 (1.52%)	Iraq	883 (2.07%)
15	Egypt	353 (1.13%)	China	620 (2.65%)	Egypt	470 (1.43%)	Angola	856 (2.01%)
16	China	349 (1.12%)	Egypt	485 (2.07%)	Qatar	458 (1.40%)	Kazakhstan	815 (1.91%)
17	Oman	267 (0.86%)	Oman	472 (2.02%)	Canada	405 (1.24%)	Oman	761 (1.78%)
18	Brunei	265 (0.85%)	Canada	322 (1.38%)	Malaysia	365 (1.11%)	UK	671 (1.57%)
19	Trinidad Tobago	172 (0.55%)	Qatar	307 (1.31%)	Syria	294 (0.90%)	Yemen	368 (0.86%)
20	Gabon	165 (0.53%)	Malaysia	257 (1.10%)	Gabon	281 (0.86%)	Argentina	359 (0.84%)
	Top 2	12 671 (40.7%)	Top 2	5 824 (24.9%)	Top 2	11 213 (34.2%)	Top 2	14 210 (33.3%)
	12 Muslim Nations	23 385 (75.1%)	13 Muslim Nations	13 310 (56.9%)	13 Muslim Nations	20 591 (62.8%)	12 Muslim Nations	23 740 (55.7%)
	Sum 20	30 430 (97.8%)	Sum 20	21 925 (93.7%)	Sum 20	30 702 (93.7%)	Sum 20	39 239 (92.0%)

Indonesia provides another interesting case. Indonesia's net exports of oil were 1.25 mb/day in 1980 and this ranked it number 9 in the world, as shown in Table 3.2. In 2003, however, Indonesia's net exports of oil fell to 0.085 mb/day, ranking it number 8 from the bottom among 43 net oil export countries and have disappeared from Table 3.2. Figure 3.4 shows that both Chinese and Indonesian oil consumptions have increased rapidly with China changing status from exporter to importer in 1993 and Indonesia diminishing its net exports of oil.

Indonesia is a member of the OPEC international cartel. With such a reduction in the quantity of net oil exports in 2003, Indonesia could be endangering its membership in OPEC. Dynamic change thus happens not only on the demand side but also on the supply side in global oil markets. Rapid economic growth in many emerging economies has led to increasing usage of oil. It is therefore quite possible that other oil net exporter countries will follow China and Indonesia in the near future and turn themselves into oil net importers, thereby creating pressures in global oil markets from both the supply and demand sides.

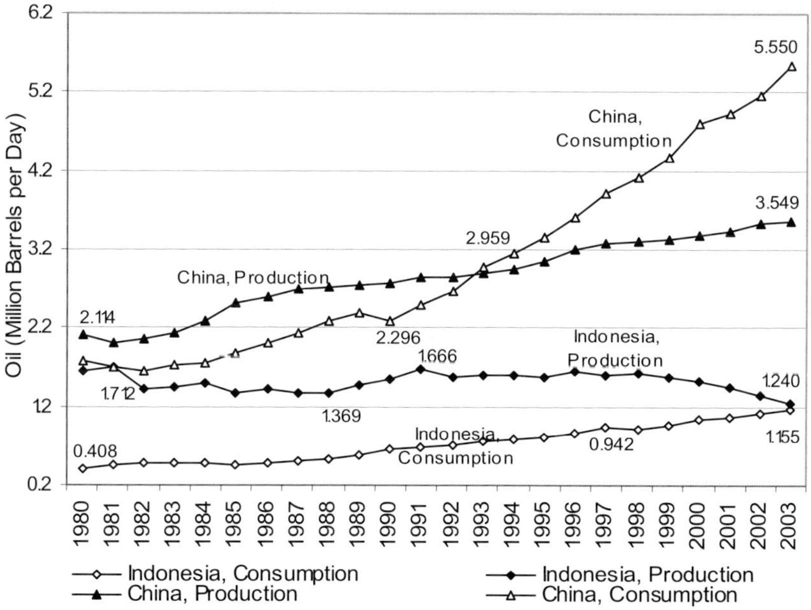

Figure 3.4: Oil Production and Consumption of China and Indonesia.

We could continue this discussion of Tables 3.1 and 3.2 to cover other items of interest. Instead, however, we move to the next topic which deals with which exporters supply oil to which importers.

3.1.2. Net Oil Imports by Origin

We now leave aside further analysis of Tables 3.1 and 3.2 in order to move to the next topic that shows which exporter supplies oil to which importer. This analysis further identifies specific relationships and connections between Muslim and advanced countries.

We start by describing the net oil import origins for the largest world net importers — the United States, Japan, OECD Europe (including Germany, France, Italy and other European countries) and South Korea. Muslim countries are represented by OPEC Muslim members since they all belong to the top 20 net exporters of oil.

These import origins are first categorized as OPEC and non-OPEC in columns 3 and 4 of Table 3.3. OPEC is then divided into the Persian Gulf group (Saudi Arabia, Iran, Iraq, Kuwait, UAE and Qatar), and OPEC Africa (Algeria, Libya and Nigeria), OPEC South America (Venezuela), and OPEC Asia (Indonesia). We use net import quantities to calculate shares of net imports from each origin

Table 3.3: Oil Import Origins of USA, OECD Europe, Japan and South Korea

Net Importer	Year (1)	Net Oil Imports (mb/day) (2)	Non-OPEC (3)	OPEC (4)	Persian Gulf (5)
United States	1991	6.626	2.711 (40.9%)	3.915 (59.1%)	1.833 (27.7%)
	1995	7.886	3.906 (49.5%)	3.980 (50.5%)	1.563 (19.8%)
	2000	10.419	5.237 (50.3%)	5.182 (49.7%)	2.483 (23.8%)
	2004	12.097	6.094 (53%)	5.688 (47%)	2.489 (20.6%)
OECD Europe	1991	9.092	2.319 (25.5%)	6.772 (74.5%)	3.686 (40.5%)
	1995	7.825	1.531 (19.6%)	6.295 (80.4%)	3.422 (43.7%)
	2000	7.926	1.955 (24.7%)	5.971 (75.3%)	3.240 (40.9%)
	2004	9.080	3.715 (40.9%)	5.364 (59.1%)	2.831 (31.2%)
Japan	1991	5.375	1.311 (24.4%)	4.064 (75.6%)	3.410 (63.4%)
	1995	5.709	1.206 (21.1%)	4.503 (78.9%)	4.025 (70.5%)
	2000	5.526	1.062 (19.2%)	4.464 (80.8%)	4.158 (75.2%)
	2004	5.340	0.722 (13.5%)	4.618 (86.5%)	4.288 (80.3%)
South Korea	1993*	1.735	0.665 (38.3%)	1.070 (61.7%)	0.975 (56.2%)
	1996	2.187	0.307 (14.0%)	1.880 (86.0%)	1.673 (76.5%)
	2000	2.228	0	2.243 (100%)	2.077 (93.2%)
	2004	2.201	0.002 (0.09%)	2.199 (99.91%)	2.033 (92.4%)

Net Importer	Year (1)	Saudi Arabia (6)	OPEC Africa (7)	Indonesia (8)	Venezuela (9)
United States	1991	1.796 (27.1%)	0.956 (14.4%)	0.106 (1.6%)	1.020 (15.4%)
	1995	1.343 (17.0%)	0.860 (10.9%)	0.087 (1.1%)	1.468 (18.6%)
	2000	1.571 (15.1%)	1.121 (10.8%)	0.047 (0.45%)	1.53 (14.7%)
	2004	1.557 (12.9%)	1.611 (13.3%)	0.043 (0.36%)	1.548 (12.8%)

(*continued on next page*)

Table 3.3: (*continued*)

Net Importer	Year (1)	Saudi Arabia (6)	OPEC Africa (7)	Indonesia (8)	Venezuela (9)
OECD Europe	1991	2.231 (24.5%)	2.836 (31.2%)	0.002 (0.02%)	0.250 (2.74%)
	1995	1.955 (25.0%)	2.577 (32.9%)	0.016 (0.02%)	0.280 (3.58%)
	2000	1.416 (17.9%)	2.536 (32.0%)	0.003 (0.03%)	0.194 (2.45%)
	2004	1.437 (15.8%)	2.389 (26.3%)	0.008 (0.009%)	0.144 (1.59%)
Japan	1991	1.342 (25%)	0.011 (0.2%)	0.670 (12.5%)	0.010 (0.2%)
	1995	1.310 (22.9%)	0.026 (0.5%)	0.479 (8.4%)	0.002 (0.04%)
	2000	1.262 (22.8%)	0.018 (0.3%)	0.287 (5.2%)	0.012 (0.2%)
	2004	1.320 (24.7%)	0.104 (2.0%)	0.228 (4.3%)	0.013 (0.2%)
South Korea	1993*	0.477 (27.5%)	0	0.095 (5.47%)	0
	1996	0.886 (40.5%)	0.096 (4.37%)	0.123 (5.63%)	0
	2000	0.900 (40.4%)	0.035 (1.55%)	0.148 (6.63%)	0
	2004	0.844 (38.4%)	0.046 (2.08%)	0.132 (6.02)	0

*South Korea's data start with 1993.

in percent terms for each net importer country for the four years, 1991, 1995, 2000 and 2004. These results are presented in Table 3.3.[1]

From Table 3.3, one can observe that US total net imports of oil rose from 6.6 to 12.1 mb/day during 1991–2004. This is shown in column (2) while column (3) shows that 40.9%–53% came from non-OPEC exporters and column (4) shows that 59.1%–47% came from OPEC. Even though the net import share of OPEC was reduced, the net imported oil quantity from OPEC increased from about 3.9 to 5.7 mb/day from 1991 to 2004. By 2004 the US managed to import more than half of its oil from non-OPEC exporters, but rapidly increasing net oil imports has made the US still heavily dependent with nearly 5.7 million barrels of oil per day coming from OPEC. US net imports of oil from Saudi Arabia were re-

[1] As China and India are not OECD members, their oil import origin data are not available in the EIA (Energy Information Administration) database. Table 3.3 therefore does not include China and India.

duced from about 1.8 to 1.6 mb/day during 1991–2004 and the Saudi share was also reduced (from 27% to 13%) as shown in column (6). The same thing happened to net imports from Indonesia, as shown in column (8), with both import quantity and share declining substantially. US net import quantities of oil from OPEC, Africa and Venezuela increased by nearly 50% over 1991–2004, but the percentage shares fell slightly. These numbers show that US net imports of oil from non-OPEC origins increased much faster than from OPEC countries. (Later we will see which oil exporters have taken over OPEC's market share of US net imports of oil.)

Net imports of oil by OECD Europe fluctuated but did not increase over 1991–2004. Starting at 9.09 mb/day, falling to 7.8 mb/day in 1995 it returned to 9.08 mb/day in 2004. But net import oil quantity by OECD Europe from non-OPEC exporters increased from 2.3 mb/day in 1991 to 3.7 mb/day in 2004 while the corresponding share rose from 25.5% to nearly 41%. Similarly net imports from OPEC were reduced from 6.8 mb/day to 5.4 mb/day and the OPEC share fell from 74.5% to 59%. This reduction in both net import quantities and shares was true for all of the OPEC origins listed in Table 3.3 except for Indonesia, which was not a significant import origin for OECD Europe during this period. Nevertheless, by 2004 OECD Europe still imported as much as 5.4 mb/day of oil from OPEC, which was slightly less than the US net imports of oil from OPEC (5.7 mb/day). Comparing OECD Europe's share of OPEC origin (59%) with the US share of OPEC origin (47%), one can see that OECD Europe depends on OPEC more than the United States in these proportions.

Japan stabilized its net imports of oil at around 5.5 mb/day during 1991–2004. But its net imports of oil from OPEC origins increased from nearly 4.1 mb/day to 4.6 mb/day with the OPEC share rising from 75.6% to 86.5%. Japan focused its oil imports on the Persian Gulf region and raised its net imports of oil from this region from 3.4 mb/day in 1991 to 4.3 mb/day in 2004, with the share rising from 63% to 80%. Japan stabilized its net imports of oil from Saudi Arabia at about 1.32 mb/day and 1.28 mb/day from UAE (not shown in Table 3.3). Japan's rising net imports of oil from the Persian Gulf region emanated from Iran and Kuwait. Japan's import share from Iran also rose from 7% in 1991 to 12% in 2004, and the share of Kuwait rose from 1.1% to 9.0%. Japan's increase in net imports of oil also had other OPEC origins — except for Indonesia, from which Japan imported 0.67 mb/day (or 12.5% of Japan's total net imports) in 1980 but only 0.23 mb/day in 2004 (4.3%) in 2004. Hence Japanese dependency on OPEC continues to be heavy and growing.

South Korean oil net import data start with almost 1.74 mb/day in 1993 and increase to more than 2.2 mb/day in 2004. This included a persistent shift in net imports of oil into OPEC that raised the OPEC share to 99.9% by 2004. Like Japan, South Korea has also concentrated its oil imports in the Persian Gulf region with a net import quantity rising from 0.98 mb/day (56.2% of its total net imports of oil) in 1993 to 2.03 mb/day (92.4%) in 2004. Saudi Arabia is the major source of imported oil to South Korea with net imports of 0.48 mb/day (27.5%) in 1993 and 0.84 mb/day (38.4%) in 2004. Other significant origins are UAE, Kuwait and Iran which respectively account for 24%, 13% and 8.6% of South Korean net imports of oil in 2004. As of 2004 about 6% of net imports of oil for South Korea still came from Indonesia, with 2% from Nigeria and Algeria, but none from Venezuela. Thus South Korea, the world's fourth largest oil importer, depends almost completely upon OPEC, particularly Saudi Arabia, UAE, Kuwait and Iran, to meet its increasing demand for oil.

The above analysis shows that the Western world and emerging economy-countries like South Korea are all heavily dependent on the ten Muslim countries of OPEC for their oil imports. The United States, however, has diversified its increasing net imports of oil to non-OPEC origins. Although the percentage is declining, the quantity of US net imports of oil from OPEC keeps rising.

Table 3.4 shows that the United States has diversified its oil imports to non-OPEC countries in North America, South America and Africa. Canada is the

Table 3.4: Origins of US Net Imports of Oil in 2004

Origin of Net Imports of Oil	Net Imports of Oil (1 000 barrels per day)	Net Import Share of Origin
Total Net Imports of Oil	12 097	100%
OPEC	**5 688**	**47.02%**
Saudi Arabia	1 557	12.87%
Venezuela	1 548	12.80%
Nigeria	1 139	9.42%
Iraq	656	5.42%
Algeria	452	3.74%
Kuwait	250	2.07%
Libya	20	0.17%
United Arab Emirates	18	0.15%
Qatar	5	0.04%
Non-OPEC	**6 409**	**52.98%**
Canada	1 980	16.37%
Mexico	1 456	12.04%
United Kingdom	366	3.03%
Virgin Islands, US	330	2.73%
Angola	316	2.61%
Russia	298	2.46%
Other	269	2.22%
Norway	242	2.00%
Ecuador	236	1.95%
Colombia	173	1.43%
Gabon	142	1.17%
Argentina	95	0.79%
Trinidad and Tobago	85	0.70%
Brazil	77	0.64%

largest origin for non-OPEC US oil imports and accounts for nearly 16.4% of the total net US imports. This share is greater than the 12.87% share of Saudi Arabia. Thus social eruptions or political disturbances in Canada, Saudi Arabia, Venezuela, Mexico and Nigeria could substantially affect US oil imports since more than 1 million barrels of oil every day flow into the US from each of these five countries.

3.2. Strategic Geography of the Muslim World

Following up on this last point, we turn to geographic locations since this can have strategic importance in the case of political instability or similar considerations. From Chapters 1 and 2 and the previous Section 3.1, one can see that major oil producer and exporter countries are located in the Persian Gulf region, the Muslim countries in Africa and Central Asia as well as Russia. The major oil consumer and importer countries are located in North America, Europe and East Asia. Thus crude oil and oil products must travel from production origins to destination countries around the globe. Security and safety of oil transportation and pipelines have become increasingly important in global oil markets. Because major oil producer and exporters are located in Muslim countries, we start our examination with them.

This section describes geographic features of the Muslim world that can affect oil flows around the world. Today, there are 49 countries in which Muslims have an overall population majority. The total area occupied by these 49 Muslim-majority nations is about 31.120 million square kilometer or 12.016 million square mile, which is larger than the combined areas of China, Canada and the United States.

3.2.1. An Overview of the Muslim Land via Map 3.1

The Muslim world starts from its Islamic origin in the Arabian Peninsula and stretches northward and southward, eastward, and westward, in a long belt surrounding the middle portion of our planet. It envelops all countries in the Middle East (usually defined as the area between North Africa and the India subcontinent) except for Israel and Malta. It includes Saudi Arabia, Yemen, Oman, Qatar, United Arab Emirate, Bahrain, Kuwait, Iraq, Iran, Jordan, Lebanon, Syrian Arab Republic, and Palestine (or West Bank and Gaza). Toward the west of this region, the Muslim world stretches across all of the North African countries: Egypt, Libya, Tunisia, Algeria, and Morocco. The Sahara, the world's largest desert, with its 3.5 million square miles of sand spreading from the Atlantic Ocean to the Red Sea, separates North Africa from the rest of Africa (usually labeled sub-Sahara Africa). It is so difficult to travel in this desert that it forms a divide between North Africa and sub-Sahara Africa with the former linking up closely with the other Muslim countries in the Middle East. It is therefore common to regard this geographic configuration in a manner that separates the two regions of Africa one of which combines North Africa into a broad Middle East and North Africa region. In this region there are 19 Muslim-majority countries today with a combined area of about 11.067 million square km (or 4.273 million miles). Except for Iran the other Muslim nations in this region form the main part of the Arab world.

The Sahara desert did not stop further expansion of the Muslim world within Africa, where it reaches out to 16 sub-Sahara nations. This includes the 8 larger nations of Mauritania, Mali, Niger, Nigeria, Chad, Sudan, Ethiopia, and Somalia, as well as 8 smaller African countries of the Gambia, Senegal, Sierra Leone, Guinea, Cote d'Ivoire, and Guinea-Bissau on the western coast of Africa, and Eritrea and Djibouti on the east side of Africa and the southern coast of the Red Sea. The pooled area of these 16 Muslim-majority nations in sub-Sahara Africa is about 11.318 million square km (or 4.37 million square miles), with a population of 308 million in 2000.

Toward the north and east, the Muslim world spreads over 8 central Asian countries: Turkey, Albania, Azerbaijan, Turkmenistan, Uzbekistan, Tajikistan, Kyrgyzstan, and Kazakhstan — where the last six countries were split off from the former Soviet Union. These 8 Muslim-majority nations have an area of 4.89 million square km (or 1.89 million square miles) and a population of 136 million in 2000.

The Muslim world is also present in the northwest provinces of China and extends into other countries in Asia, like Afghanistan, Bangladesh, Pakistan and the Maldives, as well as Malaysia, Brunei, and Indonesia. In terms of geographic configuration, four Muslim-majority nations — Afghanistan, Bangladesh, Pakistan and the Maldives — belong to the South Asian region with a combined area of about 1.596 million square km (or 0.616 million square miles) and with a population of 302 million in 2000. Indonesia and Malaysia are Muslim-majority nations in South East Asia. The area of these two nations is about 2.249 million square km (or 0.868 million square miles), and was inhabited by approximately 235 million people in 2000.

Map 3.1 exhibits the geographic distribution of Muslim populations over these 49 countries and other non-Muslim countries of the world.

There are two major sects of the Islamic religion, Sunni and Shi'ite, which have become the main denominations since the early creation of this religion. The overwhelming majority of Muslims in the world belong to the Sunni sect. The Shi'ite are the majority only in (1) Iran, accounting for about 89% of its total population, in (2) Iraq about (60–65)%, and in (3) Bahrain about 70%. A traditional Shi'ite regime holds power in Iran, while a Sunni minority held political power in Iraq until the recent end of Saddam Hussein's regime.

From the Muslim-majority countries identified above and the accompanying description in Chapter 2 it becomes manifest that the Muslim world occupies many of the most important geo-political and geo-economic regions of the world. The control of access to the land, water, air and outer space, as well as the natural

Map 3.1: The Muslim Land.

and human resources of those regions can have significant impacts on the security of global oil markets and the economic prosperity of many other nations including the United States, Japan, China, India, and the European countries.

As the above map shows, the Muslim world stretches from the Pacific to the Atlantic and links the three continents of Europe, Asia and Africa together. Geographic features in these lands, mountains, lakes, rivers, and shore lines have provided natural pathways and barriers that affect not only oil transportation, but also economic and military operations as well.

3.2.2. North Africa and Middle East

There are 18 Muslim-majority countries located in the Middle East and North Africa. The strategic position of this region determines access to routes and to oil and natural gas resources. These locations can facilitate or impede oil transportation and military conflicts, as well as economic and cultural interactions of many countries. The entire southern coast of the Mediterranean Sea belongs to Muslim countries. With Morocco on the south side of the strait of Gibraltar, which is the western outlet of the Mediterranean Sea to the Atlantic Ocean, the Muslim world is on a vital link for all Mediterranean to Atlantic countries and with Egypt on the east it holds the Suez Canal, the outlet to the east. Southern European NATO members such as France, Italy, Spain, and Greece are located on the northern coast of the Mediterranean Sea separated by only a short maritime distance from the North African Muslim countries, as shown in Map 3.2.

North Africa

There are five major Muslim countries located in North Africa: Egypt, Libya, Algeria, Morocco and Tunisia. The 4200-mile long Nile River flows through the

Map 3.2: Middle East and North Africa.

Muslim countries of Sudan and Egypt, with headwaters in Tanzania, Uganda and Ethiopia. The Nile's long and winding path ties the fates of all these countries together. It supplies much of the region's water needs for agriculture and navigation, while also creating both economic and political threats to Egypt if the Nile were diverted or its flow reduced.

The Nile floods in the summer every year, bringing nutrients and minerals that make the soil around the Nile fertile and ideal for farming while threatening the population along the river with floods that can wipe out farmlands and cotton fields. To control the flood waters, the British in 1902 completed construction of a dam, known as the Aswan Low Dam today, which straddles the river at the city of Aswan in the south of Egypt. Due to dam overflows in 1946, the Nasser government of Egypt decided to build a second dam in Aswan in 1952 with an expected loan of $270 million from Britain and the US. Both nations, however, cancelled their offers in 1956.[2] In the struggle for influence in Africa, the Soviet Union stepped in and provided technicians and heavy machinery and paid nearly one third of the cost of the dam.

Construction of this second dam was completed in July, 1970 and the dam was called the Aswan High Dam. This dam is considered the greatest man made work in Egypt since the Pyramids. Hydroelectric outputs from power stations provide nearly 15% of Egypt's electricity and the dam mitigates the effects of dangerous

[2] A secret Egyptian arms agreement with the USSR and Egyptian recognition of the People's Republic of China are cited as possible reasons for the cancellation.

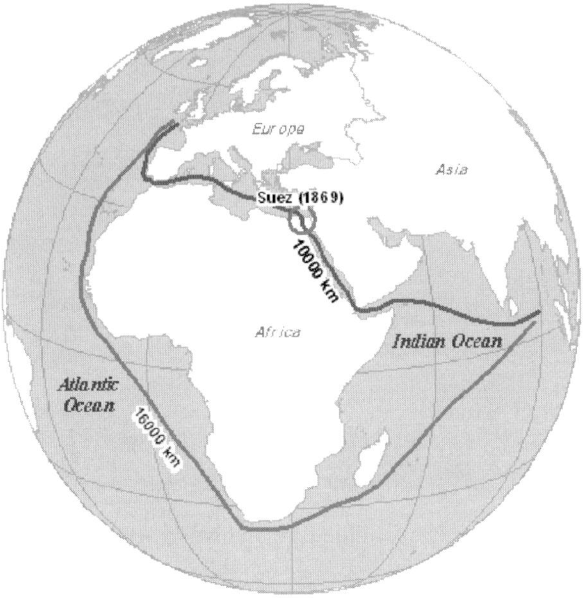

Map 3.3: The Strategic Position of the Suez Canal. With permission from: Rodrigue, J.-P., et al. (2006) The Geograhy of Transport Systems, Hofstra University, Department of Economics & Geography, http://people.hosftra.edu/geotrans.

floods and droughts. In addition to these benefits, however, the dam produces environmental effects such as erosion of farmlands downriver and erosion of coastlines along the eastern Mediterranean due to a lack of the sand that was once brought there by the Nile. About 95% of Egypt's population lives within 12 miles of the Nile so that destruction of the dam would flood the entire Nile valley and lead to a catastrophe for the nation. This dam is therefore also viewed as a strategic threat to Egypt's national security.

Egypt's Suez Canal and the Sinai Peninsula constitute an important maritime choke point at the eastern outlet of the Mediterranean to the Red Sea. The Suez Canal was planned by the French but constructed by the British, and opened in 1869. It is one of the most significant maritime "shortcuts" ever built, reducing the journey (see Map 3.3) from Asia to Europe by about 6000 km (around Africa). It allows Persian Gulf oil to be transported to many oil consumer countries in Europe and to cross the Mediterranean Sea for the United States, the largest oil consumer. Its strategic value was demonstrated by the British–French invasion in 1956 following nationalization of the Suez Canal by Egyptian President Nasser. Thus Egypt controls the most important choke point on the busiest lane of the global oil transportation network. Although Egypt is not a major oil producer or consumer country, the Suez Canal allows Egypt to play a critical role with respect

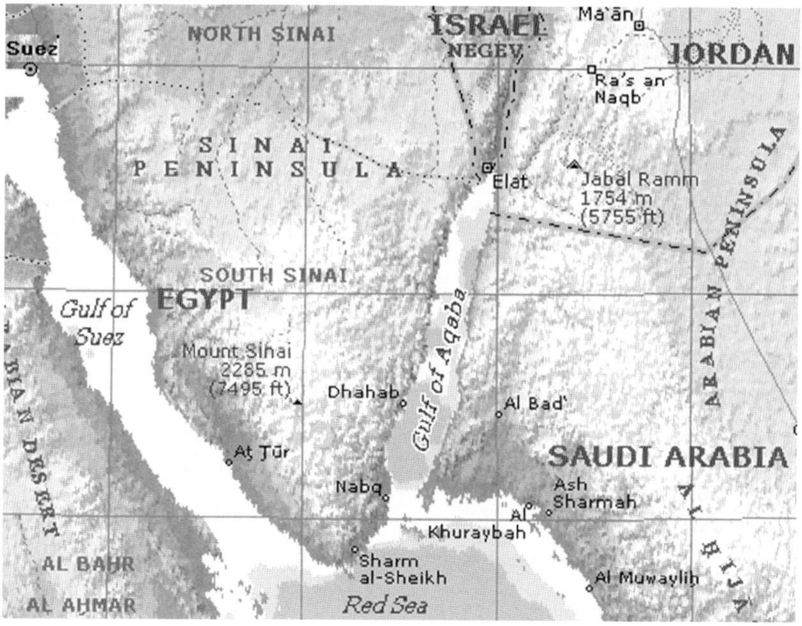

Map 3.4: The Gulf of Aqaba.

to the safety of the global oil transportation network and the security of global oil markets.

The Middle East

As Map 3.4 shows, the Gulf of Aqaba is an arm of the Red Sea, running to the east of the Sinai Peninsula and west of the Arabian mainland, touching Egypt, Israel, Jordan, and Saudi Arabia. This Gulf is 160 km long, and has a maximum width of 24 km. It passes through the Straits of Tiran where it joins the Red Sea. It is an important maritime route for Israel to reach the Red Sea, but Egypt occupies a choke point in the straits of Tiran. In fact, closure of this route to Israeli shipping contributed to the full-fledged war between Israel and the Arab nations in 1967.

The strait of Bab el Mandeb is located between the African Muslim countries of Djibouti and Eritrea and the Muslim country of Yemen on the Arabian Peninsula (Map 3.5). It is also a choke point at the junction of the Red Sea and the Gulf of Aden, the Arabian Sea and the Indian Ocean. The Gulf of Aden, the western arm of the Arabian Sea, meets the Red Sea at the strait of Bab el Mandeb. In a West–East direction, the gulf runs between Yemen and Somalia, meeting Djibouti at the western end. It is about 900 km long and 500 km wide at the eastern end, between Ra's Asir of Somalia and the city of al-Mukalla of Yemen. The strait of Bab el Mandeb is one of the most active shipping lanes in the world. Its closure

Map 3.5: The Gulf of Aden and the Strait of Bab el Mandeb.

would keep oil tankers from reaching the Suez Canal, and divert them around the southern tip of Africa and the Cape of Good Hope. This would affect global oil markets by greatly increasing transportation time and cost, shortening oil supplies, and probably affect global inflation and economic growth.

The Persian Gulf Region

In the Persian Gulf region there are eight Muslim-majority countries, Bahrain, Iran, Iraq, Kuwait, Qatar, Saudi Arabia, the United Arab Emirates and Oman, all sharing the coast line. These countries hold nearly two-thirds of world crude oil reserves, and produce nearly one-quarter of world oil. The Persian Gulf, a 600-mile-long body of water (Map 3.6), separates the Muslim country of Iran, which is non-Arab, from the Arabian Peninsula, which is the home of the richest oil countries of the world: Saudi Arabia, United Arab Emirates and Qatar.

More than 80% of oil produced by the Persian Gulf countries is exported by tankers through the Strait of Hormuz, which is located between Iran, the United Arab Emirates (UAE) and Oman. The Hormuz Strait is the world's most important oil choke point, because its closure would require use of alternative routes at much higher transportation cost and longer times (such as use of the East–West pipeline across Saudi Arabia to the Red Sea). Every day, more than 10 million barrels of oil transit the Strait of Hormuz to the rest of the world — eastward to India, Japan, China and South Korea, and westward, via the Suez Canal, to Europe and the United States. The strategic importance of the Persian Gulf results from world reliance on its oil supply. Any threat to the stability of the Persian Gulf en-

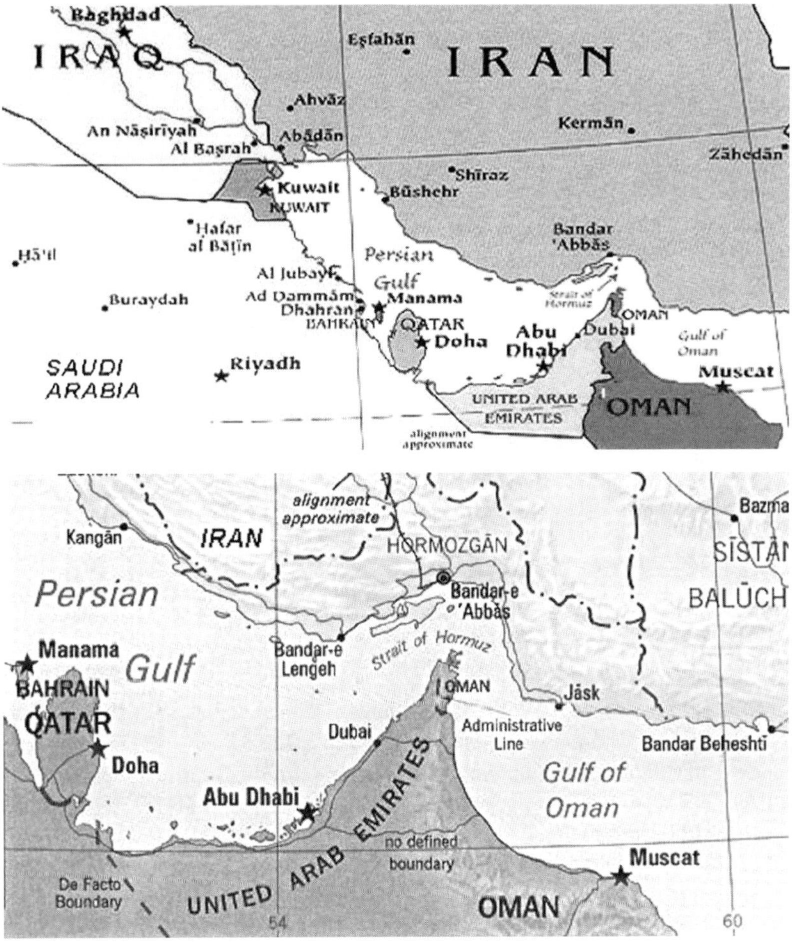

Map 3.6: The Persian Gulf and the Strait of Hormuz.

dangers production and flow of oil from this region, which is the lifeblood of the global economy. Security of the oil road provided by the Persian Gulf has been the focus of much attention due to growing concerns that Islamist terrorist groups plan to attack oil facilities and tankers because their leader, Osama bin Laden, has identified energy facilities in the region as one of the strategic targets in his war against the West.

3.2.3. South East Asia

Malaysia, Brunei, and Indonesia are Muslim-majority countries in Southeast Asia. They also have significant oil production and exports. The Strait of Malacca, one

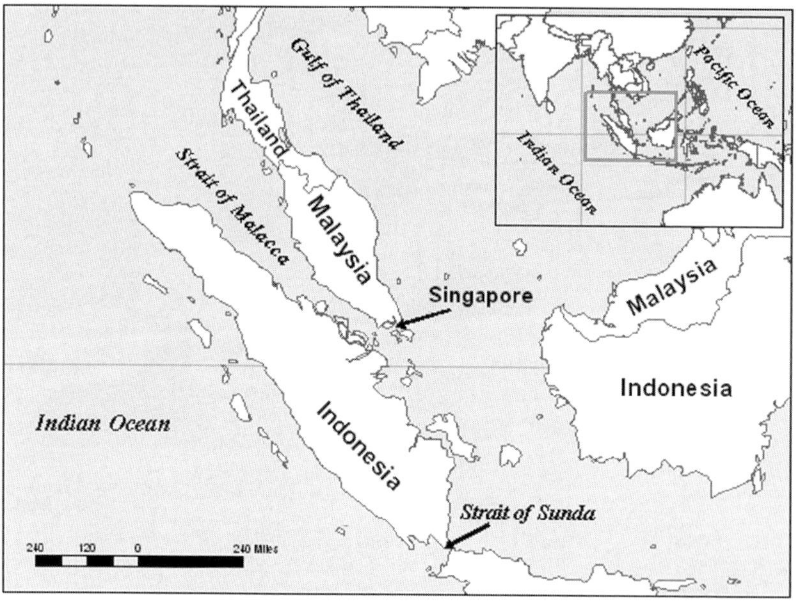

Map 3.7: The Strait of Malacca.

of the world's most important sea passages, is located between the Malaysian Peninsula and the Indonesian island of Sumatra (Map 3.7).

The Strait of Malacca links the Indian Ocean with the South China Sea as indicated by the square drawn in the inset on the upper right in Map 3.7. It is a strategic waterway used by oil tankers from the Persian Gulf to reach the Asian markets of Japan (about 80% of Japan's oil imports come from the Persian Gulf), South Korea (about 92% of its imported oil come from the Persian Gulf), China (surpassed Japan in 2002 as the World's second-largest oil user) and other Asian countries and regions with rapidly growing economies. The Malacca Strait, however, was previously a place for pirates and the reviving activities of pirates in the Strait may encourage terrorists to seek them as allies in a possible shift from land to sea-based targets directed against commercial shipping. The transnational combination of terrorism and crime in national and international waters presents a challenge to international commerce and the security of the global community in this important part of the Muslim world.

3.2.4. Europe/Central Asia

The northeastern outlet of the Mediterranean lies completely in the territory of Turkey, another Muslim country. Turkey is located in Southeastern Europe and Southwestern Asia, bordering the Black Sea, the Aegean Sea and the Mediterranean Sea, and belongs to the Europe/Central Asia group according to World

Map 3.8: Turkey and the Straits of Bosporus and Dardanelles.

Bank's "World Development Indicators". Turkey is considered to be an increasingly important country in the world because of its geographic location between Europe, the Middle East and Asia, and its easy access to strategically important regions and major energy resources. The Turkish Straits of Bosporus and Dardanelles connect the Black Sea and the Mediterranean (Map 3.8).

These are key maritime routes for East European countries located on the coast of the Black Sea. These countries include Russia, Ukraine, Romania, and Bulgaria, for which these routes provide access to the Mediterranean and the Atlantic Ocean for exports of oil, grain and other commodities. Russia, in particular, relies on these routes to transport its oil from the Black Sea to the Mediterranean and then to world markets — even though the narrow waters of the Straits can cause delays and significant losses in stormy weather.

Turkey has introduced tougher shipping restrictions due to concerns over safety and pollution, and, in order to reduce congestion, Turkey has advised oil exporters such as Russia to find routes other than the Bosporus and Dardanelles straits for their crude oil. Any closures of the Turkish Straits would hamper crude oil exports and raise shipping costs and oil prices in the global energy market and would likely affect the global economy. Thus Turkey's strategic geography allows it to play a critical role similar to that of Egypt in the global oil transportation network.

With the emergence of six independent republics (Azerbaijan, Kazakhstan, Kyrgyzstan, Tajikistan, Turkmenistan and Uzbekistan) from the breakup of the Soviet Union, the countries of the Muslim world now span the Caucasus and Central Asia in what is called the Caspian region as shown in Map 3.9.

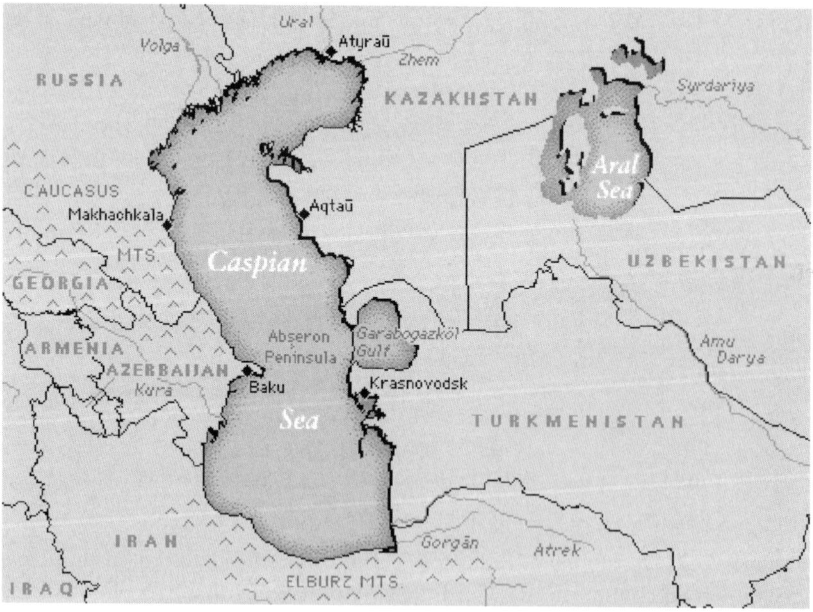

Map 3.9: The Caspian Region. From "Caspian Sea", Microsoft® Encarta® Online Encyclopedia 2007. All Rights Reserved.

Russia, and the now independent nations of Georgia, Armenia, and Azerbaijan comprise today's Caucasus. The Caucasus Mountains lie in the neck of land dividing the Black and Caspian seas. To the south are Turkey and Iran, with Iraq nearby, and to the north lies the Russian republic of Chechnya, which is entrenched in a long-lasting conflict with the Russian central authority. The Caucasus region forms a part of the traditional border between Europe and Asia and is called Eurasia. The Caucasus Mountains, with its 5642-meter high peak Elbruz and the Hindu Kush mountain ranges in Afghanistan restrict Russian entry to the Middle East and the Indian Ocean. These barriers have had a profound impact on the history of the region that was manifested as recently as World War II, when the German and Russian armies engaged in major battles in the Caucasus area.

The rich proven reserves of oil and natural gas in the Caspian Sea region, particularly in the sea's shallow shelf, have made the sea's demarcation lines the topic of long-standing disputes among the five Caspian Basin states: Azerbaijan, Iran, Kazakhstan, Russia, and Turkmenistan. These disagreements have substantially slowed regional energy development and exports, including oil exploitation and oil-pipeline construction. Russia, Turkey, and Iran are the largest and strongest countries with significant political, cultural and religious influences, and substantial economic interests in this region. The Caucasus and the Caspian Sea, however, separate these three regional powers from one another. Today's geo-political setting in the Caspian region is reminiscent of the eighteenth and nineteenth century struggles between three powerful empires: the Tsarist, Ottoman, and Persian empires.

3.2.5. South Asia

According to some geographic categorizations the four Muslim-majority countries of Afghanistan, Pakistan, Maldives and Bangladesh constitute the South Asian region. Bordering Iran, India, China, and three Muslim dominated independent republics from the former Soviet Union (Turkmenistan, Uzbekistan and Tajikistan), Afghanistan and Pakistan occupy especially important strategic positions in today's geo-political arena.

Afghanistan

Afghanistan has frequently been a center of fierce battles between powerful neighbors trying to extend their zones of influence (see Map 3.10). In the 19th century, Great Britain projected its power from colonial India into Afghanistan that frequently involved clashes with the neighboring power of Russia.

As recently as 1979 the USSR invaded Afghanistan and inspired a guerrilla war against their occupying force. After expulsion of the Soviet forces, a civil war ensued and al-Qaeda training camps for international terrorism kept this country strategically important.

Map 3.10: Afghanistan.

Huge oil and gas reserves in neighboring countries provide great opportunities for using west Afghan land to build oil pipelines from Tajikistan, Kazakhstan and Turkmenistan to Pakistan for use in exporting oil and gas to India, Japan and China. More recently, toppling the Taliban regime in Afghanistan by the US and allied forces and pursuing al-Qaeda and Taliban terrorists provides the Western world a foothold in the middle of this politically and economically important region that is surrounded by countries like Russia, Iran, China, India, Pakistan, and the independent and former Soviet Republics in the Central Asia.

Pakistan

Pakistan lies in the western part of the Indian subcontinent between Iran, to the west, Afghanistan, to the northwest, India, to the east, and China, to the northeast, and with a southern frontier on the Arabian Sea as exhibited in Map 3.11.

Map 3.11: Pakistan.

This has let Pakistan play an important role as an intermediary for the United States in recent years. There is also a longer history. In the early 1950s, US military bases in Pakistan were used to launch U-2 spy planes that flew over important USSR space stations and strategic missile bases that are located in today's independent ex-Soviet Republics in Central Asia. President Nixon also used the Pakistani channel to make contact with China in his visit to Beijing in 1972 in his effort to obtain rapprochement after decades of hostility between China and the United States. Pakistan also helped the US in defeating the Soviet Union in Afghanistan. But Pakistan later supported the Taliban regime and made Afghanistan its client state.

The terrorist attacks on 9/11 in New York and Washington brought Pakistan back into the US camp to oppose transnational terrorism. Pakistan's close proximity to the Persian Gulf, Iran, Afghanistan, China, and India, as well as its profound

Map 3.12: Bangladesh.

religious influences in nearby Muslim countries continues to affect regional stability in South Asia.

Bangladesh and Maldives

Bangladesh came into existence in 1971 when Bengali East Pakistan seceded from union with West Pakistan. This Muslim country lies in Southern Asia where it borders the Bay of Bengal, between Burma and India (Map 3.12). The Maldives is located in Southern Asia where it includes a group of islands in the Indian Ocean, southwest of India as shown in Map 3.13. These two Muslim countries can help balance military and economic relations between the US and Pakistan and between the US and India.

The above descriptions of the geo-strategic positions of the countries and regions dominated by the Muslim populations clearly show their strategic importance. Oil and natural gas reserves and production, as well as the routes that carry those energy resources from the Muslim world to global markets command world attention and influence political struggles and military confrontations between and

Map 3.13: Maldives.

among Muslim nations, as well as non-Muslim nations. Other issues are also involved, of course, but the central importance of oil and natural gas produced in Muslim countries and exported to advanced countries and emerging-economy countries made it desirable to discuss this topic in some detail.

Summary of Chapter 3

This chapter provides an analysis of international trade in oil, showing relationships between the West and the Muslim world in terms of individual country export and import. It also describes strategic geographic features of the Muslim world that can affect oil flows around the world. Our analysis is based on oil net export and import data for individual countries and their aggregates. We can emphasize the following:

(1) World net oil imports (exports) increased from 24.2 mb/day in 1985 to 43.1 mb/day in 2003, which is consistent with our analysis of the accelerating worldwide demand for oil in Chapter 1 of this book.

(2) As of 2003, the percentage of the world total net oil exports was 55.5% for the 48 Muslim countries, and 39.8% for Gulf countries. Twelve Muslim countries

were in the rank of top 20 largest net exporters of oil in 2003, including Saudi Arabia (number 1), Iran (number 4) and UAE (number 5). The combined net oil exports of these 12 Muslim countries accounted for about 55.7% of world net oil exports in 2003.

(3) The United States has become and remained the largest net oil importer in the world since 1985, with its net oil imports reaching 11.236 mb/day (or about 26.1% of world net oil imports) in 2003. Japan and Germany have been the second and third largest net oil importers since 1980. South Korea and China became the fourth and fifth largest net oil importers in 2003. Our analysis shows that the Western world and emerging economy countries like South Korea and China are all heavily dependent on the Muslim countries of OPEC for their oil imports although the United States has diversified its oil imports to non-OPEC countries in North America, South America and Africa.

(4) The total area occupied by the 49 Muslim-majority countries is about 31.12 million square kilometer, which is larger than the combined areas of China, Canada and the United States. Stretching from the Pacific to the Atlantic, the Muslim world has strategically important geographic locations that can dominate the oil and natural gas reserves and production as well as the routes and seaways that carry those energy resources from the Muslim world to global markets. The global oil transportation network consists of many important choke points in the Muslim countries in Middle East and North Africa, South East Asia, Central Asia and South Asia, which can control oil and natural gas flows from production locations to consumption destinations. Hence the Muslim world has also become important for geo-political and geo-economic regions with significant impacts on the security and prosperity of many other nations including the United States, Japan, China, India, and the European countries.

Summary of Part I

This concludes Part I of this book which provides a detailed analysis of global oil and natural gas markets and discuses changes in both demand and supply as well as international trade of oil. The time frame of this analysis extends from 1960 to 2004 and the energy sources and consumptions are projected into 2025. We now summarize main conclusions of Part I as follows:

(1) Oil and related products have been and will continue to be the single largest fuel in the energy mix in the world over the forcseeable future. This includes oil, natural gas, coal, renewable energy and nuclear energy. Oil consumption now accounts for about 39% of world total energy use and it is projected to be 38% by 2025. World use of natural gas has tripled in the last thirty years, and demand for natural gas is projected to grow at a greater rate than for any other primary fuel. The combined consumption of oil and natural gas accounts for more than 60% of total energy use worldwide. In the next twenty years — i.e. until 2025 — oil and natural gas will remain the main energy sources and serve as the lifeblood for modern industries and civilizations.

(2) World demand for oil and natural gas is driven by economic growth and social development across the globe. World oil consumption increased almost fourfold in the last 45 years. It reached 82.5 mb/day in 2004 and is projected to be 86 mb/day by 2006. The United States has been and remains the largest oil consumer and US oil consumption has accounted for nearly one quarter of worldwide oil consumption. China has replaced Japan as the second largest oil consumer, next only to the US.

India has become the sixth largest oil consumer, worldwide. The combined oil consumption of nine emerging economies (China, South Korea, India, Brazil, Saudi Arabia, Egypt, Iran, Indonesia and Turkey) has now exceeded the oil consumption of OECD Europe. The combined oil consumption of the 48 Muslim countries was nearly twice as much as Japanese oil consumption in 2003. The entire world has become heavily dependent upon oil and natural gas and is therefore heavily dependent on Muslim country policies and performance.

(3) The United States was once the world's largest oil producer. This top position has been taken over by Saudi Arabia. The OPEC cartel controlled 38.6% of world total oil production (crude oil plus natural gas plant liquids and other liquids) in 2003 and also controlled about 42% of world crude oil production in 2004. The 48 Muslim countries produced about 42.5% of the world total of oil in 2003. Thirteen Muslim countries entered the top 25 world oil producer list with a combined production share of 38.7%. Hence world oil production is concentrated in the Muslim world, particularly in the ten Muslim OPEC members of Saudi Arabia, Kuwait, UAE, Qatar, Iran, Iraq, Algeria, Libya, Nigeria and Indonesia.

(4) World production of natural gas has nearly doubled in the last twenty five years and reached 95 trillion cubic feet in 2003. The 48 Muslim countries produced about one quarter of the world total of natural gas in 2003. Russia and the US were the world's top two producers of natural gas in 2003 with combined production share of 43%. Three Muslim countries were ranked as number 5 (Algeria), 6 (Iran) and 7 (Indonesia). Significant emerging producers of natural gas are two Muslim countries, Turkmenistan and Uzbekistan.

(5) The latest estimates of petroleum resources show that 48 Muslim countries hold (55–64)% of world total oil reserves and (42–55)% of total world natural gas reserves. Seven Muslim countries in the Persian Gulf (Saudi Arabia, Kuwait, UAE, Qatar, Iran, Iraq and Bahrain) hold (42–55)% of world total oil reserves and (28–35)% of world total natural gas reserves. Thus the Muslim world, in general, and the Persian Gulf states, in particular, will continue to be strategically important to the security and prosperity of the entire world.

(6) World net imports of oil increased from 24 mb/day in 1985 to 43 mb/day in 2003, of which 26% was taken by the United States — the largest oil net importer in the world. Saudi Arabia has been the world's largest oil net exporter and Russia the second largest net oil exporter since 1992. The net exports of oil from the 48 Muslim countries reached 24 mb/day in 2003 or about 56% of world total net exports of oil. The seven Muslim states in the Persian Gulf exported oil at 17 mb/day or about 40% of world total net export. Twelve Muslim countries entered the top 20 list of world net exporters of oil in 2003 with a combined market share of 56%. Thus the Muslim world has dominated global oil markets from the supply side. Advanced countries such as US and OECD Europe have attempted to diversify their oil import origins to non-OPEC producers, but nearly half of their net imports of oil still came from OPEC, and about (20–30)% came from the Persian Gulf in 2003. Japan and South Korea had (80–92)% of their net imports of oil coming from the Persian Gulf.

(7) Oil-rich Muslim countries of OPEC have dominated world oil production and international trade in oil and continue to do so. Muslim countries without huge oil or natural gas production and reserves, such as Egypt, Turkey and Malaysia, possess geographic features that can control flows of oil from the Persian Gulf to Europe, North America and East Asia. Any interruptions to the global oil transportation network could generate panic in global oil markets, push oil prices higher and affect economic activity worldwide.

(8) Security and stability of global oil markets is mainly determined by stability in the Muslim world. The first oil crisis in 1973–1974 put an end to the era of cheap oil and opened a new age of high prices, high consumption and high production of oil. Demand-side disruptions caused by the Asian financial crisis in 1997–1998 pulled down oil prices and production, temporarily, but the supply-side disruption in 1979 and 1980–1985 damaged both producers and consumers in both the Muslim and Western world for a longer time period. A peaceful and stable Muslim world is key to stable and growing global oil markets.

In conclusion, we note that many Muslim countries have been involved in the development of oil production and the global oil transportation network. Abundant oil from the Muslim lands not only allows Western countries to sustain their military strength, increase their economic and commerce power and enhance their living standard, but also helps newly industrialized countries, like South Korea, China, and India, catch up with the advanced Western countries. However, many countries in the Muslim lands could not help themselves to develop their economies and advance their societies. Except for a few countries, the Muslim world has become poor, weak, ignorant and unstable, falling behind even some of the less developed countries in terms of military strength, economic prosperity, and human rights developments. This makes us interested in what has happened and what is likely to happen for the Muslim world in the foreseeable future and we therefore next turn to the demographic transitions that influence many of these developments.

We believe that significant demographic changes and economic development have always served as the foundation of any societies with a long-lasting impact on the status of a nation in the world. Hence, in the next part of this book — Part II — we turn to demographic transformation for the Muslim world and the future characteristics of the Muslim populations. We also speculate on their impact on both world peace and prosperity. Then, in another book, we will also study economic transformations in the Muslim world.

Part II

Demographic Changes and Social Instability

Introduction

Islam, the second largest religion in the world, will continue to grow in the foreseeable future if only because of the rapidly increasing population in the Muslim world. As estimated by some Islamic organizations and religion information websites,[1] Christians accounted for 30% of the total world population in 1980, while Muslims accounted for 16.5% (for a nearly 2 to 1 ratio). Those percentages increased to 33% for Christians and 22% for Muslims in 2002. However it is forecasted that by 2025 the percentage of Christians will probably reduce to 25%, while the percentage of Muslims could increase to 30%. This means that in the next twenty years Islam will probably become the largest (i.e., most populous) religion of the world and likely reverse a relationship to Christianity that has lasted for nearly about a millennium.

Compared with other religions of the world, Islam is relatively new. Before the birth of Islam in 610 AD, Christianity had already become widely accepted in Europe and the Middle East, and it has sustained this favorable status for almost a millennium. The rapid growth of Muslim populations across the world is expected to reverse that situation in the very near future, as we just indicated. This brings us to the topic of this, Part II of this book, which is devoted to demographic analysis of the Muslim world.

As discussed in Part I of this book, advanced and emerging-economy countries have been heavily dependent on Muslim countries for supplying abundant and affordable oil to sustain their industries, economies and high standards of living, and this dependency is projected to continue in the 21st century. The majority of populations in many Muslim countries, however, have lived in economic poverty and social turbulence. The Muslim world seems unable to improve the standard of living for the majority of its populations even with the enormous wealth generated by precious energy resources — oil and natural gas. This has led to a bifurcation between the modern world and the Muslim world and has been used by international terrorists to pursue their political agenda against the United States and Western countries. Hence, this bifurcation threatens world peace and prosperity, and has been the cause of great concern across the globe.

Part I spelled out one reason why it is important to study the Muslim world; and Part II begins with fundamentals in the demographic transformation of the Muslim world that have important implications for the future. We believe that:

---

[1] http://muslim-canada.org/index.html, "Muslim Population Statistics", by the Canadian Society of Muslims. Also http://www.adherents.com/Religions_By_Adherents.html, "Major Religions of the World Ranked by Number of Adherents" by Adherents.com.

> "All human affairs — political, social, economic, cultural, religious, and commercial — are conducted by human beings. People's faiths, motivations, ingenuity and creativity ultimately determine success or failure in all these human affairs. After all, it is men and women who produce goods and services, and who feed, cloth, shelter, entertain, and govern themselves. In both production and consumption, demographic factors play important roles in any form of societies and economies. As a part of an interlocked system, economic development and social modernization change patterns under demographic transition. As an underpinning force, demographic factors feed back into the process of economic growth and social progress".[2]

Estimating the size of Muslim communities has also become a contentious political issue and some Islamic groups have accused researchers (who had conducted a study of all faith groups in America) of releasing falsely low population numbers to help diminish Islamic influence and to continue marginalizing Muslims. Others have accused Muslims of exaggerating their numbers in order to obtain more political clout. As a matter of fact, accurate estimates of Muslim populations are few and hard to find in the public information domain where many conflicting numbers repeatedly occur regarding the Muslim population size and its relative percentages. This is particularly true for some of the Muslim-minority countries like China and India.[3] Given the difficulties in getting accurate statistics about Muslim communities in Muslim-minority countries, we focus our attention on the national demographic analyses of the 49 Muslim-majority countries in the world, with their Muslim population greater than 50% of the total, and thus bypass issues involved in estimates for other, non-Muslim, countries — like China. The aggregations for specific regions and for the entire Muslim world are thus based on the national populations of the 49 Muslim-majority nations, without subtracting

[2] Embracing the Global Demographic Transformational, 1950–2050, an IC^2 Institute Monograph, University of Texas, by George Kozmetsky and Piyu Yue, 2000.

[3] The authors believe that there is a serious mistake in some of the existing estimates of the number of Muslims in China. According to http://www.islamicweb.com/begin/population.htm, the number of Muslims in China was given as 133.1 million, accounting for 11% of the Chinese population (no specific year was given). However, China's national population censuses have reported the number of Muslims as 4.473 million in 1964, and 7.219 million in 1982, accounting for 0.65% and 0.75%, respectively, of the total Chinese population. Officially, the average annual growth rate was 2.7% for Chinese Muslims versus 2.1% for the national population during 1964–1982. China's population growth has been significantly reduced since 1978, and so has the growth rate of Chinese Muslims. For instance, if the Chinese Muslim population had continued to increase at the rate of 2.7% after 1982, the number of Muslims in China would have been 10.206 million in 1995, 11.661 million in 2000, and 12.632 million in 2003. As the total Chinese population was 1286.975 million in 2003, the population share of Chinese Muslims would have been 0.98% in 2003. This clearly makes the estimates of 133.1 million and 11% from http://www.islamicweb.com/begin/population.htm of questionable value. This mistake from this website has also significantly inflated the number of Muslims to 1022.692 million in Asia and to a world total of 1482.597 million, contributing to a claim by the above cited website that "Among every four humans in the world, one of them is Muslim".

non-Muslim cohorts in those nations,[4] and without bringing in Muslim cohorts from Muslim-minority nations like India (Hindu 80.5% and Muslim 13.4%) and large Muslim cohorts from countries like Bosnia/Herzegovina (Muslim 40%, Orthodox 31%, Roman Catholic 15%, other 14% — from World Factbook of CIA). Two sources of demographic data are employed in our analyses: (1) World Development Indicators CD-ROM by the World Bank, and (2) World Population Prospects by the Department of International Economic and Social Affairs of the United Nations.

Part II contains four chapters (Chapters 4, 5, 6 and 7). Chapter 4 provides Muslim country population estimates over the period 1950–2000 and projections from 2005 to 2050. Population growth rates and percentages are analyzed for regions and individual Muslim countries. Chapter 4 also describes different patterns of Muslim population transition processes via vital parameters such as the birth rates, death rates, total fertility rates, and the life expectancy at birth.

Chapter 5 discusses the changing age structure of Muslim populations with a focus on three cohorts: children aged 0–14, working-age people from 15 to 64 years old, and the elderly, aged 65 and over. It also separately analyzes a specific population cohort, which we refer to as the "troublesome" cohort of male youngsters in ages from 15 to 29 in order to help understand why some populations behave more violently or manifest disturbances in certain time periods.

Chapter 6 focuses on the swift urbanization process now occurring in the Muslim world and does so by examining the scope and speed of increasing urban Muslim populations as well as the rise of Muslim mega-cities.

Chapter 7 provides an appraisal of the "intellectual" quality of Muslim populations along with a portrayal of Muslim education systems. Illiteracy rates are analyzed for male and female adult cohorts and for male and female youngster cohorts in the 49 Muslim-majority countries for the last three decades, 1970–2000. The Muslim education systems are also the focus of this chapter in which we investigate the economic base for education in the Muslim countries and the situation of school enrollment at three education levels. Our interest is directed to religious education and the madrasas system, and the two education systems in the Muslim world: religious and secular education systems. We also take a close look at Saudi Arabia's activities in promoting Islamic education across the world. We then draw conclusions from these analyses of the demographic transformation of the Muslim world in the last section where we also summarize Part II.

[4] This can be justified, we think, because it is the Muslim majority that guide the fortunes and behaviors of these nations.

Chapter 4
Population Sizes, Birth and Death Rates

This chapter consists of two sections. Section 4.1 presents population sizes for the 49 Muslim-majority countries and the distribution of Muslim populations over five geographic regions. It also provides population projections for 2000–2050 and population growth rates for the Muslim world and for selected individual Muslim countries over the periods 1950–2000 and 2000–2050. Section 4.2 describes the demographic transition that has taken place in Muslim countries. Four vital parameters — the crude birth rates, crude death rates, total fertility rates (TFR), and life expectancy at birth — are used to show the dynamic underpinnings that drive these demographic transition processes for Muslim countries.

4.1. Population Size and Distribution

In our analyses of population size and distribution, we use official population estimates and projections published in the 2002 Revision by the Population Division of the Department of Economic and Social Affairs of the United Nations Secretariat.[1] The estimates cover the time period from 1950 through 2000, and the projections are from 2000 up to 2050. The population projections are based upon assumptions about future trends in fertility, mortality and international migration. Three variants are published for each country — low variant, medium variant and high variant — in which total fertility rates (TFR[2]) in the high and low variants is projected to be 0.5 children above and 0.5 children below the total fertility rates of the median variant.

4.1.1. Population Expansion in the Muslim World

We employ population estimates and median variant projections for each of the 49 Muslim-majority nations and aggregate them to yield the total population of the 49 Muslim nations that represent the Muslim world with which we are concerned.

Figure 4.1 displays population estimates and projections of the Muslim world compared with world total population. As shown in this figure, the population

[1] United Nations Population Division, World Population Prospects: The 2002 Revision, Volume II: The Sex and Age Distribution of Population".

[2] Total fertility rate (TFR) can be defined as the average number of children a woman would have in her lifetime, assuming that current age specific birth rates remain constant throughout her childbearing years.

International Symposia in Economic Theory and Econometrics, Vol. 19
William W. Cooper and Piyu Yue

ISSN: 1571-0386/DOI: 10.1016/S1571-0386(07)00014-2

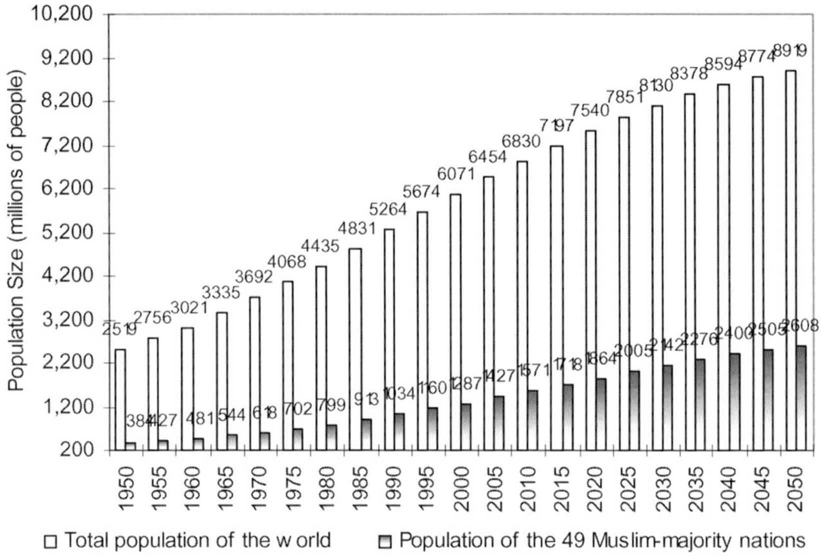

Figure 4.1: World Total Population vs. the Muslim Population.

of the 49 Muslim-majority countries increased from about 384 million in 1950 to 1287 million in 2000, while the total population of the world rose from 2519 million to 6071 million in the same 50-year period. These numbers show that the Muslim population expanded 3.35 times, while the world total population increased by 2.41 times in the last fifty years. Thus, the growth rate of the Muslim population was greater than that of world population as a whole (including the Muslim population) during this 1950–2000 period.

For the next fifty years, world total population is expected to continue an ascending trend, increasing 1.47 times to 8919 million by 2050. The total population of the 49 Muslim-majority nations is projected to increase 2.03 times, reaching 2608 million by 2050. Thus the Muslim population is forecasted to continue to grow faster than world population.

Figure 4.2 depicts annual growth rates for total world population and the 49 Muslim-majority nations. The population data for the time period of 1960–2000 come from the database "World Development Indicator", and the population data for the time periods 1950–1960 and 2000–2050 come from "World Population Prospects: The 2002 revision".[3] We use annual population estimates to calculate

[3] The publication, "*World Population Prospects: The 2002 Revision*", does not provide annual population data for nations and the world. Instead it reports estimates and projections for every 5 years, starting with 1950. The database of "The World Development Indicator"

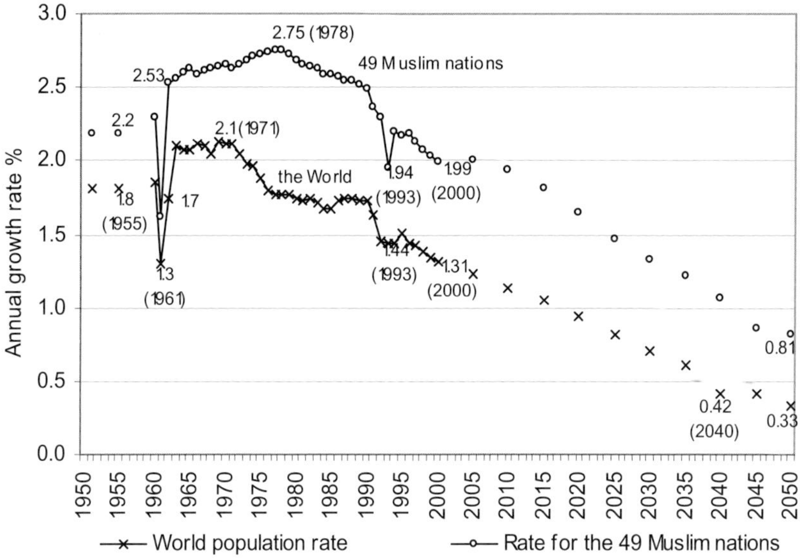

Figure 4.2: Annual Growth Rate of Population.

annual growth rates of populations and also use population projections to calculate average annual growth rates for each 5-year sub-period for the period 2000–2050.

As Figure 4.2 shows, the world total growth rate began to decline about 1971 while the growth rate of the Muslim countries began to decline about 1978. However, the growth rate of the Muslim population stays well above the growth rate of world total population over the entire one-hundred-year span and this leads to a relative expansion of the number of Muslims. During the 1950s, world population grew at a rate of 1.8% annually, while the Muslim population rose 2.2% per year. In the 1960s, world population accelerated its growth rate to 2.1% — except for the single year of 1961 when the rate dropped to 1.3%, due to a reduction of the Chinese population by nearly 6.8 million.[4] The growth rate of the Muslim popula-

provides annual population estimates for the time period 1960–2000, but no data for population projections. The authors have found the two data sources for the majority of nations in the world to be consistent and feel justified in combining them to calculate the annual population growth rate for the period 1950–2050.

[4] China's "Great Leap Forward" movement in 1958–1959 resulted in mass starvation throughout China. No one really knows how many people died during the 1960 famine. It is estimated that at least 20–25 million Chinese died during 1959–1960 and this is in addition to normal deaths of 6–7 million (G. Kozmetsky and Piyu Yue, *Embracing the Global Demographic Transformation, 1950–2050*, Published by the IC2 Institute, the University of Texas at Austin, 2000).

tion, however, accelerated to 2.5% in 1962 and reached an all time high of 2.75% in 1978, after world population had already begun its decline.

In 1993 there was a sudden drop to 1.93% in the growth rate of the Muslim population. This was due to reduction of increments in Ethiopia and Somali populations. During the 1990s, the population of Ethiopia increased by 1.5–1.8 million every year with the exception of 1993, when its population decreased by 1.5 million. The Somali population rose by 0.35 million per year in the early 1990s. It stopped increasing in 1993 and declined in 1994–1995 by about 0.4 million. These two nations are among the poorest and least developed countries in the world with the majority of their population earning a living directly or indirectly from agricultural activities. Severe drought caused acute starvation which was associated with a sharp increase in mortality and a population decline in both countries. Somali has also engaged in a long lasting civil war that claims large civilian casualties.

As forecasted by the United Nations Population Division, world population is expected to increase at a rate of 1.2% in the first decade of the twenty first century, and at rate of 1.0%, 0.8%, 0.6% and 0.4%, respectively, for the following four decades. Meanwhile, the population of the 49 Muslim-majority nations is expected to continue expanding at a greater rate than that of world population growth. By 2050, growth rate of the Muslim population is projected to be 0.81%, which is two times larger than the 0.33% projected growth rate of world population.

This faster expansion of the Muslim population has resulted in a continuing increase in the Muslim share of world population. Figure 4.3, portrays the changing population share of the 49 Muslim-majority nations, compared with shares of the top three most populous nations of the world, China, India and the United States.

In 1950, the total population of the 49 Muslim nations was slightly greater than the population of India, and significantly less than that of China. In 2000, however, the size of Muslim population approached the size of the Chinese population (1287 million versus 1322 million), with its population share increasing from 15.2% in 1950 to 21.2% in 2000. According to the population projections made for all nations of the world by the United Nations Population Division, the share of the 49 Muslim nations is expected to rise continuously and to reach 29.2% by 2050. See the top right hand corner of Figure 4.3. Thus, by 2050 in every 100 people on the Earth, including men, women and children, there are expected to be on average about 29 people from the 49 Muslim nations, 17 from India, 16 from China, 5 from the USA, and only 33 from the rest of the world.

4.1.2. Population Distribution of the Muslim World

The Muslim population is geographically distributed over five regions: (1) Europe/Central Asia, (2) South-East Asia, (3) South Asia, (4) Middle East & North Africa, and (5) sub-Sahara Africa. These geographic regions are defined by "World Development Indicators" of the World Bank. As is shown in Table 4.1

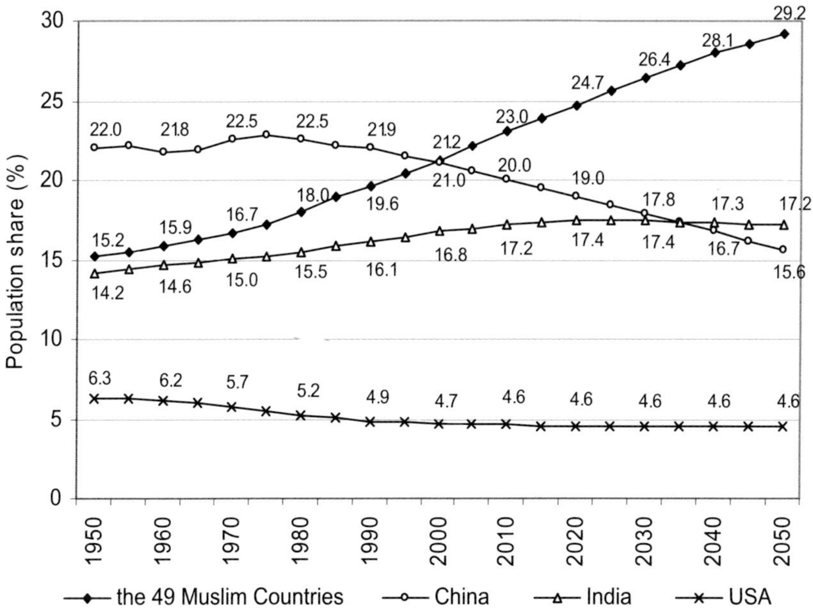

Figure 4.3: World Population Shares (%) of the 49 Muslim Countries vs. China, India, and USA.

each of these regions contains a different number of Muslim-majority nations. Some regions like North America, Europe, the Caribbean and South America, and Eastern Asia do not have any Muslim-majority nation. We have therefore excluded them from Table 4.1 even though some Muslim-minority nations such as China and India have substantial Muslim populations in their societies.

As the percentages in Table 4.1 show, in 1950 the Muslim population was fairly evenly distributed over these regions except for Central Asia where the Muslim share was 11.2% for Europe/Central Asia compared to 21%–23% for the other four regions. However, changes in population shares become apparent in 2000. The share increased for the regions of sub-Sahara Africa and Middle East & North Africa, and decreased for the regions of Europe/Central Asia and South East Asia, while remaining approximately unchanged for South Asia. By 2050 it is expected that the largest Muslim population share will belong to the sub-Sahara Africa region at about 30.1%, while the largest decline in population share will occur in South-East Asia (from 18.1% in 2000 to 12.8% by 2025). The changing distribution of the Muslim population is graphically displayed in Figure 4.4 for the entire period from 1950 through 2050.

As Figure 4.4 shows, the regions of Central Asia and South-East Asia have experienced a declining trend in their Muslim population share since 1970 and this is expected to continue during the next five decades.

Table 4.1: Geographic Distribution of the Muslim Population

Regions*	Muslim-Majority Nations	Population (in million) and Regional Distribution (%)		
		1950	2000	2050
Europe and Central Asia (8)	Albania, Azerbaijan, Kazakhstan, Kyrgyz Republic, Tajikistan, Turkey, Turkmenistan, Uzbekistan	43.095 (11.2%)	135.757 (10.5%)	188.458 (7.2%)
South-East Asia (2)	Indonesia, Malaysia	85.648 (22.3%)	234.560 (18.2%)	333.348 (12.8%)
South Asia (4)	Afghanistan, Bangladesh, Maldives, Pakistan	89.675 (23.4%)	302.288 (23.5%)	673.635 (25.8%)
Middle-East & North Africa (19)	Algeria, Bahrain, Djibouti, Egypt, Iran, Iraq, Jordan, Kuwait, Lebanon, Libya, Morocco, Oman, Qatar, Saudi Arabia, Syria, Tunisia, Yemen, United Arab Emirates, West Bank and Gaza	80.983 (21.1%)	306.397 (23.8%)	627.591 (24.1%)
Sub Sahara Africa (16)	Burkina Faso, Chad, Cote d'Ivoire, Eritrea, Ethiopia, Gambia, Guinea, Guinea-Bissau, Mali, Mauritania, Niger, Nigeria, Senegal, Sierra Leone, Somali, Sudan	84.517 (22.0%)	308.234 (24.0%)	784.749 (30.1%)
Muslim World (49)	The above 49 Muslim-majority nations	383.918 (100%)	1,287.236 (100%)	2,607.781 (100%)

*The parenthesized figures show the number of Muslim countries in each region.

Their population size, however, has increased and is projected to continue expanding. Thus the declining population share of Europe/Central Asia and South East Asia reflects the fact that their population expansion is proceeding at a slower pace than that of other regions. As the top line in Figure 4.4 shows, the most rapid expansion of Muslim population is now occurring in sub-Sahara Africa where the Muslim population has increased 3.6 times — from 84.5 million in 1950 to 308 million in 2000 — and is projected to reach about 785 million by 2050, which is about equal to the total population of the 49 Muslim-majority nations in 1980. The regions in South Asia and Middle East & North Africa have also witnessed a rapid population expansion in terms of both size and share. The population size tripled during 1950–2000 in both regions and is expected to double in the next five decades. The population share for Middle-East & North Africa and South Asia, however, is projected to remain at about 24% and 25.8% after 2025, respectively. (See Figure 4.4 and Table 4.1.)

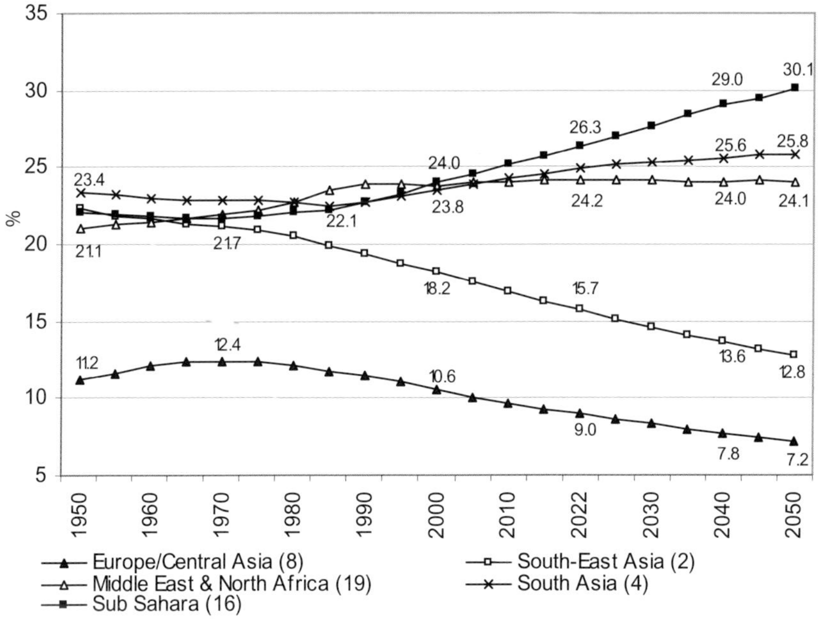

Figure 4.4: Geographic Distribution of Muslim Population Share.

Table 4.2 lists the 12 most populous Muslim nations with their population size. In the parentheses it also shows the percentage of the total population of the 49 Muslim-majority nations for each nation. These twelve nations are ranked in the order of their projected population size for 2050. Pakistan is expected to become the largest Muslim nation of the world by 2050 with 348.7 million people, accounting for 13.4% of the total population of these Muslim countries. Pakistan had about 40 million people in 1950 — a population size that was smaller than both Indonesia and Bangladesh. Its fast population growth rate made Pakistan the second largest Muslim country of the world in 2000. It was then next in size to Indonesia, whose population is expected to rise continuously but, nevertheless, will fall behind Pakistan after 2035.

Figure 4.5 graphically portrays the growth path for the top eight Muslim-majority nations over the 100-year time period 1950–2050. This includes Bangladesh, Pakistan, Indonesia, Nigeria, Ethiopia, Egypt, Turkey, and Iran. Indonesia had the largest population (79.5 million) in the Muslim world in 1950, followed by Bangladesh (41.7 million), Pakistan (39.7), Nigeria (29.8 million), Egypt (21.8 million), Turkey (21.5 million), Ethiopia (18.4 million) and Iran (16.9 million). All of these populations expanded rapidly in the last five decades. By 2000 Indonesia was still on top (211.6 million); Pakistan (142.7 million) exceeded

Table 4.2: The Most Populous Muslim Countries

Muslim Countries	Population Size (in million) and Population Share (%)		
	1950	2000	2050
Pakistan	39.659 (10.3%)	142.654 (11.0%)	348.700 (13.4%)
Indonesia	79.538 (20.7%)	211.559 (16.4%)	293.797 (11.3%)
Nigeria	29.790 (7.7%)	114.746 (8.9%)	258.478 (9.9%)
Bangladesh	41.783 (10.9%)	137.952 (10.7%)	254.599 (9.7%)
Ethiopia	18.434 (4.8%)	65.590 (5.1%)	170.987 (6.5%)
Egypt	21.834 (5.7%)	67.784 (5.2%)	127.407 (4.9%)
Iran	16.913 (4.4%)	66.443 (5.1%)	105.485 (4.0%)
Turkey	21.484 (5.6%)	68.281 (5.3%)	97.759 (3.7%)
Yemen	4.316 (1.1%)	18.017 (1.4%)	84.385 (3.2%)
Afghanistan	8.151 (2.1%)	21.391 (1.7%)	69.517 (2.7%)
Sudan	9.190 (2.4%)	31.437 (2.4%)	60.133 (2.3%)
Iraq	5.158 (1.3%)	23.224 (1.8%)	57.932 (2.2%)

Bangladesh (138.0 million); Turkey (68.3 million) exceeded Egypt (67.8 million); and Iran (66.4 million) exceeded Ethiopia (65.6 million).

These populations are all projected to continue their ascending paths but at different paces. The momentum exhibited by Pakistan, Nigeria and Ethiopia is expected to continue over the next five decades. The momentum in the other five populations has begun to slow and is projected to continue along relatively flat paths, particularly for Egypt, Turkey, and Iran. By 2050 Pakistan will have the largest population in the Muslim world (about 348.7 million) followed by Indonesia (293.8 million), Nigeria (258.5 million), Bangladesh (254.6 million), Ethiopia (171.0 million), Iran (105.5 million) and Turkey (97.8 million). With the exception of Turkey, these nations will all have populations greater than 100 million by 2050.

The combined size of these populations was 269 million in 1950 and it has already increased 3.2 times in the last five decades, reaching 875 million in 2000. This number is projected to increase another 1.9 times in the next five decades and reach 1657 million by 2050. This rapid population expansion has already

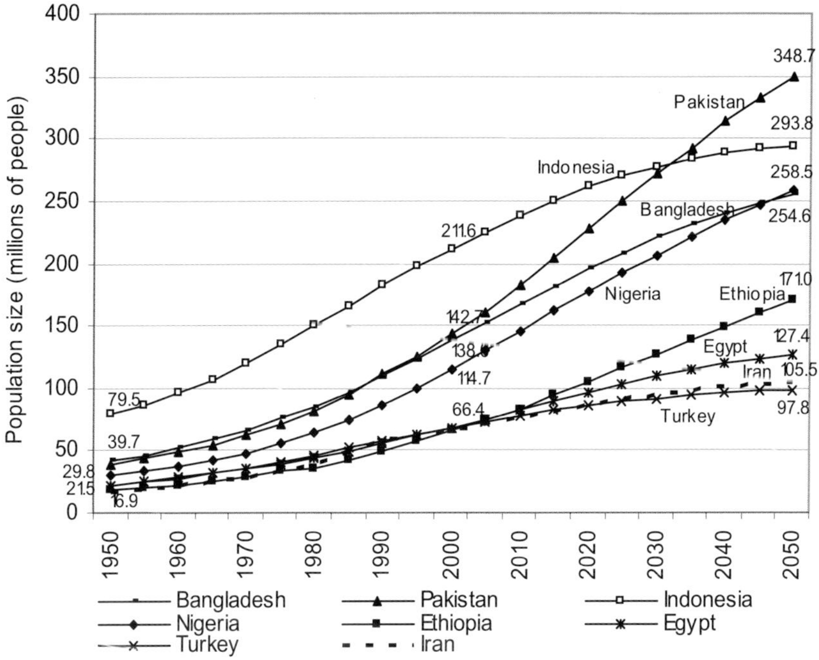

Figure 4.5: Population Sizes of the Large Muslim Countries.

created many economic and social problems for these countries. The continuing population growth certainly will be a great burden and offer obstacles to economic development and social progress for these Muslim countries.

4.1.3. Fastest Population Growth in the Muslim World

In the past several decades the fastest population growth occurred in some of the smaller Muslim nations rather than the large Muslim nations displayed in Figure 4.5. We therefore compute average annual population growth rates for all 49 Muslim countries for four time periods, 1950–1975, 1975–2000, 2000–2025, and 2025–2050 (each with a 25-year span). We also calculate two ratios for each Muslim country — population at 2000 to population at 1950 and population at 2050 to population at 2000.

Table 4.3 lists the 15 fastest growing Muslim populations in the first five decades, 1950–2000, along with their average annual growth rates and the associated population sizes and ratios for the two time periods, 1950–1975 and 1975–2000.

In Table 4.3 the first column covering the period 1950–1975 shows that UAE had the highest rate of population growth, 10.7% per year, while Yemen had the

Table 4.3: The Fastest Growing Muslim Populations in 1950–2000

Countries	Average annual growth rate (%)		Population (in million)		Population ratio 2000/1950
	1950–1975	1975–2000	1950	2000	
UAE	10.7%	11.5%	0.070	2.820	40.29
Qatar	9.49%	6.60%	0.025	0.581	23.24
Kuwait	9.33%	4.44%	0.152	2.247	14.78
Djibouti	5.76%	5.63%	0.062	0.666	10.74
Jordan	6.61%	4.17%	0.472	5.035	10.67
Saudi Arabia	3.57%	5.09%	3.201	22.147	6.92
Bahrain	3.73%	4.13%	0.116	0.677	5.84
Oman	3.02%	4.65%	0.456	2.609	5.72
Cote d'lvoire	3.90%	3.86%	2.775	15.827	5.70
Libya	3.8%	3.54%	1.029	5.237	5.09
Syria	3.33%	3.44%	3.495	16.56	4.74
Iraq	3.28%	3.27%	5.158	23.224	4.50
The Gambia	2.72%	3.74%	0.294	1.312	4.46
Niger	2.78%	3.44%	2.500	10.742	4.30
Yemen	1.98%	3.86%	4.316	18.017	4.17
49 Muslim Countries	**2.57%**	**2.61%**	**382.913**	**1287.236**	**3.36**
World	**2.01%**	**1.73%**	**2518.629**	**6070.581**	**2.41**

lowest rate, 1.98% per year. Comparing these values with the rates in the last two rows, one can see that all Muslim countries in Table 4.3, except for Yemen, experienced faster population expansion in 1950–1975 than the world and the 49 Muslim countries as a whole. In the second column for the period 1975–2000, UAE was still first at 11.5% per year and Iraq was the last at 3.27% per year. However, all of these values exceed the rate of 2.61% for the 49 Muslim countries and 1.73% for world population.

The next two columns under the heading "Population" show population sizes for 1950 and 2000, and the last column shows the ratio of their population sizes in 2000 compared to 1950. As can be seen, Iraq had the biggest population in both 1950 and 2000, while Saudi Arabia was the fourth largest in 1950 but second in size in 2000. As shown in the last column, however, population ratios of both Iraq and Saudi Arabia are not the largest. Indeed, the most rapid population expansions occur in smaller Muslim countries like UAE, Qatar, Kuwait, Djibouti and Jordan with population sizes increasing more than 10 times for each over 1950–2000.

Table 4.3 also shows that among these fifteen fastest growing Muslim populations of the world for the period 1950–2000, twelve belong to the Middle-East and the North African region, while the other three, Cote d'lvoire, The Gambia, and Niger, are located in sub-Sahara Africa. The Middle-East and North African region contains 19 Muslim-majority countries, but only six had population sizes exceeding the 20-million mark in 2000. These six include Egypt (67.784 million),

Table 4.4: The Fastest Growing Muslim Populations in 2000–2050

Countries	Average annual growth rate (%)		Population (in million)		Population ratio 2050/2000
	2000–2025	2025–2050	2000	2050	
Niger	3.81%	3.32%	10.742	53.037	4.94
Yemen	3.82%	3.00%	18.017	84.385	4.68
Somalia	3.82%	2.83%	8.720	39.669	4.55
Mall	3.27%	2.60%	11.904	45.998	3.86
Guinea-Bissau	3.03%	2.36%	1.367	4.719	3.45
Burkina Faso	3.11%	2.42%	11.905	42.373	3.56
Afghanistan	3.06%	1.93%	21.391	69.517	3.25
Eritrea	2.93%	1.63%	3.712	10.539	2.84
Maldives	2.88%	1.70%	0.291	0.819	2.81
Oman	2.71%	1.56%	2.609	6.812	2.61
Ethiopia	2.49%	1.70%	65.59	170.987	2.61
Iraq	2.57%	1.46%	23.224	57.932	2.49
Saudi Arabia	2.63%	1.43%	22.147	54.738	2.47
Pakistan	2.44%	1.48%	142.654	348.700	2.44
Guinea	2.21%	1.57%	8.117	19.591	2.41
49 Muslim Countries	**1.90%**	**1.17%**	**1293.986**	**2611.539**	**2.02**
World	**1.11%**	**0.57%**	**6070.581**	**8918.724**	**1.46**

Iran (66.443 million), Algeria (30.245 million), Morocco (29.108 million), Iraq (23.224 million), and Saudi Arabia (22.147 million). Except for Tunisia (9.519 million in 2000), Lebanon (3.478 million), and West Bank and Gaza (2.966 million), which are not listed in Table 4.3, the other small populations in the Middle-East and the North African region grew rapidly and all are in the list of top 15 fastest growing Muslim populations in 1950–2000, as shown in Table 4.3.

Table 4.4 displays the 15 Muslim countries with fastest growing populations for the next fifty years in the same manner as Table 4.3. See the last column in Table 4.4 for the ranking. This includes eight countries in sub-Sahara Africa (Niger, Somalia, Mali, Guinea-Bissau, Burkina Faso, Eritrea, Ethiopia and Guinea), four countries in the Middle East and North Africa (Yemen, Oman, Iraq and Saudi Arabia), and three countries in South Asia (Afghanistan, Maldives, and Pakistan).

Comparing Table 4.4 with Table 4.3 reveals that the Muslim population growth rate is expected to slow significantly in the next five decades, and that growth momentum will probably shift from smaller Muslim countries in the Middle-East and North Africa to sub-Sahara Africa and South Asia. Thus more black and Asian men and women may become followers of Islamic religion due to the natural growth of Muslim populations in Africa and South Asia. In particular, Pakistanis will become the largest ethnic group of the Muslim world and exceed Indonesians. The last column of Table 4.4 shows that the total population of the 49 Muslim countries is expected to increase 2.02 times in 2000–2050 and the top 15 countries will increase 2.41–4.94 times versus an increase in world population of 1.46 times.

4.2. Demographic Transition of the Muslim World

The just discussed Muslim population estimates and projections provide a demographic profile of the Muslim world. The fundamental force that determines population sizes and their evolutions over time is the dynamic population process in what is called "demographic transition".

4.2.1. What is Demographic Transition?

Demographers investigating the development of populations of Western European nations in the last two centuries discovered a demographic transition process that was experienced by all of the developed countries. At beginning of the Industrial Revolution, both birth and death rates in Western Europe were high — about forty births and thirty seven deaths per thousand people per year. Economic development and social and technological progress gradually raised the standard of living and reduced the death rate significantly. The birth rate, however, remained high and this resulted in rapid population expansion. This period of population expansion lasted for several generations and was characterized by a high birth rate and low death rate. This resulted in a high population growth rate.

Continuously improving living conditions and medical care made people realize that children, once born, now had a good chance to survive. Prolific reproduction was no longer necessary to assure a few surviving children, and a large number of children actually became a burden on the parents. The idea gradually prevailed that having fewer children could make a family better off. As a result, the birth rate began to decline, while the death rate remained low, so the population growth rate declined gradually. This, the second expansionary phase of population transition, was thus characterized by a low death rate and a declining birth rate which resulted in a slowly increasing population size.

Ideally the birth rate would approach the replacement rate of about 2.1 children per woman in her life, and population would reach a stationary state with a constant age structure and a constant population size. In reality, however, many developed nations have completed the second phase of demographic transition but have not yet reached the stationary state because the total fertility rate has not stayed at 2.1. Rather, it keeps falling below the replacement rate. This has led to population decline for Russia and will do so for other developed nations. Most developing nations, on the other hand, are still in the first phase of their demographic transition with a high birth rate and a low death rate, resulting in rapid population growth. Hence, the birth rate and death rate as well as the population growth rate can be used to describe demographic transitions.

We now provide an analysis of demographic transitions in the Muslim world. This will be done with four vital parameters — (1) the crude birth rate, (2) crude death rate, (3) total fertility rate (TFR), and (4) life expectancy at birth. The averages we use for these vital parameters are calculated from vital parameters for individual Muslim countries. These values are compared with world averages as well as averages of high-income countries of the world in order to relate the demographic transition of the Muslim world to these other countries.

4.2.2. Vital Parameters of Muslim Countries

The main vital parameters used in demography and population analysis include the four we use, crude birth rate, crude death rate, total fertility rate, and life expectancy at birth as well as others measures that we will explain. These primary demographic parameters provide crucial information about population dynamics and take form in population models that can be used to estimate and predict population sizes and growth rates.

Figure 4.6 graphically depicts the average crude birth rates and crude death rates of the 49 Muslim-majority nations over the period 1960–2000, compared to the corresponding average rates of the high-income countries and the world.

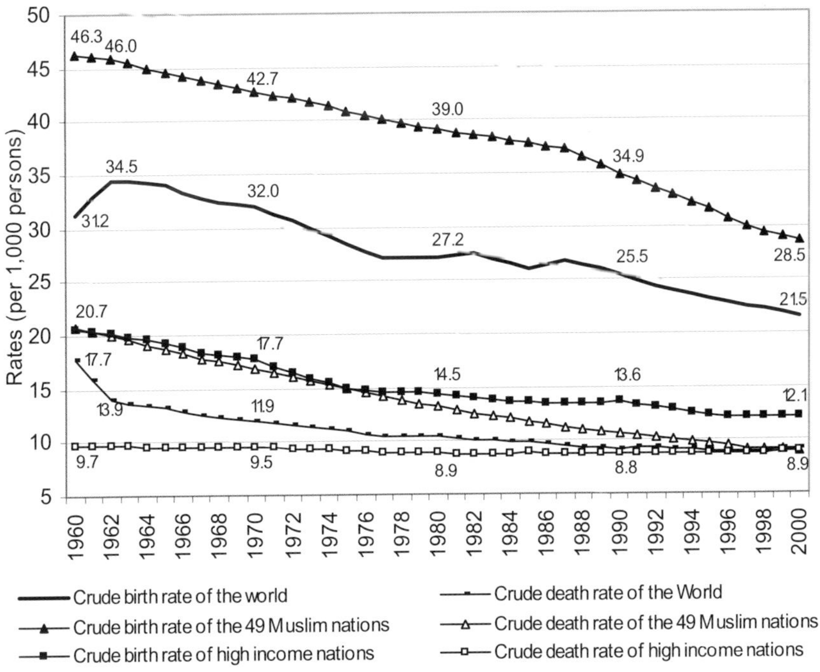

Figure 4.6: Crude Birth and Death Rates.

The original data come from the database of "World Development Indicators" for individual nations and are used to calculate average rates for the 49 Muslim nations.

As Figure 4.6 shows, the average crude birth rate of the Muslim world was significantly higher than the world average — 46.0 versus 34.5 in 1962 and 28.5 versus 21.5 in 2000. At 21.5 per thousand, the crude birth rate of the world in 2000 was close to the high-income-country level in 1960 (about 20.7) and far above the current crude birth rate level of 12.1 for high income countries. The average crude death rates of the Muslim world and the entire world reduced dramatically in the 1960s and 1970s and converged to coincidence with the crude death rate of the high-income countries in the 1990s.[5]

At about 8.9–9.1 per thousand the three death rates in Figure 4.6 were very close to each other in 2000, and the average mortality rate for the world has remained even at the relatively low level. This is true for different reasons. In high-income countries the crude death rate was already low by 1960, and stayed at this low level for decades, reflecting both continuously rising standards of living and advances in medical science. For Muslim countries it was the increasing proportion of young people in the Muslim world that kept the average death rate low while the increasing proportion of elderly in high-income countries kept the average death rate from falling further. However, the average crude death rate of high-income countries has changed slightly from 9.7 in 1960 to 8.9 in 2000.

Figures 4.7(A) and 4.7(B) depict infant mortality rates. The curves in Figure 4.7(A) show a huge gap in infant mortality rates between high-income countries and the world average. This reflects the significant impact of different living conditions on infant mortality. In every 1000 live births in 1960 about 31 babies would on average die before their first birthday in high-income countries. However, this number was 126.5 for the world average and 145 for the Muslim country average. During the last four decades the infant mortality rate declined substantially. Across the world, it dropped to 5.7 per thousand in high-income countries in 2000, to about 53.8 in the world average, and to 53.2 in the Muslim world. Since 1996, the average infant mortality rate of the 49 Muslim countries reduced to the world average and has kept falling. In 2000, however, the world infant mortality rate was still more than nine times larger than the rate for high-income countries.

Figure 4.7(B) presents individual Muslim country infant mortality rates in 2000 versus their corresponding real GDP per capita measured in terms of 1995 US

[5] In Figure 4.6, the average world birth rate shows a sharp increase from 31.2 in 1960 to 34.5 in 1962 and the average death rate declined sharply from 17.7 in 1960 to 13.9 in 1962. The huge size of the Chinese population has a great impact on world averages. Hence, we believe that these abnormal changes were due to the Chinese population rebounding from the 1959–1960 famine. See, for instance, the "World Development Indicator", which shows that China's crude birth rate was 20.86 in 1960 and jumped to 37.01 in 1962, and the crude death rate for China was 25.43 in 1960 and dropped to 10.02 in 1962.

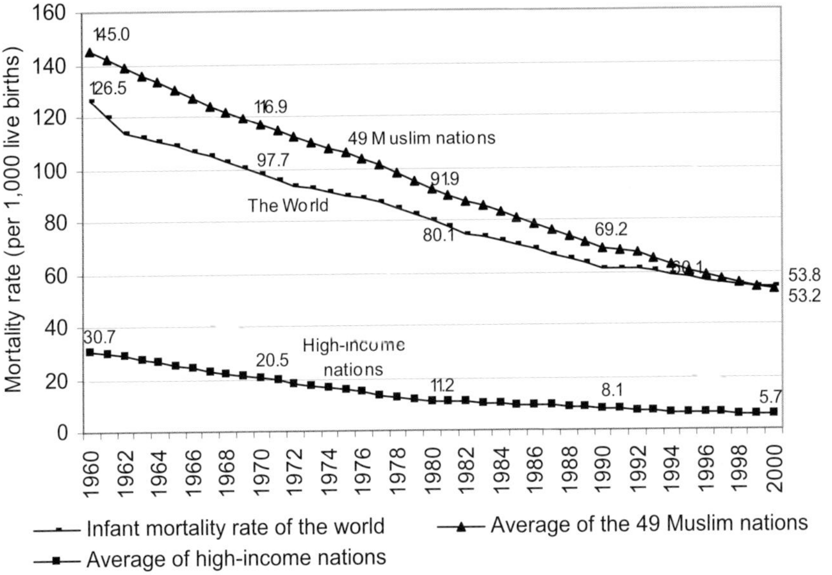

(A)

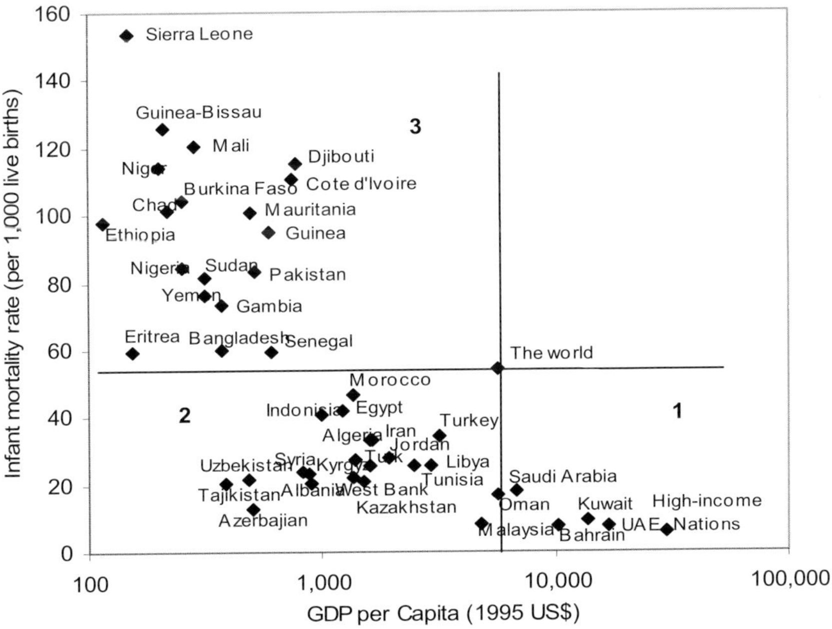

(B)

Figure 4.7: (A) Comparison of Infant Mortality Rates. (B) Infant Mortality Rate vs. GDP per Capita of Muslim Countries (2000).

dollars. For comparisons the world average is also shown (at the intersection of the horizontal and vertical lines) and the average of high-income countries of the world (shown on the far lower right region of the diagram). Figure 4.7(B) thus portrays a general trend: higher GDP per capita leads to lower infant mortality rates.

The Muslim countries can be divided into three groups. The first group, shown in the lower right of Figure 4.7(B), exhibits higher GDP per capita and lower infant mortality rates than the world average. This group includes five high-income Muslim countries: UAE, Kuwait, Bahrain, Saudi Arabia and Oman. However, all have higher infant mortality rates than the average in the high-income countries of the world as shown on the right. The second group, shown in the lower left, has both lower GDP per capita and lower infant mortality rate than the world average. These Muslim countries are in South-East Asia, Central Asia, and the Middle East & North Africa. All of the Muslim countries in sub-Sahara Africa belong to the third group, shown in the upper left, with lower GDP per capita and higher infant mortality rate than the world average. This group also contains Pakistan and Bangladesh, the most populous nations in South Asia, with Bangladesh showing both a lower infant mortality rate and a lower GDP per capita than most of the other Muslim countries of this group.

As was noted in Figure 4.6, the death rate of the Muslim world has already reduced and stabilized at around the world average, and its birth rate has declined continuously since 1960. Thus, the Muslim world is characterized as being in the second phase of its demographic transition, with lower death rates and declines in both birth rates and population growth rates. (See Figures 4.2 and 4.6.) However, the birth rate of the Muslim world is still higher than the world average, implying that this demographic transition has proceeded much slower than in other parts of the world. Several generations may be needed before the birth rate of the Muslim world falls to the world average and even then it will stay well above the level of high-income countries.

To portray the different fertility patterns, we provide the total fertility rates (TFR) over 40 years for the three populations in Figure 4.8(A).[6] The term, total fertility rate (TFR), is defined for a given population as the average number of children a woman would have assuming that current age-specific birth rates remain constant throughout her childbearing years, usually considered to be 15 to 49. Since 1973 the TFR in high-income nations has been below the replacement rate of 2.1, and reached 1.7 in 2000. This means that the population of high income countries is expected to decline in the future. The declining trend in the TFR of the Muslim world was not as steep as the world population in the 1960s and

[6] China's TFR was 3.39 in 1960 and jumped to 7.55 in 1962 due to the population rebound explained in notes 4 and 5. China's impact caused the irregular change in the world TFR in 1960–1962 that is shown in Figure 4.8(A).

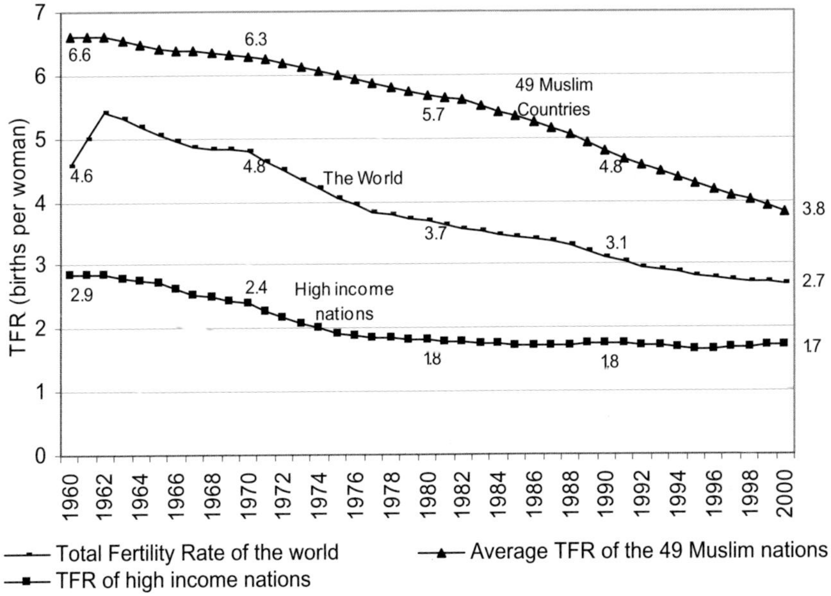

(A)

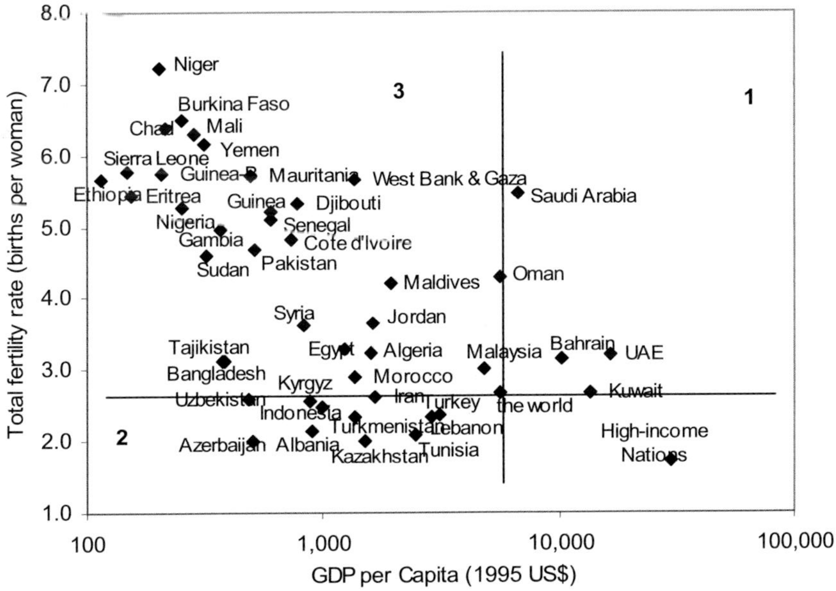

(B)

Figure 4.8: (A) Total Fertility Rates (TFR). (B) Total Fertility Rate vs. GDP per Capita of Muslim Countries (2000).

1970s, but began to catch up with the world trend in the early 1980s. However, the average TFR of Muslim countries remained above the world TFR as can be seen on the right side of Figure 4.8(A). In 2000, the TFR of the Muslim countries (3.8) was still greater than the world average (2.7), but both are well above the replacement rate of 2.1 per woman, indicating a continuing population expansion both for the world and especially for all the Muslim countries in the 21st century with a TFR of 3.8 in 2000.

Figure 4.8(B) shows the individual Muslim country Total Fertility Rate (TFR) in 2000. Like Figure 4.7(B) the portrayal is related to their real GDP per capita (in 1995 US dollars) and presented along with the world average at the point of intersection and the high-income country average in the lower right hand cell. Similar to Figure 4.7(B), Figure 4.8(B) shows a general trend: higher GDP per capita is associated with lower TFR.

These Muslim countries can also be divided into three groups in Figure 4.7(B). The first group, as shown in the cell on the upper right, contains the same five high-income Muslim countries as Figure 4.7(B), but their relative positions have changed. All except Oman have both higher TFR and higher GDP per capita than the world average, and all have both higher TFR and lower GDP per capita than the average of high income countries of the world. Compared with Figure 4.7(B) there has been some movement from the second group in the lower left cell into the third group in the upper left cell of Figure 4.8(B). Malaysia, Tajikistan, Jordan, Algeria, Egypt and Morocco all belong to group 2 in Figure 4.7(B) but have moved upward into group 3 in Figure 4.8(B) due to their higher TFR than the world average. As Figure 4.8(B) shows most Muslim countries still have higher total fertility rates than the world average even when account is taken of their lower GDP per capita.

The last vital parameter is life expectancy at birth. This is defined as the average number of years a newborn infant can expect to live given the current mortality pattern of the population. As Figure 4.9(A) shows, the life expectancies at birth of both female and male for all three populations — the world, Muslim countries and high-income countries — have risen steadily over the last four decades. This reflects economic, social, and technical (including medical) developments in all three groups. Female life expectancy at birth was greater than the corresponding male expectancy in all three populations (the world, Muslim countries and high-income countries) as shown in Figure 4.9(A). As shown by the bottom two curves, this sex gap in life expectancy widens over time for the Muslim countries. Also, the average life expectancy of both female and male was shorter in the Muslim world than the corresponding world average and much shorter than that of high-income countries. This occurred even though life expectancy increased faster over time for the Muslim countries than for the world and faster also than for the high-income countries, as shown by the steeper slops of two curves at the bottom of Figure 4.9(A).

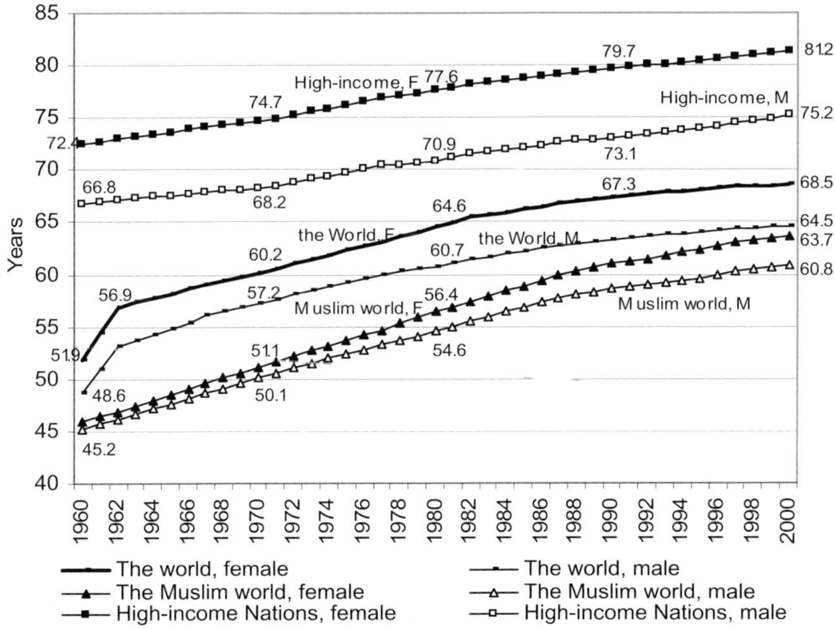

(A)

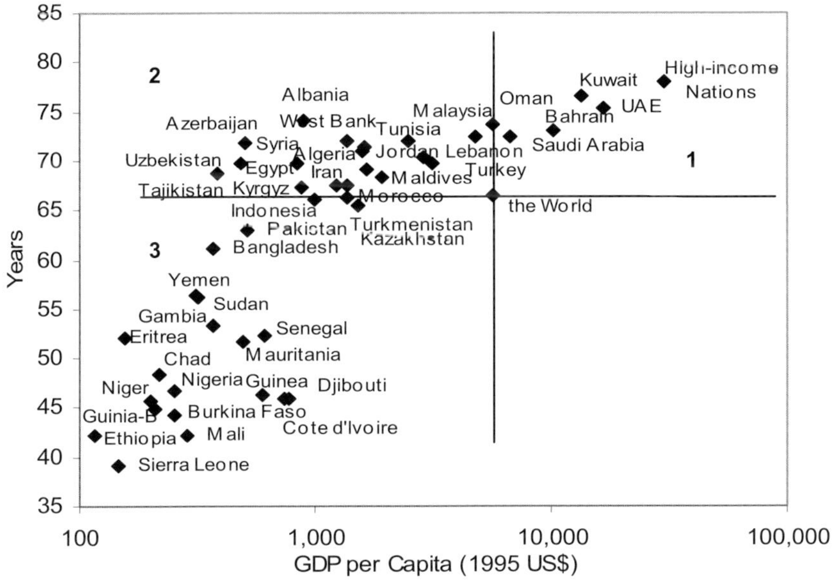

(B)

Figure 4.9: (A) Life Expectancy at Birth. (B) Life Expectancy vs.GDP per Capita of Muslim Countries (2000).

Table 4.5: Vital Parameters Averaged Over 1990–2000

	Crude Birth Rate (per 1000 People)	Crude Death Rate (per 1000 People)	TFR	Life Expectancy at Birth (year)	
				Female	Male
World Average	23.31	9.07	2.86	68.00	63.97
High-income Countries	12.57	8.79	1.70	80.42	74.04
49 Muslim Countries	34.04	13.87	4.44	62.36	59.69
Europe/Central Asia	22.74	16.16	3.82	72.00	64.99
South-East Asia	26.72	8.71	3.02	65.90	65.81
South Asia	39.07	13.92	5.48	57.16	56.18
Middle East & North Africa	33.09	10.23	4.61	68.52	65.96
Sub-Sahara Africa	48.57	20.35	5.26	48.24	45.91

Figure 4.9(B) portrays individual Muslim country life expectancy at birth for both sexes in 2000 in terms of GDP per capita and relates this to the world average and to the high-income country average. As in both Figures 4.7(B) and 4.8(B) the trend is for higher GDP per capita to result in higher life expectancy. As shown in the upper right hand cell of Figure 4.9(B) the same five high-income Muslim countries as in Figures 4.7(B) and 4.8(B) have both higher GDP per capita and higher life expectancy than the world, but all are still below the high-income nations of the world. Similar to Figure 4.7(B) the upper left cell of Figure 4.9(B) shows lower GDP per capita but higher life expectancy than world average. Again, Muslim countries in sub-Sahara Africa and South Asia, as shown by group 3 in the lower left cell in Figure 4.9(B), experienced both lower GDP per capita and lower life expectancy than the world average. A large life expectancy gap exists between high-income and low-income Muslim countries. This is shown by Sierra Leone, Ethiopia and Mali with their life expectancy less than 43 years versus high-income Kuwait with its life expectancy of 77 years.

Table 4.5 summarizes the four vital parameters for the Muslim world of 49 countries and each of its five geographic regions. These values are compared with the world average and the high-income country average in the top two rows. On average, the Muslim population in Europe/Central Asia has the lowest crude birth rate (22.74) and the longest female life expectancy (72.0) among the Muslim countries, but its crude death rate (16.16) is greater than other regions with the exception of sub-Sahara Africa The Muslim population in sub-Sahara Africa has both the highest crude birthrate and the highest crude death rate (48.57 and 20.35), and the lowest life expectancy at birth for both females and males (48.24 and 45.91). South Asia is next to sub-Sahara Africa with both a high crude birth rate and short life expectancy for its Muslim population. The Muslims in the Middle East and North Africa experience longer male life expectancies (65.96) than Muslims in other regions and this life expectancy is accompanied by a relatively low crude death rate (10.23) during 1990–2000.

Table 4.6: Muslim Country Vital Parameters Averaged Over 1990–2000

	Crude Birth Rate (per 1000 People)	Crude Death Rate (per 1000 People)	TFR	Life Expectancy at Birth (year)	
				Female	Male
49 Muslim Countries	34.04	13.87	4.44	62.36	59.69
Muslim Countries with High Birth Rate					
Niger	53.47	21.16	7.43	47.22	43.74
Somalia	51.88	21.08	7.21	45.28	42.74
Mali	48.79	18.84	6.66	44.87	42.79
Afghanistan	48.41	21.54	6.85	42.53	42.09
Ethiopia	47.23	20.00	6.29	45.18	42.84
Sierra Leone	47.08	26.93	6.21	37.73	35.07
Chad	45.90	17.39	6.75	49.29	46.01
Burkina Faso	45.82	18.76	6.81	46.24	44.02
Guinea-Bis	44.25	21.05	5.94	45.13	42.17
Mauritania	43.34	15.66	6.00	51.81	48.61
Muslim Countries with Low Birth Rate					
Kazakhstan	17.25	9.42	2.30	71.34	60.95
Qatar	19.04	2.88	3.43	74.40	73.10
UAE	19.79	3.02	3.65	75.91	73.39
Azerbaijan	20.31	6.48	2.4	74.22	66.59
Albania	20.90	5.37	2.53	74.77	69.12
Tunisia	21.17	5.62	2.62	73.28	69.49
Kuwait	22.59	2.24	3.01	77.78	73.78
Turkey	22.65	6.67	2.71	70.72	65.80
Bahrain	22.77	3.66	3.42	74.75	70.11
Indonesia	23.93	7.92	2.79	65.90	62.28

Table 4.6 lists the 10 Muslim countries (in its top 10 rows) with the highest birth rates and the 10 Muslim countries (in its 10 bottom rows) with the lowest birth rates for the period 1990–2000. With the exception of Afghanistan, all the top 10 high-birth-rate Muslim countries are located in sub-Sahara Africa. Niger, a sub-Sahara African country, had the highest birth rate at 53.47 per thousand, and it also had the highest total fertility rate (TFR), 7.43, over the period 1990–2000. Sierra Leone, another sub-Sahara African country, had the highest death rate, 26.93 per thousand, and the lowest life expectancy at birth, 37.73 years for females and 35.07 years for males. Both are less than half the average life expectancy at birth in high-income countries (80.42 and 74.04 as shown in Table 4.5). One might also observe that life expectancies at birth of all of the top 10 high-birth-rate Muslim countries were far below the average for the Muslim world: 62.36 and 59.69 years for females and males, respectively (see Table 4.6).

The bottom half of Table 4.6 displays the 10 Muslim countries which had the lowest birth rates in 1990–2000. Five of them (Qatar, United Arab Emirates, Tunisia, Kuwait and Bahrain) are located in the Middle East and North Africa, while Kazakhstan, Azerbaijan, Albania and Turkey belong to Europe/Central Asia, and Indonesia is in South-East Asia. Kazakhstan has the lowest birth rate (17.25) and the lowest total fertility rate (2.3). This is nearly half the corresponding averages of the Muslim countries (34.04 and 4.44) shown at the top of Table 4.6. Four Muslim countries in the Persian Gulf (Kuwait, Qatar, Bahrain and United Arab Emirates) experienced extremely low crude death rates (about 2.24–3.66 per thousand). This is less than one third the average death rate of the 49 Muslim countries (13.87) shown at the top of Table 4.6. They also experienced moderate birth rates of 19.04–22.77, at approximately two thirds the average birth rate of Muslim countries (34.04), and slightly less than the world average 23.31 (Table 4.5).

Recall the discussion in Section 4.1 where we observed the tremendous population expansion in the small oil rich nations in the Persian Gulf (see Table 4.3 in Section 4.1.3). The high birth rates and low death rates exhibited in Table 4.6 are the forces underlying this rapid population expansion over the last four decades in the Persian Gulf region.

4.2.3. Muslim Countries in Demographic Transitions

We select seven populous Muslim countries (Indonesia, Iran, Egypt, Turkey, Saudi Arabia, Pakistan and Nigeria) and exhibit their different demographic transitions over the last four decades. The Indonesian population has been experiencing the fastest demographic transition in the Muslim world, so we use it as a basis of comparison with the six other Muslim countries.

For the past three decades, the Indonesian government has been implementing its family planning program through the National Family planning Coordinating Board. The Board has effectively provided family planning services, such as contraception and follow-up care, to Indonesian women. Local clinics have become the locus for birth control efforts with affiliated fieldworkers, who advocate birth control methods door-to-door. Various incentive programs, "target or quota" programs and other special drive programs are implemented to create new contraceptive acceptors. These efforts have resulted in a significant decline in Indonesia's crude birth rate, from 41.4 per thousand in 1972 to 21.7 per thousand in 2000, as shown in Figures 4.10, 4.11 and 4.12. This has made demographic transition in Indonesia more expeditious than other Muslim countries'.

As the top part of Figure 4.10 shows, the birth rates of Egypt and Iran have declined since 1962 and moved toward the birth rate of Indonesia in 2000. However, the birth rates of these two countries in the 1980s were significantly larger than the birth rate of Indonesia, and only converged to Indonesia in the 1990s. The death rates of Egypt and Iran were slightly below the death rate of Indonesia in the 1960s and 1970s and then fluctuated around the Indonesian death rate. Rates of both countries approached Indonesia's level of 21.7 for birth rates and 7.4 for death rates in the late 1990s.

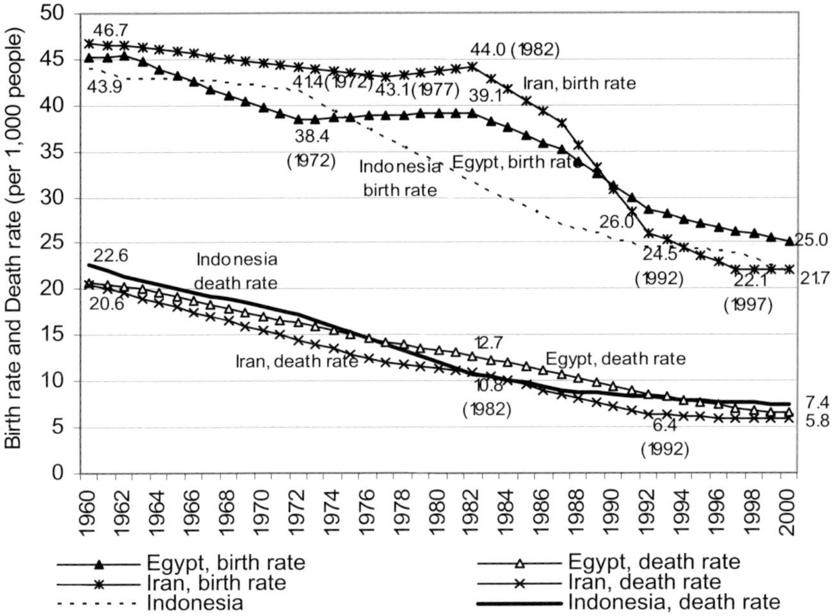

Figure 4.10: Demographic Transitions of Egypt, Iran and Indonesia.

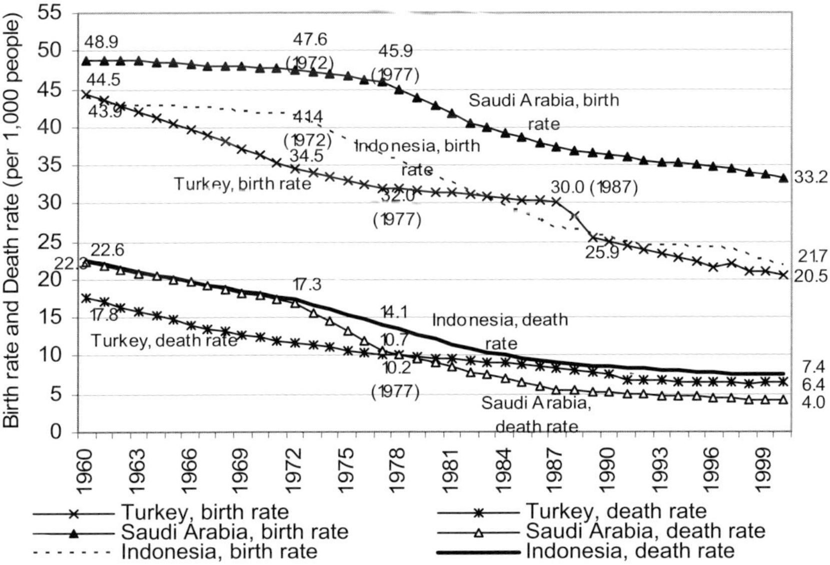

Figure 4.11: Demographic Transitions of Turkey, Saudi Arabia and Indonesia.

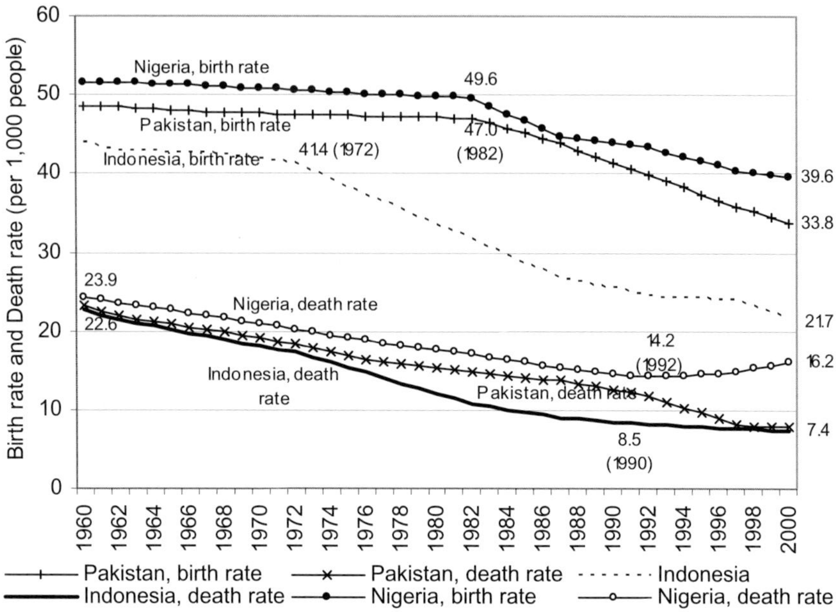

Figure 4.12: Demographic Transitions of Pakistan, Nigeria and Indonesia.

The death rates of these three nations, Iran, Egypt and Indonesia, have moved downward uniformly, as shown in Figure 4.10, but the birth rate behaviors differ. For Indonesia, the second phase of its demographic transition began before 1960, and accelerated in the period 1972–1992; for Iran the demographic transition started in 1982 and has since accelerated, while for Egypt the demographic transition started in 1962 and accelerated in 1982–1992.

The two curves of birth and death rates for Iran show a steeper decline over the period 1982–1992 with the birth rate falling from 44.0 in 1982 to 26.0 in 1992, and the death rate falling from 10.8 to 6.4 shown in Figure 4.10. During the 1980–1988 Iran–Iraq war, more than one million Iranians were killed. The heavy casualties and hardships of the war were reflected in rapid declines in Iran's birth rate.

Historically, Iran's first family planning policy was introduced in 1967 under Shah Reza Pahlavi, aiming at accelerating economic growth and improving the status of women. Implementation of this policy resulted in a slow decline in Iran's crude birth rate, from 46.7 in 1960 to 43.1 in 1977. However, Iran's declining fertility reversed its course during the Islamic Revolution, when the Iranian health officials were ordered not to advocate contraception, and family planning programs were criticized as under Western influence and were, therefore, dismantled. In particular, during Iran's war with Iraq in 1980–1988, a large population was

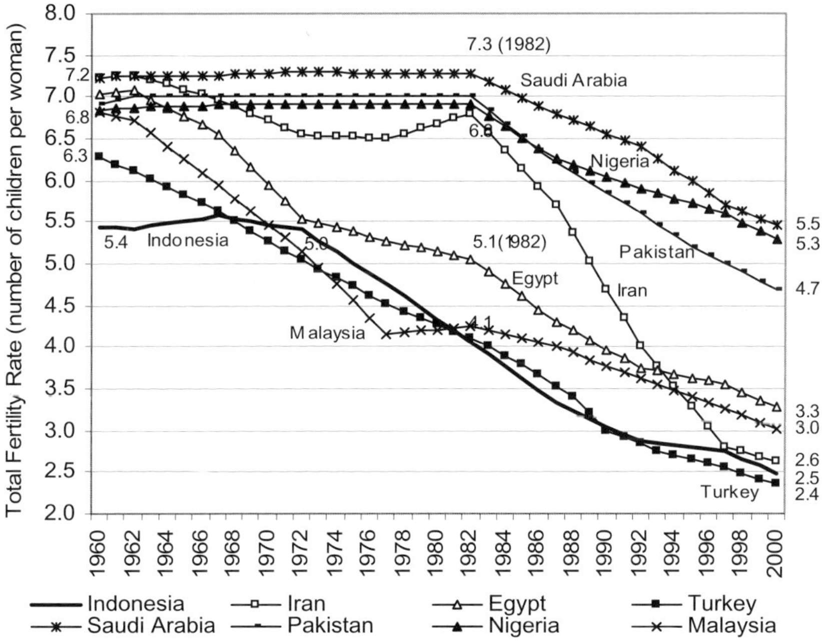

Figure 4.13: Total Fertility Rate of Seven Muslim Countries.

viewed as a comparative advantage, and Iran's supreme leader Ayatollah Khomeini pushed procreation for "an army of 20 million" of "soldiers for Islam". This strong pro-high-fertility policy led to an increase in Iran's birth rate to 44.0 in 1982 shown in Figure 4.10.

The resulting rapid population growth, however, generated many problems for Iran's post-war reconstruction, including overly crowded and polluted cities, severe job shortages and a faltering economy. By the end of 1989, Iran revived its national family planning program, viewing its rapid population growth as an obstacle to development. In 1993, the Iranian government passed a national family planning law that effectively encouraged couples to have fewer children by restricting maternity leave benefits after three children. Iran's religious leaders and media have also become involved with the promotion for smaller families, raising awareness of population issues and family planning programs and citing them as a social responsibility. The Iranian government has also covered 80 percent of family planning costs. These multiple efforts have facilitated Iran's demographic transition with a birth rate quickly declining from 44.0 in 1982 to 21.7 in 2000 as shown in Figure 4.10 and the TFR decreasing from 6.8 to 2.6, in the same time frame. See Figure 4.13.

Egypt is the most populous Arab country, and, with a population of 67.784 million in 2000, ranks above Iran (see Table 4.2). Although family planning was introduced for the first time in Egypt's Five Year Plan in 1961 as part of the economic program, a separate population planning program began to be carried out in 1966 with a centralized drive to reduce the birth rate. About two thousand birth control clinics were set up to offer a variety of contraceptives and educational information on birth control. A propaganda campaign was undertaken by the media and in the mosques where the clergy preached in favor of birth control.[7] After a few months of these hasty and short-lived efforts, no further attempts were made to implement birth control programs from the government due to the government's inability to deal with Egypt's worsening economic situation and the internal and external pressures, including the involvement in the civil war in Yemen, and the Six-Day War with Israel. Egypt's birth rate stopped declining and began to rise in 1973 and it reached 39.1 in 1982, as shown in Figure 4.10.

In the 1980s, however, the Egyptian birth rate returned to its declining trend with a particularly rapid decline in birth rate, from 39.1 in 1982 to 25.0 in 2000, as shown in Figure 4.10. In Egypt, like in other Muslim countries, almost all births occur within marriage. Postponement of marriage is a central aspect that influences fertility levels. The opportunity of Egyptian girls to receive education has significantly improved in the 1980s and 1990s. Girls who reach secondary school are more likely to delay marriage and childbearing. Urbanization also helps Egyptian women find jobs in urban areas in which socio-economic structural change, mortality and fertility declines, and acceptance of birth control have much stronger impact on family planning decisions than in rural areas. Participation of women in the labor force, particularly in urban areas, has changed reproductive behavior and speeds up the demographic transitions in Egypt.

Figure 4.11 portrays demographic transitions for Turkey and Saudi Arabia in comparison with Indonesia. The government of Turkey encouraged population growth from the establishment of the republic in 1923 until the early 1960s. When rapid population expansion became an evident factor that hurt Turkey's economic development, a family planning law was passed in 1965 for the establishment of the Family planning Division within the Ministry of Health and Social Assistance. Birth control information and services were extended to as many couples as possible. A 1967 law decriminalized abortion, and under legislation passed in 1983 a pregnancy could be lawfully terminated under certain specific conditions. The primary focus of birth control in Turkey has been on limiting and spacing births, and family planning is combined with maternal and child health services. Strong government support for family planning led to the rapidly declining birth rate in

[7] The Egyptian clergy are state employees and their power and authority stem directly from the regime that is in power.

Turkey shown in Figure 4.11, from 44.5 per thousand people in 1960 to 32.0 in 1977.

During 1977–1986 Turkey's birth rate became stationary at above 30, which caused government concern about the continuing high birth rate. The Ministry of Health launched a new population control campaign in 1986 that concentrated on rural areas. In high fertility rural areas, many new health clinics were established to focus on training medical professionals in family planning, counseling and distribution of birth control information and services. The Turkish Family Health and Planning Foundation was also established by the private sector to supplement the population control efforts in the public sector through financial support and nationwide television advertisements. Even Sunni Muslim religious leaders in Turkey have stated that Islam does not prohibit married couples from trying to space births or limit the size of their families. However, there was a consensus among religious leaders that resort to sterilization or abortion as a means of birth control was not permissible under Islam. Nevertheless, Turkey's birth rate began to decline again after 1987 and reached 25.9 in 1989 and 20.5 in 2000, and, as shown in Figure 4.11, this was smaller than Indonesia's birth rate of 21.7.

Saudi Arabia experienced a rapid population expansion with population size increasing from 3.201 million in 1950 to 22.147 million in 2000. The annual rate of population growth in Saudi Arabia also increased from 3.57% in 1950–1975 to 5.09% in 1975–2000 (see Table 4.3 in Section 4.1.3), making it one of the highest growth rates in the world. There is virtually no family planning and birth control in Saudi Arabia. Its birth rate was 48.9 in 1960 and 45.9 in 1977 and then declined to 33.2 in 2000. The declining birth rate of Saudi Arabia was due to age structure changes that affect fertility patterns over time as well as improvements in the Saudi health care system that raised the survivor ratio of new-born babies and caused less additional babies to be wanted to replace lost ones. In fact, the Saudi infant death rate plummeted from 65 deaths per 1000 live births in 1980 to only 19 per 1000 in 2000 (see Figure 4.7(B) in Section 4.2.2), making it one of the lowest death rates in the Muslim world.

As Figure 4.11 shows, death rates of Saudi Arabia declined from 22.6 in 1960 to 10.7 in 1977 and 4.0 in 2000, and this was smaller than that of Turkey (6.4) and Indonesia (7.4). High birth rate and low death rate will keep the Saudi population rising continuously for the next several decades. According to the projection by the Population Division of the United Nations, the Saudi population is expected to be 37.919 million in 2020 and 59.812 million in 2050. A very serious water supply problem for the increasing Saudi population is already looming in the Kingdom, leading to the suggestion of some inevitable form of "population rationalization", but this is still not a popular idea in Saudi Arabia. Without family planning or birth control programs supported by the government, the Saudi demographic transition may take many generations to see its fertility rate falling very slowly, while the Saudi population size continues increasing rapidly.

Figure 4.12 portrays demographic transitions for Pakistan and Nigeria, which are compared with Indonesia. Pakistan ranked number two in the Muslim world, behind Indonesia, in terms of population size in 2000. Pakistan is expected to exceed Indonesia as number one among the populous Muslim countries in the world in 2050 with population size about 348.7 million. (See Table 4.2 in Section 4.1.2.) Its rapid population expansion is due to high fertility and a slow demographic transition.

Pakistan has a non-governmental organization, Family Planning Association of Pakistan (FPAP), which took family planning initiatives as early as 1953. The Pakistani government put the Population Welfare Program in its second five-year plan (1960–1965) for the first time and in the successive five-year national development plans. However, political support for family planning did not produce visible results in reducing birth rates, which remained above 47.0 during 1960–1982. Pakistan's high birth rate stems from religious, social and cultural norms. A low literacy rate, particularly among women, is also a major impediment to family planning.

Various strategies have been adopted in Pakistan since the early 1980s with special attention to rural areas where fertility is still very high. These new measures include expansion of family planning services in rural areas through village family planning workers, acceleration of training for health services personnel, and intensification of motivational campaigns through TV, radio and other media. The latest Population Welfare Program (1998–2003) is aimed at reducing TFR to 4.2 and a population growth rate under 2.0%. As of 2000, Pakistan's birth rate stood at 33.8, slightly above that of Saudi Arabia (33.2). In Pakistan the rates of contraceptive use and participation in family planning services are low, compared with other Muslim countries like Indonesia, Turkey, Iran and Egypt. Traditional beliefs and misconception may play a big role in this situation because a large number of the population continues to believe that uses of artificial contraceptives for family planning are against nature and also against Islam.

Some observers suggest that the reason for the failure of Pakistan's family planning program was due to religious leaders being neglected, so they are not involved in the population campaign. Religious leaders are very important for the distribution of knowledge to the people at the community and grassroots levels. In May, 2005, the "International Ulama Conference on Population and Development" was held in the Pakistani capital of Islamabad. The conference attracted many participants of key religious leaders and scholars from Muslim communities in 22 countries.[8] The most important consensus reached in the conference was that family planning could be carried out in the Muslim world, as long as the methods used are not against Islamic teachings. Even if Pakistan finds ways

[8] *Pakistan: Debating Islam and Family Planning*, IRIN news, UN Office for the Coordination of Humanitarian Affairs, http://www.irinnews.org/report.

to acquire the support of religious leaders and involves communities in its family planning programs, the two-decade delay in the demographic transition during the 1960s and 1970s has already led to an unusual population size and it may take generations to stop the population growth.

We now turn to Nigeria. Nigeria is the most populous Muslim country in sub-Sahara Africa. Number four in the Muslim world in 2000, it is expected to become number three in 2050, with a population size increasing from 114.746 million to 258.478 million in the next five decades. Figure 4.12 shows that the birth rate of Nigeria stood above 50 during 1960–1982 and only began to decline, very slowly, after 1982. Its death rate remained high but also declined slowly until 1993, when, as shown in Figure 4.12, the death rate began to rise. This rising death rate does not offset the very high birth rate, however, so Nigeria's population is expected to continue increasing well into the 21st century.

Nigeria's high fertility stems from its poor economic and educational conditions, social values and lifestyles. Their beliefs also play a major role in favor of high fertility and large families. Like many sub-Sahara African countries, some Nigerians believe in African tribal religions that lead to the belief that a woman who has many children is virtuous and whose main job is to provide the husband with children. African men want larger families because larger families with more workers prosper in a typical agriculture community like Nigeria. Family size is commonly considered the decision of the husband, and Nigerian women do not have the choice of using birth control devices. In addition, Africa's levels of polygamy are ten times as high as those in "typical" "polygamous" societies in Asia. This often results in larger families with many siblings and different mothers.

During 1988–1994, the World Bank, the USA and other Western donors launched an intensive campaign of population control in Nigeria. The objective was to serve a national policy of population control at all government levels. Massive and extraordinary propaganda was conducted in the mass media to help break resistance to birth control. The campaign ended in 1994 as a total failure. Nigerian hostility to Western concepts of family planning was actually greater than when the programs started. It was widely believed that the Western interest in birth control is based on a fear of large Muslim populations. Some Nigerian scholars argued that a growing population was necessary for development and blamed international aid agencies for undermining economic development in Nigeria.[9] Social values and people's beliefs, like in Nigeria, occur in other parts of sub-Sahara Africa and form obstacles to population control that are very hard to overcome. In any case, Nigeria's birth rate remained above 40 in the 1990s and reached 39.6 in 2000. Without birth control and family planning, Nigeria's demographic transi-

[9] *When Propaganda Backfires, Nigeria*, http://www.theunjustmedia.com/Propaganda.

tion is likely to follow a very slow natural process, while its population continues to increase rapidly.

Figure 4.13 depicts evolving paths of the total fertility rates (TFRs) of these Muslim nations over the period 1960–2000. Indonesia, Malaysia, Egypt and Turkey started the second phase of their demographic transition before 1960 with TFR declining from 5.4, 6.8, 7.0 and 6.3 in 1960 to 2.5, 3.0, 3.3 and 2.4 in 2000, respectively. Iran's demographic transition was interrupted by the Islamic Revolution and the Iran–Iraq war. This postponed the second phase of its transition to 1982, with Iran's TFR decreasing from 6.8 in 1982 to 2.6 in 2000, which, as Figure 4.13 shows, is close to those of Turkey and Indonesia. As noted earlier, Pakistan had an ineffective population control program that also delayed its second phase of transition until 1982, with Pakistan's TFR declining from 7.0 in 1982 to 4.7 in 2000. Nigeria and Saudi Arabia are at the top of Figure 4.13. Nigeria did not impose a population control program, and Saudi Arabia has virtually no population control. Demographic transitions are proceeding very slowly for both countries with still high TFR, 5.3 and 5.5 in 2000. From Figure 4.13 one can clearly see the effect of family planning policies on TFR and the diversity of demographic transitions in these Muslim countries.

Summary of Chapter 4

The 49 Muslim-majority countries have experienced rapid population expansions for the last four decades. The total population of these Muslim countries increased from 384 million in 1950 to 1287 million in 2000 and is projected to reach 2608 million by 2050. The world population share of these Muslim countries also increased from 15.2% in 1950 to 21.2% in 2000 and is projected to be 29.2% by 2050. During the 1950–2000 period the fastest population growth took place in some of the smaller Muslim countries in the Middle-East and North Africa. However, the fastest population growth is projected to occur in some of the Muslim countries in sub-Sahara Africa and South Asia for the next five decades.

The average birth rate of the 49 Muslim countries has been declining since 1960, but it is still higher than the world average and much higher than the average of high-income countries. The average death rate of the 49 Muslim countries has decreased since 1960 and approached the world average as well as the average of high-income countries by 2000. The vital parameters of individual Muslim countries are closely correlated to GDP per capital. Hence, the general trend is: higher GDP per capita which leads to lower infant mortality rates, lower total fertility rates (TFR), and higher life expectancy at birth.

Many Muslim countries have been in the second phase of their demographic transition, which is characterized by declining death rates and substantially declining, but still high, birth rates. This results in rapid population expansion. The process of demographic transition in the Muslim world varies substantially for different countries. Indonesia, Malaysia, Egypt and Turkey entered the second phase about twenty years earlier than the other Muslim countries. The birth rates and TFR for these three countries have declined faster than the others, counted as a result of effective family planning policies and programs. However, birth rates and TFR for many Muslim countries have remained high, particularly in sub-Sahara Africa, even though death rates for these countries declined and stayed low. Thus populations of the 49 Muslim countries are expected to grow continuously for the next five decades, along with their percentage shares in the world population total.

Chapter 5

Changing Age Structure of the Muslim Population

Age structure is another important demographic feature that we need to bring into the demographic transformation in the Muslim world. The age structure of a population is defined, relative to the total population, as, respectively, the proportion of children, youngsters, adults, and the elderly.

This chapter consists of two sections. Section 5.1 presents the age structure for three age groups for Muslim countries in five geographic regions: Europe/Central Asia, Middle East and North Africa, South Asia, South East Asia, and sub-Sahara Africa. It also analyzes population dependency for the Muslim world, where "dependency" refers to the age groups that are dependent on other groups for their support. Section 5.2 focuses on a specific population cohort that we refer to as "troublesome", consisting of male youngsters age 15–29, which we examine for Muslim countries in five geographic regions as well as for individual Muslim countries. This is important because the relatively large size of this cohort is correlated to social instability. For perspective on this troublesome cohort behavior we will discuss past experiences of some non-Muslim countries such as the United States and China and compare their troublesome cohorts with present situations for the counterpart cohorts for the comparing cohorts in the Muslim world.

5.1. Age Structure

5.1.1. Three Population Cohorts

To simplify our analysis, we choose three age groups (or population cohorts): (1) the cohort of children aged 0–14, (2) the cohort of youngsters and adults aged 15–64, and (3) the cohort of elderly age 65 and over. Using individual country age-distribution data from United Nations Population Division, 2004 *World Population Prospects, Volume II*, we calculated the number of people in each of these three cohorts for individual Muslim-majority countries and aggregated them for each of the five geographic regions defined in the previous chapter. The geographically aggregated number of people in each cohort is then divided by the total population of the Muslim-majority countries in corresponding regions to obtain the percentage of each cohort in the total Muslim population of the region. These calculations cover the one-hundred-year period, 1950–2050. The results we obtain are used to analyze the changing age structure of the Muslim population for the five geographic regions.

International Symposia in Economic Theory and Econometrics, Vol. 19
William W. Cooper and Piyu Yue

ISSN: 1571-0386/DOI: 10.1016/S1571-0386(07)00015-4

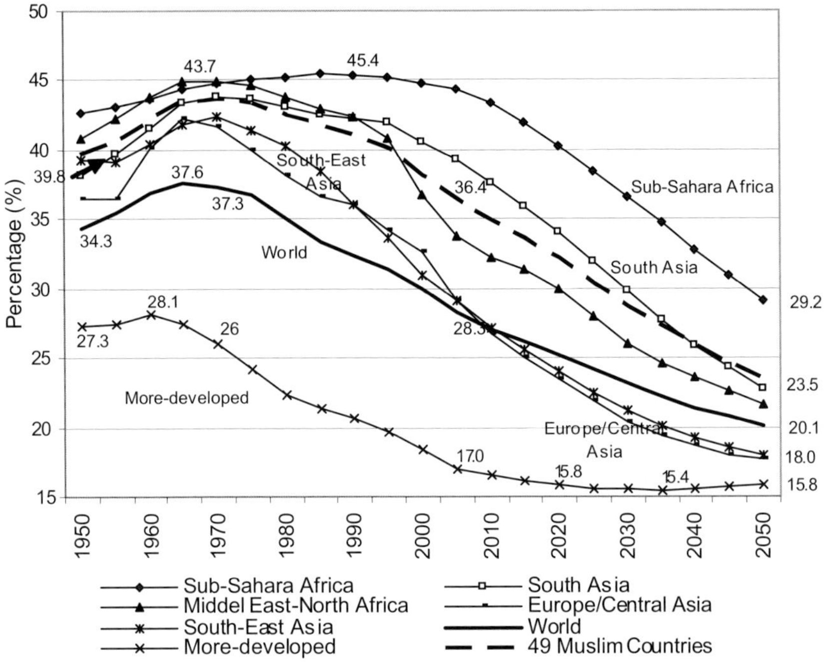

Figure 5.1: Percentage of Cohort Aged 0–14.

We, similarly, calculate the proportions of these three age cohorts in the total population for (1) the 49 Muslim-majority nations, (2) the world population and (3) the aggregate population of the more-developed region of the world.[1] In order to make our comparisons we depict in Figures 5.1, 5.2 and 5.3, respectively, evolving curves of different population percentages for each of the cohorts over the 100-year period (including extrapolation) from 1950 to 2050.

Figure 5.1 depicts percentages of the children cohort, age 0–14, for the world, the more-developed region, the 49 Muslim countries and the Muslim countries located in the five geographic regions we have been considering. Proportions of this cohort declined first in the more-developed region, around 1960, and rapidly decreased from 28.1% in 1960 to 17.0% by 2005 and is projected to be flat at around 15.8% over 2020–2050. The proportion of children for world population increased from 34.3% in 1950 to 37.6% in 1965 and has since been declining. It

[1] The more-developed region contains four sub-regions: Europe, North America, Australia/New Zealand and Japan. The aggregated population and age components of the more developed region are provided in World Population Prospects, Volumes II.

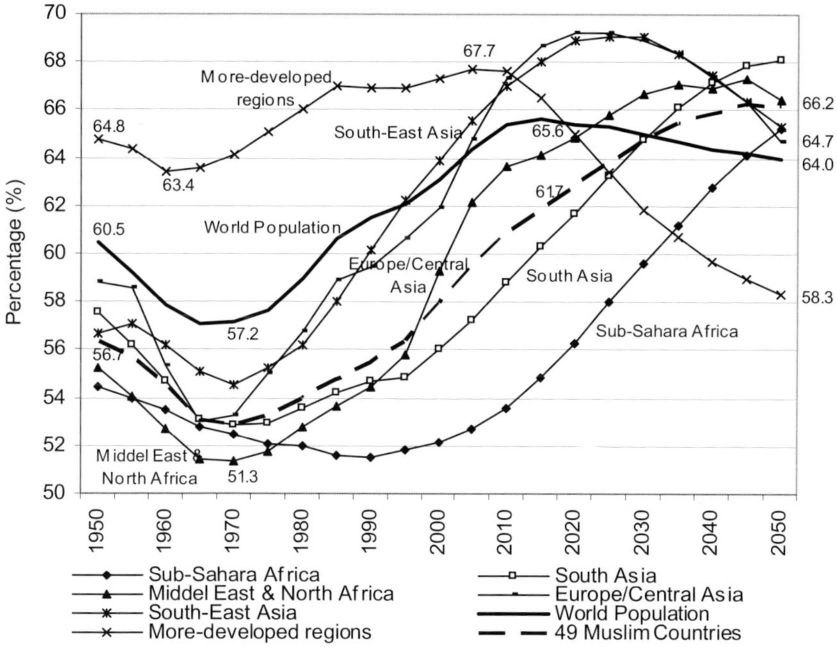

Figure 5.2: Percentage of Cohort Aged 15–64.

was 28.3% by 2005 and is expected to continue declining in the next five decades, reaching 20.1% by 2050.

For the 49 Muslim countries, this proportion follows the world average with about a (5–10)-year lag. The number of children aged 0–14 in the 49 Muslim-majority countries accounts for a greater percentage of the total Muslim population than in the world population over the entire time period — 39.8% vs. 34.3% in 1950, 43.7% vs. 37.3% in 1970, 36.4% vs. 28.3% in 2005 and 23.5% vs. 20.1% by 2050. Proportions of children for Muslim countries in all the five regions, with the exception of sub-Sahara Africa, have declined since 1970, but at different paces, and are expected to continue their declining trend. The proportion of children in sub-Sahara African Muslim countries shown in the top curve of Figure 5.1 peaked at 45.4% in 1990 and then began to decline, but at a slower pace than Muslim countries in the other regions. This is projected to continue to 2050 when its 29.2% value is still higher than for any other regions.

Before 2005 the percentages of children in Muslim countries of all five regions were greater than that of world population and much greater than that of the more-developed region. After 2005, however, percentages of children in the Muslim-majority countries in Europe/Central Asia and South East Asia are expected to fall below the world average and approach the level of the more-developed region.

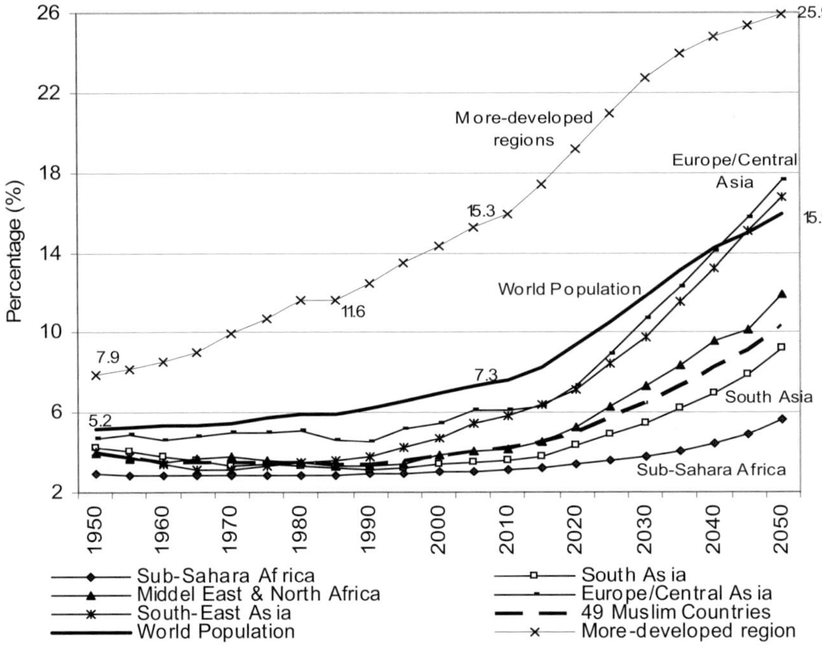

Figure 5.3: Percentage of Cohort Aged 65 and Above.

Proportions of children in Muslim countries of the other regions — sub-Sahara Africa, South Asia, and Middle East and North Africa — are projected to decline but stay above the world average.

Comparing proportions of children for the world and all regions in 2005 we find that on average for every 100 people there are 28.3 children in world population, 36.4 children in the 49 Muslim countries and only 17 children in the more-developed regions. Thus the Muslim population is younger than the world population and much younger than the population of developed countries. When a large number of children grow up and enter the age of reproduction, more newborn babies will make a population expand even faster in future. On the other hand, when the number of children is too small to replace grandparents or parents, the size of a population will shrink in the future. This is the situation faced by many developed countries in Europe and by Japan and Russia.

Figure 5.2 displays percentage curves of the 15–64 age cohort for the world, the more-developed region, the 49 Muslim countries and Muslim countries in the five geographic regions. This cohort represents working-age people in a population, who are able to conduct productive activities and earn income or generate wealth to support their children and the elderly in their families. Thus this cohort includes both youngsters and adults and is the most active and productive segment of the population.

As Figure 5.2 shows, all the percentage curves of this cohort decreased in the 1950s, began to rise in the 1960s and are expected to arrive at their peaks in different years. For the more-developed region the peak is 67.7% by 2005, for the world population, it is 65.6% by 2015, and for the 49 Muslim countries it is 66.2% by 2050. After passing these peaks, the proportions of this cohort in all three populations are projected to decline. By 2050, it is expected to be 58.3% for the more-developed region, 64% for the world, and 66.2% for the 49 Muslim countries.

The Muslim populations in the two regions of Europe/Central Asia and South-East Asia are expected to follow this pattern and to peak at around 69% by 2025 and then to decrease to about 65% by 2050. The Muslim population in the Middle-East and North Africa is also projected to peak at 67.3% by 2045. The Muslim populations in South Asia and sub-Sahara Africa, however, will not see their peak proportions of youngsters and adults before 2050. Their proportions are expected to continue increasing beyond 2050, because of the transformation of their large number of children in the 1990s and 2010s into youngsters and adults. This transformation will not be completed before 2050. (See the top two curves in Figure 5.1.)

Figure 5.3 displays the changing percentages of older people aged 65 and over for the world, the more-developed regions, the 49 Muslim countries and their populations distributed in the five regions. From this figure one can observe an ascending trend in all curves after 1985, reflecting the fact that all populations in the world are becoming older. For world population, the proportion of old people increased from 5.2% in 1950 to 7.3% in 2005, and is projected to increase to 15.9% by 2050. For the more-developed region, as portrayed in the top curve, the old cohort increased even more rapidly, from 7.9% in 1950 to 15.3% in 2005 and is expected to be 25.9% by 2050. Thus, on average, in more-developed countries, for every four people there will be at least one who is 65 years old or over by 2050.

For the 49 Muslim countries, the old cohort percentage decreased from 3.9% in 1950 to 3.5% in 1970, stayed flat over 1970–1990, and began to increase in 1995. It was 4.1% in 2005 and is projected to increase to 10.3% by 2050. This means that by 2050 the proportion of old people in the Muslim world will reach the 1970 level of the more-developed region, so the lag is about eighty years, or four generations. Only Europe/Central Asia and South-East Asia are expected to approach the world average of 15% by 2045 and to exceed it by 2050. Proportions of old people in Muslim countries of sub-Sahara Africa, South Asia, Middle-East and North Africa are all projected to be significantly lower than the world average throughout the entire time period, 1950–2050.

Population aging has emerged as a serious problem since the 1990s for many advanced nations with the elderly accounting for 15–18% and children account-

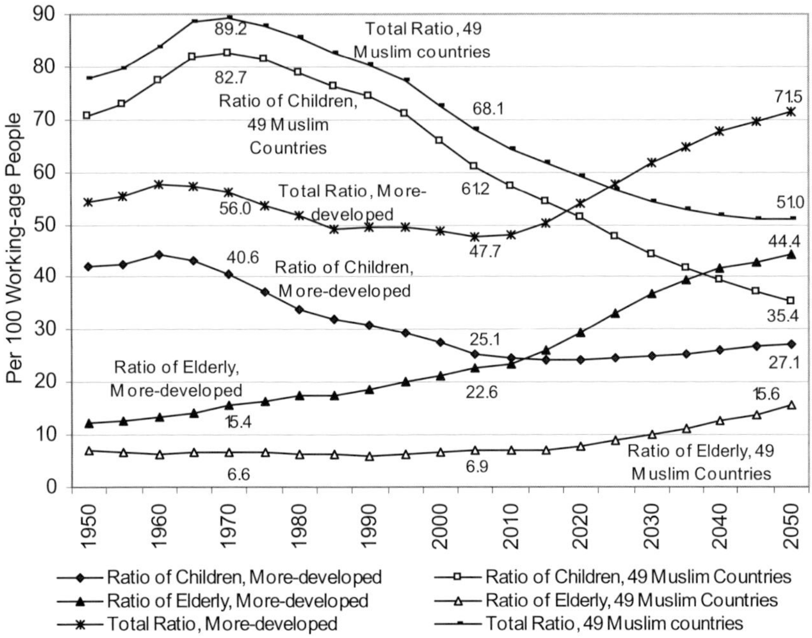

Figure 5.4: Dependency Ratios of Children and Elderly.

ing for 16%–18% of their total population. By 2050 the more developed nations are expected to see their proportion of elderly rise to 25.9% and their proportion of children reduced to 15.8% (see Figure 5.1). The 49-country Muslim world, on the other hand, is expected to have the elderly accounting for only 10.3% by 2050 while children are projected to be 23.5%. In contrast to the more-developed countries, the Muslim world is facing the prospect of having to provide for raising and educating a continuously increasing number of children.

5.1.2. Population Dependency

Youngsters and adults aged 15–64 are usually considered to be working-age people engaged in productive activities. Children aged 0–14 and elderly aged 65 and over are considered as non-working population who require support by working-age people. This raises the question of "dependency ratios". The dependency ratio of the child population is defined by number of people aged 0–14 per 100 persons in the working ages of (15–64), and the dependency ratio of elderly is defined by number of elderly (65 and over) per 100 persons in the working ages. Adding these two ratios yields the "total dependency ratio".

Figure 5.4 graphs these dependency ratios for the combined population of the 49 Muslim-majority countries, and for the combined population of the more-developed region. As Figure 5.4 shows, the two curves of total dependency ratio for the Muslim world (the top curve) and for the more-developed region (third curve from the top) will cross by 2025. This will reverse the situation of greater total dependency in the Muslim world compared to the more-developed region during 1960–2025. As shown in the bottom part of Figure 5.4, the dependency of elderly for the more-developed region will exceed dependency of children by 2012. For the Muslim countries, however, this situation will not occur during the period covered. The two curves of dependency for children and the elderly in the Muslim world never meet before 2050 even though these two curves move toward each other. Hence total dependency in the Muslim world has been and will continue to be dominated by the dependency of children for the foreseeable future.

The dependency ratio of elderly for the 49 Muslim countries, shown at the bottom of this figure, was less than 10% in 1960–2005 and is projected to rise gradually and reach about 15.6% by 2050. However the dependency ratio of children for the Muslim world was particularly large in 1970: on average every 100 working-age person had to support 89.2 dependents, in which 82.7 were children under 15 years old. In this same year, every 100 working-age person in the more-developed countries had to support 56 dependents, including 40.6 children under the age of 15. This heavier dependency for the Muslim world continued in 2005 with 68.1 dependents (61.2 children) in the Muslim world versus 47.7 dependents (25.1 children) in the more-developed countries. However, the rapidly increasing number of the elderly in the more-developed countries will cause the total dependency ratio to exceed their counterpart in the Muslim world by 2025.

By 2050, as projected, every 100 working-age person in the more-developed region will probably have to support 71.5 dependents, in which 44.4 will be at least 65 years old. This contrasts with the Muslim countries where the number of dependents to be supported by every 100 Muslim working-age person by 2050 is projected to reduce to 51, in which 35.4 will be children under 15 years old. Thus, in the next five decades major demographic changes in the more-developed region will cause population aging with associated social, economic and political challenges. Even though the dependency ratios of the 49 Muslim nations are projected to decline, the major demographic changes occurring in the Muslim world will involve a continuously increasing number of children who need to be supported.

Figure 5.5 exhibits this phenomenon in the Muslim world by showing that the number of Muslim Children aged 0–14 has increased by three fold — from 152 million in 1950 to 488 million in 2000 — and is projected to reach 619 million by 2040 and only then will it begin to decline to 609 million by 2050. To put this in perspective we may note that in 1950 there were 17 Muslim children for every 100 children aged 0–14 in the world, and 27 Muslim children for every 100 children in the world in 2000. This ratio is projected to increase to 34 per 100 by 2050, so that for every three children in the world there will be at least one child from the

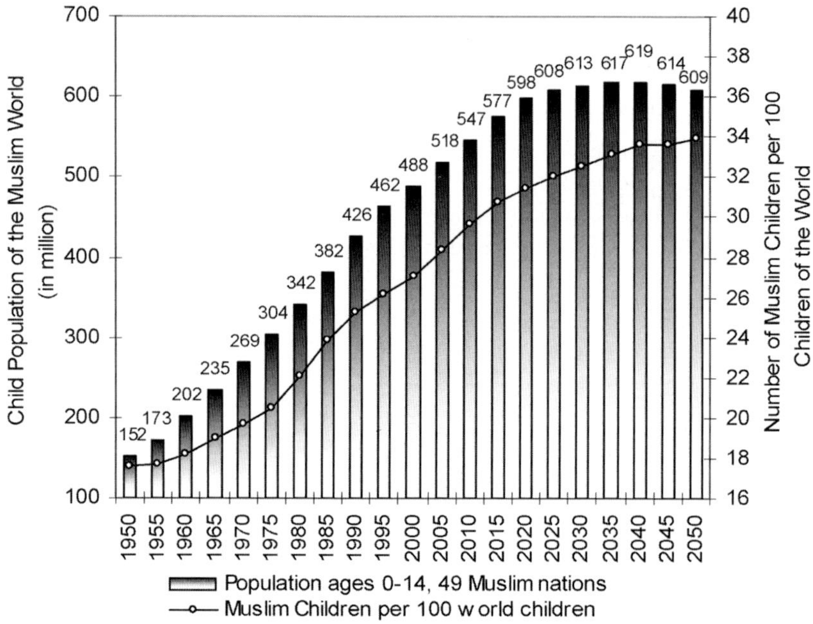

Figure 5.5: Size and Ratio of Children in the Muslim World.

Muslim world. To state this differently, the 49 Muslim countries will have to raise and support more than one third of the world's children aged 0–14 by 2050.

We might recall that the total population of the 49 Muslim-majority countries is expected to account for nearly 29% of the world total population by 2050, while the number of Muslim children is projected to be 34% of the total number of world children. Hence these proportions also reflect the younger age structure of the Muslim population relative to the world population. We therefore turn to some future implications of this development in the next section.

5.2. Increasing Size of Troublesome Male Youngsters

The rapidly increasing number of Muslim children in the last five decades has been and will continue to be transformed into an increasing number of youngsters and adults in the next several decades. This has many implications that are related to some of the problems such as "terrorism" that now confront the world.

In many Muslim nations, the rapid population growth has not been accompanied by a growing economy that could have provided food, clothing, health care, housing and the basic education needed to support a growing number of children. Indeed, many Muslim economies have been in a state of stagnation, which we will cover in Part III in of this book. People grow up in poor villages without jobs and without future prospects. As a result many have migrated into cities in search for opportunities. These migrating populations are largely young, poorly-educated males, who have to leave their families behind and work long hours under difficult conditions for low wages, if they are lucky enough to find a job. This can make them dissatisfied and bitter. These young male populations are much harder to control and much easier to manipulate politically. They could be very active in forming new organizations such as labor unions and self-help groups that could demand reforms, and challenge the existing authorities. They are also easy targets for recruitment by drug sellers, criminals, suicide bombers, militant activists, and transnational terrorists. Evidence points ominously in the latter direction.

World news programs and TV channels frequently report mass demonstrations in Iran and Pakistan, suicide bomb explosions in the West Bank and Gaza, terrorist attacks in Iraq, Turkey, Indonesia and Pakistan, as well as labor and other strife in Nigeria. The faces on these news programs are typically young men between the ages of 15 and 30, with burning eyes and angry voices. This cohort of the population tends to become troublesome in general and for the Muslim world, in particular.

To quantify this "troublesome cohort" we aggregate the number of males age 15–29[2] for the 49 Muslim-majority countries by using population estimates and projections (from the Population Division of the Department of Economic and Social Affairs of the United Nations), and calculate the population share of the troublesome cohort and the ratio of the number of Muslim male youngsters to the number of male youngsters in the world population. Similar calculations are carried out for Muslim populations in the five geographic regions and for the 49 individual Muslim-majority nations. We present these results in the following sub-sections.

5.2.1. Size of Troublesome Male Youngsters

As calibrated on the left-hand axis, Figure 5.6 shows that the number of males aged 15–29 in the 49 Muslim-majority countries has more than tripled in the last five decades — increasing from about 51 million in 1950 to 184 million in 2000. It is also expected to continue to grow in the next five decades, reaching 270 million in 2025 and 308 million in 2050. Comparisons with the total world male youngsters aged 15–29 show that the number of Muslim male youngsters has increased much faster. This is reflected in the ratio of these two numbers, shown

[2] In the "*World Population Prospects: The 2002 Revision*, Volume II: The Sex and Age Distribution of Population", the United Nations Population Division has published age-distribution data for the cohorts of 0–4, 5–9, 10–14, 15–19, 20–24, 25–29, 30–34, . . . , etc. We select three cohorts, 15–19, 20–24, and 25–29 to form the 15–29 cohort for quantitative analyses.

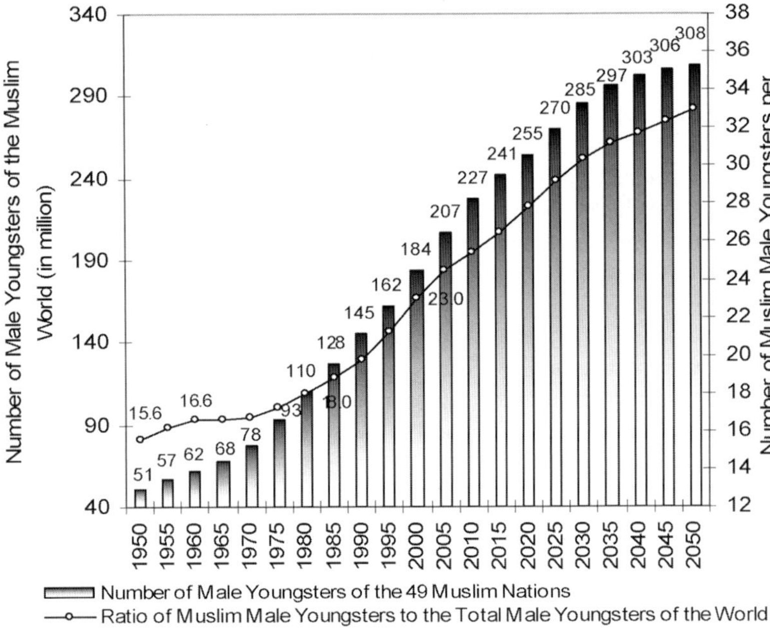

Figure 5.6: Size and Ratio of Male Youngsters.

by the curve calibrated by the vertical axis on the right in Figure 5.6. In every 100 male youngsters there were 15.6 Muslims in 1950, 18.0 in 1980, and 23.0 in 2000. This ratio is projected to continue rising and to reach 29 Muslim male youngsters per 100 world male youngsters in 2025 and 33 in 2050, and this trend is expected to continue for the next five decades. This suggests an increasing potential for instability in Muslim societies around the world.

Figure 5.7 presents population shares of male youngsters aged 15–29 in the five geographic regions of the Muslim world as well as for the 49 Muslim-majority countries and the world. In terms of the world average, male youngsters accounted for 13.1% of the total population in 1950, reached a high of 14.0% in 1985, and fell back to 13.2% in 2000. This share is projected to begin a rapid decline around 2010, falling to 11.8% by 2025 and then to 10.5% by 2050. The population share of young male Muslims in the 49 Muslim countries closely follows the world average until 1990, after which the world average share of young males began to decline while the share in the 49 Muslim countries continues to rise. This divergence is expected to continue until 2010, after which the population share of young males in the 49 Muslim countries begins to decline. In the next five decades, the share of young male Muslims will probably exceed the world average by about (1.5–2.0)%, reflecting the gap between the solid-line curve and the dashed-line curve in Figure 5.7.

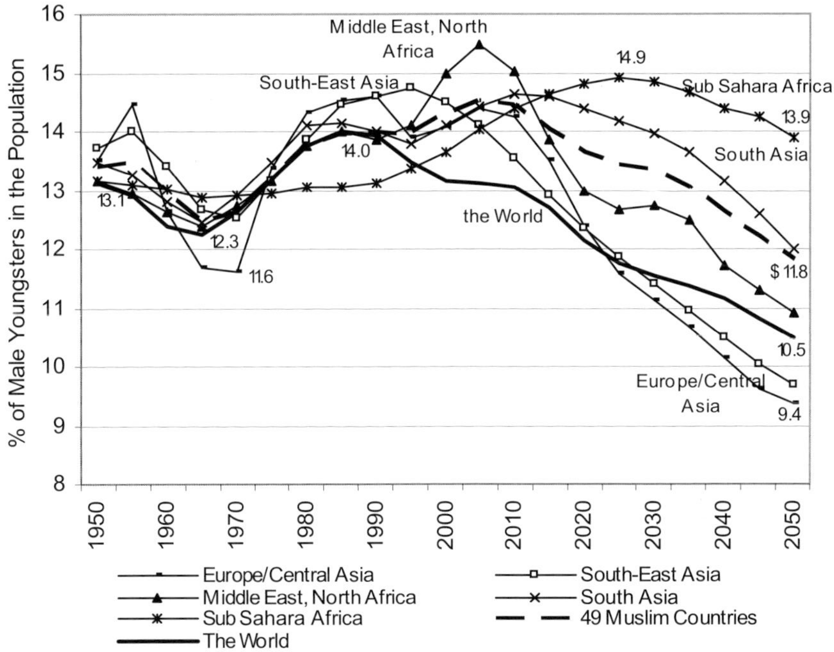

Figure 5.7: Population Shares of Male Youngsters Aged 15–29.

As shown in Figure 5.7, in the 1980s and 1990s, Muslim populations in Europe/Central Asia and South-East Asia had the largest shares of young male populations, but these shares are expected to decline from around 14.4% in 2000 to 9.5% by 2050. From 2000 to 2010, young males are estimated to account for (15–15.5)% of total population in the Middle-East and North Africa. This represents the highest share for all regions in the one-hundred-year period, 1950 2050. This offers a prospect for increasing unrest, violence and instability in the Middle-East and North Africa over the next decade.

After 2015, the highest young male population share is projected to shift to sub-Sahara Africa and South Asia, where the young male Muslims will account for more than 13.9% and 12.0%, respectively, of their total Muslim populations by 2050. Thus, violence and instability of Muslim societies in Africa and South Asia may also appear in the first half of the 21st century. The distribution of the troublesome male youngsters of the 49 Muslim countries over the five geographic regions is further illustrated in Figure 5.8.

As Figure 5.8 shows, about 11.3% of young males in the Muslim world lived in the eight Muslim countries of Europe/Central Asia before 1990 and the rest were more or less evenly distributed in the other four regions. Since 1990 a divergence appears with increasing shares in sub-Sahara Africa, South Asia, and the Middle-

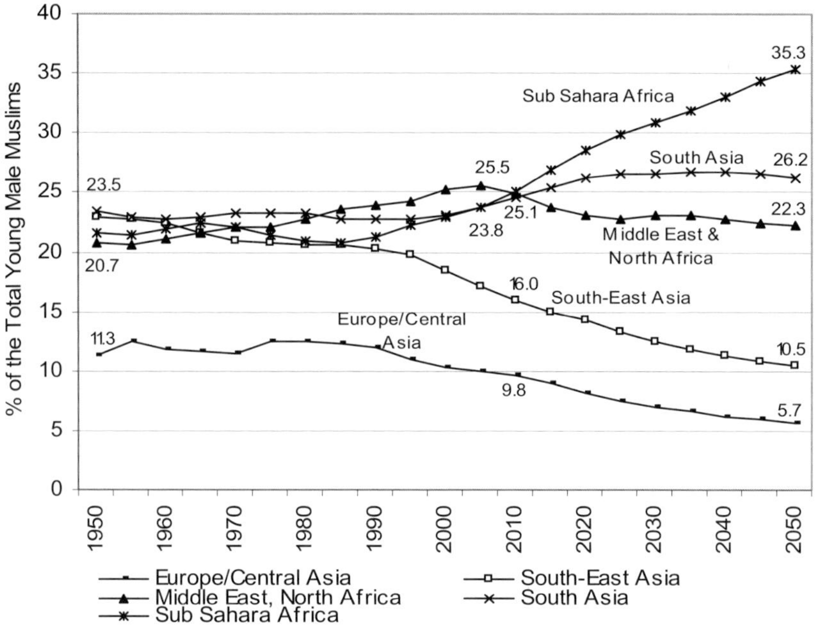

Figure 5.8: Distribution of Young Male Muslims.

East and North Africa, accompanied by decreasing shares in Central Asia and South-East Asia. By 2010, only 9.8% of total young males in the Muslim world are projected to live in Europe/Central Asia and 16.0% in South-East Asia, with about 25.1% living in each of the other three regions. Another divergence is projected to occur after 2010, with a rapidly increasing share in sub Sahara Africa, a gradually rising share in South Asia, and a declining share in the Middle-East and North Africa region. These larger shares of the troublesome cohort of Muslim populations, shown in both Figures 5.7 and 5.8, suggest an overall potential for social instability in the Muslim world. The currently increasing violence and turmoil in the Middle-East is closely related to its larger share of the troublesome population cohort and the situation may carry on in the next decade until this share of young male Muslims begins to decline. More trouble is also likely to be brewing in South Asia and sub-Sahara Africa with their shares of young Muslim males expected to increase significantly in the next five decades.

5.2.2. Troublesome Cohort of Muslim Countries

We conduct a similar analysis for individual Muslim countries to identify potentials for violence and instability in some of the Muslim-majority countries. For each Muslim country, we calculated the share of young male Muslims for five years: 1970, 1990, 2000, 2025 and 2050. The 49 Muslim countries were then ranked in the order of their shares of young male Muslims for each year. These results are presented in Table 5.1.

Table 5.1 displays the top fifteen Muslim-majority nations ranked by their proportions of the troublesome cohort for each of five distinct years. For comparisons, the bottom four rows of Table 5.1 display the population shares of young males at age 15–29 for the world, India, China and the United States in these same years. Except for China in 1990, the percentages in these Muslim countries all exceed that of the world and the three reference countries.[3] Table 5.1 also shows that in both 1970 and 1990, ten of the top fifteen Muslim countries with high potential for violence were all located in the Middle-East and North Africa region, where wars between Israel and the Arab world and struggles over Palestine have generated seemingly endless social unrest and violence. In 2000, twelve Muslim nations in the Middle-East and North Africa were in the top-15 list along with Bangladesh, Turkey and Indonesia at the bottom of this column. The demographic character, especially the proportion of the troublesome generation, is thus seen to be closely correlated with radical and dramatic changes accompanied by violence in Muslim societies of the Middle-East and North Africa region, including Oman, Libya, Jordan, Iran, Syria and Algeria. However, Qatar and Lebanon disappeared from the list after 1990.

As shown in the columns for 2025 and 2050, the demographic transition during the 21st century is projected to move the Muslim nations in sub-Sahara Africa into the top list of Table 5.1, replacing Muslim countries in the Middle-East and North Africa, which appeared in the 1970, 1990 and 2000 lists. Thirteen out of the fifteen top Muslim countries ranked in the order of population share of the troublesome cohort for both 2025 and 2050 are projected to be in sub-Sahara Africa, including such populous countries as Nigeria, Ethiopia and Sudan. For 2025, Pakistan and Maldives, two Muslim countries in South Asia, move into the column while Yemen and Afghanistan enter the list of top fifteen for 2050. Thus, after 2025, Muslim countries in sub-Sahara Africa may become the center of radical social changes and disturbances.

After 2025 all Muslim countries in the Middle-East and North Africa, except for Yemen, are projected to experience declining population shares of the troublesome cohort and therefore be ranked below the top fifteen. This points to relief from the troublesome social violence that is associated with these demographic forces. Yemen is an exception because its population share of young males is projected to increase from 12.68% in 1995 to 14.7% by 2050, and move it into 7th place in the 2050 ranking. Similar to Yemen, Afghanistan is also projected to have

[3] This was the period, 1989, in which the Tian-An-Men Square disturbances occurred in China, which were associated with the increase in the troublesome cohort, from 13.24 in 1970 to 15.90 in 1990, followed by persistent decline and by social stability thereafter.

Table 5.1: Muslim Countries Ranked by the Population Share of Troublesome Cohort (1970–2000)

1970		1990		2000	
Country	Young males % of total	Nation	Young males % of total	Nation	Young males % of total
UAE	22.67	UAE	17.2	Oman	16.98
Qatar	21.62	Bahrain	15.92	Libya	16.86
Kuwait	16.4	Kuwait	15.59	Jordan	16.15
Bahrain	14.09	Saudi Arabia	15.45	Iran	16.02
Jordan	13.99	Jordan	15.43	Syria	15.87
Mauritania	13.92	Qatar	15.42	Algeria	15.48
Libya	13.9	Lebanon	15.38	Kuwait	15.4
Saudi Arabia	13.59	Bangladesh	14.71	Morocco	15.31
Mali	13.55	Albania	14.69	Bahrain	15.21
Oman	13.52	Mauritania	14.66	Tunisia	15.13
Iraq	13.51	Indonesia	14.65	UAE	14.79
Afghanistan	13.51	Turkey	14.65	Bangladesh	14.68
Yemen	13.45	Algeria	14.63	Turkey	14.57
Eritrea	13.29	Morocco	14.47	Indonesia	14.56
Sudan	13.25	Tunisia	14.46	Saudi Arabia	14.48
World	**12.62**	**World**	**13.93**	**World**	**13.17**
India	**13.04**	**India**	**14.41**	**India**	**14.00**
China	**13.24**	**China**	**15.90**	**China**	**12.95**
USA	**12.06**	**USA**	**11.81**	**USA**	**10.51**

Muslim Countries Ranked by the Population Share of Troublesome Cohort (2025–2050)

2025		2050	
Country	Young males % of total	Nation	Young males % of total
Nigeria	15.42	Chad	24.06
Eritrea	15.4	Mali	15.07
Cote d'Ivoire	15.05	Burkina Faso	14.88
Djibouti	15.02	Niger	14.78
Guinea	14.98	Guinea-Bissau	14.75
Sierra Leone	14.8	Somalia	14.73
Ethiopia	14.76	Yemen	14.7
Burkina Faso	14.74	Sierra Leone	14.38
Maldives	14.67	Afghanistan	14.22
Mali	14.65	Ethiopia	14.00
Senegal	14.52	Djibouti	13.48
Sudan	14.49	Nigeria	13.26
Chad	14.46	Eritrea	13.25
Pakistan	14.45	Guinea	13.00
Gambia	14.38	Cote d'Ivoire	12.60
World	**11.77**	**World**	**10.50**
India	**12.85**	**India**	**10.35**
China	**9.88**	**China**	**8.78**
USA	**10.18**	**USA**	**9.83**

an increasing share of the troublesome population which will rise from 13.81% in 1995 to 14.22% by 2050 and place it 9th in the ranking for 2050.

5.2.3. Correlation Between the Troublesome Cohort and Social Instability

We use two cases — the United States and China — to illustrate the correlation between the troublesome cohort and social instability. The "*World Population Prospects: The 2002 Revision, Volume II: The Sex and Age Distribution of Population*, 2004" provides us with original data for calculating the share of young males at age of 15–29 for the United States, China and the world. Figure 5.9 presents the result.

As Figure 5.9 shows, the US troublesome population cohort share reached its trough in 1960 and thereafter began to rise rapidly when the first patch of "baby boomers", born in 1946–1950, entered the troublesome cohort in 1965. It rose to a peak in 1980, when baby boomers, born from 1946 through 1964, all came into the age cohort of 15–34. The increasing proportion of young males for the 1960s and 1970s was associated with many chaotic events involving violence and social unrest, including the flourishing of anti-war and civil-rights protest groups in the late 1960s and 1970s in the United States.

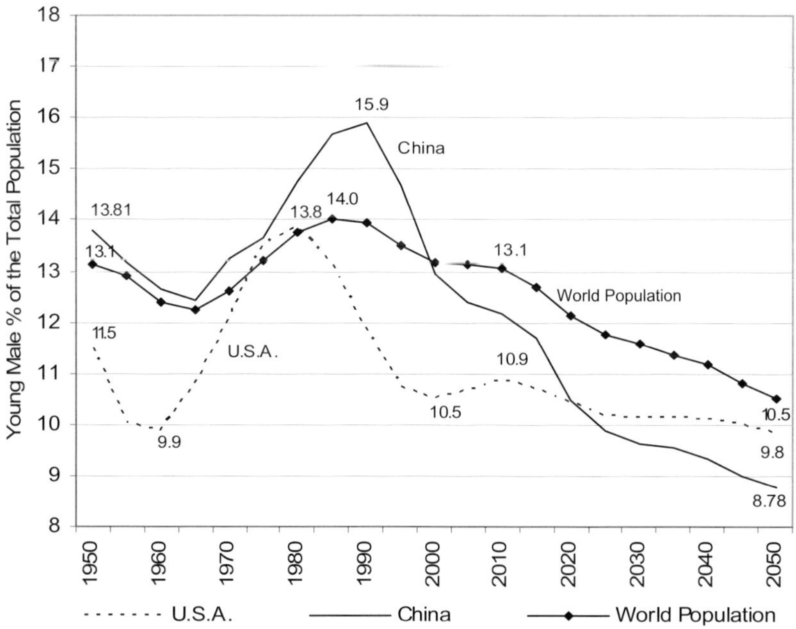

Figure 5.9: Population Shares of the Troublesome Cohort.

Since 1980 the US population troublesome cohort share declined with the first two patches of baby boomers moving out of the troublesome cohort in 1990 and all of the baby boomers leaving this cohort in 2000.[4] Also of interest is that "The United States in the 1990s has experienced the greatest sustained decline in violent crime rates since World War II"[5] as compared with the boom in crime of the 1960s and early 1970s. The US young male population share has remained beneath the world average curve since 1980 and is expected to stabilize at around 10% in 2025–2050, while the world average is projected to decrease from 13.1% in 2010 and approach 10.5% by 2050. Thus the likelihood of social violence from this indigenous source on a scale similar to the 1960s and 1970s is very small in the United States during the next five decades.

China provides another example to show the relation between an increasing troublesome cohort population proportion and increasing social unrest and violence. As shown in Figure 5.9, China's proportion of young males increased from a trough of 12.5% in 1965 to a peak of 15.9% in 1990. This percentage was also well above the peak, 14.0%, of the world average reached in 1985. The large percentage of young males during 1985–1995 provided a potential for instability in Chinese society. As a matter of fact, the largest scale of social violence, since the establishment of New China in 1949, took place in 1989 when mass demonstrations erupted in many Chinese cities and eventually led to the Tian-An-Men Square demonstration of June, 1989.

China's troublesome cohort proportion has since declined and this decline is projected to be dramatic for the next five decades due to China's radical one-child–one-family policy that has been in place since the beginning of the 1978 reform. By 2050, the Chinese young males aged at 15–29 are expected to account for only 8.78% of the total Chinese population — which is smaller than the projected world average of 10.5% and the US projection of 9.8%. From the perspective of population changes, the probability for the following five decades seems very small for outbursts of large scale social violence similar to what occurred in China in the late 1980s. China's population policies and family planning programs have dramatically reduced the momentum of its population growth and significantly changed its population age structure and will also substantially affect both economic growth and social development.

The United States and China are very different countries with different histories, political systems, cultural traditions and stages of economic development. But demographic factors affected social behavior of these two different societies

[4] See Chapter 6: US Population in the Post-Transitional Period in the Book, *The Economic Transformation of the United States, 1950–2000*, by George Kozmetsky and Piyu Yue, Purdue University Press, 2005, pp. 183–187.

[5] Gary LaFree, *Declining Violent Crime Rates in the 1990s: Predicting Crime Booms and Busts*, Annu. Rev. Soc. 25 (1999) 145–168.

in a very similar manner with a larger proportion of the troublesome cohort being associated with radical behavior and social violence, unrest and instability.

To see how population proportion of the troublesome cohort for individual Muslim countries evolves over time, we use the proportions for two groups of Muslim countries and compare them with China, the United States, India, and the world in Figures 5.10(A) and 5.10(B). The countries of the first group in Figure 5.10(A) includes the six Muslim countries of Indonesia, Turkey, Iran, Algeria, Libya and Syria, which are compared with China and the United States. These countries share a common feature in that the population proportion of the troublesome cohort is estimated to reach its peak before 2010 and then to decline rapidly and fall below the world average by 2050. However, as displayed in Figure 5.10(A), the time of peak occurrence differs for individual countries.

Linkage between population proportion of the troublesome cohort and social instability indicates a high probability for continuation of the current violent behavior of Muslim populations in the Middle-East and North Africa, with population proportion of the troublesome cohort in Iran, Libya, Syria and Algeria estimated to be at all time highs (15.8%–17.6%) in 2000–2010. However, the demographic factors associated with the current severe social violence and confrontations in the Middle-East and North Africa are expected to diminish after

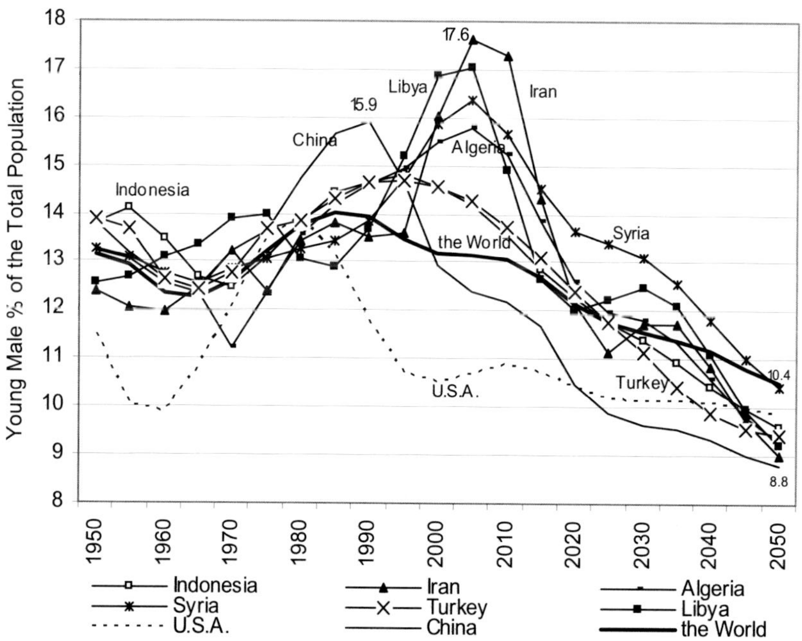

(A)

Figure 5.10: (A) Troublesome Cohort Shares. (B) Troublesome Cohort Shares.

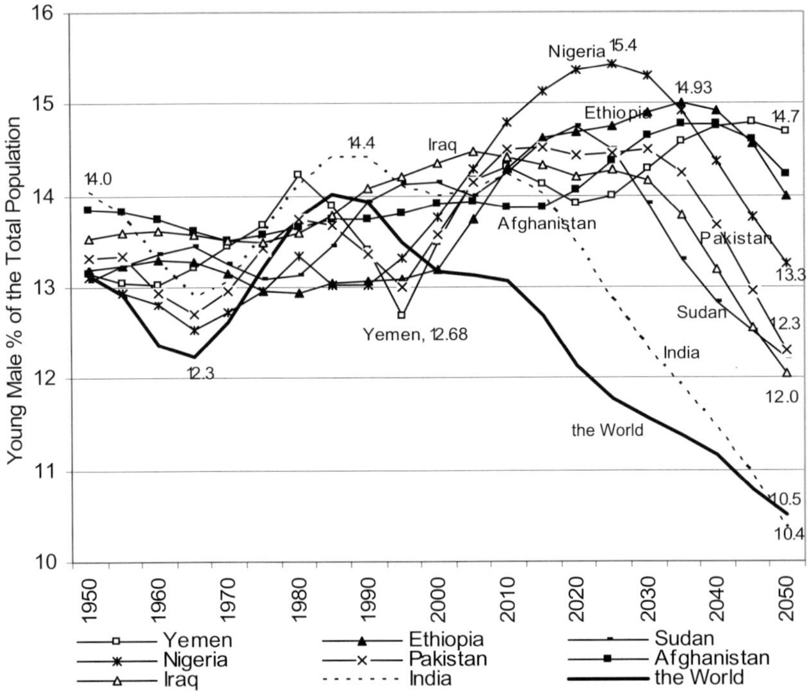

(B)

Figure 5.10: (*continued*)

2015, when proportions of the troublesome cohort are projected to continue falling until they are below the world average by 2050. Troublesome cohort proportions of Turkey and Indonesia increased to their peak in 1995 and have since declined gradually. They are projected to fall below the world average after 2025. This source of potential social unrest in Turkey and Indonesia was relatively higher in 1985–2005 than in other years but not as high as in Iran, Syria, Libya and Algeria due to their smaller proportion of the troublesome cohort.

Countries displayed in Figure 5.10(B) include India, Pakistan and Afghanistan in Asia, Iraq and Yemen in the Middle-East, and Ethiopia, Nigeria and Sudan in sub-Sahara Africa. Population proportions of the troublesome cohort of these nations are projected to rise for the next two or three decades before reaching their peaks. India's proportion is projected to begin to decline by 2015 and to continue falling to the world average by 2045. All other countries exhibited in Figure 5.10(B) are expected to have their proportions stay well above the world average curve in the next five decades. Of perhaps special interest is that this demographic factor points toward violent behavior and social instability in Iraq, Pakistan and Sudan over the next three decades and in Nigeria, Ethiopia, Afghanistan and Yemen for the next five decades.

Summary of Chapter 5

This chapter has described the changing age structure of populations in Muslim countries. The increasing number of children in the Muslim world has constituted a great challenge for providing economic support and education to children and this situation is projected to continue during the next five decades. The increasing number of children has also transformed into increases in the troublesome cohort of Muslim populations and this has been and will continue to be associated with increasing radical behavior, social violence and instability of Muslim societies. This is also not the end of this potential for trouble. In the following Chapter 6 we will describe urbanization, another demographic factor that could generate social instability in the Muslim world.

Chapter 6

Rapid Urbanization and Its Problems

The process of people migration from rural areas into cities, usually in search for better jobs and a better life, is known as urbanization. This is a companion phenomenon in the development of an industrialized economy and a modern society. Unlike the Western countries which experienced a gradual urbanization during the Industrial Revolutions, the urbanization in Muslim countries has proceeded with great speed and has and is occurring on a large scale due to the rapid expansion of Muslim populations and the accelerating growth of young Muslim males.

Rapid urbanization in the Muslim world results from two factors: natural increase in population due to excess of births over deaths, and migration of individuals, households or groups of people from rural to urban areas, within borders (internal migration), and across borders (international migration). Both factors have contributed to rapidly increasing urbanization but migration seems to have played the most significant role. This will be demonstrated with empirical statistics in this chapter.

6.1. Increasing Size of Urban Population

We use population time-series data for individual countries from the *World Development Indicators* CD-ROM to calculate aggregate rural and urban populations for the 49 Muslim-majority countries over the five geographic regions that represent the Muslim world. Figure 6.1 shows that total urban population of these 49 Muslim countries[1] increased from about 96 million in 1960 to 554 million (5.8 times) in 2000, and total rural population increased from 380 million to 725 million (1.9 times) in the same time period. The total population of these 48 Muslim countries rose from 476 million in 1960 to 1279 million (2.7 times) in 2000.

Different paths of population expansion can be compared with a "population index", which is defined as a "normalized population size" with index value of 100 in base year 1960.[2] Figure 6.2 displays the growth paths of the urban, rural and total populations of the 48 Muslim nations as stated in terms of their index. It shows that the urban population in the Muslim world increased much faster than

[1] West Bank and Gaza, one of the 49 Muslim countries, is excluded from the analysis in this section due to a lack of population data divided into urban and rural sections.

[2] A normalized population size equals the population size in each year divided by the population size of the base year and then multiplied by 100.

International Symposia in Economic Theory and Econometrics, Vol. 19
William W. Cooper and Piyu Yue

ISSN: 1571-0386/DOI: 10.1016/S1571-0386(07)00016-6

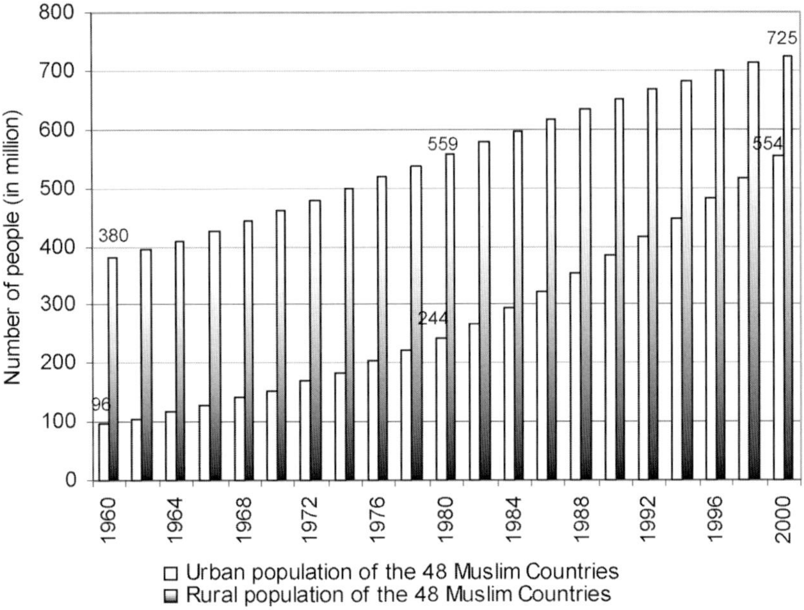

Figure 6.1: Urban and Rural Populations of the Muslim World.

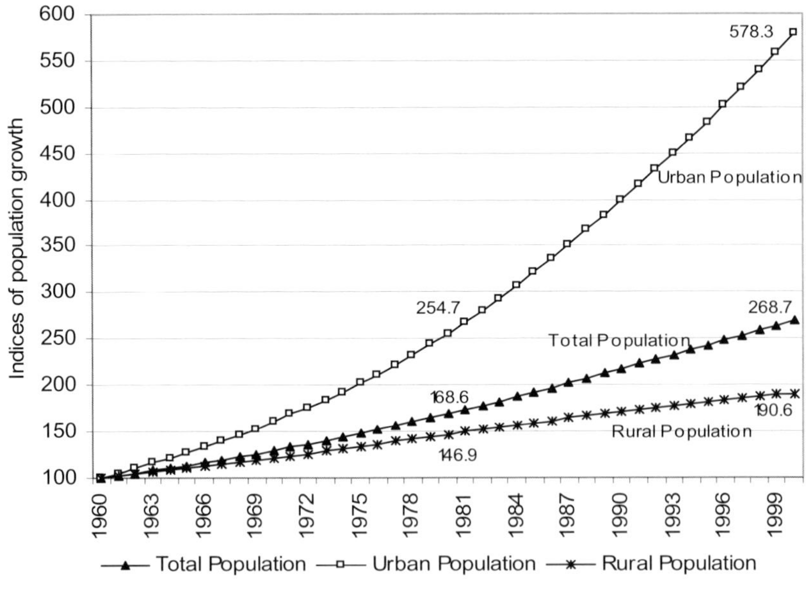

Figure 6.2: Indices of Population Growth of the Muslim World.

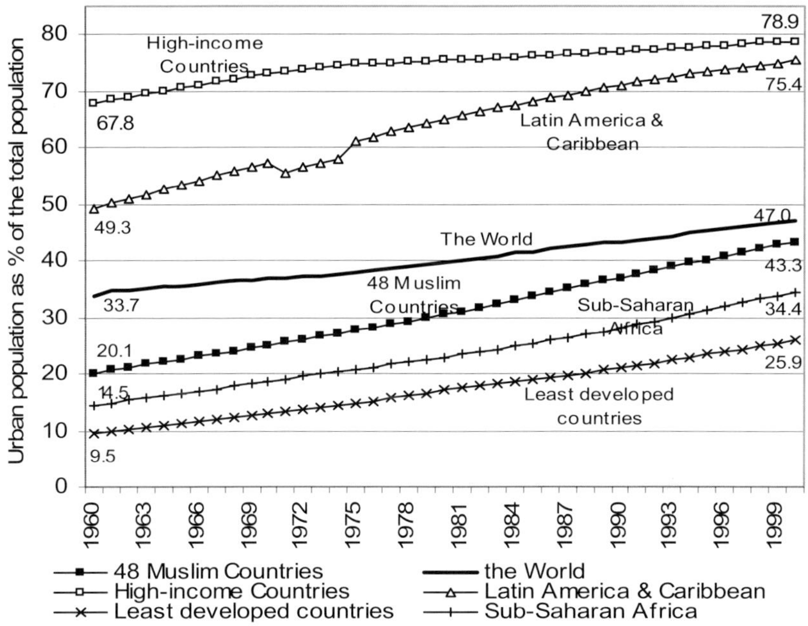

Figure 6.3: Urban Population Percentages.

both the rural population and the total population during the last four decades (from 1960 to 2000). In general, the birth and death rates of urban areas are both lower than corresponding rates in rural areas due to better living conditions in urban areas. Conditions are also generally better for the education and health care of women in urban areas. Natural increases in urban population should, therefore, not be much greater than for rural population. Hence, the explosion of urban population shown on the top curve in Figure 6.2 is due to the migration of people from rural areas into cities.

How fast has urbanization proceeded in the Muslim world? What is the level of its urbanization? A comparative analysis can provide some answers to these questions. Figures 6.3 and 6.4 depict the urbanization process of the Muslim world, compared with the world as a whole and some selected regions of the world such as the high-income countries as well as Latin America and the Caribbean, and, finally, the Least-developed countries and sub-Sahara Africa. Figure 6.3 displays urban populations as percentages of the corresponding total populations, while Figure 6.4 exhibits the expanding paths of these urban populations in terms of population indices.

World total urban population increased from about 1017 million in 1960 to 2848 million in 2000, and, as shown on the left-hand axis, the urban population percentage rose from 33.7% in 1960 to 47.0% in 2000. In Figure 6.3 the

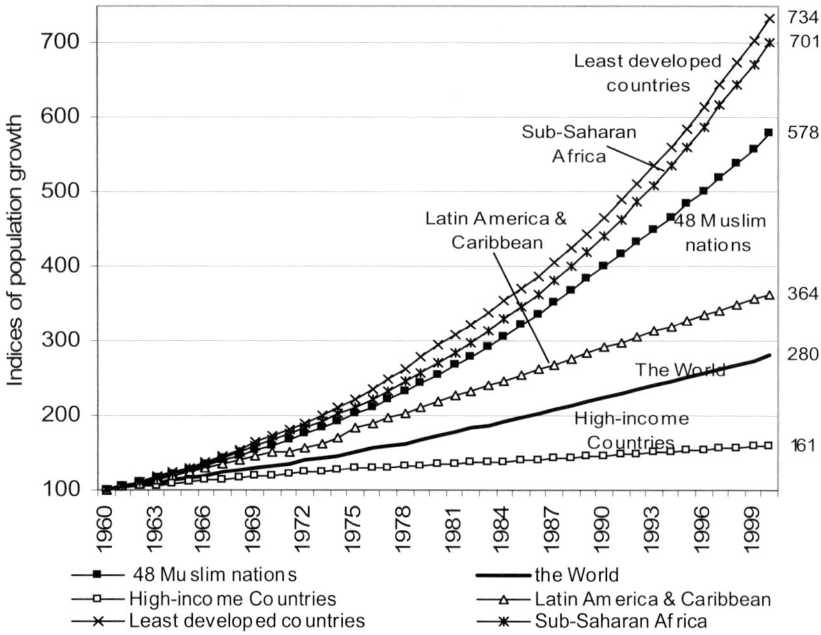

Figure 6.4: Indices of Urban Population Growth.

high-income countries, which includes highly industrialized countries in North America, Western Europe and Japan, are shown to have had the highest level of urbanization in the world in 1960, with over 67% of their population living in urban areas. At that time, as shown on the bottom curve, the Least-developed countries had slightly less than 10% of their inhabitants living in cities and towns. Converging to the high-income country percentage of 78.9% by 2000, Latin America and the Caribbean region had the second largest percentage of urban population at 49.3% in 1960 and 75.4% in 2000. Reference to Figure 6.3 shows that the urban population shares of both the high-income countries and Latin America and the Caribbean region have been well above the world average for the last four decades.

As was shown in Figure 6.1 the aggregate urban population of the 48 Muslim-majority countries increased from less than 100 million to over 550 million (more than five times) in the last four decades (1960–2000), and the urban population percentage more than doubled from 20.1% to 43.3% in the same time period (see Figure 6.3). Urban population percentage growth was less rapid than the growth in urban population size due to the rapid increase in total population from 476 million to 1279 million (2.7 times). Thus this increase in total population, which serves as a denominator in our percentage indicator, has reduced the growth in urban population percentage. As Figure 6.3 shows, even though the urban population percentage in these Muslim countries was smaller than the world average, the gap between them has significantly decreased over time. As this figure also shows, the urban population percentage of both sub-Sahara Africa and the Least-developed region were smaller than that of the 48 Muslim countries throughout the entire 1960–2000 time period. In 2000 the urban population percentage was 43.3% for the Muslim countries, 34.4% for sub-Sahara Africa and 25.9% for the Least-developed countries. Thus the level of urbanization increased worldwide, including sub-Sahara Africa and the Least-developed countries, but their urban population percentage remained well below the world average.

Differences in the pace of urbanization are revealed by the urban population indices depicted in Figure 6.4. As noted above, the urban populations of the world, the 48 Muslim countries and the selected regions are all normalized to 100 by reference to the base year 1960. The index of an urban population is defined as normalized urban population size, and this definition is applied to the world and selected regions in Figure 6.4.

As the top two curves in Figure 6.4 show, the Least-developed region and sub-Sahara Africa experienced the fastest urbanization for the four decades, 1960–2000, during which their urban population increased more than seven times. The Muslim world urban population increased by 5.78 times in the last forty years, compared with 3.64 times for Latin America and the Caribbean, 2.8 times for the world average and 1.61 times for the high-income countries.

Presently industrialized countries have reached such high levels of urbanization that more than 75% of their total populations inhabit urban areas as of 2000. However, this urbanization took over a hundred years. During the 19th and early 20th centuries, the Industrial Revolutions generated many new job opportunities in cities and motivated mass movements of population away from countryside. Migrants both within borders and across borders provided cheap and plentiful labor for the emerging factories in urban areas. This resulted in structural changes along with economic growth in these economies and urbanization of these societies.

The new wave of globalization has created circumstances in developing countries similar to the early stages of development in modern industrialized countries. In addition, low labor costs in the developing world, to which many Muslim nations belong, are attractive to companies from advanced countries. Global capital has reaped benefits from and contributed to the rapidly increasing urban populations in developing countries, including many Muslim nations.

6.2. Urbanization Process of Muslim Countries

Figure 6.5 shows that regional differences in the level and speed of urbanization are quite pronounced. In 1960 the urban population percentage of Muslim countries in Middle-East and North Africa and Europe/Central Asia was slightly above

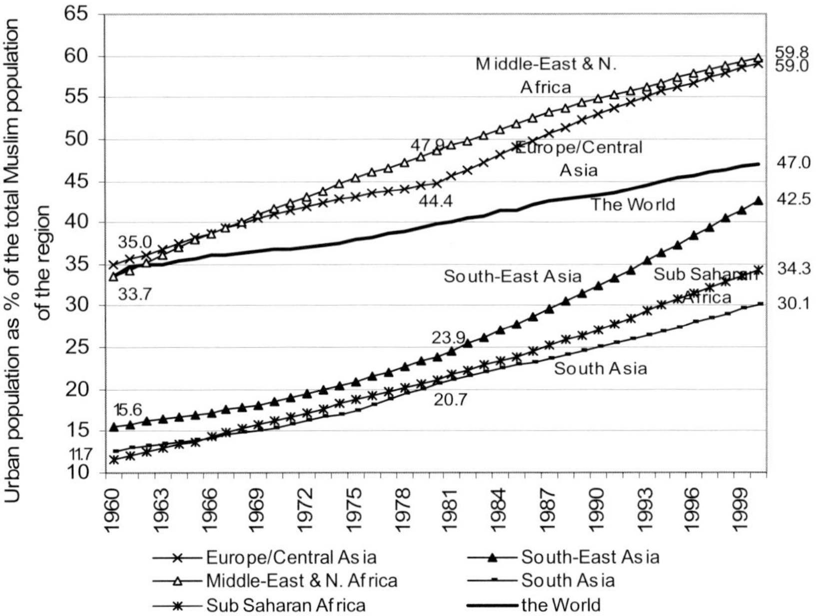

Figure 6.5: Urbanization of Muslim Populations in Five Regions.

the world average of 33.7%. About one third of their populations lived in urban areas and two thirds in rural areas. In 2000, however, nearly 60% of their people resided in urban areas and only 40% in rural areas. In addition, their urban population percentages were much greater than the world average of 47.0%.

As displayed in Figure 6.5, the steeper slopes of the urban population curves for Muslim nations in South-East Asia, South Asia and sub-Sahara Africa were caused by a great speedup of urbanization during this time period. Although the level of urbanization in these latter three regions was still below the world average in 2000, the discrepancy between their urban population percentages and the world average decreased substantially over the period 1960–2000. The urban population percentage of South-East Asia (Indonesia and Malaysia) is likely to exceed the world average in the near future, but the Muslim countries in sub-Sahara Africa and South Asia will take more time before this occurs.

Urbanization processes for individual Muslim countries differ in both level and speed. During the last four decades, the Muslim countries displayed in Figures 6.6(A) and 6.6(B) experienced especially fast urbanization and a large percentage of the population became urbanized.

Figure 6.6(A) exhibits the evolving urbanization of smaller Muslim countries in the Middle-East and North Africa region. These eleven smaller Muslim countries in Figure 6.6(A) are Kuwait, Qatar, Bahrain, Lebanon, Libya, UAE, Saudi

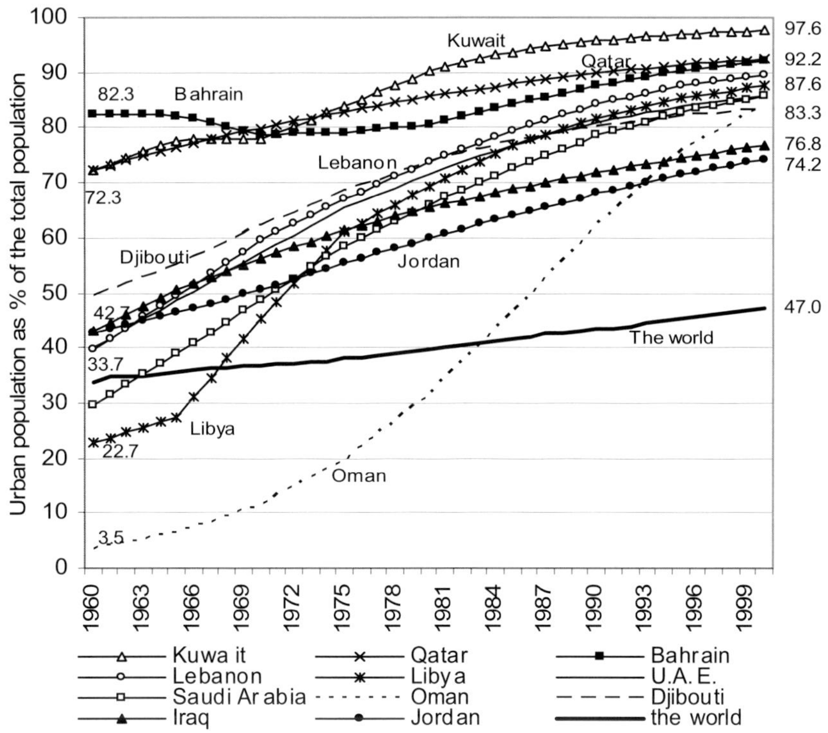

Figure 6.6(A): Urbanization of Small Muslim Countries.

Arabia, Oman, Djibouti, Iraq and Jordan. Urban population percentages for these Muslim countries ranked in the top ten among all of the 48 Muslim-majority nations in 2000. Kuwait, Qatar and Bahrain had their urban population accounting for more than 90% of the total population in 2000. Lebanon, Libya, UAE, Saudi Arabia, Oman and Djibouti also had more than 83% of their total population residing in urban areas by 2000. The urban population percentage for these nine smaller Muslim countries was even greater than that of many advanced countries in the world (see Figure 6.3 which shows that high-income countries had 78.9% of their population urbanized in 2000). Iraq and Jordan had almost identical urban population percentages at 43% in 1960 with percentages that reached 76.8% and 74.2%, respectively, in 2000 — thus approaching the urbanization level of high income countries.

As shown on the bottom left in Figure 6.6(A), Oman, Libya and Saudi Arabia all had urban population percentages rising from below the world average (3.5%, 22.7% and 30%) in 1960 to 84%, 88% and 86%, respectively, and substantially above the world average of 47.0% in 2000. Oman, in particular, as shown in Figure 6.6(A), experienced a spectacular speed up in urbanization. See the dotted-line

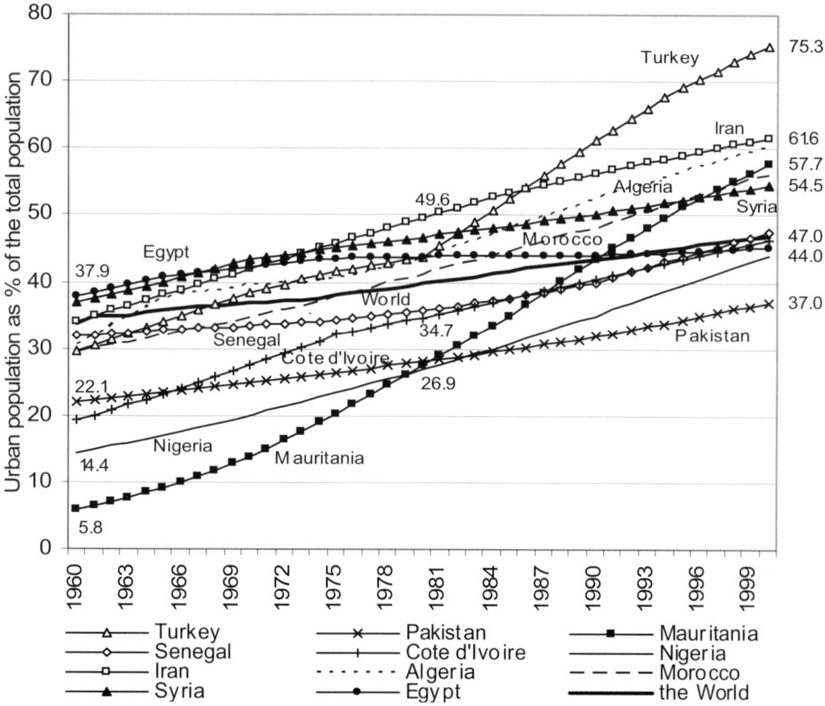

Figure 6.6(B): Urbanization of Large Muslim Countries.

curve at the bottom of Figure 6.6(A), which shows that Oman's urban population accounted for only 3.5% of the total population in 1960, but reached 84% in 2000.

Figure 6.6(B) depicts urbanization for some of the larger Muslim countries. These larger countries include Iran, Syria, Egypt, Algeria, and Morocco in the Middle-East and North Africa; Nigeria, Senegal, Mauritania and Cote d'Ivoire in sub-Sahara Africa; Turkey in Europe/Central Asia; and Pakistan in South Asia. The urban population percentages of six of these nations, Turkey, Iran, Syria, Algeria, Morocco and Mauritania, exceeded the world average in 2000. Egypt and Senegal experienced only a moderate rise in their urban population percentages, from 37.9% and 32% in 1960 to 45% and 47% in 2000 which put them close to the world average of 47% in 2000. Nigeria and Cote d'Ivoire moved to close their gap with the world average in 2000. Pakistan is the only nation in this group with an urban population percentage substantially below the world average over the entire time period, with an urban population percentage of 22.1% in 1960 rising to 37% in 2000. Turkey and Mauritania exhibited the largest gains. We see in Figure 6.6(B) that Turkey evolved from being less than 30% urbanized in 1960 to more than 75% urbanized in 2000, and Mauritania from 5.8% to 57.7% in the same period. The large increases in the urban population percentage of these two countries reveal an accelerating momentum in their urbanization process.

Not shown in Figures 6.6(A) and 6.6(B) are the ten Muslim countries which were ranked at the bottom in terms of the urban population percentage for 2000. This includes six countries in sub-Sahara Africa (Ethiopia, Burkina Faso, Eritrea, Niger, Guinea-Bissau and Chad), three countries in South Asia (Afghanistan, Bangladesh and Maldives) and one in the Middle-East, Yemen. In 1960 at least 90% of their populations resided in rural areas and in 2000 the rural population still accounted for about (74–82)% of the total population in these ten least-urbanized Muslim countries.

Another way to look at urbanization of Muslim countries is to study them relative to the growing number of big cities. Over the 20th century the world population became increasingly concentrated in highly urbanized areas known as "urban agglomerations". Global urbanization has given rise to "mega-cities", which are urban agglomerations with a population of 10 million or more. The following section studies urban agglomerations in the Muslim world.

6.3. Mega-Cities in the Muslim World

According to *World Urbanization Prospects, the 2001 Revision* published by the United Nations Population Division, in 1950, there was only one mega-city in the world, New York, with a population of about 12 million. In 1975 there were five mega-cities, Tokyo, New York, Shanghai, Mexico City, and Sao Paulo, all with urban populations exceeding the 10-million mark. At that time (1975) Cairo was the only city in the Muslim world with a population (6.075 million) exceeding five million people. In 2000, however, three cities in the Muslim world (Dhaka in Bangladesh, Jakarta in Indonesia, and Karachi in Pakistan) became mega-cities with population sizes greater than ten million. Another three cities, Cairo in Egypt, Istanbul in Turkey, and Lagos in Nigeria, were close to reaching mega-city status each with populations exceeding 8.6 million people in 2000. Another two Muslim cites, Teheran in Iran and Lahore in Pakistan also had populations exceeding the five-million mark in 2000. As forecasted by the United Nations Population Division, the Muslim world will see six cities become mega-cities and another nine will have populations above the five-million mark by 2015. See the last column in Table 6.1.

Table 6.1 lists all of the Muslim cities that are expected to have 5-plus million populations by 2015, and compares them with the top urban agglomeration cities of New York, London, and Tokyo. Tokyo has been the fastest growing urban agglomeration in the developed world over the last four decades. Its population overtook the top two cities of New York and London by 1975, and it is expected to remain at the top with about 27.2 million city residents by 2015.

Table 6.1: Evolution of Urban Agglomerations

Nation	City	Population (million)			
		1950	1975	2000	2015
United States	New York	12.339	15.880	16.732	17.944
United Kingdom	London	8.733	8.169	7.640	7.640
Japan	Tokyo	6.920	19.771	26.444	27.190
Bangladesh	Dhaka	0.417	2.173	12.519	22.776
Indonesia	Jakarta	1.452	4.814	11.018	17.268
Pakistan	Karachi	1.028	3.990	10.032	16.197
Nigeria	Lagos	0.288	1.890	8.665	15.966
Egypt	Cairo	2.410	6.079	9.462	11.531
Turkey	Istanbul	1.077	3.601	8.953	11.362
Pakistan	Lahore	0.826	2.399	5.452	8.721
Iran	Teheran	1.042	4.274	6.979	8.178
Saudi Arabia	Riyadh	0.111	0.710	4.549	7.536
Iraq	Baghdad	0.579	2.815	4.865	6.549
Bangladesh	Chittagong	0.290	0.969	3.651	6.360
Cote d'Ivoire	Abidjan	0.059	0.960	3.790	6.076
Afghanistan	Kabul	0.216	0.674	2.602	5.397
Indonesia	Bandung	0.511	1.493	3.409	5.245
Saudi Arabia	Jidda	0.119	0.594	3.192	5.183

In terms of growth pace, however, many Muslim cities displayed in Table 6.1 dwarfed Tokyo's expansion record. Witness, for instance, Dhaka in Bangladesh. Dhaka, the capital of Bangladesh, had less than a half million population in 1950. Its population grew to 2.2 million in a 25-year period from 1950 to 1975 and accelerated further to 12.5 million in another 25-year period from 1975 to 2000. This growth is projected to continue. Dhaka is expected to add an additional 10 million residents in the next fifteen years and become the second largest city, next to Tokyo, by 2015. This kind of extraordinary growth in urban populations can also be found in Indonesia, Pakistan, Saudi Arabia, and Nigeria. Even though Tokyo is expected to be the largest city in the world by 2015, its population growth has significantly slowed down (it will add only about 0.75 million people in the next fifteen years), while many Muslim cities are projected to continue their rapid growth.

As already noted, migration has been the major contributor to urbanization. Worsening economic conditions in rural areas act as "push factors", while job opportunities, income disparities among regions, and possibilities for a better life in cities and towns become "pull factors" in a process that has led to swift urbanization in many Muslim countries. Swift urbanization has generated many social problems and resulted in environmental deterioration. Rapid growth of cities strains their ability to provide services such as energy, transportation, sanitation and physical security, as well as education and health care. It often overwhelms their ability to absorb new urban dwellers on a large scale. Many people migrating into big cities do not find the jobs they had come to look for and are forced into part-time, temporary and subcontractor relations in employment and also engage in illegal, black market and criminal activities.

Another major effect of rapid urban growth is the creation of scattered developments in urban outskirts, which give rise to what is known as "urban sprawl". Migrants flooding into cities often live in impoverished slums and squatter settlements, where high density settlements often pollute air and water. Lack of electricity, running water, trash pickups and paved roads have caused many big Muslim cities to become areas of massive urban sprawl with widespread poverty, high levels of disease incidence, significant juvenile delinquency, frequent crimes, and social violence. Swift urbanization, combined with increasing numbers of young males migrating into cities with already unemployed labor forces has turned big city sprawls into fertile soil for the emergence of social problems. This includes creation of militants and terrorists. Addressing and solving problems associated with such big and sprawling cities like Cairo, Karachi, and Jakarta have become important for achieving social stability.

6.4. Summary of Chapter 6

In summary, this chapter has analyzed another important demographic dynamic in Muslim countries — swift urbanization over the last forty years (from 1960 to 2000). Rapid urbanization in the Muslim world is closely associated with the rapid population expansion that was discussed in Chapter 4. It is also related to increasing proportions of children and young people, and the "troublesome cohort" described in Chapter 5. We noted some of the economic and social problems that resulted from these demographic changes, such as poverty and social instability of Muslim society, and such as the potential for transnational terrorism in mega-cities and urban sprawls. Up to this point the analyses have been mainly "quantitative" in nature with a focus on quantity of people. For instance, we have discussed numbers of people living in different countries or regions, and different age or sex cohorts or numbers of people living in urban or rural areas. In the following Chapter 7 we move to an analysis that deals with "quality" of populations, especially intellectual quality, in Muslim countries.

Chapter 7

Population Quality: Illiteracy and Education

The quality of a population and its lifestyles can be assessed in two ways: (1) physical conditions and (2) intellectual levels. For example, population vital parameters, such as infant mortality, death rates and life expectancy as well as population age structures, that we discussed in Chapters 4 and 5, can be used to measure overall health and physical conditions, but are not suitable measures for the intellectual quality of a population. Other social and economic criteria are involved in defining and evaluating a population's intellectual quality.

In economics and the business world, individuals are treated as human resources of inputs or capital. Workers are carriers of skills, knowledge, and abilities that can be employed to create wealth. In this view human skills, knowledge, and abilities are regarded as assets that can be supplied by workers and professionals in the form of various services. Hence, human capital is not equivalent to people per se, but is dependent on their acquiring skills and knowledge, and performing productive services. In other words, these resources are dependent upon a population's intellectual level. Measuring a population's intellectual level is therefore akin to measuring human capital. However no single index has been agreed upon as the measure of a society's human capital stock. At the national level three approaches to measuring human capital have been promoted by OECD (Organization for Economic Development and Cooperation). These include measures of educational attainment and adult skills directly, as well as estimates of the market value of human capital.[1] Unfortunately, these measurements are incomplete even for some advanced countries and not available from public information resources for many developing countries.

This chapter is devoted to the intellectual quality of Muslim populations in which we use available data to show their intellectual level over the last three decades, from 1970 to 2000. It contains two sections. Section 7.1 analyzes illiteracy rates of adults and young Muslim male and female population cohorts for the 49 Muslim-majority countries. Section 7.2 discusses education systems in the Muslim world.

[1] See *Embracing the Global Demographic Transformation, 1950–2050*, An IC2 Institute Monograph, University of Texas, by George Kozmetsky and Piyu Yue, 2000, pp. 82–106. Also see Chapters 7, 8, and 9 in: *The Economic Transformation of the United States, 1950–2000*, by George Kozmetsky and Piyu Yue, Purdue University Press, 2005, pp. 198–239.

International Symposia in Economic Theory and Econometrics, Vol. 19
William W. Cooper and Piyu Yue

ISSN: 1571-0386/DOI: 10.1016/S1571-0386(07)00017-8

7.1. Illiteracy Rates of the Muslim Populations

The only available data to analyze the intellectual quality of Muslim populations generally is illiteracy. This is an indicator of human capital stock because it is related to the skills and competence of a population. Illiteracy, however, has different meanings in different countries.[2] For the more developed world, sophisticated measures have been developed to gauge skills and competence in areas such as prose literacy, document literacy, and quantitative literacy. In the less developed world, illiteracy is widely used in national population censuses and surveys. An illiterate person is defined as someone who cannot both read and write a short, simple statement, with understanding, about his or her everyday life. This definition constitutes a minimum for reading and writing. It does not measure the degree of functional skills and competence for work and life. It is, however, a reasonable measure of educational achievement for the less developed world, where the opportunity for formal education has been low and where many people remain in a state of illiteracy even by this definition.

In Table 7.1, we present both the top and bottom fifteen Muslim countries in terms of illiteracy rates for males and females. For purpose of comparison, illiteracy rates of the upper-middle-income, low-middle-income, and low-income groups of the world are also provided at the bottom of Table 7.1.

Illiteracy rate is correlated with a nation's income level. Many high income nations have nearly no illiterate adults in their societies because they provide at least elementary education for all their citizens. Low income nations, however, encounter difficulties in financing elementary education for rapidly increasing numbers of children, and this has resulted in large numbers of illiterate men and women.

World Bank estimates of GNI (Gross National Income) per capita in year 2000 US dollars are used to classify countries into the following average income groups: low income group ($745 or less), middle income group ($746–$9 205), and high income group ($9 206 or more). The middle income group is further divided into two subgroups: low-middle income group ($746–$2 975), and upper-middle income group ($2 976–$9 205). The illiteracy rates of these groups provide benchmarks for Muslim populations.

The top 15 Muslim countries in Table 7.1 belong to different income groups: two of them were the former Soviet states; two of them are in the high-income group, five in the upper-middle income group and six in the low-middle income group. Uzbekistan and Tajikistan belong to the low income group, although their illiteracy rates over 1970–2000 were the lowest (0.41% and 0.42% for male and

[2] See *Embracing the Global Demographic Transformation, 1950–2050*, An IC2 Institute Monograph, University of Texas, by George Kozmetsky and Piyu Yue, 2000, p. 91.

Table 7.1: Muslim Countries Ranked by Illiteracy Rate of Adults

Top 15 Muslim Countries Ranked by Illiteracy Rate of Adult Males in 2000

Nation	Male (%)				Female (%)			
	1970	1980	1990	2000	1970	1980	1990	2000
Uzbekistan	1.09	0.75	0.54	0.41	5.22	3.46	2.11	1.16
Tajikistan	4.67	2.01	0.84	0.42	13.53	6.53	2.78	1.18
Maldives	10.94	7.94	5.40	3.38	14.53	9.72	5.59	3.21
Jordan	27.79	17.98	9.99	4.93	65.56	46.45	28.90	16.14
Turkey	26.88	17.10	10.76	6.52	60.37	46.04	33.49	23.45
Lebanon	24.05	17.34	11.65	7.86	49.22	37.09	26.88	19.65
Albania	33.58	21.16	13.19	7.87	63.39	47.37	33.28	23.02
Indonesia	31.19	20.86	13.24	8.18	56.09	40.54	27.41	18.00
Malaysia	29.79	19.87	13.05	8.57	54.10	37.54	25.53	16.57
Bahrain	38.37	21.48	13.15	9.07	63.01	40.69	25.33	17.41
Libya	44.55	28.69	17.12	9.18	87.83	69.52	48.81	31.80
Syria	39.34	27.81	18.15	11.73	78.99	66.18	52.49	39.54
Kuwait	34.40	26.95	20.59	16.00	54.70	40.54	27.37	20.33
Iran	54.23	38.79	27.54	16.80	76.89	61.39	45.64	30.71
Saudi Arabia	50.74	34.83	23.65	16.94	83.50	67.65	49.81	33.08

Bottom 15 Muslim Countries Ranked by Illiteracy Rate of Adult Males in 2000

Nation	Male (%)				Female (%)			
	1970	1980	1990	2000	1970	1980	1990	2000
Egypt	53.60	46.27	39.64	33.38	83.23	75.35	66.41	56.20
Iraq	61.75	52.49	43.02	34.40	86.88	78.33	66.76	54.13
Morocco	68.19	57.95	47.25	38.15	91.84	84.53	75.07	63.92
Cote d'Ivoire	77.13	67.78	57.37	45.50	93.73	87.11	76.63	61.37
Pakistan	67.91	59.50	50.70	42.54	91.15	86.13	79.87	72.14
Guinea-Bissau	78.94	68.80	57.49	45.61	96.66	93.31	87.15	76.68
Bangladesh	64.57	59.14	53.74	47.69	88.46	83.10	76.87	70.14
Chad	85.21	75.41	63.02	48.43	95.94	90.69	81.17	65.98
Mauritania	63.55	59.54	53.68	49.25	82.52	82.50	76.09	69.93
Mali	90.32	80.71	67.10	51.09	96.79	91.47	81.28	65.60
Senegal	76.69	69.54	61.78	52.69	93.86	88.31	81.41	72.36
Ethiopia	80.18	71.54	62.49	52.81	93.39	88.25	80.16	96.06
Gambia, The	87.07	78.84	68.16	55.99	93.32	88.28	80.42	70.59
Burkina Faso	88.03	82.40	74.98	66.07	97.79	95.74	92.04	85.92
Niger	89.45	86.46	81.99	76.23	98.77	97.33	94.89	91.57
Upper middle income	18.47	14.20	11.00	8.44	28.52	21.68	16.38	11.95
Low middle income	29.07	20.11	13.59	9.23	50.71	39.17	28.87	21.50
Low income	49.80	42.10	34.94	28.35	72.75	64.94	56.12	47.02

Data source: *World Development Indicators*, the World Bank, 2003 and 2004.

1.16% and 1.18% for female adults in 2000). This is likely the result of a mandatory education system under the former Soviet regime, although there are no illiteracy data for other former Soviet Muslim states to verify this. Bahrain and Kuwait are two high-income countries in the Muslim world. However, illiteracy rates for these two countries are even greater than the average of the upper-middle income group, so their illiteracy rates do not match their income status.

Five countries in the upper part of Table 7.1 belong to the upper-middle income group: Turkey, Lebanon, Malaysia, Libya, and Saudi Arabia. As of 2000, the illiteracy rates of Turkey (6.52%) and Lebanon (7.86%) were below the average for the upper-middle income group (8.44%), while Malaysia (8.57%), Libya (9.18%) and Saudi Arabia (16.94%) remained above that average. The illiteracy rates of female adults for the five upper-middle income Muslim countries were significantly greater than the average for the upper-middle income group over the entire period. There was an illiteracy gap between female and male adults, but this gap was much larger for the Muslim counties than for the average of upper-middle income group. For instance, as shown at the bottom of Table 7.1, in 2000, the average illiteracy rate for the upper-middle income group was 11.95% for female adults versus 8.44% for male adults, but, as shown in the top 15 in Table 7.1, it was 23.45% for female adults versus 6.52% for male adults in Turkey and 33.08% versus 16.94% in Saudi Arabia.

The last six countries, Maldives, Jordan, Albania, Indonesia, Syria and Iran in the "top 15" list are members of the low-middle income group. In 2000 the illiteracy rates of male adults in these countries were all below the average of 9.23% for the low-middle income group, with the exception of Syria (11.73%) and Iran (16.8%). The illiteracy rates of their female adults, however, remained above the average for low-middle income group over the entire time period, except for Jordan in 2000 (16.14% vs. 21.5%), Indonesia (18.00% vs. 21.50%) and Maldives. Maldives is a small island Muslim country in South Asia with female illiteracy rate of 14.52%–3.21% over 1970–2000 outperforming the average of the low-middle income group (50.71%–21.50%) shown at the bottom of Table 7.1.

Among the bottom 15 countries listed in the lower part of Table 7.1, Iraq is a high-income country; Egypt, Morocco and Cote d'Ivoire belong to the low-middle income group. The others are members of the low income group. The illiteracy rates of both male and female adults for all these 15 countries were greater than the average rates of the low income group (28.35% for male versus 47.02% for female in 2000). Large discrepancies between male and female adult illiteracy rates are also apparent in all 15 countries in the lower part of Table 7.1.

With few exceptions, like Maldives and Jordan, and the two split ofls from the former Soviet Union, these Muslim countries have high illiteracy rates relative to world income groups. The gap in illiteracy rates between male and female adults is also much larger in Muslim countries than in the world income groups. Nevertheless, in the period from 1970 to 2000, significant reductions were apparent in the illiteracy rates of these countries for both male and female adults. This reflects social developments and progress that have been made in the Muslim world over the last three decades.

Comparing numbers on the right side to numbers on the left side of the upper part in Table 7.1, one can see that Muslim females were generally about 20 years behind Muslim males — see 1970 for male versus 1990 for female — in terms of illiteracy rates in higher income Muslim countries. Similarly, a comparison of the lower part of Table 7.1 reveals that Muslim females were nearly thirty years behind Muslim males in these lower income countries. This high illiteracy of Muslim females reflects practices that are widespread in the Muslim world. It has adverse effects on demographic transitions in the form of keeping total fertility rates high and accelerating population growth. Muslim women also bear a heavy responsibility to raise and educate their children. Being semi-illiterate and discriminated against, females become subordinate and under performing in Muslim countries. From an economic standpoint, this wastes large amounts of human resources; it also affects the next generation of Muslims. The issue of women in the Muslim world is highly controversial. Some believe Muslim women did not benefit from the general Islamic principles and were doomed forever to remain in inferiority.[3,4] Some believe the status of women in Islam is one of equality and honor; but some believe that this is misunderstood and incorrectly portrayed in the western world.[5]

It seems generally agreed that the rights granted to women in the Quran and by the prophet Muhammad were a vast improvement in comparison to the situation of Arabian women in pre-Islamic age. The Quran does not subscribe to the view that Eve was created from the crooked rib of Adam and thus is of inferior status, and shows that there is no superiority for one sex over the other. The equality of women in Islam is evident by woman's legal rights defined in the Quran, such as both men and women have equal rights to contract a marriage or a divorce, to pursue any profession including political positions.

The Quran and Islamic history provide ample evidence of women undertaking various forms of political involvement from fighting in battles to influencing political decisions. Benazir Bhutto, elected Prime Minister of Pakistan in 1988, was the first woman to lead a post-colonial Muslim state. Tansu Ciller was Turkey's first female Prime Minister in 1993–1996.

Nowadays, however, the majority Muslim women do not enjoy such equal rights because much of these rights granted by the Quran and much of the original Islamic practice and history have been ignored, while laws and practices have

---

[3] See *What Went Wrong? Western Impact and Middle Eastern Response*, by Bernard Lewis, Oxford University Press, 2002, pp. 67–69.

[4] *What Went Wrong? Western Impact and Middle Eastern Response*, by Bernard Lewis, Oxford University Press, 2002, p. 157.

[5] Noha Ragab (Duke University), *The Record Set Straight: Women in Islam Have Rights*, November 16, 1995, http://www.jannah.org/sisters/noha.html.

moved in the opposite direction. Much of the present laws in Muslim countries have deviated from or totally unrelated to the origins of Islam. Instead, many practices are based on cultural or traditional customs which are either residues of old pre-Islamic tribal traditions, where women were not entitled to the same rights as men, or civil laws imposed during European colonization. Consequently, the condition of women in the Muslim world has often reverted back to pre-Islamic norms.

Muslim women often have to suffer from the laws which are legislated and enforced by men to suit political agendas, such as the Saudi's ban on women to drive. Many problems of concern for Muslim women include family laws with the rights of the husband superseding those of the wife, violence against women in the home and community, restrictions on women's contribution to society beyond childbearing, subjecting women to harassment, intimidation, or discrimination, and abusing certain Islamic practices that affect women negatively, such as polygamy and temporary marriage, and others. The Muslim world today is facing great challenges and calls for changes to revitalize Islam. The emancipation of Muslim women might be important and urgently needed for changes that could restore the original Islamic Image of the Muslim woman as communicated by God in the Quran of a liberated, vital human being who can work in cooperation with men to contribute to family, community, society, nation and the world.

In order to gain more insight into the potentials for the future of the Muslim world, we present illiteracy rates of young people aged 15–24.[6] Table 7.2 displays the top 15 and bottom 15 Muslim countries in a fashion similar to Table 7.1. Two countries (Kuwait and Saudi Arabia) in Table 7.1 have dropped out of the top 15, and another two (Oman and Tunisia) have been added in Table 7.2. The bottom 15 nations in Table 7.1 all remain in the bottom part of Table 7.2.

As of 2000, the illiteracy rates of young males in the top 15 Muslim countries, with an exception of Iran (3.72%) and Syria (4.64%), were all less than their counterpart in the world upper-middle income group (3.23%). Nine out of these fifteen top Muslin countries in 2000 also had their young female illiteracy rates below the counterpart in the upper-middle income group (4.26% in 2000). Tunisia and Syria were the only two countries in the top 15 that showed a double-digital percentage of young female illiteracy rates in 2000 (10.82% and 21.21%). Comparing Tables 7.1 and 7.2, one can observe that impressive progress has been achieved in education of children and youngsters in these top Muslim countries over the three decades 1970–2000. In the next two or three decades — when the youngsters of 2000 replace their parents and grand parents in the adult cohort — the top 15 Muslim countries could reach an adult illiteracy level similar to the upper-middle

[6] The original data for illiteracy rates come from the "*World Development Indicators*" database of the World Bank. In this database the "young cohort" is defined as persons of ages from 15 to 24 and thus differs from the troublesome cohort discussed in Chapter 5.

Table 7.2: Muslim Countries Ranked by Illiteracy Rate of Youths

Top 15 Muslim Countries Ranked by Illiteracy Rate of Young Males (15–24) in 2000

Nation	Male (%)				Female (%)			
	1970	1980	1990	2000	1970	1980	1990	2000
Tajikistan	0.23	0.21	0.20	0.20	0.65	0.40	0.24	0.20
Libya	16.68	4.72	1.05	0.20	72.66	38.59	17.18	6.86
Uzbekistan	0.32	0.31	0.31	0.28	0.58	0.40	0.40	0.40
Oman	43.89	17.68	4.58	0.45	88.61	64.48	24.58	3.74
Jordan	8.50	3.87	1.79	0.67	37.02	15.01	4.47	0.70
Albania	9.64	4.32	2.58	0.89	30.59	16.34	8.06	3.56
Turkey	7.77	4.30	2.93	1.17	35.73	20.17	11.73	5.96
Maldives	5.40	3.80	2.17	1.19	5.51	3.46	1.70	0.61
Indonesia	12.45	6.97	3.38	1.69	28.07	14.78	6.58	2.86
Bahrain	11.60	6.94	3.78	1.83	31.13	13.47	5.01	1.44
Malaysia	11.73	7.30	4.67	2.55	25.35	12.43	5.78	2.33
Tunisia	29.73	14.41	7.17	2.61	65.37	41.85	24.82	10.82
Lebanon	10.16	6.82	4.50	2.76	26.40	17.80	11.41	6.98
Iran	29.83	16.77	8.13	3.72	57.37	36.50	18.78	8.43
Syria	20.67	12.55	7.78	4.64	63.95	47.17	33.10	21.21

Bottom 15 Muslim Countries Ranked by Illiteracy Rate of Young Males (15–24) in 2000

Nation	Male (%)				Female (%)			
	1970	1980	1990	2000	1970	1980	1990	2000
Iraq	48.65	38.62	29.42	21.67	77.39	64.04	48.05	32.55
Egypt	42.30	35.78	29.11	23.57	72.36	61.52	48.92	37.30
Morocco	50.61	42.87	31.94	23.87	82.84	72.32	57.97	41.71
Chad	72.78	58.03	41.59	26.61	90.78	80.15	62.31	40.10
Guinea–Bissau	63.04	48.84	37.44	26.78	93.04	85.69	73.69	56.60
Mali	81.53	65.61	45.95	27.57	92.73	82.11	63.35	39.76
Pakistan	56.31	48.20	37.44	28.88	85.68	78.51	69.37	58.08
Cote d'Ivoire	63.63	51.93	40.49	29.73	87.16	75.61	59.33	40.35
Gambia, The	76.75	63.99	49.17	34.37	87.28	78.55	66.24	51.21
Ethiopia	69.74	57.96	48.40	38.85	87.71	78.03	66.07	51.58
Bangladesh	56.64	52.12	45.31	39.07	81.86	74.23	67.69	60.17
Senegal	66.16	58.49	49.99	40.40	87.37	78.64	69.88	58.27
Mauritania	59.99	52.61	44.49	42.88	79.73	83.49	63.95	59.35
Burkina Faso	80.80	73.06	64.29	54.18	95.63	91.96	86.04	76.68
Niger	86.78	81.96	75.14	67.67	97.63	94.83	90.74	86.28
Upper middle income	10.64	6.62	4.52	3.23	16.52	10.20	6.91	4.26
Low middle income	11.08	7.61	6.06	4.41	28.21	17.19	10.29	6.58
Low Income	37.72	30.14	23.88	18.28	62.65	50.97	40.22	30.81

income group for the world. The intellectual quality of these Muslim populations will then have improved significantly and this could move their economies and societies forward.

The bottom 15 Muslim nations display quite a different situation. In this case all of the national illiteracy rates of both male and female youngsters in 2000 were still higher than the average of the world low-income group. This indicates that these 15 Muslim countries can expect their adult illiteracy rate to stay above the world low income group over the next two or three decades.

Overall, the illiteracy of Muslim youngsters improved significantly, but unevenly, during the last three decades, with a larger gain in the top 15 Muslim countries and a smaller gain in the bottom countries. There is also a larger gain in males compared to females. Hence disparities in illiteracy rates are likely to carry over into adult illiteracy in the next two or three decades that will keep the fertility level high with large effects on the future of the Muslim world.

7.2. Education Systems of the Muslim Nations

The quality of a population is determined by social-economic-political conditions of a society in which education system occupies center stage. The future of any society depends on educated younger generations and the education system has a great long-term impact on its economic wealth, cultural prosperity, and social stability. An education system does not exist in a vacuum but in the contemporary social-economic and political climate of a country. It responds to changes and challenges in both the internal and external environments. Education also costs money and resources for both nations and families. Richer nations or families generally spend more on educating their children and poorer nations or families spend less.

As was discussed earlier in Chapter 5, Muslim-majority countries all have younger age structures for their populations than the rest of the world. Their child cohorts are expanding much faster than the other population cohorts. For every 100 children aged 0–14 in the world there were on average 27 Muslim children in 2000. This number is expected to rise to 34 by 2050, so that on average there will be at least one Muslim child for every three children in the world. The Muslim world will have to raise and educate more than one third of the world's children from very limited economic and intellectual resources as well as fragmented education systems.

7.2.1. Economic Base of Education in Muslim Countries

Table 7.3 lists the population of children for thirty Muslim-majority countries along with average GNI (Gross National Income) per capita, and education and military expenditures per capita for three decades, 1970s, 1980s and 1990s. The three rows at the bottom of the table provide corresponding aggregates for high-income countries, low-income countries[7] and the world average in order to facilitate comparisons. The GNI per capita is stated in current US dollars for the year being considered and the percentage of GNI is used to calculate the education and military expenditures per capita in order to exhibit differences among Muslim countries in terms of US dollars per capita. All data in Table 7.3 are annual data and all are averaged over corresponding time periods. The original data are from the 2002, 2003, and 2004 versions for the "World Development Indicators" database published by the World Bank. All the GNI (Gross National Income) and expenditure data are measured in current US$. The GNI per capita data of Libya, Afghanistan and Somalia are for the 1980s due to missing data for the 1990s.

The first three columns of Table 7.3 present the numbers of children at age 0–14 for the last three decades of the twentieth century. This population cohort represents the need and the demand for basic (elementary) education services. As shown at the bottom of the lower part of Table 7.3, the total number of children in the world increased by 20% in three decades, from 1 468 million in the 1970s to 1 756 million in the 1990s. This increasing trend was even sharper in the low-income nations, which exhibited increases in number of children by nearly 45% — rising from 588 million to 850 million in these three decades. The high-income nations, on the other hand, exhibited a declining trend with their number of children reducing by 11%, from 176 million in the 1970s to 156 million in the 1990s.

The percentage numbers in parentheses of the two bottom rows denote the percentage ratio of the number of children in the income groups to the number of children in the world. It shows that during the 1970s nearly 40% of world children were raised and educated by low-income nations, compared with only 12% by high-income nations. During the 1990s, that percentage increased to 48% for the low-income countries and decreased to less than 9% for the high-income countries. Therefore, increasing pressure for providing basic education has been concentrated in the low-income nations, mainly due to the demographic nature of a younger age structure.

As discussed earlier in Chapter 5, this changing age structure reflects a continuously increasing number of children in the Muslim populations. The total number of age 0–14 Muslim children increased from 269 million in 1970 to 488 million in 2000. It is expected to reach 619 million by 2040 and then to level off (see Figure 5.5). It is therefore not surprising that the Muslim-majority countries listed in Table 7.3 have all shown increasing numbers of age 0–14 children, regardless of

[7] The world groups by income were classified according to World Bank estimates of 2002 GNI per capita. This amounted to $9 076 or more for the High-income group, and $735 or less for the Low-income group. See *World Development Indicators* by the World Bank, 2004.

Table 7.3: Muslim Countries Ranked by Education Expenditure

Top 15 Muslim Countries Ranked by Annual Education Spending per Capita

Nation	Population ages 0–14 (in million)			GNI per capita	Education spending per capita		Military spending per capita	
Time period	1970s	1980s	1990s	1990s	1980s	1990s	1989–1995	1995–1999
Kuwait	0.440	0.651	0.679	19 023	654	791	7 419	1 739
Qatar	0.057	0.102	0.142	16 626	709	539	1 855	1 869
Saudi Arabia	3.276	5.394	7.964	7 275	526	436	1 412	1 059
Bahrain	0.109	0.136	0.177	9 593	304	428	864	760
Libya	1.138	1.697	1.844	7 426^{+}	375	na	536	453
UAE	0.161	0.405	0.662	19 080	350	324	1 093	851
Oman	0.390	0.624	0.937	5 252	154	205	1 056	888
Malaysia	5.140	6.039	7.340	3 468	107	151	104	81
Tunisia	2.488	2.868	2.995	1 835	66	110	46	36
Iraq	5.147	6.949	8.860	2 170	120	100	360	117
Jordan	0.868	1.262	1.726	1 491	87	87	141	130
Algeria	7.637	9.599	10.666	1 751	136	85	44	65
Turkey	16.009	18.424	19.593	2 873	28	83	106	124
Iran	14.946	20.706	24.579	1 703	117	59	72	48
Morocco	7.977	9.007	9.781	1 160	41	57	55	48

Bottom 15 Muslim Countries Ranked by Annual Education Spending per Capita

Nation	Population ages 0–14 (in million)			GNI per capita	Education spending per capita		Military spending per capita	
Time period	1970s	1980s	1990s	1990s	1980s	1990s	1989–1995	1995–1999
Pakistan	29.852	39.702	51.752	445	6.1	10.2	29.8	26.8
Guinea	1.877	2.304	2.952	498	3.6	7.3	6.7	7.7
Niger	2.353	3.284	4.573	218	7.6	6.5	2.7	2.2
Mali	2.738	3.457	4.428	255	7.0	6.2	5.4	5.3
Guinea-Bissau	0.267	0.354	0.461	211	5.7	5.6	6.8	5.7
Bangladesh	34.105	41.966	48.762	319	3.2	5.5	4.0	4.1
Chad	1.751	2.299	3.084	238	3.4	5.3	7.8	5.8
Indonesia	54.73	62.245	64.513	797	5.5	5.3	11.2	10.0
Burkina Faso	2.962	3.852	4.862	232	4.9	4.5	5.4	3.6
Afghanistan	6.164	7.164	9.599	260^{+}	4.4	na	na	na
Sudan	7.444	9.609	11.471	309	17.4	4.0	20.2	15.5
Ethiopia	14.781	19.476	25.595	105	na	2.9	6.2	4.2
Nigeria	27.755	38.231	50.886	253	6.0	1.9	3.8	2.9
Sierra Leone	1.248	1.559	1.975	164	5.5	1.8	4.7	7.1
Somalia	2.119	3.188	3.666	123^{+}	0.6	na	na	na
World average	1468	1611	1756	4811	132	218	148	118
High income	176 (12%)	161 (10%)	156 (9%)	25 027	653	1199	753	593
Low income	588 (40%)	718 (45%)	850 (48%)	415	11.2	12.2	11.3	10.5

the level of their GNI per capita. As a matter of fact, there are four Arab nations in the Middle East that belong to the high-income group — Kuwait, Qatar, Bahrain and the United Arab Emirates (Saudi Arabia was classified as an upper middle income country by the World Bank in terms of 2002 GNI per capita). Unlike other high-income countries of the world, all of the Muslim high-income countries have increasing numbers of children even though their population sizes are relatively small.

Large Muslim countries, such as Nigeria, Pakistan, Bangladesh, Ethiopia, Indonesia and Iran have also shown big increases in number of children. As shown in the bottom portion of Table 7.3, over the last three decades, the number of children increased by nearly 23 million in Nigeria, 22 million in Pakistan, 15 million in Bangladesh, 11 million in Ethiopia, 10 million in Indonesia and, in the top portion of the table, 10 million in Iran. Over the same time period, the number of Saudi children more than doubled, increasing by 4.7 million. The other Muslim countries that showed a more-than-2-million increase in their numbers of children include Sudan (4 million), Iraq (3.7 million), Yemen (3.7 million), Turkey (3.5 million), Afghanistan (3.4 million), Algeria (3 million), Cote d'lvoire (3 million), Uzbekistan (2.8 million), Syria (2.7 million), and Niger (2.2 million). From these numbers one can see the urgency of providing basic education for the rapidly expanding population of Muslim children.

The capability of the Muslim world to meet this escalating need for children's basic education has been constrained by the lower economic wealth generated by many Muslim countries. As Table 7.3 shows, only the top seven Muslim-majority countries had a GNI per capita greater than the world average ($4 811) during the 1990s. Five of them are OPEC member countries — Kuwait, Qatar, Saudi Arabia, Libya and the United Arab Emirates — and this is largely due to their oil export revenues.

In the lower part of Table 7.3 there is only one nation (Indonesia) that had a higher GNI per capita ($797) than $735, which was the dividing mark between the high-income and low-income countries in 2002. Only two Muslim countries (Pakistan and Guinea) had a slightly larger GNI per capita than $415, which was the average GNI per capita of the low-income group during the 1990s shown at the bottom of the Table 7.3. The other twelve Muslim countries in the lower part of Table 7.3 showed a significantly lower GNI per capita than the average of the low-income group.

Economic reality confronts education in much of the Muslim world. On the one hand, younger populations in Muslim countries have produced increasing numbers of children, year after year, and these children need to be raised and educated. However, only a very few relatively small, oil-rich, Muslim nations have adequate economic resources for their education systems. The great number of Muslim countries, particularly populous nations like Pakistan, Indonesia, Bangladesh, Nigeria and Ethiopia, spend very little GNI per capita for the education needs of their children.

Education expenditures are shown in Table 7.3 under "Education spending per capita" in two columns: one for the 1980s and one for the 1990s. For purposes of comparison, military spending per capita in the two halves of the 1990s are also provided in the two right-most columns. The data on education spending refer solely to public spending, consisting of government spending on public education plus government subsidies for private education. The data exclude foreign aid for education and expenditures by religious schools, which play a significant role in the Muslim-majority countries, and which will be separately discussed later in this chapter.

As shown at the bottom of Table 7.3, the world average expenditure on education per capita increased from \$132 in the 1980s to \$218 in the 1990s. For the high-income nations it rose from \$653 to \$1 199, compared to from \$11.2 to \$12.2 per capita for the low-income nations in the same time period. Military expenditures declined during the 1990s, from \$148 to \$118 per capita for the world average, from \$753 to \$593 per capita for the high-income nations, and from \$11.3 to \$10.5 per capita for the low-income nations. These data therefore show a trend of increasing education expenditures and decreasing military expenditures in the 1990s. That trend was less pronounced although also applicable to many Muslim nations. The incessant confrontations and wars in the Muslim world, which will be discussed in Part III of this book, have kept military expenditures relatively high and education expenditures relatively low in many of these Muslim countries.

In the upper part of Table 7.3, there are two nations, Kuwait and Qatar, with education spending per capita comparable to that of the high-income nations of the world during the 1980s (\$654 and \$709 versus \$653 in the 1980s), but their education spending was significantly lower than that of the high-income group in the 1990s (\$791 and \$539 versus \$1 199 in the 1990s). During the 1990s, the top seven Muslim nations in Table 7.3 spent more income per capita on boosting their military power than on educating their children. Iraq's invasion of Kuwait in 1990 and the war with Iraq was the main motivation for increasing military expenditures in Persian Gulf nations in the first half of the 1990s. Although there was some reduction, military spending remained high for this region in the second half of the 1990s.

As the top portion of Table 7.3 shows, education spending, except for Bahrain, was only one third, or nearly so, of their military spending, while Bahrain's education expenditure was approaching one half of its military spending in the 1990s. Among the top 15 Muslim nations in Table 7.3 there are only five (Malaysia, Tunisia, Algeria, Iran and Morocco) that spent more income per capita on education than on the military — although their absolute expenditure numbers are both relatively small. Some Muslim nations experienced a significant decline in their education spending. For example, the education expenditure per capita was reduced from \$526 in the 1980s to \$436 in the 1990s in Saudi Arabia, from \$120 to \$100 in Iraq, from \$136 to \$85 in Algeria and from \$117 to \$59 in Iran.

The lower part of Table 7.3 shows these per capita expenditures all at much lower levels. From its meager $445 GNI per capita during the 1990s Pakistan spent $29.8–$26.8 per capita per year on the military and only $6.1–$10.2 per capita per year on education. Indonesia's annual military expenditure was $11.2–$10.0 per capita versus education expenditures of $5.5–$5.3 per capita. Sudan has been entangled in civil war for many years, with military expenditures of $20.2–$15.5 per capita per year and education expenditures of only $17.4–$4 per capita per year. Sudan's GNI per capita was only $309 during the 1990s. Ethiopia and Nigeria, the most populous Muslim nations in sub Sahara Africa, had GNIs per capita of only $105–$253 during the 1990s, with education spending at less than $3 per capita per year in the 1990s. Somalia had the lowest GNI per capita at $123 and education expenditures of only $0.6 per capita per year during the 1980s, with no figures available for the other years.

Except for Indonesia, all countries listed in the lower portion of Table 7.3 showed a GNI per capita in the 1990s of less than $2 a day. Pakistan and Guinea had an income per capita of only about $1.2–$1.4 a day, and other countries in the lower part of Table 7.3 had incomes per capita of less than $1 a day. A dollar a day is a minimum living standard for survival. Nations with income per capita of less than a dollar a day are considered to be "extremely poor" or "chronically poor". Many Muslim countries are in chronic poverty with deeply seated problems in their economic and social structures.

They are also poor because of increasing population pressure combined with degraded resources and stagnant economies. The marginal resources on which such poor people subsist are much more vulnerable to natural calamities such as droughts and floods, which can easily push them into starvation. In many poor Muslim nations, an inequitable distribution of land and a feudal, ethnic or tribal system further accentuates this chronic poverty. Such chronic poverty keeps many Muslim countries spending little money for education. Consequently, illiteracy rates of their adults and youths are the highest of the world (see Tables 7.1 and 7.2). Without quality human resources, many Muslim countries have been trapped in a vicious cycle: lower education–lower quality of labor–lower productivity–lower income–lower education, and so on.

7.2.2. School Enrollment

There is mounting evidence that the intellectual quality of a population is correlated with individual earning, productivity and economic growth of a nation. The acquired useful ability of members of a society is one of the factors of production that make up the general stock of capital for a society. Adam Smith, the founder of modern economics, points out,

> The acquisition of such talents, by the maintenance of the acquirer during his education, study, or apprenticeship, always costs a real expense, which is a capital fixed and realized, as it were in his person. Those talents, as they make a part of his fortune,

> so do they likewise of that of the society to which he belongs. The improved dexterity of a workman may be considered in the same light as a machine or instrument of trade which facilitates and abridges labor, and which, though it costs a certain expense, repays that expanse with a profit.[8]

Other production factors (machines, buildings and improved land) belong to the owner-firms in the form of physical resources and can be purchased and sold in markets. Acquired and useful abilities are human resource capital that belongs to workers and employees — carriers of productive skills and abilities. Therefore, skills and abilities can be considered to be assets provided by workers via services. They are not equivalent to people per se, but they are dependent on people to acquire skills and perform productive services. Thus formal schooling is important in educating children and youngsters and imbuing them with proper spirit, advanced knowledge and useful skills to create human resources. The school enrollment ratio therefore becomes a pertinent measure of educational achievement and indicates the potential progress a nation could make in its economy and society.

In the "*World Development Indicators*" database of the World Bank there are three levels of school enrollment: primary school, secondary school, and higher education. Even though school age differs among countries due to different education systems, the primary school age is generally considered to be 6 to 11, the secondary school age 12 to 17, and the tertiary education age 20 to 24. Basic education begins at the primary and ends at the secondary level. It aims at laying foundations for lifelong learning and human development by offering both subject- and skill-oriented instruction. A minimum condition for entry to higher education is successful completion of the secondary education or proof of equivalent knowledge or experience.

The gross enrollment ratio is defined as the ratio of total enrollment regardless of the age to the age cohort that officially corresponds to the level of education. For countries with universal primary education, the gross enrollment ratio of primary schools may exceed 100 percent because some pupils may be below or above the official primary school age. Likewise, the gross enrollment ratio of secondary schools for some countries may also be above 100 percent.

Table 7.4 presents school enrollment ratios at three levels (primary, secondary and tertiary) in 1970,1990 and 2000 from available data for 45 Muslim countries, along with school enrollment ratios of three country income groups (low, middle and high) listed in the three bottom rows of Table 7.4. All 45 countries are ranked in order of the tertiary enrollment ratio for 2000. A synoptic view of Table 7.4 reveals that school enrollments in all three categories have, in general, improved significantly over the last three decades, from 1970 to 2000.

---

[8] Adam Smith, *An Inquiry into the Nature and Causes of the Wealth of Nations* edited with an introduction and commentary by Kathryn Sutherland (Oxford; New York: Oxford University Press, 1993).

Table 7.4: School Enrollment of 45 Muslim Countries (%)

Nation		Primary			Secondary			Tertiary		
		1970	1990	2000	1970	1990	2000	1970	1990	2000
1	Libya	110.5	105.2	114.6	20.8	86.0	104.8	2.9	14.6	48.4
2	Lebanon	121.4	120.3	102.5	41.5	72.9	75.5	21.0	29.0	42.3
3	Kyrgyzstan	na	111.1	101.4	na	100.1	85.6	na	14.3	41.1
4	Uzbekistan	na	81.4	102.6	na	99.4	98.6	na	30.4	37.4
5	Egypt	67.6	93.8	96.6	28.4	76.2	85.3	6.9	15.8	36.7
6	Kazakhstan	na	87.3	97.0	na	98.0	88.9	na	40.1	33.2
7	Jordan	72.0	70.9	97.0	32.8	44.6	86.1	2.1	16.1	27.5
8	Malaysia	88.7	93.7	96.9	34.2	56.3	69.3	na	7.3	26.3
9	Qatar	96.2	97.3	106.2	36.3	80.7	88.7	na	27.0	23.8
10	Turkey	107.5	99.1	91.9	26.0	47.3	73.3	5.0	13.1	23.8
11	Azerbaijan	na	113.7	92.9	na	89.9	79.7	na	24.2	22.7
12	Saudi Arabia	45.3	73.3	68.3	12.1	44.0	68.7	1.6	11.6	22.1
13	Tunisia	100.4	113.3	112.9	22.7	44.9	77.6	2.6	8.5	21.3
14	Kuwait	88.1	60.2	93.7	63.4	42.9	88.4	4.0	na	20.9
15	Bahrain	98.4	110.0	98.3	51.3	99.7	94.7	1.4	17.7	20.7
16	Iran	72.8	112.2	93.0	27.1	55.2	82.4	2.9	10.0	20.2
17	Turkmenistan	na	91.3	109.0	na	107.5	112.0	na	21.7	19.5
18	Algeria	76.1	100.2	107.4	11.2	60.8	68.4	1.8	11.4	15.1
19	Albania	105.6	100.2	106.6	34.9	78.3	78.4	14.1	6.9	15.1
20	Indonesia	80.0	115.2	109.7	16.1	44.0	56.8	2.5	9.2	14.4
21	Tajikistan	na	91.0	104.3	na	102.1	78.5	na	22.1	14.0
22	Iraq	68.8	111.3	98.8	24.4	47.0	38.3	4.8	12.6	13.5
23	Yemen	na	58.3	79.2	na	58.0	46.3	na	4.1	10.5
24	Morocco	51.5	66.9	101.2	12.6	35.3	40.9	1.4	10.6	10.3
25	UAE	94.6	104.3	90.6	21.8	67.0	80.4	na	9.2	10.2
26	Oman	na	86.1	84.3	na	45.7	76.5	na	4.1	7.5
27	Sudan	37.9	52.8	58.2	7.4	24.0	31.8	1.1	3.0	6.8
28	Cote d'Ivoire	58.8	67.1	77.9	9.1	22.0	22.8	1.0	3.2	6.7
29	Bangladesh	54.3	71.6	98.9	na	19.0	46.1	1.9	4.2	6.4
30	Syria	77.5	108.4	108.6	38.1	51.9	42.8	8.3	18.2	5.7
31	Nigeria	43.7	91.4	96.5	5.2	24.9	30.3	0.5	4.2	4.0
32	Senegal	38.8	58.9	74.1	9.3	16.2	17.3	1.4	3.2	3.7
33	Pakistan	35.8	60.7	73.2	12.8	22.7	25.8	1.8	2.9	3.5
34	Mauritania	14.6	48.7	85.4	2.1	13.7	21.6	na	2.8	3.5
35	Somalia	8.0	10.5	9.6	3.7	6.4	5.7	0.3	2.9	2.5
36	Sierra Leone	34.8	50.2	78.9	9.0	17.3	16.5	0.5	1.3	2.1
37	Afghanistan	26.9	27.0	15.1	7.5	8.9	12.5	0.6	1.8	1.9
38	The Gambia	24.8	63.9	78.9	8.2	18.8	34.3	na	na	1.9
39	Mali	23.2	26.5	54.0	4.9	7.0	13.6	0.2	0.6	1.8
40	Ethiopia	14.4	32.7	60.5	3.6	14.2	17.0	0.2	0.8	1.5
41	Niger	13.3	28.8	35.8	1.1	6.6	6.5	na	0.7	1.5
42	Guinea	31.2	37.1	67.0	12.4	10.0	13.9	0.6	1.1	1.3
43	Burkina F.	12.2	33.3	43.6	1.4	7.2	10.2	0.0	0.7	0.9
44	Chad	34.7	54.4	73.4	2.0	7.8	11.5	na	0.8	0.9
45	Guinea-Bissau	40.1	55.7	69.7	8.2	9.3	17.8	na	0.6	0.4
Low income		66.0	88.5	93.5	17.6	35.4	45.6	3.1	5.4	9.6
Middle income		94.0	113.6	111.4	27.3	56.5	75.3	3.9	13.1	22.0
High income		99.8	102.7	101.9	75.0	93.8	106.0	26.2	47.4	61.1

In 1970 at the primary education level only 66% of children in the relevant age cohort enrolled in schools in the low-income group, shown at the bottom of Table 7.4; they were almost fully enrolled in the middle-and high-income groups (94.0% and 99.8%). In 2000, 93.5% of children in the relevant age cohort attended primary schools in the low-income group and this enrollment ratio was about equal to the 1970 enrollment ratio for the middle-income group (94.0%). This evidences significant improvement in primary education across the world during 1970–2000. However, 14 Muslim countries at the bottom of Table 7.4 — from Senegal (number 32) to Guinea-Bissau (number 45) — exhibited significantly lower enrollment ratios than the low income group for all three years. Besides these 14, Saudi Arabia (number 12), Yemen (number 23), Oman (number 28), Sudan (number 27) and Cote d'lvoire (number 28) also exhibited lower enrollment ratios than the low-income group.

As of 2000, only 9.6% of Somalia (number 35) children aged 6–11 were enrolled in elementary schools. Only 15.1% of Afghan (No. 37) children and 35.8% of Niger's (No. 41) children were enrolled in primary education. However, significant progress in primary education was made by Egypt (No. 5), Jordan (No. 7), Iran (No. 16), Algeria (No. 18), Indonesia (No. 20), Iraq (No. 22), Morocco (No. 24), Bangladesh (No. 29), Syria (No. 30) and Nigeria (No. 31), each with the primary enrollment ratios rising from less than 80% in 1970 to around 95% in 2000.

At the secondary education level, shown at the bottom of Table 7.4, the enrollment ratio rose from 17.6% in 1970 to 45.6% in 2000 for the low-income group, from 27.3% to 75.3% for the middle-income group, and from 75.0% to 106.0% for the high-income group. The bottom 15 Muslim nations in Table 7.4 from Nigeria (No. 31) to Guinea-Bissau (No. 45) plus Cote d'lvoire (No. 28), Sudan (No. 27) and Morocco (No. 24) all experienced lower secondary education enrollment ratios than the average for the low-income group of countries for all three years, 1970, 1990 and 2000.

The top 26 Muslim countries, from Libya (No. 1) to Oman (No. 26), in Table 7.4, showed large improvements in secondary education. In some cases their enrollment ratios doubled or tripled during 1970–2000. Many of them showed secondary school enrollment ratios exceeding the counterpart for the middle-income group in 2000 (75.3%). For instance, Egypt's (No. 5) secondary enrollment ratio rose from 28.4% in 1970 to 85.3% in 2000 while Qatar's (No. 9) secondary enrollment ratio increased from 36.3% in 1970 to 88.7% in 2000. In 2000, the secondary enrollment ratios for some middle-income Muslim countries were still below the counterpart for the middle-income group of the world (75.3%). These countries include Malaysia (No. 8), Turkey (No. 10), Saudi Arabia (No. 12), Algeria (No. 18), Indonesia (No. 20), Iraq (No. 22), Yemen (No. 23) and Morocco (No. 24).

Progress in secondary education occurred in most Muslim countries during 1970–1990. An exception is Kuwait (No. 14). Kuwait's secondary enrollment ratio reduced from 63.4% in 1970 to 42.9% in 1990 probably due to Iraq's invasion in 1990. During 1990–2000, declines in secondary education enrollment ratios are observed for some former Soviet republics like Kyrgyzstan (No. 3) (from 100.1% to 85.6%), Kazakhstan (No. 6) (from 98.0% to 88.9%) and Azerbaijan (No. 11) (from 89.9% to 79.7%). Nevertheless, these former Soviet republics exhibit relatively high enrollment ratios in all three levels of education. During 1990–2000, Iraq (No. 22), Yemen (No. 23) and Syria (No. 30) also showed significant decreases in enrollment ratios of secondary education: from 47.0% to 38.3% for Iraq, from 58.0% to 46.3% for Yemen, and from 51.9% to 42.8% for Syria.

At the level of higher education, great progress was made by the high-income group of countries, as shown at the bottom of Table 7.4, with their tertiary school enrollment ratios rising from 26.2% in 1970 to 61.1% in 2000. Significant progress was also made by the middle-income and low-income groups with their ratios increasing from 3.9% to 22.0% and from 3.1% to 9.6% respectively. In 1970, a relatively high tertiary enrollment ratio was exhibited by a few Muslim countries such as Lebanon (No. 2), (21.0%), Albania (No. 19), (14.1%) and Syria (No. 30), (8.3%). In 2000, however, the top 12 Muslim nations from Libya to Saudi Arabia in Table 7.4 exhibited rising tertiary enrollment ratios and these ratios exceeded the middle-income group in 2000 (22.0%).

In 2000, the four high-income Muslim countries — Qatar (No. 9), Kuwait (No. 14), Bahrain (No. 15) and United Arab Emirates (No. 25) — showed much lower tertiary education enrollment ratios (23.8%, 20.9%, 20.7% and 10.2%) than the high-income group (61.1%). The eight Muslim countries in the upper part of Table 7.4 exhibit declining tertiary education enrollment ratios. These countries include Kazakhstan (No. 6), (from 40.1% to 33.2%), Qatar (No.9), (from 27.0% to 23.8%), Azerbaijan (No. 11), (from 24.2% to 22.7%), Turkmenistan (No. 17), (from 21.7% to 19.5%), Tajikistan (No. 21), (from 22.1% to 14.0%), Morocco (No. 24), (from 10.6% to 10.3%), Syria (No. 30), (from 18.2% to 5.7%) and Nigeria (No. 31) (from 4.2% to 4.0%).

Tertiary enrollment ratios of the bottom 20 Muslim nations from Oman (No. 26) to Guinea-Bissau (No. 45) in Table 7.4 were still below the low-income group of countries (9.6%). The bottom 10 Muslim countries include the 9 sub Sahara African countries plus Afghanistan. Tertiary enrollment ratios of these 10 Muslim countries were less than 2.5% in 2000 which is a very poor showing even though they increased from less than 1% in 1970.

From Table 7.4 one can observe the following pattern: During the last three decades (1970–2000) significant progress in primary education was made by almost all 45 Muslim countries, except for Somalia (No. 35) and Afghanistan (No. 37). Major improvements in secondary education occurred in the top 26 countries, plus Bangladesh (No. 29) and minus Iraq (No. 22). A large gap in secondary education exists between sub Sahara African countries and the other Muslim countries with sub Sahara Africa falling further behind. With few exceptions (Lebanon (No. 2) and Albania (No. 19)), Muslim countries had very low tertiary education enrollments in 1970. This situation improved in 2000 for the top 16 Muslim countries, from Libya (No. 1) to Iran (No. 16) in Table 7.4, but remained very low in the Muslim countries of sub Sahara Africa and in Pakistan (No. 33), (3.5%).

Overall, many Muslim countries continue to fall behind their peer income groups in tertiary education. In today's world, higher education has become ever more important. Higher education is central to science and technology development. It is necessary for creation, dissemination and implementation of advanced knowledge. Without higher education, no nation can advance its technical and professional capacities any more and the shortfall in tertiary education of many Muslim countries will have long-term impacts on their relative economic growth and social development.

7.3. Fragmentation of Muslim Education System

Education in the Muslim world is fragmented into two parallel systems: a system of religious and a system of secular education. These two systems are further divided into a variety of sectarian, philosophical and geographic differences and affiliations. There is no single uniform and harmonious system of education at the national level in most of the Muslim-majority countries. Their education systems are fragmented into various strata, groups and sects of the Muslim societies in which they occur. The Muslim education system resembles a mirror that reflects not only the current social and political fragmentation of the Muslim societies but also inherited legacies from the Islamic Empires, the colonial age and the Post-Colonial struggles. As Nazeer Ahmed states in his article, *Modern Issues in Islamic Education*,

> ... At the outset, a clarification in terminology must be made, and a differentiation established between maktab, madrasa and jami. A maktab is any school, whether it is secular or religious. Every child who attends school goes to a "maktab". A madrasa is usually a religious school in which Arabic is taught as part of a religious curriculum. A jami is a university in which advanced religious studies are pursued and graduate degrees are granted.[9]

The following section provides a brief description of the madrasa[10] system of religious education in the Muslim world.

---

[9] Nazeer Ahmed is the Director of the American Institute of Islamic History and Culture. His article "*Modern Issues in Islamic Education*" is posted by Islamic Research Foundation International, Inc. in the website: http://www.irfi.org.

[10] Madrasa, also madrassah, is a group of buildings used for teaching Islamic theology and religious law, typically in a mosque.

7.3.1. Religious Education — the Madrasa System

Originally there was no secular splitting off of religious matters in terms of culture and education in Muslim societies. The Islamic faith is not only a religion, but also a unified way of life (both religious and secular) at all levels of individual, community, society and national activities. There is no official authority who decides whether a person is to be accepted or dismissed from the community of believers or the Ummah (the Muslim community). Islam is open to all, regardless of race, age, gender, or previous beliefs. It only requires a Muslim to believe in the central beliefs of Islam and to perform five main duties described as (1) recital of the Creed: "There is no god but God and Muhammad is the Prophet of God". (2) Prayer, (3) fasting, (4) almsgiving, and (5) a pilgrimage to the Kaba at Mecca in Saudi Arabia. These are the "Five Pillars" of Islam. It is a personal responsibility for every Muslim to know the principles and fundamentals of Islam in order to practice them properly in his/her everyday life. Every Muslim must therefore get some basic religious education during their formative years through schools, seminaries and mosques.

In the older traditional societies, governments did not supply education services and religious establishments ran the educational system. The word 'madrasa' means school in the Arabic language as well as other languages of Muslim nations such as Persian, Turkish, and Indonesian. The Islamic madrasa refers to an Islamic religious school for Muslims in a manner analogous to the parochial schools for Catholics in the western world. In older days, the madrasa was a mosque-based religious school similar to the bible schools attached to churches in the western world. Madrasas now have the purpose of teaching Muslim children about Islam as well as providing a general education. No reliable statistics exist on the number of madrasas in the Muslim world. According to some media estimates, however, about forty thousand madrasas have blossomed in Pakistan, and tens of thousands in Indonesia, Bangladesh, and India.

> At independence in 1947, there were only 137 Madrasas in Pakistan. According to a 1956 survey, there were 244 Madrasas in all of West Pakistan (present-day Pakistan). Since then, even by official accounts, their number has doubled every ten years. It is speculated there are presently around 47 000, but nobody is sure how many actually exist.[11]

As the ICG[12] Asia Report No. 36, 29 July 2002 indicates,

---

[11] *Pakistan's Madrasahs: Consequences for Democracy and Free Society: Some Public Policy Options*, International Policy Fellowship-2004-OSI, Proposal, Dr. Syed Tauqir Hussain Shah (Pakistan).

[12] ICG stands for the International Crisis Group, an independent, non-profit, multinational organization, with its headquarter in Brussels and over 100 staff members on five continents. Based on information and assessments from field analyses, ICG produces regular reports and recommendations targeted at key international decision-makers.

> Madrasas provide free religious education, boarding and lodging and are essentially schools for poor. About a third of all children in Pakistan in education attend madrasas.[13]
> ... Nobody is sure how many madrasas actually exist. (The ministry of education in 1995 estimated the figure at 3 906, which increased to 7 000 in 2000.) Pakistan's minister for religious affairs, Dr. Mahmood Ahmed Ghazi, puts the figure at 10 000, though he acknowledges the problem of definition and suspects it could be higher, with as many as one million to 1.7 million students attending classes as least for short periods....[14]
> All that said, madrasas do serve many useful functions for about a third of all children in education....[15]

This assessment of a high and increasing enrollment in Pakistani madrasas has recently been challenged by researchers from the World Bank, Pomona College and Harvard University. Their paper, *Religious School Enrollment in Pakistan: A Look at the Data*,[16] uses published data sources and a census of schooling choices to show that the above estimates of Pakistani students enrolled in madrasas is inflated by an order of magnitude. We quote from their report as follows:

> These data sources show that around 200 000 children were enrolled full-time in madrasas before 2001. Since 2001, our school census suggests that these numbers may have increased somewhat, although the experience varies across districts. To put this number in context, total primary enrollment (grades 1–5) in public and private schools stood at 17.4 million in 2003. (Government of Pakistan, Ministry of Finance, 2003.) The choice of madrasa schooling viewed as either the percentage of eligible children or the percentage of enrolled children, is statistically insignificant for the average Pakistani household. Enrollment in madrasas accounts for approximately 0.3 percent of all children between the ages of 5 and 19. Given that the overall enrollment rate for this age group is roughly 42 percent, this represents less than 0.7 percent of all enrolled children, an order of magnitude less than the 33 percent cited by the International Crisis Group report (2002).[17]

According to the authors of the above cited report, madrasas are most popular in the Pashtun belt of Pakistan bordering Afghanistan. The biggest jump in madrasa

---

[13] *Pakistan: Madrasas, Extremism and the Military*, Executive Summary and Recommendations ICG Asia Report No. 36, 29 July 2002, page i.

[14] *Pakistan: Madrasas, Extremism and the Military*, Executive Summary and Recommendations ICG Asia Report No. 36, 29 July 2002, p. 2.

[15] *Pakistan: Madrasas, Extremism and the Military*, Executive Summary and Recommendations ICG Asia Report No. 36, 29 July 2002, p. 3.

[16] Tahir Andrabi, Jishnu Das, Asim Ijaz Khwaja and Tristan Zajonc, "*Religious School Enrollment in Pakistan: A Look at the Data*", Faculty Research Working Papers Series, RWP05-024, John F. Kennedy School of Government, Harvard University, March 2005.

[17] Tahir Andrabi, Jishnu Das, Asim Ijaz Khwaja and Tristan Zajonc, "*Religious School Enrollment in Pakistan: A Look at the Data*", Faculty Research Working Papers Series, RWP05-024, John F. Kennedy School of Government, Harvard University, March 2005, p. 4.

enrollment is for the cohort born between 1979 and 1983. This corresponds to those children who would start attending school around the years of the Soviet invasion of Afghanistan. Their estimate of lower madrasa enrollment indicates a changed educational landscape of Pakistan over the last decade. Their substantially lower estimate of madrasa enrollment is explained by the authors as due to an explosion of private schools that have become an important choice for Pakistani households in the 1990s. The huge gap between estimates of Pakistani madrasa enrollment may reflect unreliability of Pakistan government information about their educational system and its evolution over time. As these authors point out,

> ... Given the spatial and temporal patterns of overall madrasa enrollment we found, and the very small percentage of children enrolled in madrasas, the only reliable way to capture such enrollment and the correlates of madrasa use is with very large-scale surveys, perhaps even censuses, in a representative sample of villages throughout the country. This would be a costly affair.[18]

Madrasas teach Muslim children reading and writing in the local language and introduce them to elementary Arabic in order to facilitate memorization of the Holy Quran and Hadith.[19] In some areas, such as Afghanistan, madrasas are the sole means of education for children, and have made the difference between literacy and illiteracy of their populations. As we showed in the previous section of this chapter, in many poor Muslim countries governments do not spend much money on education, and poor Muslim families cannot afford the cost of a secular education at private schools. They bring their children to the madrasa to get at least an elementary education in the religious disciplines. Many students, however, quit the madrasa and enter the work force as teenagers to support their family. A great majority of madrasas are poor and located in rural areas, but some are well endowed with land and money contributed by local landlords and businessmen; some have received foreign donations from Saudi Arabia for building school infrastructure at the cost of changing their teaching instructions into the Saudi version of Islam. Many of the madrasas even offer free education, boarding and lodging for orphans and the destitute as an important part of social welfare for the poor Muslims that governments do not support.

As a matter of fact, many non-Muslim nations of the world consider literates as people who complete education of at least the primary level. In Muslim society, moreover, a person who can read and write is considered to be literate. If the non-Muslim standard were applied to Muslim nations, the illiteracy rates we reported

---

[18] Tahir Andrabi, Jishnu Das, Asim Ijaz Khwaja and Tristan Zajonc, "*Religious School Enrollment in Pakistan: A Look at the Data*", Faculty Research Working Papers Series, RWP05-024, John F. Kennedy School of Government, Harvard University, March 2005, p. 23.

[19] Quran (or Koran), the sacred text of Islam, is considered by Muslims to contain the revelations of God to Muhammad. Hadith is a collection of the sayings or actions of Muhammad or his companions.

earlier would have been much higher because many students of madrasas do not receive a standard knowledge from elementary education except for reading, writing and recalling the Holy Quran.

A traditional madrasa system separates males and females into different classes to teach them Islamic studies in different contexts. It typically offers two kinds of courses of study that correspond to madrasas' two functions: elementary Islamic education and restructuring of character. The courses of elementary Islamic education are for teaching Muslim children to memorize the Quran and to become a "Hafiz". The term "Hafiz" is used for those Muslims who have completely memorized the Holy Quran. The title "Hafiz" is certified only to those Muslims who are tested for the accuracy of their recall by being asked to continue the reading of a passage taken randomly from the Quran. Currently, the number of Hafiz in the world is estimated to be more than ten million. Muslim countries often hold competitions of Holy Quran recitations; an Iranian boy came first in a recent recitation competition held in Saudi Arabia, and was said to become Hafiz at age six.[20]

The second kinds of courses are for teaching Muslim children and youths to become a scholar or mullah (mullah is a male Muslim teacher, or leader, or the head of a mosque), who is trained in the doctrine and law of Islam. To become a mullah requires more than twelve years of studying the Islamic tradition and law and this is done under very strict and harsh disciplines. The second function of madrasas, namely the molding of character, is what distinguishes a religious school from a secular school. Whether a graduate of a madrasa becomes an extremist or Islamist depends on the molding process that the head and teachers of a madrasa imparts to a student.

A regular curriculum of madrasas includes Arabic language, memorization and interpretation of the Holy Quran, Islamic law, Hadith, and the history of Islam, without teaching modem topics such as mathematics, science and technology. The Hadith (Arabic for "report") is a body of legends and stories about the Prophet Muhammad's way of life, which contains narrations of the Prophet's sayings, deeds, and actions of his approved companions. For most Muslims in the world, the Hadith is an authoritative exposition of the meaning of the Quran, and Islamic law is derived from the acts, statements, opinions, and ways of life of the Prophet Mohammad. The Hadith, however, was handed down orally in the Arab society until the mid 700s. After that point, collections of Hadith were written, edited and corrected, and some texts later found to be fallacious were discarded. Over time many Hadith collections were developed, covering topics such as belief, prayer, fasting, marriage, laws, etc., with regard to different social, religious and political considerations.

---

[20] *Unique Hafiz-e-Quran boy fascinates reception*, staff report, Daily Times of Pakistan, November 10, 2003, http://www.dailytimes.com.pk.

By the 9th century, six collections of Hadith were accepted as reliable. Only two of them are now said to be authentic. The other four collections are referred to as Sunnah (the Arabic word Sunnah means "the way of the Prophet" or Prophet's traditions). These four do not have a claim to authenticity but nevertheless provide judgments on the degree of authenticity of the Hadiths — such as authentic, acceptable, rare, weak, etc. Sunnah includes the deeds, sayings and approvals of Muhammad. Whatever Muhammad said, did, or approved of as the Prophet and Messenger of Allah is considered a Sunnah — which Muslims are to follow. For Muslims, the Qur'an is considered as the only authentic revelation of Allah to humanity and the authentic source of Islamic law, and the Sunnah is considered to be the second source of Islamic law after the Qur'an. All collections of the Hadiths are considered to be divine directives for Muslims worldwide. Together these are supposed to constitute a moral example for Muslims to study, discuss, and emulate. They are also considered as essential teaching materials in madrasas across the Muslim world.

Except for Saudi Arabia, Islamic madrasas are sectarian, privately-run, not supported by public finance, and not supervised or accredited by the Education Department of state governments. They are generally of poor or inadequate quality. In many Muslim countries, the Islamic madrasas have neither a uniform curriculum nor a standard of educational performance. The madrasas in these countries are as diverse as various denominations of Islamic religion, and as distinct as many different schools of Islamic thought, as well as depending on the background and training of their operators and teachers. A madrasa of Sunni sect of Islam is very different from a Shia sect, and the Egyptian strain of Sunni Islamic madrasas differs from the Saudi Arabian type. The religious and doctrinal differences of these schools are generally irreconcilable. Based on sectarian identities, madrasas are mutually exclusive, aiming to promote a particular sect and to reject the others. "In the foundations of the traditional madrasa are the seeds of factional, political, religious, and cultural conflict".[21]

Political struggles in the Muslim world have had a great impact on the madrasa system. Many local religious leaders push their own political agendas by preaching distorted Islamic principles and promoting hatred toward Jews and Christians. Some Islamic mosques and madrasas have become breeding grounds for religious intolerance and abhorrence. Saudi Arabia provides a typical example to illustrate the Islamic religious education. In December 2002, the Middle East Media Research Institute (MEMRI[22]) released a special report on Saudi Arabia's education

[21] *Pakistan: Madrasas, Extremism and the Military*, ICG Asia Report No. 36, 29 July 2002.
[22] The MEMRI was founded in 1998 to inform the debate over US policy in the Middle East. It is an independent, non-partisan and nonprofit organization, with headquarters in Washington, DC, and branch offices in Berlin, London, and Jerusalem. MEMRI research is translated into English, German, Hebrew, Italian, French, Spanish, Turkish, and Russian.

system.[23]. That report provides an overview of Saudi Arabia's official position on education policy and Saudi school curricula. It reports that the contemporary Saudi education policy aims at promoting Wahhabism, which dates back to the 18th century. Its founder, Muhammad ibn abd al-Wahhab, taught that absolutely every idea added to Islam after the third century of the Muslim era (about 950 AC) was false and must be expunged with a strict interpretation of Islam. The Saudi types of Islamic schools have a common curriculum primarily based upon the teachings of Wahhab, calling for the return of Muslims to the fundamentals of Islam as preached by the Prophet Muhammad.

The special report by MEMRI also provides some translations from Saudi schoolbooks. A textbook for the 8th grade students interprets a Hadith of the conversation between the Prophet and a companion as "the most important activity is Jihad (a holy war) for the sake of Allah and the convocation of Allah's religion on this earth". A textbook explains that Jews and Christians have sinned by accepting polytheism and therefore incurred Allah's wrath. To punish them, Allah has turned them into apes and pigs. In a schoolbook for the 9th grade, the Hadiths of ancient stories about the Prophet and his companions are always accompanied by a number of statements with contemporary contexts, such as "It is Allah's wisdom that the struggle between Muslims and Jews shall continue until the Day of Judgment". "The Jews and the Christians are the enemies of the believers. They will not be favorably disposed toward Muslims and it is necessary to be cautious in dealing with them". Saudi religious school curricula and courses are full of such texts inciting hatred toward not only other religions but also other Muslim sects. Those kinds of teaching and instruction are imparted to numerous Saudi youths and disseminated to other Muslim teenagers in many Saudi supported madrasas across the Muslim world. This has promoted anti-Western religious fanaticism and a resurgence of Islamic militants around the globe, which is especially attractive to the increasing proportion of the "troublesome" population cohort that we discussed in Chapter 5.

Madrasas in Pakistan played an important role in the Afghan War against the former Soviet Union and in helping the development of Bin Ladin's international terrorist network, al-Qaeda. The late dictator of Pakistan, General Zia ul-Haq, initiated a program directed to building several thousand madrasas along areas bordering Soviet-occupied Afghanistan and used them as an ideological barrier against the threat of Soviet expansion. Taking advantage of the US–Pakistani–Saudi entente to drive the Soviets out of Afghanistan, the Saudi clergy and wealthy Saudis poured some $300 million a year into this program. Hundreds of thousands of young Muslim men from some thirty countries were molded by the teaching of Wahhabi that we will discuss in the next section in those Pakistani madrasas

[23] www.memri.org/release *MEMRI Special Report — Saudi Arabia*, December 20, 2002, No. 12 by Steven Stalinsky

and became extremists. Many also went to al-Qaeda camps in Afghanistan for military training and actively joined in fighting the Soviets.

The Pakistani madrasas were also a spawning ground for a resurgent Taliban in Afghanistan. The leaders of the Taliban regime migrated into Pakistan with millions of other Afghans after the Soviet invasion. Most of those leaders were graduates from Pakistani madrasas. The madrasas in Afghan refugee camps received Saudi funds and scholarships. These religious schools supplied hundreds of thousands of Islamist militants to fight jihads in Afghanistan and the disputed territory of Kashmir.

Ever since the fall of the Taliban regime by the end of 2001, Pakistani madrasas have continued churnning out Jihadi-prone Muslim male teenagers, with hateful views of the western world, particularly America, Israel and also India. They continue to support al-Qaeda and Taliban remnants in Pakistan.

An immense impact of Pakistani religious education on the domestic political scene has also emerged. For the first time in the country's history, an alliance of six major religious parties won power in two provinces in the October 2002 elections, vowing to Islamize state and society through Taliban-like policies and targeting President Pervez Musharraf for his pro-US policies. We quote from "*Pakistan's Madrasahs: Consequences for Democracy and Free Society*" by Syed Tauqir Hussain Shah,

> A practical manifestation of how Madrasas education in Pakistan is influencing the larger society is the sweeping election victory of religious extremists in 2002 general elections. Recent political developments in Pakistan are expected to have immense impact on democratic policy. The fact that approximately 60 (25%) of newly elected parliamentarians are either Madrasa graduates or managers (this ratio in the Senate is 35%). The Chief Minister and the cabinet in NWFP[24] belong to religious parties dominated by Madrasa graduates. In Baluchistan nine Ministers are Madrasa graduates and were actually managing Madrasas before being elected to Public office. This has serious implications for free debate, political dissent, secular thought, civil society and minority and women's rights in Pakistan.[25]

In January, 2002, Pakistani President Pervez Musharraf admitted that the madrasas had become breeding grounds for intolerance, hatred and militancy. The President also strongly criticized the country's Islamic leaders for misleading Pakistanis and turning mosques into breeding grounds of sectarian violence. He outlined a new madrasas strategy that would put several government regulations into the religious schools and mosques. It required that madrasas must be registered and must reform their curriculum to include English, Pakistan studies

[24] NWFP means the Northwest Frontier Province, bordering on Afghanistan.

[25] This quotation is from "*Pakistan's Madrasahs: Consequences for Democracy and Free Society: Some Public Policy Options*", International Policy Fellowship-2004-OSI, Proposal, Dr. Syed Tauqir Hussain Shah (Pakistan).

and science and technology to enable their students to enter universities and compete for jobs. In the face of stiff political resistance, this reform of the madrasas has been ineffectual. According to media reports, as of June, 2003, out of about 8 000 madrasas, only 1 000 have registered and the remaining 7 000 have refused. Recognizing the importance of the troubled Pakistani education system, the United States announced a donation, in 2003, of $US 100 million over five years to support the reform of Pakistan's education system, including reforming religious schools. Despite their many problems, madrasas still provide a useful service in teaching poor Pakistani children how to read and write, and they occupy a key place in Pakistan's religious and social life.

7.3.2. Islamic Education of Saudi Arabia

Since the oil crises of the 1970s, rapidly increasing oil prices in global markets has made Saudi oil revenues available, that can enable the Kingdom of Saudi Arabia to fulfill its ambitions of spreading the Wahhabi vision of Islam to every corner of the world. In fact, for the last two decades the Kingdom has been engaged in an extensive effort to promote Islamic fundamentalism by creating, financing and supporting numerous mosques, Islamic centers and schools in many Muslim-majority nations as well as non-Muslim nations throughout the world A weekly news magazine, Ain-Al-Yaqeen, published online by the Saudi royal family, reported in its 03/01/2002 issue[26] that "as the Custodian of the Two Holy Mosques,[27] the Saudi King Fahd Ibn Abdul Aziz has directed many billions of US dollars to financing Islamic institutions worldwide".

According to this 2002 report, the Islamic institutions, wholly or partly financed by Saudi money, include some 210 Islamic centers, more than 1 500 mosques, 202 colleges and almost 2 000 schools all over the world. The Saudi Kingdom has supported and fully financed mosques and Islamic centers in many African nations such as Mali, Nigeria, Tunisia, Ghana, Chad, Cameroon, Sudan, Somalia, Gabon, Burkina Faso, Tanzania, and Senegal. A Saudi-built modern mosque or Islamic center usually comprises a large mosque, a library, a school, a lecture hall and housing, costing millions of dollars to build. This structure is usually considered to be the largest and the most beautiful mosque in each of these African nations. Saudi Arabia has also built 10 mosques in Egypt, which, together, can simultaneously accommodate approximately one million worshipers. Saudi Arabia has established and supported a large number of mosques and Islamic centers in Pakistan, Maldives, Indonesia, Japan and South Korea, as well as the Taiwan

---

[26] http://www.ain-al-yaqeen.com/archives2.htm, The issue May 1, 2002 in Archives.

[27] Custodian of the Two Holy Mosques is a title given to the King of Saudi Arabia. After the abolition of the Islamic Caliphate, the title was created to give legitimacy to the King as a protector of the two holy cities of Mecca and Medina, which had traditionally been the role of the Caliph.

province of China. It has given support to Islamic institutions in Australia (the State of Victoria, and Queensland), New Zealand, the Isles of Fiji and other parts of the eastern world.

The Kingdom of Saudi Arabia has vigorously spread Islamic fundamentalism by building mosques, schools and Islamic centers not only in the eastern world but in the western world. Saudi Arabia has also given support to many Islamic organizations and mosques in the world The Ain-Al-Yaqeen report (see note 18) has listed Saudi-supported Mosques and Islamic centers in the states of California, Missouri, Michigan, New Jersey, New York, Maryland, Ohio and Virginia, and in the cities of Washington D.C., Chicago and Los Angeles. Saudi Arabia has also donated millions of US dollars to support Mosques and Islamic centers in Toronto and Quebec in Canada. The Kingdom has supported and contributed to the establishment of many Mosques and Islamic centers in Europe, including Brussels in Belgium, Geneva in Switzerland, Madrid in Spain, London in England, Edinburgh in Scotland, Rome in Italy, Mont La Jolie in France, and in the Gibraltar territory of the UK. Many Saudi-contributed Mosques and Islamic centers in Europe have a very capacious Mosque, a prayer hall for women, a library, a school, a lecture hall and a medical clinic. The cost of the Mosque of the Custodian of the Two Holy Mosques in Gibraltar, for example, exceeded 30 million Saudi riyals (exchange rate was 3.745 Saudi riyals per US dollar in 2003), even though Gibraltar's Muslim population accounted for less than 7% of the 27.8-thousand total.

Saudi Arabia's efforts to build mosques and Islamic centers have reached afar into South America, in such cities as Brasilia, Sao Paulo, Santo Amaro, and Santos of Brazil, as well as the capital city of Buenos Aires in Argentina. Again Muslims represent very small portions of these populations where Roman Catholics account for 80% of the Brazilian population and 92% of the Argentine population. Besides many Saudi-built Mosques and Islamic centers across the world, the Kingdom of Saudi Arabia and King Fahd in person have donated a great deal of money to indigenous Mosques in France, Chad, Ghana, Senegal, Cameroon, Tanzania, Mali, Egypt, United States, and Britain. King Fahd also established a number of scholarships and academic chairs at some prominent Western universities and colleges, such as the University of California at Santa Barbara, the College of Law at Harvard University, University of London, and University of Moscow.

Saudi Arabia has established Islamic academic programs in major world capitals. These academies are institutes designed to provide Muslim children in the western world with opportunities to attend an institution of academic excellence and thus reinforce their commitment to Islamic religion, language and culture while at the same time communicating Muslim values and points of view to the societies in which they live. Among these academies is the Islamic Academy in Washington D.C. with 1 200 students at a cost of over 100 million Saudi riyals for a 10-year period, 1984–1994. The King Fahd Academy in London has 1 000 students who are Arab and Muslim children living in London and belong to 40 nationalities. King Fahd Academy in Moscow not only educates Muslim children in Islamic studies and Arab culture, but also aims to promote Islamic religion and culture among the Russian people. The King Fahd Academy in Bonn opened in 1995 at a cost of nearly 76 million Saudi riyals to build. It combines education in Islamic religion and culture with promoting Arab and Islamic culture in German society.

Among other extensive educational efforts by Saudi Arabia that are intended to promote Islamic fundamentalism, Saudi King Fahd in 2002 directed the distribution of 1 260 084 copies of the Holy Quran to pilgrims and governmental and private organizations outside the Saudi Arabia Kingdom. It has been reported that every pilgrim leaving the Kingdom had the right to obtain a copy of the Holy Book in any one of 14 different languages.

Those huge efforts are intended to match Saudi ambitions to spread Islam to every corner of the world. It is also a part of a Saudi propaganda effort to counteract the western world — particularly the Western media that has promoted negative images of Islamic religion and culture as being backwards and breeding terrorists. The Saudi educational campaign is intended to promote the Wahhabi brand of Islamic religion, and to demonstrate the contribution of Arab culture and Islam to the history of mankind and thus counteract a negative view in the western world about their religion and culture. Dr. Nazeer Ahmed, the Director of the American Institute of Islamic History and Culture in Concord, California, describes the linkage between the Saudi educational campaign and the surge of Islamic extremists around the globe in the following passage:

> Since the 1960s, the Saudis have made substantial investments into madrasas and masjids [mosques] around the globe. While the infusion of oil money did help in the construction of the much needed infrastructure, the price paid was the abandonment of the spiritual Islam that has grown over a thousand years and its replacement by a largely ritualistic, puritanical Islam emphasizing rigidity over flexibility, intolerant to the core, riding roughshod over history and culture alike. Dissent was not tolerated. Contempt for other religious traditions was openly expressed by word and in print. The result was the creation of a religious edifice without spirit, a body without soul. Into this spiritual vacuum, the extremists walked in, hoisting their political agendas, creating mayhem around the globe.[28]

The Saudi royal family, however, did not concede the linkage between al-Qaeda terrorism and Wahhabi missionaries engaged in teaching anti-Western religious fanaticism until May 2003 when Islamist terrorists bombed three housing compounds in Riyadh that killed 35 people. Another suicide attack against a Saudi housing compound took place in November 2003, killing 17 people. In response the Saudi government launched a massive crackdown against Islamist militants.

[28] *Why Do People Call Us Terrorists*? by Nazeer Ahmed, posted in the website of the IRFI (Islamic Research Foundation International, Inc.), http://www.irfi.org/articles/.

Saudi security and intelligence reported that almost 1 000 Saudi clerics are either linked to, or in sympathy with, al-Qaeda.[29] According to Pakistan's Daily Times, those clerics have been fired or banned from addressing worshipers after Friday prayers. The Kingdom has prohibited any reference to jihad in radio and television broadcasts. The Royal family is also drafting new regulations that would actually remove elements of Wahhabi doctrine as it is presently taught in mosques and schools. Crown Prince Abdullah, the leading reformist in the Saudi Kingdom, has told educators to avoid promoting extremist concepts within the school system and to stick to teaching the Muslim Holy book, Quran. Many people suspect, however, that there is little hope for change in the near future because Islamists still control the education of the country.

As previously noted, Islamic education emphasizes the humanities and Islamic studies at the expense of mathematics, science and technology. It relies on rote memorization rather than encouraging students to be creative and innovative in solving problems of the real world. The ancient Islamic education exposed students to a broad spectrum of disciplines. That tradition, however, has been discontinued since the colonial age. Professor Nazeer Ahmed[30] has made a comparison of today's syllabus with counterparts during the period of the Great Mogul Akbar (1543–1605 AD) — who was a descendant of Genghis Khan and succeeded in forging an Islamic empire in India that brought about a splendid period of political stability and religious tolerance. As Nazeer Ahmed states, the subjects taught in schools during the Akbar dynasty included Good Character, Arithmetic, Astronomy, History, Medicine, Public Good, Equality, Jurisprudence, Languages, Literature, Purification of the Heart, Planning, Goal Setting, Execution, Contemporary Politics, Religious Studies, Quran, Recitation, and Hadith. Today's madrasas teach much narrower topics in Arithmetic, Jurisprudence, Languages, Quran, Recitation and Hadith, and exclude modern science and technology almost entirely.

7.3.3. Two Education Systems

Since the early 17th century, the madrasas system was developed to train civil servants for Muslim rulers. That purpose and function of the Muslim religious schools was lost under the period of European colonial ruling, and the secular/religious dichotomy in the education system was imported into the Muslim nations from the western world. The colonial age (see Part III later in this book) resulted in a two-system educational setup in all Muslim-majority countries. This two-system approach is the focus of a debate today over the reform of Muslim educational systems.

---

[29] *Saudi mea culpa*, by Arnaud de Borchgrave, *The Washington Times*, July 16, 2003.
[30] *Modern Issues in Islamic Education — Part II*, by Professor Nazeer Ahmed, http://www.irfi.org/articles/.

The secular education system was bequeathed to the Muslim nations by the European colonial ruling. The foreign rulers established many secular schools in the occupied Muslim land that taught a non-Islamic curriculum. Some special schools, with English (usually) as the instruction medium and with special syllabi and facilities, were established for children and youths from families of indigenous lords, feudal leaders and the privileged. Christian missions were encouraged to set up schools in Muslim nations to attract intelligent students by imparting western cultural and religious training. These schools educated many moderate Muslims in local societies who formed a special class that tended to be loyal to the foreign rulers.

However, the Islamic religious educational system in Muslim nations, survived the foreign reigns and religious invasions. These religious educational divisions have become an important vehicle for the transfer of Islamic heritages to the next generation and meet the demands of the mass of Muslims who want to preserve their ancestral heritage, national solidarity and cultural heritage. Therefore, the Islamic religious education system, or the madrasa system, is deeply rooted in the religion, culture and society of the Muslim world.

When the Muslim world succumbed to the European occupation, western colonialists began to dismantle the traditional Islamic education systems and replace them with a public secular education system that served the ruling colonial administration. European languages (English, French or Dutch) were introduced into the public school system, and became the medium of instruction. Losing their land, power, and nation, Muslims developed a deep distrust of foreign occupiers, including the foreign languages, Western culture, philosophy, science, technology and even the mathematics that was associated with Europeans. Abandoning all subjects related to western modern science, philosophy and politics, madrasas became a narrow Islamic education in an effort to defend their religious practices and reject Western influences.

As a result of Islamic religious education, a graduate from the madrasa is expected to become a religious teacher who would start his own madrasa in some remote poor area or work for a mosque. He does not have modern knowledge or skills to work in other sectors of a modern society. Many Muslim young men become unemployable due to lack an understanding of the needs of modern society and lack of skills that are necessary to land a job other than as a religious teacher. The majority of poor Muslim children are dependent on madrasas for being able to read and write. At the end of their education, however, most of them become unemployed or underemployed. Instead of constituting human capital for their economy, these Muslim youths become a drag and a disturbing force in Muslim economies and societies. These under-educated or wrongly educated Muslim youths are vulnerable to becoming recruits for rebel political movements, religious sectarians, and international terrorism.

For perspective, we compare the current situation with the Islamic Golden Age (see Part III of this book), in which Greek philosophy found support by Arab

Caliphates (the early Islamic leaders regarded as successors of Muhammad). Religious tolerance was adopted as apolitical policy that allowed Islamic scholars to use works of conquered people in medicine, astronomy and mathematics as foundations on which to develop new fields like chemistry and algebra. Research, education and learning were widespread across the Islamic Empire, which promoted an Islamic civilization that achieved its apex. In fact, Christians in Europe used to travel to Muslim Spain to obtain higher education in medicine, mathematics, physics, chemistry, astronomy, etc. Later on, Islamic orthodoxy started rejecting Greek philosophy because it was believed incompatible with Islamic tenets. Religious tolerance was replaced by narrow-mindedness as the Islamic Golden Age came to an end.

Now Wahhabism and its likes have become pervasive throughout the Muslim world with an accompanying intolerance and militancy toward other sects of Islamic religion as well as other religions and civilizations in the world. Religious intolerance has not only destroyed the Islamic spirit of the Golden Age, it has also stifled scientific research and education in sharp contrast with the situation prevailing during the Islamic Golden Age. Only a few Muslim youths are studying science and technology in the universities of their own nations. Many highly educated Muslims have perforce been educated in western universities in order to obtain advanced or specialized knowledge in science, engineering and medicine.

Education is directly related to the development of science and technology as well as economic growth and social progress for all societies and nations in the modern world. In many Muslim nations, Islamic religion has replaced education in modern knowledge and skill. Rote recitation has replaced learning and inquiry, isolation has bred intolerance and blocked the flow of knowledge with the result that inadequately educated and unemployable youths have replaced needed human capital. As a consequence, many Muslim countries today occupy the low positions on the world ladder of development. We will deal with this issue in another book which deals with the economic transformation of these 49 Muslim-majority countries.

Summary of Chapter 7

This chapter provides an analysis of the intellectual quality of Muslim populations of the 49 Muslim-majority countries over the period of 1970–2000 with the following conclusions:

(1) Muslim countries exhibited higher illiteracy rates for male adults than the averages of world income groups with some exceptions, and their illiteracy rates for females were all above the averages of world income groups. The illiteracy rates of many of these 49 Muslim countries are high and do not match their income status in the world. There was an illiteracy gap between female and males, but this gap was much larger for the Muslim countries than for the averages of world income groups.

(2) In the 1970–2000 period, Muslim countries made significant reductions in the illiteracy rates for both male and female adults, but Muslim females were generally about 20 years behind Muslim males. The illiteracy of Muslim youngsters also improved significantly, but unevenly, with a larger gain in middle-income countries and a smaller gain in low-income countries. There is also a larger gain in Muslim males compared to Muslim females.

(3) The higher illiteracy of Muslim females has adverse effects on demographic transitions in the form of keeping total fertility rates high and accelerating population growth. Muslim women also bear a heavy responsibility to raise and educate their children. Being semi-illiterate and discriminated against, females become subordinate and under performing in Muslim countries. This wastes large amounts of human resources and affects the next generation of Muslims.

(4) There is the urgency of providing basic education for the rapidly increasing population of Muslim children in all these Muslim countries. However, only a very few relatively small, oil-rich, Muslim countries have adequate economic resources for their education systems. The great number of Muslim countries spend very little GNI per capita for the education needs. Chronic poverty keeps many Muslim countries trapped in a vicious cycle of lower education–lower quality of labor–lower productivity–lower GNI per capita–lower education and so on.

(5) In the 1970–2000 period, in terms of school enrollment, significant progress in primary education was made by almost all these Muslim countries. Major improvements in secondary education occurred in more than half these Muslim countries. Muslim countries had very low tertiary education enrollments in 1970 and this situation improved in 2000 for nearly one third these Muslim countries. Muslim countries in sub Sahara Africa fell behind in all three levels of education enrollments.

(6) Education in Muslim countries is fragmented into two parallel systems: religious and secular education. The madrasa system is for religious education popular throughout the Muslim world. In many Muslim countries, the Islamic madrasas have neither a uniform curriculum nor a standard of educational performance. They are generally of poor or inadequate quality, and are as diverse as various denominations of Islamic religion and different schools of Islamic thought. Political struggles in the Muslim world have also had a great impact on the madrasa system. Despite their many problems, madrasas still provide a useful service in teaching poor Muslim children how to read and write, and they occupy a key place in religious and social life in many Muslim countries.

(7) Saudi Arabia has played an important role in Islamic education worldwide. With its increasing oil revenues Saudi Arabia has attempted to build mosques and Islamic centers not only in the eastern world but in the western world in order to spread Islam to every corner of the world. However the Saudi educational campaign is intended to promote the Wahhabi brand of Islamic religion. Some observers believe that there is the linkage between the Saudi educational campaign and the surge of Islamic extremists around the globe.

Summary of Part II

In this, Part II of this book, we covered demographic transformations of the Muslim world in terms of population size, age structure and intellectual quality. Through detailed quantitative analyses of population changes in the 49 Muslim-majority countries over the last five decades, 1950–2000, and projections into the next five decades, we could observe the following:

(1) The total population of the 49 Muslim countries has grown much faster than the world population in the last five decades and will continue to do so in the next five decades. As of 2000, the total population of these Muslim countries reached 1287 million and accounted for 21.2% of the world population. It is projected to be about 2608 million and account for 29.2% of the world total by 2025. With such a large population percentage the Muslim world will become increasingly important in terms of its influence and impact on the world.

(2) During 1950–2000, the more rapid population expansions occurred in smaller Muslim countries in the Middle East such as UAE, Qatar, Kuwait, Jordan, Saudi Arabia, Bahrain, Oman and etc. For the next five decades, the fastest population growth is projected to occur in Niger, Yemen, Somali, Mali, Afghanistan, Oman, Ethiopia, Iraq, Saudi Arabia and Pakistan. In 2000 there were only four Muslim countries (Indonesia, Pakistan, Bangladesh and Nigeria) with population sizes greater than 100 million, but three more Muslim countries (Ethiopia, Egypt, and Iran) are projected to join them by 2050. Also important is that Pakistan is projected to replace Indonesia as the Muslim country with the largest population in the Muslim world by 2035.

(3) Changes in population size are determined by the "demographic transition" process with both death and birth rates declining throughout the world. In the Muslim world both rates declined substantially — from 20.7 to 12.1 per 1000 persons for death rates and from 46.3 to 28.5 per 1000 persons for birth rates over 1950–2000 — but they are still above the world average (12.1 vs. 8.9 for death rates and 28.5 vs. 21.5 for birth rates in 2000). The demographic transition started much later and proceeded much slower in the Muslim world than in other countries and will keep Muslim populations growing rapidly relative to other populations in the 21st century.

(4) Populations in Muslim countries also have a younger age structure with the cohort of children aged 0–14 accounting for 36.4% in 2005 versus 28.3% for the world average and 17.0% for high-income countries. Muslim countries will exercise great influence by virtue of their population age structure.

(5) The "troublesome cohort", a special population group of male youngsters aged 15–29, will increase more rapidly in the Muslim world. This cohort is associated with radical behavior, social violence and instability. Many Muslim countries

are projected to experience the largest relative percentage of the troublesome cohort in 2000–2050 so the probability for violent behavior and social instability in the Muslim world is likely to be fairly high, particularly for countries like Iran, Libya, Syria and Algeria in 2000–2010 and for Iraq, Pakistan and Sudan in 2000–2030, for Nigeria, Ethiopia, Afghanistan and Yemen in 2000–2050.

(6) Rapid urbanization is another demographic factor that will contribute to social instability in the Muslim world where urban population increased by 5.8 times and rural population increased by 1.9 times in 1960–2000. Swift urbanization generated many urban agglomerations or urban sprawls in the Muslim world which become fertile soil for the emergence of social problems and international terrorist activities.

(7) Illiteracy rates are the only indicator available to measure intellectual quality of Muslim populations. Significant reductions in illiteracy rates were achieved in many Muslim countries over 1970–2000, but the progress was uneven. The gap in illiteracy between males and females was substantially larger in Muslim countries than in other countries in the world.

(8) Education systems could have a long-term impact on the Muslim world but the capacity to meet escalating education needs of children is constrained by low economic wealth. Muslim countries in the Middle East have high GNI, but spend more income per capita on boosting their military power than on educating their children. Many low-income Muslim countries like Pakistan and Indonesia also spend more on the military than on education even though both expenditure numbers are miniscule. For instance, in the 1990 Pakistan had an average GNI per capita of $445, of which only $10.2 was spent for education and $26.8 was for military spending (Table 7.3).

(9) At the primary education level, many Muslim countries experienced lower enrollment rates than the low-income group of countries. However, significant progress was made by Egypt, Jordan, Iran, Algeria, and others, with enrollment rates rising to 95% in 2000. Progress in the secondary education level also occurred in all the Muslim countries, but with great discrepancies. Tertiary education improved greatly in the higher income Muslim countries in the Middle East and North Africa, but remained below the level of the low-income group of countries for Muslim countries in South Asia and sub-Sahara Africa.

(10) The traditional madrasa system plays an important role in teaching Muslim children about Islam and providing education. This system also performs an important role in social welfare for the poor in many Muslim countries. However, madrasas today have become sectarian and of poor quality. Many promote hatred toward other religions such as Christianity and Judaism as well as other Islamic sects. On the other hand, the colonial heritage has bestowed a secular education system on the Muslim countries. These two conflicting education systems further complicate education reform in many Muslim countries.

As the chapters in this Part II show, large impacts are to be expected from these demographic changes that will continue long into the 21st century.

We are not aware of any significant government programs or policies that are in place or under way to deal with the problems and opportunities that will come with these changes. A useful and effective program will need to take account of the preceding history of Muslim countries in a world that experienced the 19th and 20th century colonization, occupation and domination of these Muslim territories by Western countries. This history will be addressed in Part III of this book.

Part III

History and the Contemporary Scene

Introduction

As a worldwide community, the Muslim world covered in this book consists of a variety of nations with different nationalities and races, speaking different languages. It is Islam that links together all its believers and followers across the globe to form one religious community — the Muslim world. Islam is not only a set of religious beliefs and practices; it also represents a civilization that offers Islamic values and a model for good life and good society that Muslims believe they are religiously required to obey. The Islamic faith forms the basis for cultural and societal norms in Muslim countries.

Islam is one of the youngest and largest worldwide religions. It is about 1400 years old, compared with a 2000-year old Christianity and a 2600-year old Buddhism. The term "Islam" means literally "to submit to God"; its prime message is the unity of God, expressed by the Islamic Creed: "There is no god but God and Muhammad is the Prophet of God". The Islamic faith believes that the literal words of God were revealed to the Prophet through the Angel Gabriel, and are preserved in the Islamic holy book of Allah (Arabic for God), the Quran, where they serve as the rules governing civilization and ways of life. Believers and followers of Islam are called Muslims who submit to God and have five main duties to perform: (1) recital of the Creed, (2) prayer, (3) fasting, (4) almsgiving, and (5) a pilgrimage to the Kaba at Mecca in Saudi Arabia. These are the "Five Pillars" of Islam.

The influence of religion on state affairs and daily lives in Muslim countries is extensive and greater than that found in Western nations. According to religious doctrine this is because Christ accepted the separation between God and Caesar. Christ's kingdom is heavenly and seeks the reconciliation of the sinner to God, but civil governments are of this earth and seek power and supremacy. In contemporary Christianity, the spiritual is separated from the political, and the church is separated from the state. In Islam, however, religion emphasizes its totality.

> ... Islam is not merely a religion. It is a total and unified way of life, both religious and secular; it is a set of beliefs and a way of worship; it is a vast and integrated system of law; it is a culture and a civilization; it is an economic system and a way of doing business; it is a *policy* and a method of *governance*; it is a special sort of society and a way of running a family; it prescribes for inheritance and divorce, dress and etiquette, food and personal hygiene. It is a spiritual and human totality, *this*-worldly and *other*-worldly. Consequently, religion and politics are the two sides of a single coin in Islam...[1]

[1] The totality of Islam in *Militant Islam* by G.H. Jansen, Harper & Row Publishers, 1979, p. 17.

Islam also has unique characteristics that are not shared with other worldwide religions and must be understood through its historical development. Islam is one of the most rapidly growing religions in the world and has recently become the focus of worldwide attention due to the resurgence of activities by Islamic fundamentalists, militants and terrorists. One of the basic factors shaping the perceptions and goals of Muslim nations lies in views of their common Islamic history which has frequently been recalled to justify what these nations believe and what they want in their contemporary economic, social, and political activities. Ignoring or misunderstanding Islamic history could lead not only to religious antagonism, but also to mutual hatred and distrust between the Muslim and Western worlds and could result in worldwide confrontations in the economic, political, and cultural arenas.

Although this book focuses on the economic linkage of the 49 Muslim-majority countries with the world economy through oil production and exports as well as characteristics of Muslim populations and their future trends, this chapter is intended to provide a comprehensive overview of Islamic history along with descriptions of political struggles in the Muslim world, particularly over the last fifty years. We believe that such a history provides a key to understanding not only the past but also the present and future. In particular, Islamic history provides the basis for understanding the contemporary situation of Muslim nations and their relationship to the world.

Chapter 8
The Islamic Empires

8.1. The Islamic Empires and Their Golden Age

The history of Islam begins in the Arabian Peninsula in the seventh century. The prophet Muhammad was born in A.D. 571 in the town of Mecca in Western Arabia. At age 25 he was a merchant and married a rich widow; he then worked as the manager of a caravan outfitting business owned by his wife. At 40 Muhammad began to preach the first of a series of revelations that, Muslims believe, were given him by God, or transmitted by the Archangel Gabriel, while meditating alone inside a cave in the hills above Mecca. Most of his followers were from the lower classes and the poor peasantry, but some wealthy men also became his supporters later on.

Before the time of Muhammad, Arabia was inhabited by Arabs who worshiped many idols and had contacts with Christians, and Jews, as well as numerous pagan religions. The pagan idols around Mecca became important because pilgrims visiting the idols brought trade and economic prosperity to the city. When Muhammad denounced polytheism and idols, he encountered severe opposition by residents of Mecca. In the end he withdrew along with a small band of followers from Mecca and migrated to the oasis town of Medina in 622 CE (Common Era), and established the Muslim calendar in that year. In Medina Muhammad continued to preach, while consolidating his leadership, building up a military force, and governing the new Muslim community. After winning several major battles with Mecca in 630 CE, Muhammad established his Islamic state, which covered almost all of the Arabian Peninsula. He became virtually lord of Arabia and poised for military thrusts into present-day Syria and Iraq.

Even though he conceived of Islam as heir to the two great monotheistic faiths, Judaism and Christianity, Muhammad regarded Islam as a culmination and fulfillment of those faiths and the holy book Quran as God's final revelation which corrected erroneous interpretations and uses made by Christians and Jews. Christians and Jews, however, refused to accept Muhammad as the "seal of prophecy" and the Quran as God's final revelation. During subsequent history, this religious difference developed into a great rivalry between the Muslim world and the Western world (including the European Christian nations, the United States and Israel).

Muhammad died in 632 at the age of 63 and did not designate a successor. The next three Caliphs (heads of the Islamic state) enjoyed recognition as being consensually selected by the entire Muslim community. Those leaders united all the tribes of Arabia under Islam by expelling Jewish and Christian tribes and then began the great wave of Muslim conquest. The Islamic armies won a decisive

International Symposia in Economic Theory and Econometrics, Vol. 19
William W. Cooper and Piyu Yue

ISSN: 1571-0386/DOI: 10.1016/S1571-0386(07)00021-X

victory against the major Christian power of the day — the Byzantine Empire — and then occupied Syria, Persia, Egypt, and even developed a navy base in Alexandria, Egypt. By the end of the eighth century, Islamic armies had reached far westward into North Africa, and northeastward into Asia. Within three generations, Muslimism established one of the largest empires the world has ever known. Concomitantly, Islam penetrated deeply in the new empire and led to the conversion of many of the conquered people into Muslims. In the views of Christians and Jews, Islam become the arch-enemy. Military confrontation and occupation escalated during subsequent centuries and engendered additional rivalries between the Muslim and Western worlds.

When Ali ibn Abu Talib, Muhammad's cousin and the husband of his daughter Fatima, succeeded to the fourth caliphate in 656, some Muslims believed that he should have been the first Caliph based on descent from the Prophet. They believed that the three Caliphs before him were illegitimate because they were not named by the Prophet. Supporters of this belief were known as Shiites (or Party of Ali). Shiites revere Ali as the First Imam, and his descendants continued the line of the Imams until the twelfth Imam. The Muslim majority, however, rejected this belief and insisted that the Caliph must be consensually selected. This larger faction of Muslims, known as Sunnis, has represented themselves as the orthodox Islam for centuries. Although originally political in nature, the differences between Sunnis and Shiites rapidly became theological confrontations over interpretations of true Islam, and then helped to create many religious sects in both Sunni and Shiite camps.

When the political unity of Islam began to disintegrate over time, only the first four Caliphs were recognized as rulers of the entire Islamic empire. The governor of Syria, Muawiyah, under the 3rd Caliph, Uthman, rebelled against the 4th Caliph, Ali, and fought many battles with Ali's armies. After Ali was assassinated in 661 CE, Muawiyah declared himself the Caliph of all Muslim lands, moved his capital to Damascus, and established a Sunni dynasty, the Umayyad dynasty, as the largest state in history up to that point. However, the Umayyad dynasty was overthrown in 750 and the unity of the Arab world was dissolved.

The Abbasid family took over the Caliphate of the Islam Empire in 786 CE. The Abbasid dynasty, another Sunni dynasty, constituted the beginning of what is called "the Golden Age of Islam". This religiously inspired conquest grew into a culturally eclectic empire, and Muslim control extended from Spain and Morocco in the west to India in the east. Many different areas and peoples of more advanced cultures were conquered by Arabs from Arabia, but the Abbasid leaders encouraged and facilitated the creation of a new hybrid Islamic culture that brought together elements of Arab, Latin, Greek, Persian, and Jewish societies. The Arabs in the conquered territories began to lose their Arabian identity and merge with the native population. This increased the ability of Islamic civilization to adapt to change, and produced intellectual flexibility and was reflected in Islamic thought and culture as well as openness to new ideas and influences.

For 400 years, from the mid-9th century to the mid-13th century, Islamic culture became unparalleled in its splendor and learning. The accomplishments of Islam's Golden Age are numerous, including unrivaled intellectual activities in all fields: science, technology, theology, philosophy, and literature–particularly biography, history, and linguistics. The tales of the Arabian Nights ("One Thousand and One Nights") was compiled during this period. The Muslim belief that Arabic, the language of the holy Quran, was the language of Allah himself, led to standardization of the language throughout the Islamic Empire as the language of faith and power. The so-called "Arabic" numerals began to replace the cumbersome Roman numerals, and the concept of zero was introduced for the first time. Muslim scholars also made many other important and original contributions to mathematics, astronomy, medicine, and chemistry (an outgrowth of alchemy) and studied a wide variety of minerals and compounds.

Important advances in agriculture were also made in the Golden Age, including preserved and improved ancient networks of wells, underground canals, and waterwheels. New breeds of livestock were introduced; the spread of cotton and new strains of wheat was hastened; and the art of making paper was borrowed from the Chinese. The Middle East became the center of world trade and Baghdad became a luxurious and commercial world city. Science, technology, medicine, astronomy, and architecture flourished. Literature, history, poetry, and religious studies reached great heights. The achievements of the Islamic Empire in religious mission, military success, and cultural advancement represented one of the greatest civilizations of the time.

While the Muslim world enjoyed this "Golden Age", Europe was still going through its "Dark Ages". Many advances in science and technology of the Islamic civilization later provided the impetus for the development of the European Renaissance. The Islamic civilization considered itself superior to the Christian West, which was regarded as backward in every way by Muslims. In the view of Westerners, however, Muslim rule in Christian lands was considered an act of Muslim imperialism over European people and led to further dislike and hatred between Christians and Muslims.

In 1258, the Mongol, Hulagu Khan, sacked Baghdad and one of the important centers of Islamic civilization was destroyed.[1] Abbasid's Caliph moved to Cairo where the dynasty finally disappeared. The Islamic Empire then declined and never fully recovered. Eventually scientific and technological progress came to a halt and the Golden Age of Islamic civilization reached its end.

---

[1] As Bernard Lewis notes in *What Went Wrong?* (Oxford University Press, 2002, p. 4) "... in 1252 the Khan of the Golden Horde and his people were converted to Islam". This book also provides a succinct but detailed overview of another important turning point in the disastrous defeat of the Ottoman Empire in their attempted siege of Vienna in 1683 and the treaty of Carlowitz signed in 1699, after the defeat of the Ottoman Empire.

During the Golden Age, in about year 909 C.E., a descendant of the Prophet's daughter Fatima and her husband, Ali, declared himself a "divinely guided one" and established a Shiite Islamic empire, the Fatimid Empire, with its capital in Tunisia. Conquering the surrounding areas, the empire extended its control over all of the North Africa regions, including today's Morocco, Algeria, Tunisia, Libya, and Egypt. In the end, however, Fatimid territory shrunk into only Egypt, and was taken over by the Abbasid Sunni Caliphs who terminated the Fatimid dynasty in 1171.

8.2. Crusader Wars

Turning to Europe we can start with the year 393, when the Roman Empire was divided into two halves ruled by the emperor's two sons. The eastern half was called the "Eastern Roman Empire" with its capital in Constantinople (today's Istanbul). The name, Byzantine, was invented by a French historian in the 18th century for the Eastern Roman Empire and then popularized long after the Empire had disappeared. The Byzantine Empire was a multinational state, including Greeks, Vlachs, Armenians, Jews, Egyptians, Syrians and Slavs, but dominated by Greek culture and the Christian religion.

Starting in the 5th century, the Byzantine Empire fought with Persian, Slav, and Bulgarian invaders. In the 7th century, the empire was invaded by the united Muslim Arabs, and its southern provinces were overrun by Islamic armies. Quickly, Mesopotamia (an ancient region of the Middle East between the Tigris and Euphrates rivers in modern-day Iraq[2]), Syria, and Egypt were all permanently incorporated into the Islamic Empire. Jerusalem, an ancient Middle East city of key importance to the religions of Judaism, Christianity, and Islam, was one of the Islamic Empire's first conquests, in 638, by the second Caliph Umar, who personally went to the city to receive its submission. However, attempts by the Islamic Empire to conquer Constantinople failed because of the Byzantine's superior navy. In 1071 the Muslim Seljuk Turks[3].) won a decisive victory over the Byzantine armies at the battle of present-day Malazgirt in eastern Turkey, and this

[2] See note 4 in Chapter 2.

[3] "The Seljuk Turks are regarded as the ancestors of the Western Turks, the present-day inhabitants of Turkey, Turkmenistan, Uzbekistan and Azerbaijan. The Seljuk Turks migrated from the north into Persia, while fighting and conquering various tribes along their way. They converted to Sunni Islam, zealously defended it and promoted its predominance among the branches of Islam. The lands they eventually accumulated covered present-day Kyrgyzstan, Uzbekistan, Turkmenistan, Kazakhstan, Turkey, the entire Middle East, and a part of the Arabian Peninsula, and grew into the Seljuk Empire". (Wikipedia: *Seljuk Turks*, http://www.nationmaster.com/encyclopedia, which is a web-based free content multilingual encyclopedia

led to the Byzantine emperor calling for help from the Western Roman Empire to defend his empire against the Muslim Seljuk Turks.

In 1095, Pope Urban II called upon all Christians to join a war against the Muslim Turks, which was referred to as the First Crusade. In 1099, Crusader armies conquered Palestine and Jerusalem, massacring the Jewish and Muslim populations. Several small Crusader states were created after the First Crusade, including the Kingdom of Jerusalem. In 1187, however, the Muslim army led by Saladin annihilated the crusader army and recaptured Jerusalem after just 88 years of crusader rule. During the 11th through 13th centuries nine crusades were launched and developed into territorial wars. There were also frequent minor crusades that continued into the 16th century until the Renaissance. These crusades took place not only in Palestine but also in Spain and central Europe, not only against Muslims, but also against Christian "heretics" and enemies of the Papacy.

During the European Middle Ages (from the 4th through 15th centuries), much of the European continent was united under a powerful Papacy. The Pope in Rome visualized a Christian "just war" that might enhance the wider standing of an aggressively ambitious papal leader of Europe by unleashing the mass of common people against both Muslims and Byzantines. Western hegemony would then allow the Pope to claim supremacy over the Patriarch of Constantinople. Like Muslims and Jews, Eastern Orthodox Christians also saw the Crusades as attacks by barbarians from the West and witnessed the killings and devastation of Constantinople when it fell to the Christian Crusaders in 1204.[4] The result of the Crusades was to ingrain in Muslim minds a harmful image of the West not only as culturally backward but also as aggressive and barbaric. The Muslim and West worlds developed a deep mutual dislike, mistrust, and fear of each other for the centuries to follow.

The Ottoman Empire was a great Islamic Empire. Beginning in the 14th century and lasting into the 20th century, it comprised Anatolia (the Asian portion of present-day Turkey), part of Southwest Asia, North Africa, and South-Eastern Europe. The first Ottoman rulers called themselves Gazi (Holy Warrior) because they drove out the Byzantines and crusaders from Anatolia, captured Constantinople in 1453, and pursued crusaders into Europe. The Ottoman Empire reached its apex in the 16th century when it stretched from the Persian Gulf in the east to Hungary in the west and from the Caucasus in the north to Egypt in the south. With the arrival of Arab traders during 14th and 15th centuries, Islam began a

[4] "Since the 17th century the term "crusader" has carried a connotation in the West of being a "righteous campaign", usually to "root out evil", or to fight for a just cause. In the Arab world, the equivalent term of a holy war is jihad, while "crusade" is a term that connotes a hostile and foreign invasion by "infidels", those disrespectful or defiling of the Muslim culture". This is excerpted from the term "crusade" in Wikipedia: *Crusader*, http://www.nationmaster.com/encyclopedia.

gradual infiltration into Malaysia and Indonesia, and, by the end of 16th century, it had replaced Buddhism and Hinduism as the dominant religion.

The Ottoman Empire exhibited a high tolerance of alien religions and cultures. By assimilating and absorbing cultures of some of the conquered peoples, it created an Ottoman culture consisting of the Turks' own culture plus elements of the Greek, Balkan and other European influences. The Ottoman Empire interacted with both Eastern and Western cultures throughout its 624-year history. At the end of World War I, however, the Ottoman government collapsed and the Empire was divided by the Allied Powers (France, Britain, Russia, Italy and the United Sates).

By the 16th century another two Islamic empires were the Saffavids in today's Iran, and the Moguls on the Indian subcontinent. The Saffavids ruled Iran for more than 200 years establishing it as a unified modern state. The Saffavids were Shiites and converted most of Iran to this form of Islam. The Moguls were Muslims who ruled over a Hindu majority. The founder of the Mogul Empire Babar (1482–1530), a Turkish–Mongol prince from Afghanistan, invaded India in 1526. His grandson, Emperor Akbar (1542–1605), was the greatest in building a powerful dynasty and impacting the thoughts and arts of India. Those two empires were also powerful and productive during the Middle Ages. However, their power was waning with increasing rebellions thereafter.

Summary of Chapter 8

This chapter provides a brief review of the Islamic history before the 17th century, from the creation of Islam by the Prophet Muhammad to the apex of the Ottoman Empire. We borrow words from Bernard Lewis to summarize glories and achievements of Islam during this era in the following:

> "At the peak of Islamic power, there was only one civilization that was comparable in the level, quality, and variety of achievement; that was of course China. But Chinese civilization remained essentially local, limited to one region, East Asia, and to one racial group. It was exported to some degree, but only to neighboring and kindred peoples. Islam in contrast created a world civilization, polytechnic, multiracial, international, one might even say intercontinental.
>
> For centuries the world view and self-view of Muslims seemed well grounded. Islam represented the greatest military power on earth — its armies, at the same time, were invading Europe and Africa, India and China. It was the foremost economic power in the world, trading in a wide range of commodities in Asia, Europe, and Africa; importing slaves and gold from Africa, slaves and wool from Europe, and exchanging a variety of foodstuffs, materials, and manufactures. It had achieved the highest level so far in human history in the arts and sciences of civilization. Inheriting the knowledge and skills of the ancient Middle East, of Greece and of Persia, it added to them new

> and important innovations from outside, such as the use and manufacture of paper from China and decimal positional numbering from India. . .".[5]

In the next chapter we will see the dramatically changed situation in the Muslim world. The Muslim world had become complacent and lost the dynamism that had made it great. Muslims had also become divided among themselves. This created opportunities for European imperialism to invade the Muslim lands.

[5] *What Went Wrong? Western Impact and Middle Eastern Response* by Bernard Lewis, Oxford University Press, 2002, p. 6.

Chapter 9

Colonization and Islamic Fundamentalism

After the 17th century the three Islamic Empires could no longer compete with emerging European nation states that were coming out of their "Dark Ages" and years of religious warfare and began to develop their Renaissance and scientific and industrial revolutions. Europe had successfully transited from the medieval to the modern age. European technology, military organization, and general efficiency had all surpassed that possessed by the Muslim world. In 1683, the Ottoman Empire launched its last significant offensive against the Christian West by besieging the City of Vienna, but failed.[1] It was forced to retreat from southeast Europe and finally decisively defeated by the modern European powers in World War I. The Muslim world then became a land of Western imperialism occupation and conquest with their superior technology that we now describe.

9.1. European Colonialism

The age of European expansion and imperialism began in the 15th century and lasted until the mid-20th century with dismantling of the British, French and other empires after World War II. Under attacks from European powers, the Muslim world began a downturn that led to its disintegration.

From Portugal to Britain

The Portuguese were first, coming to the Middle East in the early 16th century. This was accomplished with a superior ship-building technology that enabled their hulled ships to remain stable in high seas and make longer ocean voyages. By this means, the Portuguese found their way around the southern tip of Africa and reached the Muslim lands on the eastern side of that continent. With the help of Arab navigators they crossed the Arabian Sea and reached the west coast of India. By capturing coastal cities in Oman and Iran, and by setting up forts and customs offices to collect duties, the Portuguese began to control trade between India and Europe as well as local trade across the Arabian Sea between India and the Middle East.

---

[1] See the introduction to *What Went Wrong?* by Bernard Lewis as cited in note 2 of Chapter 8 for a description of this defeat and its consequences.

International Symposia in Economic Theory and Econometrics, Vol. 19
William W. Cooper and Piyu Yue

ISSN: 1571-0386/DOI: 10.1016/S1571-0386(07)00022-1

At that time Iran was so weak that its Shah (King of Persia) invited the British and the Dutch to drive the Portuguese out of the Persian Gulf in return for half the revenues from Iranian ports. In the end, the Portuguese were driven out and the British triumphed over the Dutch. By the beginning of the 19th century the British became the major power in the Gulf.

By the 1850s the British already controlled most of the Indian subcontinent, including present-day Pakistan and Bangladesh. In 1857, a rebellion in northern India caused the British Parliament to transfer all political power from the East India Company to the Crown, and Britain began administering most of India directly. As a Crown colony, India became "British India", the so-called "British Raj".[2]

Britain was mainly interested originally in protecting shipping between Europe and India from widespread piracy in the Persian Gulf and had no desire to take over the desolate hinterland of the latter region. The British therefore decided to support those coastal tribal leaders who promised to suppress all piracy. During the 19th century, the British signed a series of treaties with tribes in the Gulf region that had required local tribes to yield their control of foreign relations to Britain. By the end of World War I, local leaders from Oman to Iraq in the Gulf region could not make any international agreement or host any foreign agent without British consent which was directed to excluding influences in the area from other powers like Turkey and France. As a result of these concessions, Gulf tribal leaders secured British protection from their powerful neighbors, such as the Al Saud[3] in central Arabia and the Turks of the Ottoman Empire, as well as the Omani and Iranian threats. In fact, at the end of World War I, the Arab states in the Gulf region were so weak and fragile that local tribal rulers could maintain their autonomy only in small urban areas with British help.

The discovery of oil in the Gulf region drastically changed this situation. The British first found oil in Iran in 1911 and in Iraq after World War I. A US company, Standard Oil Company of California, discovered oil in commercial quantities in Bahrain in 1932, and in Saudi Arabia in 1938. With these oil discoveries, the controlling and owning of land in this region became very important. Foreign oil companies that came to explore for oil went to the area's leading families owning the land and agreed to pay fees to the heads of those families. Land ownership, however, was determined in accordance with British treaties. The many treaties signed by Britain with tribes and families in the previous one and a half centuries

[2] The "British Raj" is an informal term for the British colonial administration of most of the Indian subcontinent, or present-day India, Pakistan and Bangladesh. Also included was Burma from 1886.

[3] In 1744, Muhammad Wahhab, an Islam reformer, and Muhammad Saud, the Emir of a small town near Riyadh, swore a traditional Muslim pledge in which they promised to work together to establish a new state based on Islamic principles. This new state was set up in 1750 in central Arabia. It is the present-day Saudi Arabia.

created a bizarre division of the Gulf region in which some very small states with a small population own rich oil and gas resources (like Qatar, Kuwait, Bahrain, and UAE), while large states with a large population (like Oman and Yemen) possess only poor natural resources. The British colonial policy of "divide and rule" greatly contributed to the fragmented states of the Gulf region as well as the entire Muslim world.

Present-day Pakistan and Bangladesh were parts of British India. They won their independence in 1947, when Britain, burdened by the tremendous sacrifices it made during the World War II, could not continue to be so involved globally. British India was then divided into Hindu India and the Muslim state of Pakistan (with two sections West and East). In 1971, East Pakistan seceded and became the separate nation of Bangladesh. Britain, however, remained in the Gulf region until the early 1970s, when the Gulf nations, one after another, declared their independence, terminated the treaties connecting them with Britain, and became independent sovereign states.

In Iraq

The land area of present-day Iraq is almost equivalent to ancient Mesopotamia, which was a part of the Fertile Crescent[4] located between the two rivers, Tigris and Euphrates. The richness of the Mesopotamia plain nurtured the earliest civilizations of mankind such as the Sumerian culture which flourished about 4000 BC, and the Akkadian Empire and the Babylonian Empire, dating back to around 2400 BC. This area was incorporated into the Sassanian Persian Empire (226 AD–650 AD). In 634 AD, two years after the death of the Prophet Muhammad, Muslim armies defeated the occupying Persian force in the Euphrates delta, and completed their occupation of Mesopotamia in the 7th century. During the Abassid Sunni Islamic dynasty, the Caliphate established its capital at Baghdad.

During the 14th and 15th centuries, Mesopotamia was ruled by Turkmen and then by the Ottoman Islamic Empire until World War I. British forces invaded Mesopotamia in 1917 and occupied Baghdad. Consequently, the Mesopotamian area was separated from the Ottoman Empire and became a League of Nations[5] mandate under British control with the name "State of Iraq". Britain imposed a Hashemite Monarchy[6] in Iraq and laid out the institutional framework for an Iraqi

[4] The Fertile Crescent is a region in the Middle East, incorporating present-day Israel, the West Bank, Lebanon, and parts of Jordan, Syria, Iraq and south-eastern Turkey.

[5] The League of Nations was an international organization founded after World War I for reducing armaments and settling disputes between countries. The United Nations replaced it after World War II.

[6] Hussein ibn Ali was the Emir of Mecca and proclaimed himself king. King Hussein's branch of the Hashemite family ruled the holy city of Mecca from 1201 CE until 1925 CE, when he was defeated by Abdul Aziz al Saud. Hussein ibn Ali was the last of the

government. The Iraqi territorial boundary was defined by Britain alone without apparent concern for natural frontiers and traditional tribal and ethnic settlements. The British also supported narrowly based tribal groups instead of urban-based nationalist movements. In 1941, Britain, using its military force, wiped out Iraqi rebelling troops led by Rashis Ali Al-Gaylani, recaptured Baghdad and reinstated the last King Faisal II of Iraq.[7] The British colonial rule had deepened tribal division of the Arab world and closed windows of opportunity for consolidation leading to a stronger unified Arab state.

In Fertile Crescent

The other part of the Fertile Crescent includes present day Jordan, Lebanon, and Syria, all having a long history dating back to around 2000 BC when a great Semitic empire spread from the Red Sea north to Turkey and east to Mesopotamia. The area was subject to successive waves of invaders being occupied sequentially by Egyptians, Babylonians, Persians, Greeks, Romans, Byzantines, Arabs, Crusaders, and Mongols before being taken over by the Ottoman Turks. After World War I, the Ottoman Empire was dissolved and the League of Nations split the area between two colonist countries. Britain received the territory now comprising Jordan, Israel, the West Bank, the Gaza Strip and Jerusalem as a mandate, and France received what was to become present-day Syria and Lebanon. In 1922, the British divided its mandate into two parts and established the semiautonomous Emirate of Transjordan, ruled by a Hashemite Prince, while another part, Palestine, was still under the administration of a British High Commissioner. Transjordan became independent in 1946, and was renamed "the Hashemite Kingdom of Jordan" in 1950. It ended its special defense treaty relationship with Britain in 1957.

The land of Palestine had attracted great interest from Arab nationalists and Jewish Zionists, who sought to reestablish their ancient homeland there. During World War II, almost six million Jews in Europe were murdered in the Nazi Holocaust, which led to the demand by Zionists for an independent homeland to absorb the Jewish refugees from Europe. In 1947, the United Nations decided to partition Palestine into two states, one Jewish, and one Arab. The proposal was rejected by the Palestinian Arabs (both Muslims and Christians) and the surrounding Arab

---

Hashemites to rule the Hejaz region (the northwest part of present-day Saudi Arabia). During World War I, Hussein was an important leader in the Arab Revolt against the Ottomans. Hussein allied himself with both France and Britain, and intended to form a unified Arab state that would stretch from Syria to Yemen. In the aftermath of World War I, the sons of Hussein were made the kings of Jordan, Syria and Iraq.

[7] Faisal II (May 2, 1935–July 14, 1958) was the last king of Iraq and reigned from April 4, 1939 to 1958. He was the son of the second king of Iraq, Ghazi, who was killed in an automobile accident when Faisal was three. For most of his reign his uncle Abdul Illah ruled as regent (until Faisal came of age in 1953). (From http://www.nationmaster.com/encyclopedia.)

states, arguing that it was unfair to punish the Arabs for the war crimes of Nazi Germany that caused the Jewish refugee problem. In 1948, the Jewish population declared its independence from Palestine as the new state of Israel. The proposed Arab state, however, did not exist until 1993 when the PNA (Palestine National Authority) was established as a part of the "Oslo Accords" negotiated between the PLO (Palestine Liberation Organization) and Israel.

These developments illustrate the British colonial policy of dividing the Arab world piece by piece in order to make the heartland of the ancient and mighty Islamic Empire fragile, disintegrated, powerless, and fighting each other over territorial disputes. It also put the Jewish people, who suffered a great deal during World War II, in a place surrounded by small but hostile Arab nations that refused to recognize Israel as a legitimate sovereign state. Instead of compensating for the heavy losses of the Jewish people, the Europeans created a situation in which Jews had to defend themselves against antagonistic Arabs rather than revenging themselves against the guilty European powers. The British had, thus, sown the seeds of endless struggle and bloodshed in the center of the Muslim world for the second half of the 20th century and beyond.

British colonial rule has left the Gulf region with at least three significant consequences. First, it prevented the tribe-based Arab communities from consolidating into a few larger and stronger nation states for the modern age. Most of the Arab states are still run on a tribal basis by influential families. The governments of Oman, Saudi Arabia, and UAE are all classified as monarchies along with a traditional monarchy in Qatar, a nominal constitutional monarchy in Kuwait, and a constitutional hereditary monarchy in Bahrain. Yemen was established as a united Republic in 1990 from a combination of North Yemen and South Yemen.[8] Mod ern institutions developed in many advanced nations could not be developed in those tribal-based Arab states. This has become a major institutional obstacle to economic growth and social progress in the modern age.

Second, the arbitrary division of the Arab land by the British made every Arab nation weak. In particular, small, oil rich, Arab nations like Qatar, Kuwait and Bahrain continue to depend upon US military forces to protect their security, oil production, and export routs, even though they are all independent sovereign nations. These states are simply too small to defend themselves and too important for their oil and wealth to be ignored by many aggressors.

Third, the colonial division of the Arab land caused many conflicting claims to territories and led to potential border wars among the Arab States. For instance,

[8] North Yemen became independent from the Ottoman Empire in 1918, while South Yemen was run by a Marxist-oriented government established three years after the British withdrew in 1967. There then ensued two decades of hostility between North and South Yemen before their merger, which was due to a massive exodus involving hundreds of thousands of Yemenis from the south to the north.

Kuwait was the first one in the region to declare its independence in 1961, after which Iraq immediately claimed its territory arguing that the Ottomans had ruled Kuwait from what was then a province of Iraq. Therefore, Kuwait was a part of Iraq. Even as late as the 1970s, Iran and Saudi Arabia continued to claim the territories of Bahrain and the UAE. The British colonial heritage has thus created many obstacles and uncertainties that impede development of the Gulf region.

In Egypt

During its longest continuous history, dating back to 3000 BC, Egypt had been invaded and occupied by many foreign rulers, including Persians, Greeks, Romans, Byzantines, Arabs, Turks, and British. During 639 to 1517, Egypt was a part of the Arab world. Conquered by the second Caliph of the Islamic Empire in 639 and ruled by Turks in the name of the Arab governor during the 9th century, Egypt was occupied by the Shiite Fatimid dynasty, and then returned to the Sunni Islamic faith as subjects of the Caliphate in Baghdad during the 11th century. It was finally conquered and incorporated in the Ottoman Empire in 1517 with the Ottoman rule lasting until 1882 when the British invaded Egypt and turned it into a colony.

Before the British invasion, Egyptian rulers were under heavy influence from France and in 1856 granted a French engineer the concession for the construction of a Suez Canal. The canal was inaugurated in 1869 and jointly owned by the Egyptian government and France. Increasing external debts then forced the Egyptian government to sell its share in the Suez Canal to Britain in 1875, thus giving up Egyptian control of the waterway that played such a dramatic role in increasing European penetration of Africa and the Middle East.

In 1882 after widespread revolts involving national movements against imperialism, the British fleet bombarded the city of Alexandria and British troops suppressed the revolts. The British then occupied Egypt to protect the Suez Canal and massive British investments flowed into Egypt. Egypt was virtually included within the British Empire until 1922, when Britain unilaterally declared Egyptian independence and King Fuad was installed in Egypt. Under British colonial rule, many political forces emerged, including broadly based nationalist political organizations in the form of the communist party and the Muslim Brotherhood. In 1952, a group of disaffected army officers (the "free officers") led by Lt Col. Nasser overthrew the King, abrogated the constitution and declared Egypt a republic. Nasser became an important figure in the Muslim world who sought to promote his "Arab socialism".

In Iran

Iran is the largest Shiite Islamic country in the world. The name Iran was recognized in 1935 when the Persian Shah (King) Pahlavi formally asked the international community to call Persia by its native name, Iran. Persia was a historical nation with a long history. The first Persian state, the Achaemenid dynasty, existed in 648 BC–330 BC as the largest and most powerful empire the world had yet seen. That dynasty, however, was overthrown by the Greeks when the last Achaemenid King, Darius III, was defeated in 333 BC by Alexander III (also known as Alexander the Great) of Macedon, the ancient Greek state. Persia was ruled by Alexander and Greek colonization continued until 250 BC. The next Persian dynasty, Parthian Persia, was ruled by an Iranian tribe from today's northeastern Iran and some feudal nobles (170 BC–226 AD). During 226 AD–650 AD, it was the Sassanian dynasty that brought the country back into a native Persia. The Sassanids were the true heirs of the Achaemenids. They developed Persia as a strong centralized state, based on a revived Zoroastrian religion and a class society.

The explosive growth of the Islamic Empire in the Umayyad dynasty led to the Arab invasion of Persia. The Sassanian dynasty collapsed under rapid military assaults by the invading Arabs between 636 and 642 AD. The country changed into a completely Islamic state, with a new language, religion and culture. Islam quickly replaced Zoroastrianism, which was Persia's ancient polytheistic faith. Political unrest, however, continued.

Persia experienced the invasion of the Seljuk Turks from the northeast and the Mongol occupation in 1219–1500 AD. A new Persian empire, the Safavids dynasty (1500–1722), arose from Azerbaijan, a part of the "Great Persia" region at that time. This dynasty expanded Persia to include all of present-day Azerbaijan, Iran, Iraq, and Afghanistan, an expansion that continued until encountering the Ottomans at Chaldiran in 1514. The Safavids were followers of Shiite Islam. Under their rule, Persia became the largest Shiite Islamic country in the Muslim world, and Shiite Islamic domination remains in today's Iran.

During the 18th and 19th centuries, Persia encountered frequent invasions from the growing Russian Empire in Central Asia, and a military threat from the expanding British Empire in India. Although Persia was not directly occupied by colonial powers, both Britain and Russia enjoyed "spheres of influence" in the country and made Persia economically dependent on them. After World War I and the Russian Revolution, Britain claimed Persia as a protectorate and took control of newly discovered oilfields. Iran has not yet returned to the world power that it had once been, but it has played an important role in internal struggles in the Muslim world as well as in regional and global political battles.

9.2. Colonized Muslim Countries

By European Powers

1875, the year when Britain purchased the Egyptian shares in the Suez Canal, was the beginning of the age of a "New Imperialism". This age was characterized by aggressive competition for overseas territorial acquisitions between European powers, including the British, French, Italian, Russian and other Europeans, later joined by the Americans and Japanese in the 20th century. Imperialist conquests took place in Africa, South-East Asia and the East Asian seaboard in areas that were mostly unoccupied by European powers as late as the 1880s. Almost all of the present-day Muslim nations in the five geographic regions (Middle East & North Africa, South Asia, South-East Asia, sub-Sahara Africa, and Central Asia) became colonies of European powers during the 19th and 20th centuries as shown in Table 9.1.

Table 9.1 summarizes the colonization of the Muslim world, showing 20 Muslim colonies of Britain, 15 of France, 6 of Russia, 4 of Italy, and one of the Netherlands and one of Turkey as of 1984 when the last Muslim colony, Brunei, a British protectorate, achieved its independence. Britain scrambled for the following ten Muslim colonies in the Middle East and North Africa: Bahrain, Iraq, Jordan, Kuwait, Oman, Palestine, Qatar, UAE, Yemen and Egypt; three in South Asia: Bangladesh, Maldives and Pakistan; two in South-East Asia: Brunei and Malaysia; six in sub-Sahara Africa: Eritrea, The Gambia, Nigeria, Sierra Leone, Somali and Sudan. France took over six Muslim colonies in the Middle East and North Africa: Algeria, Djibouti, Morocco, Tunisia, Lebanon and Syria, and nine in sub-Sahara Africa: Burkina Faso, Chad, Cote d'lvoire, Guinea, Mali, Mauritania, Niger, Senegal and Somalia. Italy snatched four Muslim colonies: Libya in North Africa, and Eritrea, Ethiopia and Somalia in sub-Sahara Africa.

Russia occupied all six Mushm nations in Central Asia — Azerbaijan, Kazakhstan, Kyrgyzstan, Tajikistan, Turkmenistan, and Uzbekistan. All six of these Central Asian colonies were ruled by the Islamic Empire during the Arab conquests between the 7th and 9th centuries. Due to their important location, astride the trade routes connecting Europe to Asia, these Central Asian countries experienced numerous foreign invasions. In the end, however, these Muslim countries were formally incorporated into the Russian Empire. The October Revolution of 1917 in Russia led to the collapse of the Russian Empire and the arrival of the Red Army in Central Asia. Stiff resistance from Muslims to the Red Army after World War I was eventually suppressed, and all six nations in Central Asia became Republics of the USSR under Soviet rule. When the USSR collapsed in the 1990s, the six Muslim republics declared their independence from the USSR in 1991.

There are only four Muslim nations in the world that did not become a colony of European powers during the 18th–20th centuries; they are Iran, Saudi Arabia, Turkey and Afghanistan. Even though Iran did not completely become a colony, it was divided into areas of Russian influence in the north and British influence in the east and south according to the 1907 Anglo–Russian Convention. This convention granted each of Russia and Britain the right to occupy its area of influence if threatened by a third party. During World War II, Iran was occupied by British and Russian troops. After the war, Soviet troops were still stationed in northwestern

Table 9.1: Colonization of the 49 Muslim Countries (as of 1984)

Region	Nation	Colony of	Colonization		Current Government Type
			Started in	Ended in	
Middle East & North Africa	Algeria	France	1830	1962	republic
	Bahrain	Britain	1861	1971	constitutional monarchy
	Djibouti	France	1862	1977	republic
	Egypt	Britain	1882	1953	republic
	Iran				theocratic republic
	Iraq	Britain	1917	1932	transitional
	Jordan	Britain	1917	1946	constitutional monarchy
	Kuwait	Britain	1899	1961	constitutional monarchy
	Lebanon	France	1922	1946	republic
	Libya	Italy	1919	1951	military dictatorship
	Morocco	France	1912	1956	constitutional monarchy
	Oman	Britain	1891	1971	monarchy
	Palestine	Britain	1917	1993	none
	Qatar	Britain	1916	1971	monarchy
	Saudi Arabia				monarchy
	Syria	France	1922	1946	republic under military regime
	Tunisia	France	1881	1956	republic one party rule
	UAE	Britain	1892	1971	monarchy
	Yemen	Britain	1918	1967	republic
South Asia	Afghanistan				transitional
	Bangladesh	Britain	1857	1971	Parliamentary democracy
	Maldives	Britain	1887	1968	republic
	Pakistan	Britain	1857	1947	Republic under military regime
	Indonesia	Netherlands	1602	1945	republic
	Malaysia	Britain	1826	1957	constitutional monarchy
Sub-Sahara Africa	Burkina Faso	France	1896	1960	republic
	Chad	France	1891	1960	republic
	Cote d'Ivoire	France	1919	1960	republic
	Eritrea	Italy/Britain	1885	1993	transitional
	Ethiopia	Italy	1935	1940	republic
	The Gambia	Britain	1783	1965	republic
	Guinea	France	1850	1958	republic
	Guinea-Bissau	Portugal	1630	1973	republic
	Mali	France	1898	1960	republic
	Mauritania	France	1900	1960	republic
	Niger	France	1898	1960	republic
	Nigeria	Britain	1901	1960	republic
	Senegal	France	1898	1960	republic
	Sierra Leone	Britain	1787	1961	constitutional democracy
	Somalia	Britain/France/Italy	1875	1959	transitional
	Sudan	Britain	1898	1956	military authoritarian

(*continued on next page*)

Table 9.1: (*continued*)

Region	Nation	Colony of	Colonization Started in	Colonization Ended in	Current Government Type
Central Asia	Albania	Turks	1385	1913	emerging democracy
	Azerbaijan	Russia	1828	1991	republic
	Kazakhstan	Russia	1820	1991	republic
	Kyrgyzstan	Russia	1876	1991	republic
	Tajikistan	Russia	1865	1991	republic
	Turkey			1923	republic
	Turkmenistan	Russia	1894	1991	republic
	Uzbekistan	Russia	1865	1991	republic

Source: The World Factbook by the Central Intelligence Agency (CIA).

Iran and blocked revolts against the Iranian Shah. Soviet troops did not withdraw from Iran until 1946 after receiving a promise of oil concessions from Iran.

Saudi Arabia began as a Muslim state in 1744 in the central Arabian Peninsula, ruled by the Saudi family and supported by the Islamic reformer Al-Wahhab. Fighting with Egypt, the Ottoman Empire, and other Arabian families for control of the peninsula, the Saudi family united the area as the Kingdom of Saudi Arabia in 1927. Britain immediately recognized the Kingdom as an independent state. At that time no one imagined that Saudi Arabia would become a dominating producer of oil in the world and its wide desert plus a few oases could hardly be attractive to European powers. This lack of attraction helped Saudi Arabia escape colonization during the years of the old and new imperialism.

In 1933, Saudi Arabia signed an agreement with the American company Standard Oil of California (SOCAL) to start exploration for oil. SOCAL placed the oil concession with Saudi Arabia under a wholly owned subsidiary, California Arab Standard Oil Company (CASOC) and the company name was changed to Arabian American Oil Company (ARAMCO) in 1944. Drilling for oil began in 1935 and the valves were turned on to pump oil in commercial quantities in 1938. The first discovery of oil in Saudi Arabia did not receive a great deal of attention at this time, on the eve of World War II. The outbreak of the War further restricted exploration, drilling and shipment of Saudi Arabia oil. However, oil extraction had increased to 21.3 million barrels in 1945 from only 0.5 million barrels in 1938[9] and Saudi's absolute monarchy was able to enjoy the beginning of their fabulous oil wealth. The Saudi government acquired a 25% share of ARAMCO in 1973, increased it to 60% by 1974 and finally acquired full control of the company by

[9] *A History of Saudi Arabia* by Madawi Al-Rasheed, Cambridge University Press, 2002, p. 93.

1980. In 1988 the company changed its name to Saudi Arabian Oil Company (or Saudi ARAMCO).

Table 9.1, which we have just reviewed, does not complete the real picture of European aggressions. Many non-Muslim-majority nations also became victims of imperialism. Listed beside the 20 Muslim nations in Table 9.1, Britain also ruled India since 1858. It launched two Opium Wars against China and occupied Hong Kong as its colony beginning in 1840. Britain also had Burma, Singapore and Malaya as colonies. Thailand, although not a formal British colony, was under heavy British influence. In Africa, the British also seized the colonies of South Africa, Uganda, Kenya and Ghana (formerly Gold Coast). During the years of "New Imperialism", France acquired the Asian colonies of Vietnam, Laos and Cambodia. It also established colonial rule in Madagascar, off the southeastern coast of Africa, and in the Ivory Coast, Dahomey (now called Benin) and Gabon in Western Africa. These British and French colonies are absent in Table 9.1 as they do not belong to Muslim-majority nations.

Germany, USA and Japan

Germany, the United States and Japan were late comers as industrialized powers seeking to form their own empires in order to counter Britain's advantages in international markets. After Germany's unification in 1871 and the US Civil War in 1861–1865, both countries undertook ambitious naval expansions in the 1890s. By the end of the Spanish–American war in 1898, Germany took over various islands from Spain in the Pacific as well as control over Western Samoa. At the turn of the century, the Germans declared China's Shandong peninsula as being in their sphere of influence. They also established rule in Tanzania on the east coast of Africa and in Cameroon in South-West Africa.

The United States emerged as one of the world's leading industrial, military and imperial power after wining the war with Spain in 1898. American forces occupied Cuba in 1909, and the USA annexed the former Spanish colonies of Puerto Rico, the Philippines, and Guam.

Japan's development after the Meiji Restoration of 1868 led to industrialization and to militarism that allowed Japan to gain control of Korea in 1894 where its colonial rule lasted from 1910 to 1945. Japan also gained spheres of influence in China's North-Eastern provinces, formerly Manchuria in 1905. The Japanese invasion of China started in 1931 with the Japanese Army occupying Manchuria In 1937 Japan attacked inland China (which was the beginning of World War II in Asia) and then occupied Shanghai and Nanjing (then the capital of China), killing more than 0.3 million Chinese. Japanese troops occupied French Indochina (Vietnam) in 1940, and in 1941 conducted their air raid on Pearl Harbor, the largest US naval base in the Pacific. The Japanese also invaded and occupied the British colonies of Burma, Malaya and Singapore, as well as the American colony of the Philippines. The "Greater East Asia Co-Prosperity Sphere", as they named it, reflected an attempt by Japan to create a bloc of Asian nations by driving out the British and French. In reality, however, the subsequent brutality and hardship of Japanese occupation led to the Japanese being regarded as even worse than Western colonialists. The Japanese occupation of China and other Asian countries ended when Japan unconditionally surrendered to the Allies on August 15, 1945.

These three late comers, Germany, the United States and Japan, participated in aggressive competition for overseas territorial acquisitions. Their imperialist operations occurred in Asia and Africa, but not in Muslim-majority nations. Hence their colonizing records do not appear in the above Table 9.1.

9.3. Islamic Militant Resistance Movements

As Table 9.1, above, shows almost all Muslim-majority countries were colonized during the 19th–20th centuries. This historic heritage provides a significant cohering force that unites Muslim communities around the globe in a common cause against Western occupation and influence. Colonial rule and control nearly always encountered furious resistance from conquered Muslims in occupied colonies. All possible forms of struggle were employed, including mass protest, uprisings, rebellion, insurgency, terrorist attacks, guerrilla warfare and other militant activities. Resistance to colonialism in the 19th and 20th centuries has since encouraged militant Islamic activities around the world and set heroic examples of Islamic jihad for younger generations. In this section, we will cover some of the history of Islamic militancy against European colonialism.

In Turkey

After the Ottoman Empire was defeated by the Western Allies in World War I, an agreement between Britain and France was signed in 1916 which envisioned dividing the Ottoman Empire into several states under the control of Britain, France, Italy, Imperial Russia or Greece, with a small territory around Ankara to be left for the Turks. The Turks strongly repudiated the accord and launched the "Turkish War of Independence" against the Greeks under the leadership of a nationalist, the former Ottoman general Mustafa Kemal Ataturk, after Greece occupied some Turkish territory and was destined to acquire more under the 1916 accord. The Turkish militants won three major battles during 1921–1922 and decisively defeated the Greek army. The majority of the ethnic Greek population in Asia Minor (which corresponds to the Asian portion of present-day Turkey) was then expelled to Greece. With their victory in the "Turkish War of Independence", the Turks were able to secure their current borders and demand negotiations with the Allies. This resulted in the new "Treaty of Lausanne" and the declaration of the Republic of Turkey in 1923 as an independent state with the territory of present-day Turkey.

It was this victory of the Turkish militants that saved the nation from becoming a colony of European powers.

In Afghanistan

Afghanistan is a country geographically located at the crossroads of Central, West, and South Asia. It is bordered by Iran in the west, Pakistan in the south and east, Turkmenistan, Uzbekistan and Tajikistan in the north, and China in the easternmost part of the country. During the 19th century, present-day Pakistan was a part of British India, and all three of the neighboring nations in the north (Turkmenistan, Uzbekistan and Tajikistan) were incorporated into Tsarist Russia. This geographic location positioned Afghanistan between the expanding British and Russian Empires and took the form of spheres of influence. These spheres of influence steadily moved closer to one another until they met in Afghanistan, which was ruled by the Afghan monarchy since 1747.

In the 19th century, in a series of wars of conquest against the Muslim states in Central Asia, Russia aggressively advanced and expanded its influence in Persia (Iran). This posed a threat to the British colony of India. Control of Afghanistan became an urgent imperative to Britain if it were to stop Russia's southward encroachment and if it were to maintain its power in Persia. Britain therefore launched three Anglo–Afghan wars in 1839–1842, 1878–1880, and in 1919. The first war resulted in a British column retreating from Kabul and being wiped out by ferocious Afghan militants. This was described by a British official as "the universal hostility of the whole people of Afghanistan, united against us at the present moment in a war which has assumed a religious, as well as a national, character".[10] Many Muslims consider the 1839–1842 Anglo–Afghan war as the first indication that Western powers could be stopped in their tracks and pushed back by Muslim militants.

In the second war, a British force of about 40 000 fighting men penetrated Afghanistan and occupied much of the country. To save the rest of the country from British conquest, the Afghan ruler was forced to sign a treaty, in which control of Afghan foreign affair was relinquished to the British, and various frontier areas were ceded to Britain. An Afghan uprising opposed to the Treaty was suppressed and Britain and Russia officially established the boundaries of present-day Afghanistan. Following the Russian Revolution of 1917 the agreement between Russia and Britain broke down and the Afghan ruler seized the opportunity to launch the third war by a surprise attack against the British in 1919. Afghan forces achieved an early success when tribesmen on both sides of the Russia–British border joined forces. The military skirmishes soon ended, however, when the British recovered from their initial surprise. The "1919 Agreement" was then reached in

[10] *Militant Islam* by G.H. Jansen, Harper & Row Publishers, 1979, p. 99.

which the British returned the right of controlling foreign affairs to the Afghans. In fact, however, Afghanistan's independence did not arrive until after 1919 when Afghanistan began to establish its own foreign policy, including diplomatic relations with the new Soviet government.

In Central Asia, after 1885, a series of revolts broke out and evolved, with jihads or movements of a religious nature against Russia's occupation, even though the Russian Orthodox Church carried out no missionary or proselyting activities against Islam anywhere in the Muslim world.

In Algeria

French occupation of Algeria began in 1830 and was immediately met with a rebellion led by Abd al-Qadir (1808–1883), who was an Emir with the loyalty of a number of tribes. Abd al-Qadir was revered as a national hero of anti-colonialism as well as a symbol of Muslims who struggle in the name of Islam and for the sake of Islam. He declared war on France in 1832 as a jihad (a holy war) that was very effective in using guerrilla warfare against the French. He set up Sunnimy of 8000 infantry and 2000 horsemen, composed of Muslim militant volunteers. The French armies brutally suppressed the native population and practiced a scorched-earth policy in which Sunni indiscriminately killed children, old folks, and cattle. In the end, al-Qadir was forced to surrender. Under the rule of France, many Algerians lost their lands to colonists; the traditional educational system was largely dismantled; and social structures were stressed to the breaking point.

Struggles to survive, to co-exist, to gain equality, and to achieve independence ultimately united the Algerians in the Algerian War of Independence (1954–1962). By 1956, France had committed more than 400 000 troops to Algeria, and also sent air force and naval units to Algerian battlefields. The French army divided the country into sectors, each permanently garrisoned by troops responsible for suppressing rebel operations in their assigned territory. The French also initiated concentration camps, into which more than 2 million Algerians were removed from their villages. Hundreds of empty villages were devastated, and hundreds of orchards and croplands destroyed. Those ruthless "Nazi-Fascist" measures did not stop the guerrilla wars and militant attacks continued under the Front de Libération Nationale (or FLN), an organization of Algerian nationalists in Algeria and in exile. In 1962 the French government of Charles de Gaulle was forced to sign the "Evian Accords", which allowed the Algerians to have property rights as well as the right of participation in public affairs, and a full range of civil and cultural rights. France's 132-year colonial rule in Algeria thus came to the end.

Similarly, the 20th century wars in Sudan were colored by religion and led to nearly twenty uprisings and rebellions that were referred to as Islamic jihads against economic and social sufferings which were regarded as being brought by British colonialism. In West and West-Central Africa, French colonialism faced struggles, declared as jihads of religious duty for Muslims by Sultans (Muslim leaders or rulers) of Guinea, Mauritania, Mali, Niger and Senegal. In only a few Muslim nations, like Tunisia and Egypt, did ulema (Muslim scholars trained in Islam and Islamic law) not play a leading role in the struggle against European powers, though they did take part.

In Indonesia

The Netherlands controlled Indonesia for over 300 years — excluding short periods of British rule in parts of the islands after the Anglo-Dutch Java War. Many armed struggles took place between Indonesian Muslim militants and Dutch colonial armies during the 19th century. Prince Diponegoro was a leader in the Java War (1825–1830), who became convinced that he was chosen by Allah to lead a rebellion against the non-Muslim Dutch. When he declared a jihad, a holy war, against the occupying foreigners and called for volunteer fighters, his people, the Javanese, joined his cause in a frenzy. His militant force included ulema and village religious teachers, as well as nobility and peasants willing to commit themselves to the holy war.

The Dutch rulers were surprised by the massiveness of the rebellion and the fanaticism of Muslim fighters. In fact, it was patriotism and yearnings for independence, freedom, equity, and a better life that inspired and united these people under the religious flag of Islam. The Dutch colonial policy of "divide and conquer" was implemented in order to split and conquer the rebellion force. Peasants were promised lower leasing costs for land. The nobility was promised the rent so they would have more income. This led to losing support for the resistance. In the end, Prince Diponegoro was willing to negotiate but was nevertheless put in jail by a Dutch general. The five-year Java war then came to the end.

In Middle East

The colonial policy of "divide and rule" was implemented in the center of the Muslim world on nations like Syria, Lebanon, and Palestine, which involved separate, heterodox, various Muslim sects, and minority Christians. In order for a national movement to receive support from members of these different religious communities, neither Islam, nor Christianity nor any other religion could be used as a name for the struggle. In Palestine, the Christians joined alongside Muslims in an anti-Zionist (i.e., anti-Israeli) course of action. A Muslim-Christian Association (MCA) appeared first in Jaffa in 1918 to express popular opposition to Zionism and then became a countrywide network — or an umbrella organization — for national groups and parties. The unity of Muslims and Christians in Palestine was based on a common enemy and a common devotion to the cause of Palestine nationhood, rather than being conducted in the name of a religion and for the sake of a religion.

In Iraq there are two major Muslim communities, the Sunnis and Shiites, and the Shiites claim to be the majority. There was only one time in its history that religious leaders of both Sunnis and Shiites formally decided to cooperate. This occurred in the bloody rebellion against British rule in 1920. At all other times Iraqi national movements had no recourse to Islamic religious support.

Conclusion

In summary, the bloodiest fighting against the colonialism of Europe in the 19th and 20th centuries was carried out by Islamic militants in the Muslim world. Muslims rallied and united under the religious flag of Islam to pursue independence and freedom for political and economic reasons in the name of Islam. Witness the case of Lebanon, Syria and Palestine where it was not for Islam per se or for the sake of Islam that the movements occurred. In situations that lacked competing Muslim sects or other religions, national leaders could express their political aspirations in Islamic religious terms and declare jihads against their enemies in order to rally their people and supporters in the name of Islam, and for the sake of Islam. Jihad and Islamic militancy has become an important historical heritage bestowed on the present by anti-colonialism struggles in the Muslim world of the 19th and 20th centuries. After all, Muslims believe that Islam is the religion that embraces every aspect of human society and human lives, and that there is no distinction between religion and politics. Struggles against Western powers were thus religious in nature based on the Islamic totality, namely jihads that became the religious duty of Muslims.

In the colonial age, policies of "divide and rule" offered the indigenous ruling classes — such as monarchies and princely rulers, aristocrats, and landlord classes — favorable terms of compensation that brought them on to the sides of foreign rule Sunni in modern urban Muslim societies, the cosmopolitan freethinking and Westernized liberals are heavily represented in the ruling elites. As SUNNI Jansen indicates,

> ... They usually have Sunnile time for any sort of religion, including Islam, or they are positively anti-religious. Militant Islam in Indonesia, Pakistan, Iran, Turkey and Egypt has already identified and stigmatized this class as its enemy and in Pakistan and Iran has actively gone over to the attack to contain or destroy what it considers an antagonistic force.[11]

Village religious leaders and many mystical Islamic brotherhoods are much closer to ordinary people, who suffered most under foreign oppression and exploitation. It was local religious leaders and Islamic brotherhoods that provided their followers and members with a powerful combination of spiritual renewal

---

[11] *Militant Islam* by G.H. Jansen, Harper & Row Publishers, 1979, pp. 46–47.

and human companionship. It was the "tarikas" (mystical and semi-secret brotherhoods of Muslims) that had used the power of religion to mobilize Muslim groups for anti-imperial purposes. Godfrey H. Jansen, a writer, journalist, an expert on the Middle East, a citizen of India, and a Muslim, observes that

> A review of the close living connection between Islam and Afro-Asia nationalism highlights one strange and important factor. So many of the nationalists, the men who became the historic symbols of their country's freedom, were not merely Muslim men of religion, but members of the mystical Sufi brotherhoods, the tarikas. Beginning with the forerunner, Afghani, we have Price Diponegoro; several tarika leaders including Shamyl in central Asia; the Mahdi and Muhammad Abdallh, Abdel Qadir and Abdel Krim; and the Sanusi — clear proof of how important these partially underground groupings have been in "popular" day-to-day Islam. [12]

Colonization of the Muslim world has strengthened the link between national freedom struggles and the Islamic militants and tarikas against Western powers:

---

[12] *Militant Islam* by G.H. Jansen, Harper & Row Publishers, 1979, pp. 102–103. The names he mentioned in the cited paragraph include the following:

Tarika is an Arabic word, referring to mystical and semi-secret brotherhoods of Muslims. These groups were usually distinct from the ulema or officially mandated scholars, and often acted as informal missionaries of Islam.

Sayyid Jamal al-Din Asadabadi (1838–1897) became renowned as an Afghani. A member of one of the brotherhoods, he moved across the Middle East and Europe, teaching, exhorting, plotting and advising rulers. He exerted tremendous influence on scholars and leaders around the Muslim world.

Prince Diponegoro (1785–1855) is remembered as a great hero, a central figure in the Java War against the Dutch. He had the mystic vision of a religious leader, and mobilized both the elite and the common people of the religious community and the masses in the countryside.

Shamyl (1797–1871) was both the spiritual and military leader of the tribes of the Caucasus, who maintained the struggle for twenty-five years against the Russians.

Mahdi (in Arabic, "the rightly guided one") was established by a Sudanese,

Muhammad Abdallah, in 1881, when he declared himself the Mahdi, inspired by the Prophet to cleanse society of corruption and the infidels. He urged his followers to join him in a fight for faith, modeled after the Prophet's flight from Mecca to Medina.

Abdel Qadir (or Abd al-Kadir) (1808–1883) was an Algerian military leader who led a rebellion against France in the mid-19th century. In post-independence he is respected as a national hero.

Abdel Krim (1882–1963) was the leader of a resistance movement against Spanish and French rule in North Africa. He organized the Rif army, a tribal resistance force against foreign domination of Morocco.

Muhammad bin Ali as Sanusi (1787–1859) was the founder of the Sanusi religious order in Libya. His reputation as a scholar and holy man had spread throughout North Africa. He believed that only a return to the purity of early Islam and its insistence on austerity in faith and morals could restore the religion to its rightful glory.

> By being prepared to pay the price and joining in with the movement of the people, Islam for 150 years received successive blood-transfusions from the struggle to push Europe out of Asia and Africa and back into Europe. That struggle is politically complete, but the blood still courses through the veins of Islam.[13]

Indeed, the anti-imperialist Islamic militant movements in the 19th century and early 20th century naturally extended and further developed into Islamic jihad movements in the second half of the 20th century and continue to be significant political and militant forces in today's Muslim world.

We can summarize as follows: the colonial age represented the nadir of a gradual decline of the Muslim world, witnessing military defeat, loss of territory, corruption, and the coming of Western imperialism. The declining age of the Muslim world presents a striking contrast to the Islamic Golden Age of religious expansion, combined with military success and cultural development. In the countries we are considering, these two sides of this historical heritage have dramatically shaped perspectives of Muslims about themselves and the surrounding external world.

9.4. Westernization, Modernism and Islamic Fundamentalism

Beside fierce Islamic militant resistance against Western imperialism, the dramatic reversal of the Muslim world from the great Islamic Empires into disintegrated pieces of land ruled by Western imperialists has also brought about different reactions in Islamic intellectual circles. This includes the Islamic political elite, intelligentsia, and religious leaders who do not participate in these movements and are generally opposed to them. Different reactions reflect different perspectives and assessments about what has happened to the Muslim world for the last several centuries, why it had happened, and what needs to be done in order to restore the pride of the Islamic religion, the prosperity of the Islamic civilization, and the power of the Muslim nations.

Westernization

Political leaders and a large portion of the intellectual class have advocated that Muslims must learn from Westerners and imitate those aspects that appear to be the basis for the success of Western societies. The goal of these persons is to establish a progressive secular government, separating the religion of Islam from politics, education, and economic and legal systems. Their proposals are directly contradictory to the fundamentalists who believe in an Islamic faith that emphasizes religion as the only guide to all aspects of life for individuals, communities,

[13] *Militant Islam* by GH. Jansen, Harper & Row Publishers, 1979, p.103.

and societies. Thus, these intellectual elites are regarded as radical advocates and are called "Westernizers", who have collaborated with European colonialism and dominated national leaderships of the Muslim world during the European imperialist era and beyond. Over time and under the political, economic, and cultural influences of the West, these pro-Western elites led a series of reform movements that created secular nation-states and formed upper classes with Western tastes in politics, education, entertainment, dress, and in general outlook.

These Western notions directly challenged not only the Islamic tradition, but also the Westernization reforms. Secularizations failed to restore the Islamic pride, power and prosperity that these reformers promised. The ruling class of pro-Western elites, and a small indigenous upper class obviously benefited economically from their reformist policies. They also often enjoyed ostentatious wealth and luxurious Western lifestyles. In addition, the reforms resulted in dictatorial and oppressive secular governments or pro-Western autocratic monarchs or military dictators. These ruling elites are considered to be corruptive and to contaminate Islamic culture and traditions.

On the other hand, the middle and lower classes, composed of rural villagers and peasants, urban workers and slum dwellers, shopkeepers, and migrating rural people as well as the educated yet unemployed or underemployed, suffered the most damage from poverty, unemployment, and deterioration of living standards. Thus Westernization reforms failed to meet the economic needs of the majority of Muslim populations and their demands for more equal distribution of wealth. Poorer Muslims also held strong religious commitments to the Islamic tradition along with deep-seated resentments against Western influence which they believed was the source that had eroded and corrupted their Islamic religion, culture, and society. Consequently, the majority of Muslim populations became the basis of broad anti-government/anti-Western coalitions in many Muslim nation-states during the colonization and post-colonization eras.

Modernism

The group of so-called Islamic Modernists consisting of intelligentsia did not believe that it was necessary to Westernize the Muslim world completely. They advocated that parts of Western models of political, legal, and educational organization structures could be borrowed and made to work in ways that could reflect Islamic values and reach Muslim goals without Westernizing Islamic culture. The Modernists, however, were opposed by both the pro-Western political elites and the conservative ulema, who believed that modernization would lead to dangerous innovations in Islamic religious practice and undercut their authority as "explainers" of Islamic law and traditions.

The Modernists preached their proposals only to a relatively small group of educated Muslims who were members of their social circles and were unable to communicate with the uneducated and semiliterate Muslims. Consequently, they have had few opportunities to put their propositions for Islamic Modernism into practice.

Modernists, however, found some success in Turkey. Modern Turkey was founded in 1923 from Turkish remnants of the defeated Ottoman Empire by the national hero Mustafa Kemal Ataturk (1881–1938). Under his leadership, the country adopted wide-ranging social, legal, and political reforms. After a period of largely one-party rule, a multi-party political system was established. This occurred even while the moderate Islamic Justice and Development Party had gained an overall majority in the Turkish parliament in 2002. Turkey has continued to pursue reforms that balance Islamic values with requirements of a secular and democratic political system. Some of reformers see Christian Democratic parties of Western Europe as a model, but others oppose it. Nevertheless, Islamic Modernists have achieved some degrees of success in Turkey.

Islamic fundamentalism

In contrast, the reform movement that gained broad mass support in the Muslim world is "anti-Western Islamic fundamentalism" which is motivated not only by Islamic religion, but also by related economic, political, social, and cultural concerns. The term "Islamic fundamentalism" is used to emphasize the nature of Islamic revivalist movements in the modern Muslim world. The name, "Islamic fundamentalists", is used to describe Muslims who see themselves as adhering to the ultimate fundamentals or foundations of the Islamic faith, defined by the Muslim holy book, the Quran, and Shariah[14] law.

Various Islamic fundamentalist movements have been extremely active in many Muslim nations where they have also grown rapidly. Some of them are organized as self-help groups, community committees, grassroots organizations and political parties, including the Society of Muslim Brothers — the first modern politically, culturally, and socially oriented Islamic fundamentalist organization.[15] Their activities include not only organizing anti-government, anti-Western demonstrations and protests to defend Islamic traditions and culture, but also providing social services to the poor that have been ignored for a long time by secular governments in some Muslim nations. Their services include health care, education, basic needs for food, clothing, and shelter, as well as public safety and municipal services. The Islamic fundamentalist organizations have owned and run numerous mosques,

[14] Shariah is the body of Muslim law based on the Quran and the documented sayings and actions of the Prophet Muhammad. These "laws" or "rules of behavior" can also be formulated using the techniques of analogy, consensus, and legal opinion that flow from and are consistent with the Quran and hadiths (reports of the Prophet Muhammad's words or actions, or those of his close companions of which he approved) — from "TERMS and NAMES" of the book *Islamic Fundamentalism*.

[15] Lawrence Davidson, *Islamic Fundamentalism*, Greenwood Press, 1998.

schools, hospitals, clinics, charity organizations, and business units that help them to keep in close touch, on a daily basis, with many ordinary Muslims. These additional services have made the Islamic fundamentalists popular to middle and lower class majorities and helped to gain mass support in the electoral processes of some Muslim nations like Iran, Egypt, and Algeria.

Hundreds of millions of pious Muslims have participated in the Islamic fundamentalist mass movements with quite different mind-sets. However, they share common understandings of Islamic history and the contemporary situation of the Muslim world. This is summarized by Lawrence Davidson in the following (see note 15):

> 1. The Muslim world is in a state of disorder brought on by centuries of political and moral decay . . .
>
> 2. This decay made possible Western intrusion which, for all intents and purposes, infected the Muslim world with an alien set of immoral, secularist values and behaviors based on the defining concepts of materialism and (in terms of politics) nationalism. . . They included nationalist, pan-Arabist, socialist, and military government experiments, as well as the secularizing of law codes, courts, and schools, an opening up to Western goods and advertising, and the adoption of Western dress and ideas of gender equality . . . a new period of ignorance (jahiliyya) had dawned . . .
>
> 3. In order to combat this perceived decay and infection, the Muslim world must be re-Islamized. This entails the reassertion of classical Islamic ways, particularly the reintroduction of Shariah or Islamic law, while purging most aspects of Western cultural and political influences . . .
>
> 4. The only way to re-Islamize society is to repoliticize Islam itself . . .
>
> . . . governments must be pressured to reform themselves along Islamic lines or, if they do not, they will be taken over by the forces of Islamic fundamentalism. This, in turn, will inevitably lead to the solving of the problems of corruption and spiritual vacuousness . . . Islam, representative of a total worldview, is the path to justice and socioeconomic equity. In this regard, Islamic fundamentalists look to Muhammad's example as governor and judge at Medina.[16]

Islamic fundamentalists believe they have found the right answer to the question why the Muslim world has declined for centuries. It is because Muslims have forgotten God's instructions to live a good and pious life. As they say "God has not forsaken Muslims, rather Muslims have forsaken God". To revitalize the once great Islamic civilizations Sunni Muslims must return to the "straight path" defined by the holy book Quran and Shariah law, and follow the role model set by the life of the Prophet Muhammad and his close companions. The final goal of

---

[16] Lawrence Davidson, *Islamic Fundamentalism*, Greenwood Press, 1998, pp. 12–13.

Islamic fundamentalists is to establish a pure Islamic state guided by Quran and Shariah law.

A Leading Islamic Fundamentalist

Lawrence Davidson, the author of the already cited book "*Islamic Fundamentalism*", provides selected primary documents of Islamic fundamentalism and brief biographies of seventeen leading Islamic fundamentalists as representatives of thousands of influential Islamic activists who live throughout today's Muslim world. All of the leading Islamic fundamentalists have pursued the goal of revitalizing the Muslim world through the revival of Islamic values and traditions, but have different approaches to interpreting them and to re-Islamizing the Muslim world.

For example, Hassan al-Banna, Egypt's top fundamentalist, organized the Society of the Muslim Brothers in March 1928. The Society has developed rapidly through grassroots movements and grown to be one of Egypt's largest organizations. It still stands as an inspiration for Islamic activists not only in Egypt but throughout the Muslim world. Hasan al-Banna believed that the root cause of Muslim world problems was its deviation from a true Islamic community that resulted in the corruption of institutions, imperialist intrusion, poverty and social injustice. His goal was to bring the Muslim population back to a true understanding and practice of Islam, which means going back to a lifestyle based on the Quran and Shariah.

Members of the Muslim Brotherhood carried out many nonviolent cultural and economic activities in order to purify Muslim communities. They also conducted numerous political and aggressive operations against British imperialists and the pro-British government of Egypt. As Davidson notes, "It is uncertain whether al-Banna ever had any definite plans to take over the Egyptian state... He always asserted that an Islamic government had to await the thorough re-Islamization of the Egyptian masses".[17] The Muslim Brotherhood's confrontation with the government brought troubles to al-Banna, who was arrested several times and eventually assassinated by members of the Egyptian secret police in February, 1949. Ever since, a section of the Brotherhood, which was created by al-Banna and called the "secret apparatus", has become very active, militant, and violent in actions against the Egyptian government.

Even though the Society of Muslim Brothers supported the "Free Officers" led by Nasser who overthrew the pro-British Egyptian Monarch in 1952, al-Banna's dream of an Islam-guided state was not the same as Nasser's secular socialist state. Following a series of disagreements with Nasser's policies, the Brotherhood was ordered to dissolve in 1954 by the Egyptian government and forced to slip

[17] Lawrence Davidson, *Islamic Fundamentalism*, Greenwood Press, 1998, pp. 89–90.

into an informal mode of existence and operation, and its "secret apparatus" went underground as a paramilitary group. The government's repression led to a failed attempt to assassinate Nasser in 1954. In the end, many leaders of the Society were killed, and thousands of members were arrested and accused of seeking to establish a primitive, barbaric religious state.

Dissolution and oppression of the Brotherhood helped create militant Islamic fundamentalist organizations or tarikas (mystical and semi-secret brotherhoods of Muslims) crying for violent activity against the Egyptian government and Western influences, including the assassination of Nasser's successor, Anwar al-Sadat, in 1981. Since then, the Egyptian Muslim Brotherhood has been considered as an *Islamist* organization pursuing Islamism. "Islamism" is a political ideology derived from the conservative religious views of Muslim fundamentalism. It believes that Islam is not only a religion, but a political system that governs the legal, economic and social institutions of the state. The common goal of Islamists is to rebuild Muslim states by implementing conservative formulations of Islamic law.

A Leading Islamist

An example of a leading Islamist was Ruhillah Mussaui Khomeini, the leader of the 1979 Iranian Revolution. Khomeini developed his early career as a fundamentalist theology teacher at various religious schools and built up a considerable student following. He identified the Iranian government's policies with Western, and in particular, with American influence in Iran. He referred to Pahlavi Shah's secular reform, which included women's suffrage and a land reform, as a "United States conspiracy against Islam", and accused Americans of attempting to turn Iran into a colony. Khomeini emerged as the militant leader in violent protests across the country. He was arrested in 1964 and subsequently exiled, and then spent time in Turkey, Iraq, and Paris.

Khomeini led a group of Islamists, called the Islamic Republican party. Having some contact with the Society of Muslim Brothers in Egypt, Khomeini shared the similar goal of re-Islamizing the Muslim world. As Davidson indicates,

> Hassan al-Banna had believed that the Muslim Brothers should seek political power only when the Islamic consciousness of the Egyptian people was sufficiently reestablished. Khomeini adhered to no such qualification. ... For Khomeini, the answer was first to overthrow the impious Shah and create a government dominated by the pious ulama (Muslim scholars, jurists, and clerics). Then one would proceed to "purify" Iran of its "contamination"...[18]

Iran's Islamist revolution in 1979 offered Khomeini exactly what he wanted; the opportunity to create a pure Islamic state. Khomeini started his career as a

[18] Lawrence Davidson, *Islamic Fundamentalism*, Greenwood Press, 1998, pp. 38–39.

fundamentalist, and turned himself into an Islamist to achieve his political and religious objectives. The establishment of the Islamic Republic of Iran in 1979 was the first significant political victory for Islamic fundamentalism and Islamism. It also provided a great impetus to Islamic fundamentalist and Islamist movements throughout the Muslim world. As a matter of fact, however, there are only two countries in the whole world, Saudi Arabia and Iran, where Islamic fundamentalism is now in power. The movements in Sudan, Pakistan, Algeria, and other Muslim states have not shown much success. Instead, they witnessed either one military dictatorship after another or endless civil wars. Nevertheless, Islamic fundamentalist movements envelop various loosely connected or self-help Muslim groups, and some mystical and semi-secret brotherhoods of Muslims (tarikas). Some of them choose nonviolent approaches, and are active in religious, cultural, and social domains, while others commit acts of violence and terrorism, like the militant Palestinian *Islamist* group Hamas, while pursuing political goals. All of these movements and participating groups have continued to play important roles in the post colonial era of the Muslim world. We discuss them in the next chapter.

Summary of Chapter 9

This chapter covers the declining age and the collapse of Islamic Empires and their tragic end that turned almost all Muslim lands into colonies of European countries like Britain, France, Italy, Netherlands, Italy, Portugal and Russia. Only four Muslim countries did not become a colony of European powers during the 18th–20th; they are Iran, Saudi Arabia, Afghanistan and Turkey.

The colonial age of the Muslim world witnessed military defeats, loss of territory, corruption, depredations and the humiliations associated with Western imperialism. This presents a striking contrast to the Islamic Golden Age and has dramatically shaped perspectives of Muslims about themselves and the surrounding external world. The Islamic heritage provides a significant cohering force that united Muslim communities around the globe in a common cause against Western occupation and influence. In particular, it has encouraged militant Islamic activities around the world and has set heroic examples for Islamic jihad for younger generations.

Muslim intellectual circles have tried hard to find answers to the question why the Muslim world has declined and fallen behind for centuries. They have come up with three kinds of different answers: Westernization, modernism and fundamentalism.

The goal of Westernization is to imitate the Western world by establishing secular governments and separating Islam from politics, education, and legal and economic systems. Modernists advocated that parts of Western models of political, legal, and educational organization structures could be borrowed, modified, and made to work in ways that could reflect Islamic values and reach Muslim goals without Westernizing Islamic culture.

Islamic fundamentalists believe that Muslims have forgotten God's instructions to live a good and pious life and that this caused the decline for the Muslim world. Muslims must return to the "straight path" defined by the holy book Quran and Shariah law and follow the role model set by the life of the Prophet Muhammad and his close companions. The final goal is to establish a pure Islamic state guided by Quran and Shariah law.

Many post-colonial Muslim governments pursued Westernization and failed. Turkey has at least partially succeeded with the modernism reforms initiated by Kemal Ataturk. Saudi Arabia and Iran are the only two countries where Islamic fundamentalism is now in power with all of the other countries representing mixtures of modernism and Muslimism.

Chapter 10

The Contemporary Scene and Its Challenges

The Muslim world has constantly engaged in confrontations with the Western world in the post-colonial era. The heritage of Western imperialism led to Islamic militant hatreds and hostility toward the West. It also motivated Islamic Fundamentalist movements, which condemned the West for all of the Muslim problems, and aimed at eliminating all Western influences. Western dislike and fear of Islamic militants and terrorism is also deeply rooted in a long history of religiously based Christian hostility toward Muslims.

Within the Muslim world, brother states fight each other not so much for religious disagreements, but for purposes of controlling lands, offshore petroleum resources, and oil exporting roads and pipelines. These conflicts and crises serve as a main cause of instability and are major obstacles to economic progress and social development in many Muslim nations. They are also grave threats to world peace and prosperity. Islamic Fundamentalists and militants continue to play important roles in contemporary struggles of Muslim nations with non-Muslim nations as well as among and between Muslim nations themselves. The following sections illustrate the continuation of renewed and strengthened Islamic militant activities in the post-Colonial Age.

10.1. Arab–Israeli Conflict

The Arab world

The confrontation between Israel (Map 10.1) and the Arab world is one cause of contemporary struggles between the Muslim and Western worlds. The Arab world is at the center of a Muslim land that includes 22 Muslim-majority countries in the Middle East and Africa. Except for Iran, all Muslim states in the Middle East and North Africa belong to the Arab world and, in addition, three states in sub-Sahara Africa (Somalia, Sudan and Mauritania) also belong to the Arab world. These nations are the current members of the Arab League,[1] which was founded in Cairo

[1] The Arab League was established in 1945 as an association of independent countries whose peoples are mainly Arabic speaking. Its purposes are to strengthen ties among the member states, coordinate their policies, and promote their common interests. Currently it has 22 members: Algeria, Bahrain, Comoros, Djibouti, Egypt, Iraq, Jordan, Kuwait, Lebanon, Libya, Mauritania, Morocco, Oman, Palestine, Qatar, Saudi Arabia, Somalia, Sudan, Syria, Tunisia, United Arab Emirates, and Yemen.

International Symposia in Economic Theory and Econometrics, Vol. 19
William W. Cooper and Piyu Yue

ISSN: 1571-0386/DOI: 10.1016/S1571-0386(07)00023-3

in 1945 and has served as a forum for member nations to coordinate their political stances, to promote economic integration, and to settle Arab disputes and conflicts. The Arab nations share Arabic as a written and spoken language, enjoy similar life styles, culture and traditions, and worship in the same religion — Islam. As of 2000, total population of these 22 Arab states is about 277 million, compared to a total population of 1279 million in the 49 Muslim-majority states of the world. Most importantly, the Arab world contains the dominating oil producers and occupies crucial crossroads and seaways through which oil output reaches global markets. Hence, the Arab states constitute a core of the Muslim world in the sense that what happens in the Arab states can have far-reaching effects on other Muslim states due to common beliefs as in the Muslim Brotherhood.

Establishing Israel

The conflict between Palestinian Arabs and Jews that began around the turn of the 20th century has continued to the present, and may well extend many years into the future. Religious differences are not the sole cause of the conflict; rather it is the claims to a piece of land by both sides that have caused military confrontations and civil revolts, in which the major Arab nations and the world's superpowers of the time, Britain, France, the Soviet Union and the United States, have all been involved. That piece of land known as Palestine constitutes about 10 000 square miles (a size similar to that of the state of Maryland), with a historical site in Jerusalem of the Jewish Kingdom of Israel. That Kingdom was destroyed by the Assyrians in 722 BC and by the Babylonians in 586 BC.[2] Later the land became a part of the Roman Empire and then the Ottoman Empire. The historical site of Jerusalem is also holy to Muslims because of the Al-Aqsa Mosque and Dome of the Rock that is believed to mark the spot from which the Prophet Muhammad ascended to heaven on a winged horse.

Zionism[3] was the Jewish political movement formally founded in 1897; Theodor Herzl (1860–1904), an Austrian Jewish journalist, was the founder of modern political Zionism. In 1896 a wave of French anti-Semitism motivated Herzl to publish his book "The Jewish State" with the subtitle of "An Attempt at a Modern Solution of the Jewish Question".

---

[2] Assyria, located in north Mesopotamia, extends into four countries: Syria, Turkey, Iran, and Iraq. Mesopotamia (the land between the two rivers, the Tigris and Euphrates) is the site of the world's first civilization, and often referred to as the "cradle of civilization". Assyrian history began around 2400 BC, and its First Golden Age lasted from 2400 BC to 612 BC. After the fall of the Assyrian empire (612 BC), the ancient city, Babylon, which was situated on the Euphrates River south of Baghdad in modern Iraq, became the capital of the ancient Near East, and the Babylonian Empire, which was the most powerful state of its time in the ancient world.

[3] The word "Zionism" is derived from the word "Zion", being one of the names of Jerusalem, as mentioned in the Bible.

Map 10.1: Map of Israel.

Beginning in 1881, the Russian Empire promoted a series of massive violent attacks on Jews called "pogroms"[4] in which many Jews were murdered along with simultaneous destruction of homes, businesses, and religious centers. Anti-Semitism riots also spread throughout Eastern and Central Europe and lasted till 1945. During World War II, the Nazi genocide killed over six million European Jews. Those tragedies convinced the great majority of surviving Jews across the world that a Jewish homeland was an urgent necessity — particularly given the large population of disenfranchised Jewish refugees after World War II. Palestine was considered to be the only location that was acceptable to all strands of Jews for establishing the State of Israel. Jews who had spread across the world were en-

[4] Pogrom is Russian for "devastation".

couraged to immigrate to Palestine as a place for identification of an independent Jewish state. The majority population in Palestine, however, was Arab amounting to about 683 000 Arabs versus 60 000 Jews by the outbreak of World War I in 1914. Since 1948, many Jews have continued to identify themselves as Zionists and support the State of Israel, politically and financially, even if they do not choose to live there.

In a letter dated November 2, 1917 from British Foreign Secretary Arthur James Balfour to Lord Rothschild (a leader of the British Jewish community) led to what is called the Balfour Declaration,[5] in which Britain announced its support for the establishment of a Jewish national home in Palestine. This ignored the promise Britain had earlier made to the Arab world that it would support the establishment of an independent Arab state in the Arab provinces of the Ottoman Empire, including Palestine.

The quasi-colonial authority of Britain and France over former Ottoman territories, combined with Britain's failure to fulfill its promise, angered the Arabs and generated hostilities and clashes between Arabs and Jews over Palestine. In November, 1947, the UN General Assembly voted to partition Palestine into two states, one Jewish and one Arab, and designated the area of Jerusalem as an international zone. The Palestine Arabs and neighboring Arab states rejected the UN plan and fought against the Jewish people in Palestine.

Armed Conflicts

In May, 1948, Israel was established as an independent Jewish state. Almost immediately, the surrounding Arab states, including Egypt, Syria, Jordan and Iraq, invaded Israel. Israel won the resulting war however and conquered territories beyond the borders of the UN partition plan for the Jewish state. After the war, Palestine was divided into three parts, each under separate political control. Israel controlled over 77% of the territory, Jordan occupied East Jerusalem and central Palestine, and Egypt controlled the Gaza Strip (the coastal plain around the city of Gaza). The Palestinian Arab state of the UN partition plan was never established. Instead over 0.7 million Palestinian Arabs lost their homes and became refugees during the fighting of 1947–1949.

Israel and Egypt clashed repeatedly after the 1948 war. Even though Egypt has the longest history as a unified state, it was a British colony until 1922 when its

[5] The main body of the letter reads: "His Majesty's Government view with favour the establishment in Palestine of a national home for the Jewish people, and will use their best endeavours to facilitate the achievement of this object, it being clearly understood that nothing shall be done which may prejudice the civil and religious rights of existing non-Jewish communities in Palestine, or the rights and political status enjoyed by Jews in any other country."..., excerpted from "Balfour Declaration, 1917" in Wikipedia, the free encyclopedia, http://en.wikipedia.org.

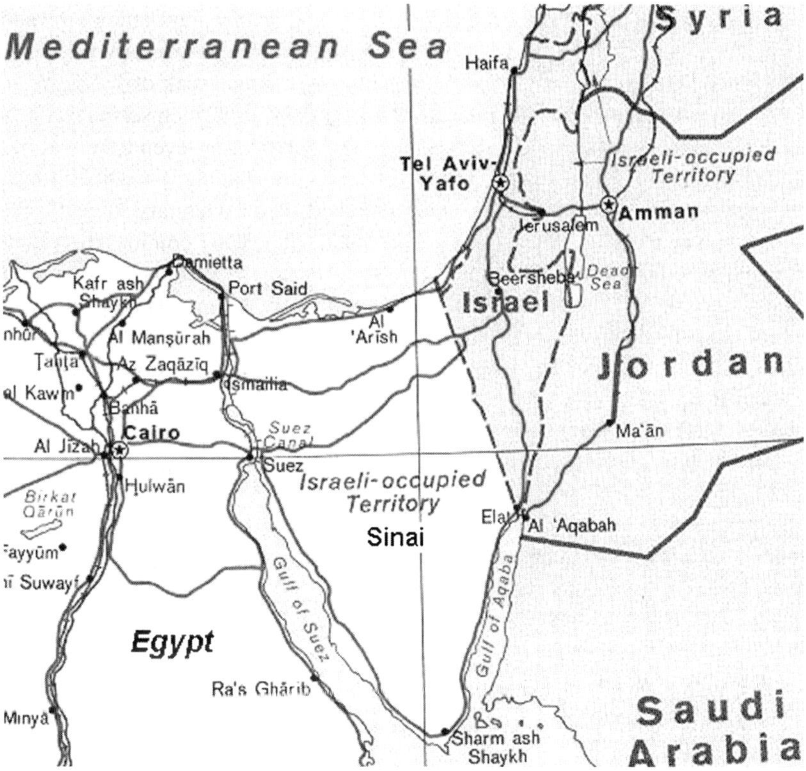

Map 10.2: Map of Suez Canal and Sinai Peninsula.

independence was granted. True self rule did not occur until 1953 with the rise to power of General Nasser. Other Arab nations also gained independence from Britain and France. These young Arab states were eagerly pursuing nationalist goals and looking for foreign aid to help develop their economies and societies. At that time the Soviet Union superpower rushed into the Muslim world, attempting to make friends and Egypt became one of them. Nasser's Egypt began to import arms from the Soviet Bloc to help build its arsenal for a confrontation with Israel.

This led to the following events. In July, 1956, Egypt nationalized the Suez Canal, which was owned by British and French private companies. Later, Egypt escalated the conflict with Israel by blockading the Strait of Tiran, the narrow waterway that is Israel's only outlet to the Red Sea. In October, 1956, Egypt signed a tripartite agreement with Syria and Jordan, placing Nasser in command of all three armies. Responding to the Arab world's actions, on October 29, 1956, Israeli troops invaded Egypt's Sinai Peninsula and raced towards the Suez Canal. See Map 10.2 of Suez Canal and Sinai Peninsula.

Two days later, the military forces of Britain and France attacked and invaded Egypt. In response, the Soviet Union threatened to intervene on Egypt's behalf. The United States, caught by surprise, was more concerned with global situations of the Cold War than with the interest of Britain and France in the Suez Canal. The United Sates pressured Britain, France and Israel to withdraw from Egypt, including the Sinai Peninsula and Gaza which had been captured by Israeli forces. It was believed that Israel, France and Britain had secretly planned the campaign to evict Egypt from the Suez Canal. The war itself lasted only for a week and ended with withdrawal of the invading forces. The Suez War led to an important consequence in that Egypt and other Arab nations began to align with the Soviet Union against Israel and the West, and this became of great importance in the global political and military struggle known as the "Cold War".

Supported by the Soviet Union, Syria clashed with Israel in the spring of 1967 and requested assistance of the Arab world. In response, Egyptian troops entered the Sinai Peninsula bordering Israel and proclaimed a blockade of the Israeli port of Elat on the Gulf of Aqaba. Jordan also joined in the fighting later on. Shocked and frightened by Egypt's actions, Israel preemptively attacked Egypt and Syria on June 5, 1967, destroying the enemy air forces on the ground within a few hours. The war lasted only six days with a decisive defeat of the Arab world. During this war, Israel occupied the West Bank of the Jordan river (including East Jerusalem), the Gaza strip, the Sinai Peninsula of Egypt, and the Golan Heights of Syria. The six-day war established Israel as the dominant regional military power and discredited the Arab regimes in general and Egypt's Nasser in particular.

When Egypt's willingness to sign a peace agreement with Israel in exchange for the return of Egyptian territory lost in the 1967 war was ignored by Israel and the United States, Egypt and Syria simultaneously attacked Israel on the Jewish holy day of Yom Kippur in October, 1973 and achieved early military successes. With US political intervention and sharply increased military aid to Israel, however, the Arab aggression was defeated again. After this so-called "Ramadan war",[6] the United States exhausted all of its potential to reach some agreement for Israeli withdrawals. There then seemed no prospect of an Arab–Israeli peace settlement over Palestine and the occupied Arab lands.

Egyptian leader Anwar Sadat,[7] who was Nasser's successor, decided to initiate a separate overture to Israel and signed an Egyptian–Israeli peace treaty in 1979. This was the first part of an agreement known as the Camp David accords worked out by Egypt, Israel and the United States at Camp David in September 1978. Under these accords the Sinai Peninsula was returned to Egypt. The second part of

[6] It is also called the "Yom Kippur War".

[7] Anwar Sadat met Gamal Abdel Nasser while in a British military school in colonial Egypt in the late 1930s. He joined Nasser for the revolution that fought colonialism and overthrew the monarchy in 1952, eventually succeeding Nasser as president in 1970.

the Camp David accords granted autonomy to the Palestinians in the West Bank and Gaza Strip and installed a five-year interim local administration. The Camp David accords were rejected by the Palestinians and other Arab nations because they believed that the accords did not guarantee Israeli withdrawal from captured areas in the 1967 war and the establishment of an independent Palestinian state. After the Ramadan war, Israel has continued to occupy Palestinian lands and build new settlements in these occupied areas. New dimensions of large-scale civil violence and terrorist attacks on civilians were then added to the confrontations between Arabs and Israelis.

Palestinians

The Arab League established the Palestine Liberation Organization (PLO) in 1964 to further Palestinian nationalism while appearing to champion the cause of independence. The PLO consists of different political and militant groups with varying ideological orientations, all loosely organized under the banner of "PLO". Yasser Arafat was the leader of the largest group "Al-Fatah" and served as PLO Chairman from 1968 to 2004.[8] The PLO's base was first established in Jordan, and then moved into Lebanon. The PLO participated in Lebanon's civil war in 1975. The PLO army grew in Southern Lebanon by building camps, training fighters, and stockpiling arms. PLO fighters also frequently crossed over the border to attack Israeli civilians, and forced thousands of Israeli residents to flee their homes.

A PLO terrorist group attempted to assassinate Israel's Ambassador to Britain, Shlomo Argov, on June 3, 1982 and this served as provocation for the Israeli invasion of Lebanon in 1982. After Israel seized control of southern Lebanon, the PLO leadership was expelled from the country and relocated in Tunisia. For a long time, Israel rejected the plan of establishing an independent Palestinian state and insisted that Palestinians should be incorporated into existing Arab states. Israel considered the PLO to be a terrorist organization dedicated to the destruction of Israel and refused to negotiate with it. However, a growing worry about radical Islam militant operations in the region and the weakness of the PLO after the Gulf War led to the end of Israel's intransigence. In 1993, Israel initiated a secret negotiation with the PLO at Oslo, Norway.[9]

In the Israeli occupied West Bank and Gaza Strip, the Palestinian population started a mass "intifada" (uprising) in 1987. It involved hundreds of thousands of people in many forms of civil revolt: massive demonstrations, general strikes, refusals to pay taxes, boycotts of Israeli products, stone throwing, Molotov cock-

[8] He died in November 2004 while still serving as Chairman.

[9] Israel initiated secret negotiations directly with PLO representatives. These negotiations produced the Israel–PLO Declaration of Principles signed in Washington in 1993.

tails, and erections of barricades to impede the movement of Israeli military forces. Israel tried to smash the intifada with military force, killing over one thousand Palestinians, including some leaders of the organizations in the occupied areas who had orchestrated the mass movement. Internal struggles involving political divisions and violence within the Palestinian community escalated, and the first intifada lost its cohesive force and faded away.

The second intifada broke out in the fall of 2000. It was ignited by Israeli General Sharon's visit to the Temple Mount and his well-known call for Israeli annexation of East Jerusalem. The large Palestinian protest in Jerusalem and an incident in which Israeli soldiers killed six unarmed protesters launched over a month of demonstrations and clashes all across the West Bank and Gaza Strip as well as in Palestinian towns inside Israel. The second intifada was extensive and bloodier than the first one. Both sides employed excessive force. Palestinian militant groups coordinated many street actions with a substantial cache of small arms which they could use to fire on Israeli troops. The Israeli military response escalated with tank shells, artillery, helicopter machine-guns and missiles. The second intifada was ended by implementation of the Oslo peace process, which provided for Palestinian self-rule in the Gaza Strip and the city of Jericho in the West Bank, and the future extension of self-rule to the rest of the West Bank. Israeli troops withdrew from Gaza and Jericho in 1994 and Arafat became the head of the Palestine National Authority (PNA), controlling Gaza and about 450 towns and villages in the West Bank.

Terrorists in the Islamic Fundamentalist Hamas[10] movement continued to use violence against Israeli civilians in order to destroy the Middle-East peace process. Hamas and Islamic Jihad terrorists have used suicide-bombers killing hundreds of citizens in Israel. Clashes between Israeli troops and PNA police forces also escalated. In 2002, Israel decided to erect security walls that would isolate Palestinians from Israelis. It was estimated that the walls may eventually cover several hundred miles at a cost of $1.5 billion dollars. The irony is that the security wall is not really an effective solution to the terrorist attacks on Israeli civilians.[11] Terrorist attacks and the security assurance to residents in both

[10] "Hamas" is the Arabic acronym for "The Islamic Resistance Movement" with leaders from the Muslim Brotherhood. It was a radical Islamic organization playing a major role in the Intifada, and operating in the Gaza Strip and the West Bank. Hamas has now become the leading perpetrator of terrorist activity throughout the territories as well as inside Israel. It is the second most powerful group, after Arafat's Fatah, and the strongest opposition group to the peace process in the Middle East.

[11] On January 13th 2005, Palestinian militants set off a large truck bomb at a vital Gaza crossing that blew a hole in the security wall between the Israeli and Palestinian sides of the crossing, killing five Israelis and wounding five others. The attack was aimed at peace efforts by the new Palestinian leader, Mahmoud Abbas, who was named as chairman of the PLO after Yasser Arafat died in November 2004, and won convincingly in the election for President of the Palestinian Authority in January 2005.

Israel and Palestine remain major issues that obstruct the peace process in the Middle East and increase instability of the Muslim world. Hamas won 74 of 132 seats in the January 2006 Palestinian legislative election and is now the majority party of the Palestinian Legislative Council. The Palestinian territories have since experienced sharp internal conflicts, in which many Palestinians were killed. Nevertheless, the Palestinians are still stateless.

Hatred Remarks

For over half a century, the Arab world has struggled against Israel with wars and intifadas over Palestine that achieved almost nothing. The situation of Palestinians today is worse than that of fifty years ago. The enduring violent Arab–Israel confrontation has intensified anti-Semitism across the Muslim world. Government officials of many Muslim countries have blamed their military, political, and economic failures and humiliations on Jews. The former Prime Minister of Malaysia,[12] Mahathir Mohamad, is noted for his speech to the Opening of the Tenth Session of the Islamic Summit Conference at Putrajaya of Malaysia on the 16th of October 2003. In his speech Mahathir asserted:

> "... 1.3 billion Muslims cannot be defeated by a few million Jews.... We are actually very strong. 1.3 billion people cannot be simply wiped out. The Europeans killed 6 million Jews out of 12 million. But today the Jews rule this world by proxy. They get others to fight and die for them
>
> We are up against a people who think. They survived 2000 years of pogroms not by hitting back, but by thinking. They invented and successfully promoted socialism, communism, human rights and democracy so that persecuting them would appear to be wrong, so they may enjoy equal rights with others. With these they have now gained control of the most powerful countries and they, this tiny community, have become a world power. We cannot fight them through brawn alone. We must use our brain also ...."

In his capacity as Prime Minister of Malaysia in 1997, Mahathir blamed the Asian financial and economic crisis on the Jewish financier George Soros. "We do not want to say that this is a plot by the Jews", he said, "but in reality it is a Jew who triggered the currency plunge, and coincidentally Soros is a Jew. It is also a coincidence that the Malaysians are mostly Muslim. Indeed, the Jews are not happy to see Muslims progress".[13] Mahathir's remarks helped fuel worldwide

---

[12] In 1948, the British-ruled territories on the Malay Peninsula formed the Federation of Malaya, which became independent in 1957. Malaysia was formed in 1963 when Singapore and the East Malaysian states of Sabah and Sarawak on the northern coast of Borneo joined the Federation. Singapore's secession from Malaysia took place in 1965.

[13] Mahathir Mohamad, "*Speech on the 10th Session of the Islamic Summit Conference*" at the Putrajaya Convention Centre on October 16th 2003, canibus-central.com/forum/lofiversion/index.php/t28485.html.

Muslim hatred against Israel, the United States, and Western nations. They also reflect the common stance of governments in the Muslim world. To blame and criticize the rest of the world, in general, Israel and the United States, in particular, for their own failed policies in both domestic and international affairs, and for use in shifting public anger toward external non-Muslim factors over their economic misery, hardship, frustration, and humiliations. The strategy of dividing the world into Muslim and Non-Muslim parts, however, seems hardly to be helping the Muslim states to form a united Muslim world. Indeed, as we shall see in the next section, conflicts and wars between Muslim states have also been extensive and as furious as the Arab–Jewish confrontation.

10.2. Iraq–Iran War

Violent confrontations have frequently occurred between Muslim countries. The war between Iraq and Iran is a recent example. Iran and Iraq have become the most influential nations in the Muslim world with their large populations and territories, huge petroleum resources, substantial oil production and export capacities, and possessing the region's leading military forces. These two nations, however, have been devastated by tribulations, conflicts, and wars for decades.

Iran's Islamic Revolution

As noted earlier, Iran was known as Persia until 1935 when Persia was officially renamed Iran. In January, 1979 hundreds of thousands of Iranian students — i.e., members of the "troublesome cohort" — stormed Tehran's streets, ousted Iran's pro-American monarch under Shah Mohammad Reza Pahlavi, and gave a hero's welcome to Ayatollah Khomeini, the head of the Shiite Islamic Fundamentalist movement, when he returned after 15 years of exile in France. This was the beginning of Iran's contemporary Islamic revolution. Three months later, Islamism came to power in Iran. Khomeini declared Iran an Islamic Republic and became the Supreme Leader, holding ultimate executive power, controlling the security forces of the country and holding the power to appoint and dismiss the leaders of the judiciary.

Following the exiled Shah's arrival in the United States, militant Iranian students occupied the US Embassy in Tehran on November 4th, 1979, held 52 Americans hostage and did not release them until January 20th, 1981 after they had influenced the 1980 US election of Ronald Reagan over Jimmy Carter. The 1979 Iranian Revolution also made manifest the political power of Islamist terror on the world scene. Since then, Islamist terrorism has spread worldwide with a powerful influence felt not only throughout the entire Muslim world but also in many places in Europe, India, Russia, and America.

Iran sought to create a purified Islamic society where citizen values, outlook, and behavior must be guided by the Shariah law. Strict Islamic laws were implemented and all non-Islamic laws created since 1906 (the year of creation of Persian parliament and a written constitution) were voided. Iran also started a cultural revolution that resulted in the closure of all universities and higher education institutes for two years. Human rights abuses such as torture and violent executions occurred. Khomeini's revolutionary regime also reversed the country's foreign policy from a pro-US stance to a vehement anti-US and anti-Israel stance, and declared the United States the "great Satan". The United States broke off relations with Iran in 1980, and Iran aimed at eliminating outside Western influences in the country as well as in the Middle-East. The Iranian revolution has led many Muslim nations to fear that radical Shiite Muslims of Iran could export their Islamic revolution and Shiite Islam into other Muslim countries where people hold different faiths on Islam such as Sunni Islam.

Iraq Attacked Iran

At that time Saddam Hussein had already become the effective leader of Iraq. He had drawn on Iraq's oil wealth to build up Iraqi military forces with increasing imports of sophisticated Soviet weapons. Except for Israel, Iran had the only army in the Middle East that could challenge Iraq. Hostility between Iraq and Iran was a continuation of the ancient Persian–Arab conflicts that had been fueled by numerous border disputes, centuries old Sunni–Shiite disagreements, and Persian–Arab ethnic clashes. Iraq considered the Iranian revolution and Iran's Islamic Fundamentalist agenda as threatening to pan-Arabism and Iraq's delicate Sunni–Shiite balance. Personal ambitions and hatreds between Saddam Hussein and Khomeini also escalated into an Iran–Iraq confrontation. However, the ultimate purpose that led Iraq to invade Iran in 1980 was to consolidate Iraq's rising power in the Arab world and to replace Iran as the dominant Persian Gulf state.

In September 1980, Iraq attacked Western Iran, launching an eight-year war in which more than one million people were killed, many more were wounded, and millions were made refugees. During the war, the two superpowers of the world, the United States and Soviet Union, supplied large-scale arms assistance to both sides. Iraq was accused of using chemical weapons against Iranian troops and against Iraq's Kurdish civilians. The war was ended in August 1988 with the acceptance of a UN Resolution. There was virtually no winner of the war and none of the disputed issues which were blamed for the war had been resolved either during the war or afterwards.

Shortly after the war, Khomeini died. Ayatollah Khamenei was selected as the new Supreme Leader of Iran by the Assembly of Experts in June, 1989. An arch-conservative dedicated to keeping political power in the hands of the politicized clergy, Ayatollah Khamenei has absolute authority in Iran. The head of state is the President, elected by popular vote for a four-year term. Over the past decade,

Iranian desires for freedom, human rights and democratization, as well as increasing dissatisfaction with the government encouraged some relatively liberal clerics to pursue moderate reforms. In recent years, however, conservative hardliners who control the judiciary used security forces to shut down newspapers that support reforms and jailed opponents and reformers. Resistance to democratic reforms and oppression of student protests by the ruling conservatives have set off further upheavals and increased instability in Iran.

Iran's Nuclear Threat

On February 9, 2003, Iran revealed a nuclear program and its efforts in building sophisticated facilities at Natanz and several other cities that would eventually produce enriched uranium. Iran's nuclear program and activities, though criticized for many years, have come into sharp focus since this announcement. The US government believes that Iran has a nuclear program that is far more advanced than has been disclosed. It believes that Iran's uranium-enrichment facility is "extremely advanced" so that enriched uranium could be used to produce nuclear weapons. Iran has confirmed its nuclear facilities and plants, but says its nuclear program is aimed at supplying electric power. The Bush administration in the US, however, considers new developments in Iran's nuclear program to be of "great concern". The US has long accused Iran of trying to develop nuclear weapons arguing that, having vast oil and natural gas reserves, Iran hardly needs nuclear energy and the primary purpose of Iran's nuclear program is developing nuclear weapons. Iran, together with Iraq and North Korea, was among the nations President Bush labeled the "axis of evil" in his State of the Union address in January 2002.

In 2006, the global powers, Britain, Germany, France, the United States, China and Russia have agreed in offering a new package of incentives to Iran in exchange for verifiable assurances that it is not pursuing atomic weapons. The United States, Britain and France have finally persuaded Russia and China to agree to a legally binding resolution that Iran suspend its efforts to produce plutonium and highly enriched uranium. On 31 July 2006, the UN Security Council approved such a resolution demanding that Iran suspend its enrichment and reprocessing of nuclear fuel by August 31, 2006 or face the threat of economic and diplomatic sanctions. Iran maintains that it has the right, under the 1970 nuclear Non-Proliferation Treaty, to enrich and reprocess uranium to fuel a nuclear energy program, but it is willing to engage in talks over their nuclear program in response to the global powers.

10.3. Iraqi Invasion of Kuwait

After the Iraq–Iran war, Iraq possessed significant military advantages over not only Iran but also all of the other Arab states in the region. Iraq's large air force and an army of more than a million military men were equipped with an extensive arsenal, including chemical weapons and extended-range Scud missiles. Iraq also attempted to develop its nuclear weapons. It was estimated that within 2–10 years Iraq would actually have a nuclear weapon. In any event, Israel felt it was too risky to wait for Iraq to develop weapons of mass destruction against its people. Therefore, on June 7, 1981, Israeli warplanes preemptively struck the Osirak nuclear facility near Baghdad in order to deny Iraq the capability of producing nuclear weapons. In one minute and twenty seconds, the reactor lay in ruins. Israel's preemptive strike against Iraq was condemned by the United Nations, although privately many governments in the Middle East and elsewhere were pleased to see this setback to Iraq.

Iraq's growing military strength fueled Saddam Hussein's ambitions to dominate the Persian Gulf and the Arab world and to control most of the world's oil supply. In August, 1990, Saddam ordered Iraqi troops to take over Kuwait, a small Arab country in the Persian Gulf that produced nearly 10% of the world's oil. The ruling family of Kuwait fled to Saudi Arabia, and Kuwait fell under Iraqi control. The Security Council of the UN voted to condemn Iraq's invasion of Kuwait and demanded the immediate withdrawal of all Iraqi forces; it also voted to set up trade and financial sanctions against Iraq. Iraq rejected the UN demand and renamed Kuwait "Province 19" of Iraq and Kuwait city "Qadima". In response a mass pro-Iraqi demonstration broke out in Syria; Iraq and Iran restored diplomatic relations that had been severed in 1980 after their eight-year war; and Yasser Arafat announced that the PLO of Palestine fully supported Iraq's enterprise in Kuwait.

In January, 1991, Iraq fired Scud missiles into Israel and the PLO announced its intention to open a "second front" in southern Lebanon against Israel in support of Iraq. Under the leadership of Saudi Arabia, the Organization of the Islamic Conference (QIC) voted to condemn the Iraqi invasion. However, four members (Jordan, Sudan, PLO and Libya) refused to vote. The Arab world was therefore obviously divided in its stance toward the Iraqi invasion of Kuwait. The Muslim world, and the Sunni Muslim community (or Ummah) in particular, was divided over Iraq's action. The reality was that a big "Muslim brother", Iraq, had, with Sunni Islamic authority, swallowed a little Sunni "Muslim brother", Kuwait. Other "Muslim brother" nations could do nothing to stop it; some "Muslim brother" nations even supported Iraq.

"Operation Desert Storm"

The United States, the only superpower left in the post cold war era, after the dissolution of the Soviet Union in 1991, led an international coalition and launched "Operation Desert Storm". The United States, Britain, and France were the predominating forces but Egypt and Syria also participated. Threatened by the possibility of Iraqi forces continuing down the Gulf coast to seize other oil-rich Arab states, Saudi Arabia and other smaller Arab states in the Persian Gulf had all volunteered use of their lands, ports and airfields as bases for the coalition forces.

On February 27, 1991, the coalition forces liberated Kuwait city three days after launching a ground assault and in response Iraqi troops set fire to more than 150 oil wells inside Kuwait. Retreating Iraqi troops also sparked a rebellion against Saddam's regime in the south of Iraq among the Shiite population. In the north, Kurdish forces also rose up against Saddam. Although the war was a decisive military victory for the coalition, Kuwait and Iraq suffered enormous property damage, and Saddam Hussein was not removed from power. In fact, Saddam was left free to turn his attention to suppressing internal Shiite and Kurdish revolts. As a result the Iraqi army put down the uprising in the south and north by killing hundreds of thousands of Shiite Muslims and Kurds.

After defeating Iraq, the United States, France and Britain established a northern "no-fly zone" over Iraq to protect the Kurds from Saddam Hussein, and a similar "no-fly zone" in the south to protect Iraq's Shiite population. In April 1991, Saddam Hussein accepted UN Resolution 687 and agreed to destroy or remove all weapons of mass destruction (WMD), including all long-range ballistic missiles and all nuclear, biological, and chemical weapons. UN arms inspectors worked inside Iraq to verify whether Iraq had disarmed itself of weapons of mass destruction. However, UN weapons inspectors left in 1998, ahead of a limited bombing campaign by coalition forces, and were then barred from returning by Iraqi authority until 2002. While economic sanctions continued, Iraq accepted the UN Security Council oil-for-food resolution in 1996. Under this resolution Iraq was allowed to sell certain quantities of oil on condition that the proceeds were to be given to the UN which would use them to pay for food and medicine for the benefit of the Iraqi people.[14]

[14] The Oil-for-Food Program was terminated in November 2003. In nearly seven years of operation, the Program had used some $46 billion of Iraqi export earnings on behalf of the Iraqi people. It was one of the largest, most complex and unusual programs funded entirely from resources belonging to the nation it was designed to help (Office of the Iraq Programme Oil-for-Food, UN). Recently allegations were raised that administrators in the UN oil-for-food program for Iraq took bribes and allowed Saddam Hussein to skim money from the program. A special CIA adviser found that Saddam was able to "subvert" the $60 billion UN program to generate an estimated $1.7 billion in revenue outside UN control from 1997–2003. (Oil-for-Food Scandal Key to CIA Report, Monday, October 18, 2004, FaxNews.) Former Federal Reserve Chairman, Paul Volcker, chaired an Independent Inquiry Committee in 2004 to investigate corruption allegations in the UN Oil-for-Food Program. The Committee released its first Interim Report on February 3, 2005, and its Second Interim Report on March 29, 2005, which controversially found "no evidence that the selection of Cotecna in 1998 was subject to any affirmative or improper influence of the Secretary-General in the bidding or selection process".

10.4. Pakistan's Conflict with India

Strategic Position of Pakistan

Pakistan's military dictator, President Musharraf, is a US ally, who abandoned Taliban in Afghanistan as Pakistan's client government and supported the US war against terrorism after the US decision to launch a military campaign in Afghanistan in 2001 to overthrow the Taliban. President Musharraf has, however, been very hesitant to clamp down on Islamist militant groups in Pakistan. These groups had been organized and trained by CIA and Pakistani intelligence to supply Islamic fighters for the Afghan jihad against the Soviets in the 1980s. Subsequently, these militant Islamists groups were used and nurtured for state purposes, such as supporting the Taliban in Afghanistan and launching a new jihad in Kashmir against India. The US-led war on terrorism overthrew the Taliban government and drove Pakistani and other international Islamist militants out of Afghanistan into Pakistan, where they have continued their long and intimate connection with al-Qaeda in fighting against the United States.

The top leader of Pakistani Islamic militants, Maulana Fazlur Rahman,[15] declared that the US must leave Pakistan immediately and it is the duty of every Pakistani Muslim to protect and offer sanctuary to members of al-Qaeda and the Taliban. The Islamist militant groups have controlled Pakistan's two most sensitive and strategic provinces in the northwest area bordering Afghanistan, which have become home to many members of al-Qaeda and Taliban as well as supplying a headquarter base for Osama bin Laden and his associates. With the help of Pakistani Islamist militants, al-Qaeda fighters infiltrated across the border and regrouped, and have now begun to infiltrate major Pakistani urban centers where some al-Qaeda leaders have been captured.[16] Recent terrorist bombings in London on July 7, 2005 were also traced to Pakistan. Three of the four alleged suicide bombers had traveled to the country in late 2004. Investigators of London bombings are trying to find out whether radicals in Pakistan provided them with training or other assistance in the London attacks that killed 56 people and wounded 700.

Pakistan has been a critically important ally to the US and has supplied geographic and strategic objectives for the last half century, when it began developing nuclear capabilities during wars of conflict with India over Kashmir. In 1990 the United States imposed ten-year sanctions on Pakistan for its nuclear program, and this generated much anti-American sentiment in Pakistan. Using that sentiment, Islamist militant groups found a broad audience, gained Pakistani public support,

[15] Maulana Fazlur Rahman heads the Islamic Party of Religious Leaders, who is known for his close ties to Afghanistan's Taliban regime. He fiercely criticized Presidents Bush and Musharraf, and threatened to launch a jihad — a holy war — against the US.

[16] Abu Zubaydah, al-Qaeda's chief of operations, top recruiter, and the third-highest-ranking al-Qaeda leaders, was captured by Pakistani police forces in March 2002.

and advanced their political and Islamist objectives. They even became leaders of opposition parties in the Pakistani central government to challenge President Musharraf's power — which is based on the Pakistani army, the arbiter of political forces in Pakistan for the last half century. Hence, Pakistan's war against terrorism as well as its security and power struggle has become extremely important to the US-led global war against international terrorism.

Conflict with India

Since its establishment as an independent state, Pakistan has engaged in a series of conflicts and wars with the neighboring state of India. This animosity has its roots in religion and history, and is epitomized by the long-running conflict over the state of Kashmir. Britain dismantled its Indian empire in 1947, and British India was divided into Pakistan and India. Since then, India and Pakistan have been arch rivals. Pakistan was intended as a homeland for Muslims in the Indian subcontinent, while India was intended as a Hindu state. Kashmir was an independent princely state and was given the option of joining either India or Pakistan. Most of the population in Kashmir is Muslim, but its ruler was a Hindu Rajah (prince), who decided to join India. Pakistan refused to accept the legality of the accession to India. As a result, the first Indo-Pakistani war broke out in 1947. A UN mediation process brought the war to a close toward the end of 1948, leaving about 30 percent of Kashmir under Pakistani control.

In 1965 the second Indo–Pakistani war began with the infiltration of Pakistani-controlled guerrillas into the Indian Kashmir area. A UN resolution called for a cease-fire and required both sides to withdraw to positions held prior to the war in 1965. Neither side won this war which killed about 3 000 Indian and 3 800 Pakistani military men.

A civil war erupted in Pakistan in 1971 in which 10 million East Pakistani Bengalis were forced to flee to India. Pakistan attacked Indian Kashmir, while India attacked both East and West Pakistan and occupied the eastern half, which declared its independence as the country of Bangladesh in 1971. Pakistan was defeated, lost its eastern half and eventually recognized Bangladesh as an independent state in 1974. Kashmir was divided by a "Line of Control" and administrated by India and Pakistan separately. Three wars did not resolve the Kashmir issue and both India and Pakistan seemed unable to win militarily.

For the last 30–50 years, India and Pakistan have been developing their nuclear weapons. In 1966 India declared that it could produce nuclear weapons within 18 months, and tested a device in a "peaceful nuclear explosion". India then conducted five underground nuclear tests and declared itself a nuclear state in 1998. Following the third war with India, Pakistan secretly decided to start its own nuclear weapon program in 1972 in order to match India's capability. Reacting to fresh nuclear testing by India, Pakistan conducted its own atomic explosions in 1998. The situation escalated into a dangerous nuclear arms race. Two long-time nuclear-armed rivals facing each other, eyeball to eyeball, across the Line of Control in Kashmir made the Kashmir region "the most dangerous place on Earth".[17]

The Kashmiri Islamic "separatist group" has claimed responsibility for several deadly attacks in India, including an attack on the Indian Parliament in December 2001. India accused Pakistan of sponsoring militant Islamic groups in India-controlled Kashmir. Pakistan rejected this claim and accused India of denying the Muslim-majority in Kashmir the right to national self-determination. India moved more than 0.5 million troops to the border and deployed its nuclear-capable missiles. In response, Pakistan sent more than 0.3 million troops to the border. This serious situation of two nuclear armed enemies standing poised for a war lasted for more than a year and a half. Intense mediation efforts by the United States and other countries, combined with realization of unthinkable consequences of a nuclear war, finally brought the two sides back to the table for peaceful negotiations.

The conflict between Pakistan and India, however, has not been solved, and the dispute over Kashmir remains the gravest threat to regional peace in South Asia. In October, 2003, New Delhi offered 12 proposals in a peace initiative that Pakistan has broadly accepted. The disputed territory of Kashmir, however, remains a stumbling block. One year later in 2004, Pakistan President Pervez Musharraf suggested that India and Pakistan should consider the option of identifying "some regions" of Kashmir to demilitarize and grant them the status of independence, joint Indian-Pakistani control either India and Pakistan or under the UN India has virtually rejected Musharraf's proposal, however, and asserted that Kashmir is an integral part of India. Newly added elements, such as al-Qaeda, Pakistani militant Islamists and the US led war on international terrorism have made the struggle between Pakistan and India more complicated and critical to US interests and world peace.

10.5. The War on Terrorism

The contemporary global Islamic militant movement started with the jihad (a Muslim holy war) against the Soviet Union invasion and occupation of Afghanistan in 1979. During a ten-year jihad to rid Afghanistan of the Soviet forces, approximately 200 000 Islamic militants from more than 30 countries around the world joined a fight against the Soviet Red Army for the liberty of Afghans. As a matter of fact, however, it was the United States that funded, armed and trained these Islamic militants on the battlefields of Afghanistan in order to

[17] In March 2000, President Clinton visited India and Pakistan. He wanted both countries to show restraint over the disputed territory of Kashmir, a region he described as "the most dangerous place on Earth".

create an anti-Soviet resistance front in the Muslim world. Over a 10-year period, the CIA invested about 2.1 billion US dollars in training Islamic fighters and supplying them with intelligence and weapons, including the hand-held Stinger anti-aircraft missiles and launchers. Among the pro-US Muslim fundamentalist forces in Afghanistan, the Taliban (meaning 'students of religion') appeared in this period and received US military and financial support that was channeled through Pakistan and Saudi Arabia. Osama bin Laden's al-Qaeda movement and various other Islamic armed movements were also established and nurtured in CIA training camps in Pakistan during the ten-year war against the Soviets.

Osama bin Laden and Al-Qaeda

Now the world's most wanted terrorist Osama bin Laden was one of the Arab fighters who, at age 23, went to Pakistan and then to Afghanistan from Saudi Arabia in the spring of 1980 to join the Islamic Mujahidin (meaning Muslim guerrilla warriors engaged in a jihad) cause. In the process he turned himself from a devout Muslim and a holy warrior into a supreme leader of international Muslim terrorists. Al-Qaeda was established by Osama bin Laden, Muhammad Atef,[18] and others in 1988 as a network originally to keep track of all Arab fighters they recruited and trained for fighting the Soviet troops. Most of them were Sunni Islamic militants and extremists. From about 1989 until the present, the group called itself "Al-Qaeda" (in the Arabic language, it is used for "the foundation" or "the base"). The al-Qaeda network is the base for the support of other Islamic militant groups in which it provides them with money, weapons, contacts and trained recruits in particular battles. According to Saudi intelligence estimates, up to 25 000 Saudi men have received military training in Afghan camps or similar experiences abroad since the Soviet Union invaded Afghanistan in 1979. Saudi Arabia was the largest source of what is called the "Arab Afghans" — militants from the Arab world, who volunteered to join the Afghan jihad against the Soviets.

When the Soviet Union withdrew its forces from Afghanistan in 1989, the jihad war was officially ended, and bin Laden returned to Saudi Arabia as a hero for defeating the Soviets. In 1990 when Iraq invaded Kuwait and threatened the neighboring Arab countries in the Persian Gulf, Osama bin Laden made an offer to the Saudi ruling family that he would form and lead an army of 30 000

[18] Atef was a member of the Egyptian Jihad group responsible for the 1981 assassination of Egyptian President Sadat. He joined the jihad in Afghanistan against the Soviet Union in the mid-1980s. A co-founder of al-Qaeda, he is bin Laden's right hand man, and the military leader of al-Qaeda. He is suspected of planning the 1998 bombings of two US Embassies in East Africa and of the September 11, 2001 attacks on the Pentagon and the World Trade Center. The United States Department of State is offering a reward of up to $25 million for information leading directly to the apprehension or conviction of Muhammad Atef.

Afghan veterans to defeat the Iraqi aggression. His offer was firmly rejected. Instead, 300 000 US troops were allowed to arrive in Saudi Arabia in order to stage the "Desert Storm" operation and liberate Kuwait.

As an Islamic militant and extremist, bin Laden saw the presence of US troops as an infidel invasion of holy land, and considered the US an essential supporter for all of the other "infidel" governments and institutions in the world — particularly the governments of Saudi Arabia and Egypt, the nation of Israel, and the United Nations. He organized strong protests across the country against the US military presence and started recruiting an army for the fight against the "American invasion".

In the end, Osama bin Laden was expelled by the authority of Saudi Arabia to Sudan in 1991, where he began to restore his al-Qaeda network, and rapidly shifted his political stance from a pro-US Arab fighter to an anti-US violent terrorist. He also began to use his Sudanese base to conduct terrorist operations against US interests worldwide. Expelled by the Sudanese authority in 1996, he returned to Afghanistan as a guest of Taliban. Forging close relations with the Taliban, Osama bin Laden sponsored, managed, and financially supported terrorist training camps in Afghanistan and Pakistan. Reportedly, more than 5 000 Islamic fighters were recruited from all over the Muslim world and trained in the use of infiltration, explosives, weapons, concealment, clandestine operations, communications, and self-sacrifice.

Osama bin Laden also used his money[19] and anti-Soviet reputation to attract leaders of Islamic militant and extremist groups from around the world and internationalize his cause against the United States and its allies. Under his guidance and financial support, al-Qaeda has become a global umbrella for Islamic extremist groups dedicated to overturning 'un-Islamic' governments. These groups include the Egyptian Islamic Jihad, which was led by Ayman al-Zawahiri,[20] and a number of jihad groups in many Muslim countries, such as Sudan, Egypt, Saudi Arabia, Yemen, Somalia, Eritrea, Djibouti, Afghanistan, Pakistan, Bosnia, Croatia, Albania, Algeria, Tunisia, Lebanon, the Philippines, Tajikistan, Azerbaijan, and the Kashmiri region of India and the Chechnya region of Russia.

---

[19] Osama bin Laden is the 17th son of 53 children of Saudi construction tycoon Muhammad bin Laden, who amassed a fortune from successful construction and contracting companies in Yemen and Saudi Arabia. Today, the bin Laden family fortune is estimated at $5 billion, of which Osama bin Laden is reported to have received an estimated $300 million before his family disavowed him. (*Tracing bin Laden's Money* by Yael Shahar, ICT Researcher, September 21, 2001, http://www.ict.org.il/articles.)

[20] Ayman al-Zawahiri was the leader of the Egyptian Islamic Jihad, which was responsible for the assassination of Egyptian President Sadat and the attempted murder of Egyptian President Mubarak. He became bin Laden's personal physician and chief ideologue in Afghanistan. It is believed that he was instrumental in turning bin Laden's attention toward global jihad, and he is now considered to be the second most powerful member of the al-Qaeda network.

To facilitate its global operations al-Qaeda also maintains cells and personnel in a number of non-Muslim countries. This includes Kenya, Tanzania, the United Kingdom, Germany, Canada, and the United States. The al-Qaeda cells operate independently of other terrorist groups and of other cells in the same country in order to avoid a mass capture. The al-Qaeda network also recruits locally among Muslims in the non-Muslim countries who have residences, passports, and language skills, and who can blend into local communities and be well placed for attacking specific targets in many different countries. Al-Qaeda's ultimate goal is to drive out Western influences, particularly the Americans, from all Muslim countries, to abolish Muslim state boundaries, and to establish a pan-Islamic Caliphate throughout the world, that is, a 'pure' Islamic government over all the Muslim lands.

A religious ruling (fatwa) was issued in the so-called "Jihad against Jews and Crusaders" — World Islamic Front Statement on February 23, 1998 by five heads of Jihad Islamic groups, including Osama bin Laden and Ayman al-Zawahiri. The ruling was also endorsed by dozens of other terrorist groups in the Muslim world. Osama bin Laden and his accomplices called upon all Muslims of the world in the following ruling: "to kill the Americans and their allies — civilians and military — is an individual duty for every Muslim who can do it in any country in which it is possible to do it, . . .". This fatwa has provoked a raft of terrorist devastation and bloodshed around the globe, including the September 11th 2001-9-11 — terrorist attacks on New York and Washington, in which the three suicide pilots came from the terrorist cell of the al-Qaeda network in Hamburg, Germany.

Osama bin Laden and his accomplices have directly planned, organized, and financed many terrorist attacks against US interests worldwide, including a truck bomb exploding in the parking garage of the World Trade Center in 1993, shooting down two US helicopters in Somalia in 1993, a truck bomb destroying the US Air Force's Khobar Towers housing complex in Saudi Arabia in 1996, bombing US Embassies in Kenya and Tanzania in 1998 with about 300 people killed and 5 000 injured. Responding to these brutal strikes, the Clinton administration launched cruise-missile raids on alleged al-Qaeda training camps in eastern Afghanistan in August 1998. The US government demanded an immediate handover of bin Laden from the Afghan Taliban government, imposed economic sanctions against Afghanistan, and held the government of Afghanistan responsible for any further terrorist acts by bin Laden and his accomplices. The Taliban government rejected these US warnings and continued supporting al-Qaeda's activities in Afghanistan, where bin Laden accelerated his international terror activities. In 2000, a suicide boat blasted the USS Cole in Yemen; on September 11, 2001 two hijacked airplanes destroyed the twin towers of the World Trade Center in New York and a third hijacked aircraft crashed into the Pentagon in Washington D.C., with approximately 3 000 people killed in these simultaneous attacks. A fourth plane destined for Washington crashed in Somerset County, Pennsylvania when the passengers rose up against the hijackers.

The War on Terrorism

In retaliation the US finally launched air strikes on Afghanistan on October 7th 2001, shutting down all the terrorist training camps and overthrowing the Taliban government that had supported them. This was the beginning of a large scale global campaign against international terrorism. "The War on Terrorism" is led by the US government and joined by its allies in Europe, Russia, Pakistan, India, and the Central Asian countries of Uzbekistan, Tajikistan and Turkmenistan. In merely two months after US air strikes, the Taliban government was removed from power, a broad based interim Afghan government was established, and the al-Qaeda network was significantly damaged. Osama bin Laden, however, escaped and has gone into hiding probably in caves of the Tora Bora Mountain on the Afghanistan–Pakistan border area. Since then, US and coalition forces have undertaken ongoing military actions in Afghanistan in order to root out remaining al-Qaeda terrorists and Taliban elements and to fulfill the main objective of bringing Osama bin Laden to justice.

The US-led invasion of Iraq in 2003 was another major endeavor carried out under the aegis of the "War on Terrorism". Military victories in that undertaking, however, represent only a preliminary success in the war on terror, because numerous terrorist cells in more than 50 countries on four continents have yet to be discovered and rooted out. It is these semi-autonomous cells that keep the al-Qaeda terrorist network active in many countries. Recent events have demonstrated that al-Qaeda remains capable of inflicting large-scale, high profile, high-casualty terrorist attacks worldwide. One is the bombing in Madrid. Al-Qaeda has claimed responsibility for the train bombings in Madrid, the capital city of Spain, on March 11, 2004, which left 192 dead and over 1 200 wounded. It has been the deadliest terrorist strike in Europe since the Lockerbie bombing in 1988[21] and the worst terrorist assault in Spanish history. Spain was one of the US allies that firmly supported the invasion of Iraq by contributing troops to the war against Saddam Hussein. The Spanish government under Prime Minister Aznar arrested 16 suspected al-Qaeda militants in January 2003. These were al-Qaeda members who had connections with terrorists arrested in France and Britain, and were preparing to conduct attacks by explosives and chemical materials. Spain also rounded up a major al-Qaeda cell, which had direct links to Atta's Hamburg group. (Atta was the ringleader of the September 11 plot, who piloted the first plane crashing into the World Trade Center.)

[21] On December 21, 1988 a bomb exploded aboard the Pan Am Boeing 747 flight above Lockerbie, a Scotland town, killing all 259 passengers and crew, including 189 Americans as well as 11 people on the ground. After one of two Libyans accused of murdering these 270 people in the Lockerbie bombing was found guilty of mass murder, the United Nations Security Council ended its 11 years of sanctions against Libya in 1999. Libya accepted responsibility for the bombing and agreed to a $2.7 billion indemnity settlement.

The effects of the bombing were striking. These bombings in Madrid occurred just 72 hours before voting started in the national election in Spain. Prime Minister Aznar's Popular Party lost out in the election and Spain's opposition Socialist Party won. As his campaign had pledged, the new Prime Minister, Jose Luis Rodriguez Zapatero, declared an end to Spain's mission in Iraq on April 28, 2004, and withdrew the last 260 Spanish solders from Iraq. International media came up with quite different opinions on the connection between the terrorist bombing and the result of Spain's election. As an urgent meeting of European ministers right after the tragedy made clear, "the scale of the latest catastrophe means that Spain and all European countries now realize that terrorists can strike as easily in Barcelona, Berlin, Birmingham or Bologna as they can in Boston or Buffalo. The need to strengthen international cooperation in law enforcement, intelligence, and, when necessary, military operation has clearly been underscored".[22]

On July 7, 2005 a series of coordinated suicide bombings struck London's public transport system during the morning rush hour. As reported 52 people were killed and about 700 injured in these attacks. The incident was the deadliest single terrorist act in the United Kingdom since the 1988 Lockerbie bombing of Pan Am Flight 103 which killed 270, and the deadliest bombing in London since World War II. This was also the first suicide bombings in Western Europe. On July 21, 2005, a second series of four explosions took place on the London Underground and a London bus. There were no casualties. All suspected bombers from these failed attacks escaped from the scenes but were later arrested.

It is evident that al-Qaeda and Islamic terrorist groups are still working, still reorganizing, still implementing attacks on civilians, and still producing mass casualties, even though some top al-Qaeda leaders have been killed or caught, and their training camps in Afghanistan and Pakistan have been destroyed. The "War on Terrorism" will continue to be a major challenge to the United States and the entire world for the foreseeable future. Some Muslim nations have played a more significant role than other nations in these terrorist activities. Pakistan and Saudi Arabia, which have been the hottest spots and bastions for al-Qaeda and Islamist militant groups, will next be discussed.

10.6. Saudi Arabia and Wahhabism

Saudi Arabia

Saudi Arabia has long been a Western business and military ally, yet the country has revealed itself as the source of financial and human resources for the al-Qaeda

[22] "*The Warning in Spain's Election*", by Ivo H. Daalder, March 18, 2004, www.americanprogress.org.

terrorist network and Islamist militant groups. Not only has bin Laden utilized his personal wealth, inherited from his rich Saudi family, to finance terrorist operations, the al-Qaeda network has also siphoned millions of dollars from Islamic charities that are supposed to help poor Muslims in Asia and Africa. The Al-Haramain Islamic Foundation, a Riyadh-based charily, is a prime example of how al-Qaeda is using Islamic charities. At its peak Al-Haramain alone raised \$40–\$50 million a year and, taken together, all Saudi charities could raise \$100 million a year or higher when there are natural disasters to be responded to in the Muslim world. These charily funds collected in Saudi Arabia should all have been channeled into Muslim countries to help poor Muslims worldwide. However, the Al-Haramain Foundation advertised for donations as a form of jihad, or holy war, to attract Islamist sympathizers, and has used its foreign branches as mechanisms for financing terrorist attacks. Islamic terrorists have used charities not only as a means for raising funds but also to provide logistical support and cover for terrorist operations.

Since 2002, the US and Saudi governments have blacklisted Al-Haramain's branches in Bosnia, Somalia, Indonesia, Kenya, Tanzania, Pakistan and the United States, and requested the governments of these nations to seize these assets and shut down their operations. Again, in June, 2004 the US and Saudi authorities jointly designated five additional branches of the Saudi-based Al-Haramain as terrorist financiers, including branches in Afghanistan, Albania, Bangladesh, Ethiopia, and the Netherlands. The name of the former leader of Al-Haramain was also put into the international list of terrorists. The US and Saudi Arabia have submitted their list of designees to the UN, which will call on all members of the global community to freeze the assets of these organizations and prohibit them from doing business. This is an important part of the battle against international terrorism. Terminating terrorist cash flows, disrupting terrorist financial networks, exposing terrorist "money trails" that may lead to unknown terrorist cells can eventually block many terrorist operations.

Saudi Arabia has also been used by Osama bin Laden and his al-Qaeda network as a continuing human resource for recruiting potential Islamist terrorists. About 25 000 Saudi men were trained in terror camps in Afghanistan and Pakistan during the 1980s and 1990s and new generations of terrorists have been nurtured through the al-Qaeda network and Saudi militant Islamic groups. To highlight how active bin Laden and his terrorist network in Saudi Arabia have been for recruiting new terrorist operatives, the FBI list of 19 hijackers in the attacks on New York and Washington includes 15 Saudi nationals.

According to "9/11 Commission" staff statement #16, the idea for the September 11 attacks was originated by a veteran jihadist stationed in Pakistan, and approved by bin Laden, who quickly provided four potential suicide operatives, two of whom had already acquired US visas, "because they wanted to participate in an operation against the United States, having been inspired by a friend of theirs who was a suicide bomber in the August 1998 attack on the US embassy in

Kenya". One of the four suicide pilots was a Saudi, who had studied in the United States and obtained his commercial pilot certificate in 1999. He piloted American Airlines Flight 77 crashing into Pentagon. The other three suicide pilots in the September 11 were young students studying in Hamburg Germany from Egypt, the United Arab Emirates and Lebanon respectively.

Besides the four suicide pilots, there were 15 "muscle hijackers" — i.e., hijackers who intimidated and controlled the passengers. 14 of them are believed to be Saudi nationals:

> "The muscle hijackers were between 20 and 28 years of age and had differing backgrounds. Many were unemployed and lacked higher education, while a few had begun university studies. Although some were known to attend prayer services regularly, others reportedly even consumed alcohol and abused drugs. It has not been determined exactly how each of them was recruited into al-Qaeda, but most of them apparently were swayed to join the jihad in Chechnya by contacts at local universities and mosques in Saudi Arabia".[23]

These facts indicate that terrorist operations as sophisticated as the September 11 attacks were the brainchild of bin Laden and his veteran accomplices, but were carried out successfully by the younger generation of terrorists who were inspired, recruited and trained by bin Laden and veteran Islamist terrorists. Why did those young Saudis believe in bin Laden and were willing, even eager, to give their lives to an operation directed to killing thousands of innocent men and women? The answer may well be rooted in the social, economic and religious environment of Saudi Arabia, in particular, and of the Muslim world in general.

Wahhabism

As we have already noted, in the Muslim world there are different schools of thought and different views about the Islamic religion. This has resulted in many Islamic sects and divisions. The two biggest are the Sunnis and Shiites. The Sunni sect is the largest and represents the vast majority in all Muslim countries except for Iran, Iraq and Bahrain, where the Shiites account for 89%, 60%–65% and 70% of all their Muslims respectively. Sunnis are considered the more "orthodox" Muslims and follow the most traditional doctrines and practices. They believe that some religious figures may exercise a great deal of political or social power, but committees of socially important believers in each community are generally responsible for management of the society.

The Shiite sect was initiated by followers of Ali (who was the Prophet Muhammad's cousin and son-in-law) and his descendants. Shiite Muslims continue to

[23] 9/11 Commission staff statement #16, as submitted to the National Commission on Terrorist Attacks Upon the United States. The report was released by the Commission on Wednesday, June 16, 2004.

hold the same fundamental beliefs as other Muslims but with additions that include an "imamate" — the distinctive institution of Shiite Islam. Sunni Muslims consider an *imam* to be a prayer leader, while Shiite Muslims believe that *the Imams* are the descendant of Ali and represent the rightful and true leadership which continues to be passed along through a sort of apostolic succession of Muhammad's descendants. Unlike orthodox Sunni Muslims, Shiites can expand and reinterpret Islamic doctrine over time. Shiite Islam has also developed its own sub-sects, such as Twelver, Ithna Ashari, Fatimids, etc. Some of these sects focus primarily on spiritual rather than temporal authority, and some are entirely non-political.

After Sunni and Shi'i, the Wahhabis, with a strict fundamentalist tradition, probably represent the most influential Islamic sect. The Wahhabis sect is dominant on the Arabian Peninsula, and has expanded its influence over the Middle East and South Asia. Wahhabis follow the teachings of their founder Muhammad ibn abd al-Wahhab (1703–1791), who was the first Islamic Fundamentalist reformer. He taught that absolutely every idea added to Islam after the third century of the Muslim era (about 950 A.D.) was false and must be expunged in order to uphold a strict interpretation of Islam. The Wahhabis converted the Saudi tribe and led the Saudi leader to the belief that it was his religious mission to wage holy war against non-Muslims and those Muslims with Islamic beliefs that did not conform to the reformer's teachings.

Wahhabism also provided an impetus to the Saudi tribe for its political consolidation. With the importance of jihad in Wahhab's teaching, military conquests of new territories became legitimate and desirable. The Saudi tribe began to take over the neighboring Shiite and Sunni tribes in 1763 and established the Saudi Empire in 1811 with religious and political power extending from the capital, Riyadh, and covering all the Arabian Peninsula except for Yemen. The Wahhabi army (Ikhwan) was a fervent and extremely militant group of Wahhabi nomadic tribe warriors. It converted Muslims by force into the Wahhabi version of Islamism, and attacked those who refused to conform to the Wahhabi interpretation of Islamic practices. The Wahhabis occupied Mecca and Medina in 1802 and destroyed the shrines and tombs of the two holy cities (they were opposed to marked graves) and massacred many residents. The Wahhabi army also raided northward into Syria and Iraq and destroyed the Shiite shrines in the holy city of Kabala, and this provided the historical roots of Saudi–Iranian and Saudi–Iraqi hostilities that last into the present. In 1818, however, Wahhabis were defeated and driven into the desert by an Ottoman expedition and the troops of Muhammad Ali's Egypt. The Wahhabis fought back, collected their power, and finally succeeded in obtaining control of the Persian Gulf coast of Arabia in 1833. Internal fighting among the tribes weakened the domain, however, and brought the Saudi family down, and finally forced them to flee for refuge into Kuwait in 1889.

The founder of the modern state of Saudi Arabia was Ibn Saud who recovered the territory of the first Al Saudi Empire and, with British support, established the new state by maneuvering a number of forces. The religious fervor that Wahhabi Islam continued to inspire proved to be extremely helpful to the royal family. The Saudi leader, Ibn Saud, captured Riyadh in 1902 and defeated an Ikhwan military rebellion in 1929, when the Wahhabi army challenged his authority and caused him problems with the British.[24] In 1932, Ibn Saud proclaimed the Kingdom of Saudi Arabia, which covered about 80% of the Arabian Peninsula, with domination over an area approximating the territory of the present state.

Saudi history exhibits two conflicting sides to the relationship between the Saudi Monarch and Wahhabis: close collaboration and harsh conflict. This has continued into the present as the ruling family pragmatically tries to make use of Western technologies and professionals and, at the same time, tries to maintain its traditional Islamic institutions. This is in the tradition of the founder, Ibn Saud — that is, to obtain "the iron of the West without its ideas".[25]

Wahhabi's teaching and the doctrine of a conservative and strict stance toward the religion did more than just lead to today's Saudi Arabia. As one of the two Muslim nations of the world with Islamic Fundamentalism in power, Saudi Arabia also initiated Islamic Fundamentalist movements that spread throughout the Muslim world from the early 19th century to present: "Wahhab taught that true Muslims must be concerned about politics and the nature of the state. If their rulers failed to behave as good Muslims, if they failed to create a state in which Shariah law was instituted, then believing Muslims had the religious obligation to replace that ruler and his un-Islamic government".[26] Wahhabi advocacy of political activism and melding of faith and violent action exerts a far-reaching influence in contemporary Islamic Fundamentalist and Islamist movements. It leads to extremist views, which have become popular today, that believes all non-Muslim elements have corrupted Islam and resulted in hardship for common Muslims and must, therefore, be eliminated.

[24] The Ikhwan had no tolerance for concessions to life in the twentieth century that Abd al Aziz was forced to make. They objected to machines, particularly those used for communication, such as the telegraph, as well as to the increasing presence of non-Muslim foreigners in the country. They also continued to object to some of the practices of non-Wahhabi Muslims. Most important, the Ikhwan remained eager to force their message on all who did not accept it. This led them to attack non-Wahhabi Muslims, and sometimes Wahhabi Muslims within Saudi Arabia and beyond its borders into Iraq. This across-border movement caused Abd al Aziz problems with the British, who would not tolerate the violation of borders that they had set up after World War I. It was largely because of this concern that Abd al Aziz found himself obliged to take on the Ikhwan militarily.... From "SAUDI ARABIA — A Country Study", Federal Research Division, The Library of Congress: http://lcweb2.loc.gov/frd/cs/satoc.html.

[25] "SAUDI ARABIA — A Country Study", Federal Research Division, The Library of Congress: http://lcweb2.loc.gov/frd/cs/satoc.html.

[26] Lawrence Davidson, *Islamic Fundamentalism*, Greenwood Press, 1998, p. 109.

Wahhabism is the official religion in Saudi Arabia. From their first day of learning in mosques and madrassas (Islamic schools), all Saudi men and women are taught Wahhab's teaching and doctrine. Like bin Laden in his formative years in Saudi Arabia, many Saudi young people are educated not to trust non-Muslims and to hate Christians and Jews just as we have discussed for the Saudi educational system in Chapter 7 of this book. Wahhabis preach that only an absolute return to the values of conservative Islam can protect the Muslim world from the dangers and corruptions of the West. Many young Saudi students have been ideologically indoctrinated to join the fight against the Soviets in Afghanistan and Chechnya, and against Jews and Americans in Palestine and Iraq. This enthusiasm of Muslim young men for the Islamic jihad is deeply rooted in fundamentalist and Islamist education and propaganda.

For example, Dr. Abdallah Azzam was an influential Islamist and an Islamic scholar, who received his Ph.D degree in Principles of Islamic Jurisprudence from Al-Azhar University in Cairo in 1973, and then taught in Universities both in Saudi Arabia and Pakistan. By practicing what he was teaching, Abdallah Azzam became one of the first Arabs to join the Afghan Jihad against the communist USSR. He devoted his full time and energy to the Jihad in Afghanistan and presented the jihad — the armed struggle to establish Islam — as an Islamic cause which concerned all Muslims around the world. He traveled to many places of the world, calling on Muslims to rally to the defense of their religion and lands. He wrote a number of books on Jihad and participated personally in the Afghan jihad. He called upon those Muslims who had not yet joined the fighting to take up arms and to follow him to the front. Partly due to his efforts, the Afghani jihad became a universal cause in which Muslims from every part of the world participated. Volunteer Islamic young fighters traveled to Afghanistan to fulfill their obligation of jihad. Dr. Abdallah Azzam and his fellow young fighters were inspired by their single goal: the establishment of Allah's Rule on earth. He believed that Jihad must be carried out until the Islamic Rule is established so the light of Islam may shine on the whole world.

In late 1989, Abdallah Azzam was killed in the explosion of a car bomb blamed on a rival Afghani faction for the attack. Many Islamic terrorist groups now continue to glorify his martyred life for Islamic jihad and his ideology. His picture and words have been placed on posters for terrorist propaganda.[27] One poster commemorated Abdallah Azzam by a quote from him exalting jihad, "Love of jihad has taken over my life, my soul, my sensations, my heart and my emotions. If preparing for jihad is terrorism, then we are terrorists. If defending our honor

[27] In January and February 2004, propaganda materials were found in the office of the Tulkarm Charitable Society and its Center for Quran Studies in Palestine by Israeli forces. These materials are displayed in the website, http://www.intelligence.org.il/eng/finance/bank_2o.htm.

is extremism, then we are extremists. If jihad against our enemies is fundamentalism, then we are fundamentalists". His ideology and words on jihad continue to exercise powerful influences on Muslim youth throughout the world.

As we earlier wrote, in his 1998 World Islamic Front Statement, bin Laden called for jihad against Jews and Crusaders and issued a "Religious Ruling" (a fatwa) to kill Americans and their allies — civilians and military. His jihad against Americans and the West is a natural extension of what Abdallah Azzam said and did in Palestine, Afghanistan, and Pakistan. Moreover, bin Laden has elevated Islamic jihad up to a global scope with emphasis on the United States. He has also intensified the brutality, sophistication, and scale of terror by killing thousands of innocent people simultaneously. It is therefore not surprising that bin Laden has honored Abdallah Azzam as his "spiritual mentor", and one of his closest "friends".

The Saudi authority's pragmatic approach toward the Western world and resistance to US President Bush's call for the war on international terrorism did not satisfy Osama bin Laden because he wants Saudis to sever their relationship with the US and its allies and to use their oil power to blow up the Western world. Al-Qaeda undertook major attacks on non-Muslims in the Saudi capital in 2003, and carried out a series of strikes targeting oil facilities in the eastern oil city of Khobar in May 2004. Islamic militants from al-Qaeda cells in Saudi kidnapped foreigners and beheaded an American hostage engineer, Paul Johnson, on June 19, 2004. He was thus a victim of an escalating campaign of violence against Westerners in order to (1) intimidate Americans, (2) drive foreign workers out of Saudi Arabia, and (3) undermine the royal Saudi family. The Saudi police actively fought back and killed the al-Qaeda cell chief, al-Muqrin, and three other militants. The Saudi King, Fahd, pledged that the kingdom would defeat terrorism. It therefore seems that the Saudi authority has begun to recognize the threat of Islamist terrorists on the security of their country — which had earlier been considered an oasis of safety.

10.7. The Ideological Roots of Islamist Terrorism

It is important to sort out linkages between the terrorist network al-Qaeda and other Islamist militant groups and fundamentalist organizations. It is equally important to locate the intellectual and ideological connections between various terrorist groups and their schools of thought, philosophies, and ideologies whether developed either in the modern age or in ancient historical periods — either in the East or in the West. This will help to provide a better understanding of the ideological origins of bin Laden and his terrorist groups and will help to establish the identity of these terrorists, what they think, and how they are motivated. To dig out the ideological roots of international terrorism will also help to anticipate future terrorist attacks. At the same time, a more correct image of Islam — once the greatest religion and civilization of the world — can then be distinguished from terrorist attitudes, beliefs, values, and motives. Many innocent Muslims can then also find answers to the question of why their faith has been used to promote and justify international terrorism by bin Laden and his accomplices.

Some scholars of Islamic studies point out that there has been an ideological attack on Islam that has been made by the media which falsely claims that Osama bin Laden and his al-Qaeda followers are adherents of Salafism.[28] A Salafi is a practitioner of Salafism, which refers to a following of the Prophet Muhammad, his Companions, and the two generations that succeeded him. Modern Salafis view the first three generations of Muslims as perfect examples of how Islam should be lived and practiced. The terms Salafi and Wahhabi are not identical, but bear similarities because "Wahhabis" are those who adhere to the way of the Salaf (the Prophet Muhammad and his Companions), and seek to "purify" modern Islam. After the 9/11 tragedy, however, the media began to use the term Salafi to describe various sects and groups sharing their views, including the Saudi-based Wahhabis and some groups of the Muslim Brotherhood. These modern Salafis are sometimes called "neo-Salafis" in order to distinguish Salafism from the early generations of Muslims.

Haneef James Oliver, the author of the book, *The 'Wahhabi' Myth, Dispelling Prevalent Fallacies and the Fictitious Link With Bin Laden*, disproves the claim that al-Qaeda is a Salafi group. Instead, he shows how al-Qaeda is a modern offshoot of one of the earliest and most dangerous of the sects in Islam, the Khawaarij,[29] and that Osama bin Laden is neither knowledgeable in Islam, nor is he attached to the principles and practices of Salafism. Haneef James Oliver observes that

> As a result of the wealth which the bin Laden Corporation generated, Osama bin Laden used his family's money to live a carefree and luxurious lifestyle. . . . he never managed to exert himself to sit with any of the Salafee scholars, really seek knowledge, or ground himself in the fundamentals of Islamic belief. . . The fact that he failed to take advantage of studying under the guardianship of the elder scholars of Saudi Arabia led him to mix instead with the newly arisen Qutbists.
> Eventually, he completely dismissed the methodology of the "Wahhabis", and expelled many of its people from the fold of Islam. Therefore, how could it be considered correct to say that Osama bin Laden is a "Wahhabi"? In actuality, Osama bin Laden and his al-Qaeda movement are not "Wahhabis", but rather, Qutbists.

---

[28] Haneef James Oliver, *The 'Wahhabi' Myth, Dispelling Prevalent Fallacies and the Fictitious Link With Bin Laden*, TROID Publications, 2004.

[29] The Khawaarij was a sect which killed the two Rightly Guided Caliphs, Uthmaan and Alee, and threatened to kill other Muslim leaders over the issue of ruling/leadership. The Khawaarij was the first sect to appear in the history of Islam and still exists today, but has split up into more than 20 different sub-sects.

> Confirming this important link, the New York Times' Robert Worth said: "... But if one man deserves the title of intellectual grandfather to Osama bin Laden and his fellow terrorists, it is probably the Egyptian writer and activist Sayyid Qutb". ...[30]

Qutbism

Sayyid Qutb (1906–1966) was a leading fundamentalist theoretician and one of the key philosophers in the Egyptian Muslim Brotherhood movement that has spread throughout the Muslim world. He first received a religious education and then a Western education in Cairo. From 1948 to 1950, he was in the United States on a scholarship to study the educational system and received a master's degree from the University of Northern Colorado. He officially joined the Society of the Muslim Brothers in 1952 and soon headed its Section for the Propagation of Call and Publishing. After the attempted assassination of Gamal Abdel Nasser in 1954, the Egyptian government imprisoned Qutb along with many others; and in 1965 he was brought to trial on charges of treason and was hanged in 1966. While in prison, Qutb wrote his two most important works: *In the Shade of the Quran*, and a manifesto of political Islam called *Milestones*. He was considered as the central theorist of twentieth-century Islamism due to the extensive influence of his books. The school of thought he inspired has become known as Qutbism.

One of the core elements of Qutbism, or "modern" Islamism, is that the unity of God and His sovereignty meant that human rule — government legislating its own behavior — is illegitimate. Muslims must answer to God alone, which means that all forms of governance over the Muslims are illegitimate except the Islamic state. The ancient Islamic tradition prohibited overthrowing a Muslim ruler; and if one Muslim falsely calls another an infidel, he could be burned in hell. Qutb was the first Sunni Muslim to find a way around this tradition by declaring that the rulers of Muslim nations today are no longer Muslims; they are infidels.[31] Qutb reached the conclusion that the Egyptian state was totally illegitimate and that statement sealed his death warrant. Decades after his death, however, Qutb's view continues to inspire radical Islamists.

His brother, Muhammad Qutb, moved to Saudi Arabia where he became a Professor of Islamic Studies. One of Muhammad Qutb's students and ardent followers was Ayman al-Zawahiri, who serves as bin Laden's second in command and is the al-Qaeda's ideological leader and was the mentor of Osama bin Laden.

Qutb's books and other writings have become the ideological foundation of international terrorism. Like Qutb in Egypt, bin Laden has declared that the Saudi

---

[30] Haneef James Oliver, *The 'Wahhabi' Myth, Dispelling Prevalent Fallacies and the Fictitious Link With Bin Laden*, TROID Publications, 2004, p. 9. Sayyid Qutb (1906–1966) was a leading Egyptian fundamentalist theoretician.

[31] Robert Worth, *The Deep Intellectual Roots of Islamic Terror*, The New York Times, October 13, 2001.

government — which took away his Saudi citizenship and expelled him while inviting American troops into the holy land during the Persian Gulf War — is totally illegitimate.

Many eminent Islamic scholars and theologians have consistently condemned the actions of the Islamist terrorist network. Two historians from Iran, Ladan Boroumand and her sister Roya Boroumand, wrote: "The truth is that contemporary Islamist terror is an eminently modern practice thoroughly at odds with Islamic traditions and ethics". They observe that:

> Before the Iranian Revolution, terrorism was typically seen as a straightforward outgrowth of modern ideologies. Islamist terrorists, however, claim to fight on theological grounds: A few verses from the Quran and a few references to the sunna ("deeds of the Prophet") put an Islamic seal on each operation. The whole ideological fabric appears to be woven from appeals to tradition, ethnicity, and historical grievances both old and new, along with a powerful set of religious-sounding references to "infidels", "idolaters", "crusaders", "holy wars", "sacred soil", "enemies of Islam", "the party of God", and "the great Satan".
>
> But this religious vocabulary hides violent Islamism's true nature as a modern totalitarian challenge to both traditional Islam and modern democracy....[32]

Specifically, the authors describe Qutbism as "Leninism in Islamist dress":

> ... Qutb's brand of Islamism was informed by his knowledge of both the Marxist and Fascist critiques of capitalism and representative democracy. He called for a monolithic state ruled by a single party of Islamic rebirth. Like Mawdudi and various Western totalitarians, he identified his own society (in his case, contemporary Muslim polities) as among the enemies that a virtuous, ideologically self-conscious, vanguard minority would have to fight by any means necessary, including violent revolution, so that a new and perfectly just society might arise. His ideal society was a classless one where the "selfish individual" of liberal democracies would be banished and the "exploitation of man by man" would be abolished. God alone would govern it through the implementation of Islamic law (Shari'a). This was Leninism in Islamist dress".[33]

Mawdudi's Islamism

Sayyid Mawdudi (1903–1979) was a Pakistani writer, one of the most influential and prolific of contemporary Muslim thinkers, and one of the chief architects of an Islamic reawakening in the twentieth century. He viewed Islam as a revolutionary force and as a way of life and a total system that has an innate tendency to activate and reinvigorate from within. Aware of the impact of ideological challenges of the Capitalist, Marxist and Fascist ideologies of the 19th century, Sayyid Mawdudi saw the Capitalist and the Socialist ideologies in the twentieth century as a failure

[32] Ladan Boroumand and Roya Boroumand, Terror, Islam, and Democracy, *Journal of Democracy* 13 (2) (2002) 5–20.

[33] Ladan Boroumand and Roya Boroumand, Terror, Islam, and Democracy, *Journal of Democracy* 13 (2) (2002) 5–20.

in answering to man's economic, social and political problems. He offered an alternative, Islamic, ideological framework and elaborated his ideas on political, economic and social dimensions of Islam in his writings. By the late 1950s he was an internationally known person speaking for Islam as the ideology of the future. Mawdudi's goal was to wage jihad until the whole natural universe is brought under the rule of Islam. He wrote:

> Islam wants the whole earth and does not content itself with only a part thereof. It wants and requires the entire inhabited world. It does not want this in order that one nation dominates the earth and monopolizes its sources of wealth, after having taken them away from one or more other nations. No, Islam wants and requires the earth in order that the human race altogether can enjoy the concept and practical program of human happiness, by means of which God has honored Islam and put it above the other religions and laws. In order to realize this lofty desire, Islam wants to employ all forces and means that can be employed for bringing about a universal all-embracing revolution. It will spare no efforts for the achievement of this supreme objective. This far-reaching struggle that continuously exhausts all forces and this employment of all possible means are called jihad.[34]

Over the past five decades, Mawdudi's ideology has played a significant role in the history and politics of Pakistan, India, Bangladesh and Sri Lanka in south Asian and Muslim communities of the Persian Gulf as well as in Muslim communities of Great Britain and North America. The Qutbism from Egypt and the contemporary international terrorism led by bin Laden have all found their ideological roots in Mawdudi's Islamism and jihad.

As Haneef James Oliver writes, bin Laden, al-Qaeda and all jihad revivalists who are oriented toward political activism are not "Wahhabees", but are, rather, adherents of a newly arisen sect, Qutbism. The Qutbists are opposed to the creed and scholars of "Wahhabism". "Wahhabee" scholars have refuted the political ideologies of Qutbism and regarded them as being based on Western revolutionary ideologies such as those of Marx and Engels, and not Islam. The "Wahhabee" scholars have been very careful about advising the Muslim youth to stay away from these so-called Jihads, because they are fought under unknown banners and much confusion and tribulation arises from them, because they are not established upon correct Shari'ah (the code of law based on the Quran) principles.[35]

Nevertheless, Islamic fundamentalism and Islamism ideas strongly appeal to the Muslim world where the vast majority of the populations are living in poverty, with consequent class tensions, that have led to various social and political movements that are widespread. Economic stagnation, social turbulence and disorder are pervasive throughout the Muslim world. The Western world, on the other hand,

---

[34] Quoted from Rudolph Peters, *Jihad in Classical and Modern Islam*, Marcus Wiener Publishers, Princeton, NJ, 1996, p. 128.

[35] Haneef James Oliver, *The 'Wahhabi' Myth, Dispelling Prevalent Fallacies and the Fictitious Link With Bin Laden*, TROID Publications, 2004, p. 103.

has embraced rapid technological, social, and economic transformations that have brought them unprecedented prosperity in the post cold-war era. The sharp contrasts that have resulted make Islamic fundamentalism attractive due to the blame they identified with flaws in Muslim societies that resulted from the influx of Western ideas. The message of revitalizing Islam by purging Western influences from the Muslim lands, combined with bin Laden's advocacy of jihad against the US and its allies, has resonated even with Muslims who do not share these extreme views and ideologies. In fact, Islamic fundamentalism has been used by international terrorists as a powerful ideological weapon to promote anti-American hatred and to advocate violent jihad against enemies in order to pursue an ambitious, but impossible, political agenda, directed to bringing the whole natural universe under the rule of Islam.

10.8. The American Invasion of Iraq

In 2001 the Iraqi Prime Minister renewed Iraq's claim that Kuwait was part of Iraq, and a few days later an Iraqi border patrol fired across the border into Kuwait. Four months later, however, at the Arab Summit in Beirut, Iraq and Kuwait announced an agreement resolving their disputes. It was highly doubtful, however, that Iraq would give up its Kuwait ambitions. In his 2002 State of the Union address, President George W. Bush labeled the regimes of North Korea, Iran and Iraq an "axis of evil" that threatened world peace. He pointed out: "By seeking weapons of mass destruction, these regimes pose a grave and growing danger. They could provide these arms to terrorists, giving them the means to match their hatred. They could attack our allies or attempt to blackmail the United States. In any of these cases, the price of indifference would be catastrophic".

The Bush Doctrine

In a subsequent series of speeches, the President articulated America's strategic security policy for the post-cold-war and sole-superpower world, which is now dubbed the "Bush Doctrine". This security policy calls for unilateral preemptive American strikes against nations found to be a threat to the United States because of their developing or stockpiling weapons of mass destruction. In his speech at the Graduation Exercise of the United States Military Academy at West Point on June 1, 2002, the President defined America's purpose, the nature of present threats to the United States and the world, and the necessity to launch preemptive strikes against terrorists, tyrants and rogue states in the following words,

> "We fight, as we always fight, for a just peace — a peace that favors human liberty. We will defend the peace against threats from terrorists and tyrants. We will preserve the peace by building good relations among the great powers. And we will extend the peace by encouraging free and open societies on every continent. . . .

> ... In defending the peace, we face a threat with no precedent.... The gravest danger to freedom lies at the perilous crossroads of radicalism and technology. When the spread of chemical and biological and nuclear weapons, along with ballistic missile technology — when that occurs, even weak states and small groups could attain a catastrophic power to strike great nations. Our enemies have declared this very intention, and have been caught seeking these terrible weapons. They want the capability to blackmail us, or to harm us, or to harm our friends — and we will oppose them with all our power....
> ... But new threats also require new thinking. Deterrence — the promise of massive retaliation against nations — means nothing against shadowy terrorist networks with no nation or citizens to defend. Containment is not possible when unbalanced dictators with weapons of mass destruction can deliver those weapons on missiles or secretly provide them to terrorist allies. We cannot defend America and our friends by hoping for the best. We cannot put our faith in the word of tyrants, who solemnly sign non-proliferation treaties, and then systemically break them. If we wait for threats to fully materialize, we will have waited too long.
> ... Yet the war on terror will not be won on the defensive. We must take the battle to the enemy, disrupt his plans, and confront the worst threats before they emerge. In the world we have entered, the only path to safety is the path of action. And this nation will act.
> ... And our security will require all Americans to be forward-looking and resolute, to be ready for preemptive action when necessary to defend our liberty and to defend our lives....

The "Bush Doctrine" laid out the basis for a US led invasion of Iraq. A military attack on Iraq was a possibility that had been under open debate and gained broad support from the American public and media. In October 2002, the United States Congress, both the House and the Senate, approved by a wide margin a resolution that gave President Bush the authority to wage war on Iraq should he choose to do so. Iraq was accused of having chemical and biological weapons, and developing unmanned aerial vehicles (UAVs) capable of delivering chemical and biological warfare agents, which could threaten Iraq's neighbors as well as American forces in the Persian Gulf. Iraq was also found in "material breach" of its commitment under UN Resolution 1441 on Iraq's disarmament of weapons of mass destruction.

This build up continued for some time and on March 17, 2003, President Bush delivered a final ultimatum, "Saddam Hussein and his sons must leave Iraq within 48 hours. Their refusal to do so will result in military conflict, commenced at a time of our choosing. For their own safety, all foreign nationals — including journalists and inspectors — should leave Iraq immediately".[36] The US military attack began in the next two days. US forces seized Baghdad in only two weeks from the start of invasion, and coalition forces occupied Saddam's birthplace, Kirkuk, and the northern part of the country. Without firing a single shot, US forces captured

[36] Remarks by the President in "*Address to the Nation, For Immediate Release*", Office of the Press Secretary March 17, 2003, http://www.whitehouse.gov/news/releases.

Saddam Hussein near Tikrit on December 13, 2003, and Saddam's regime was removed and completely destroyed. The US military invasion of Iraq lasted 43 days, from March 20th through May 1st, 2005, and was followed by a US "occupation" for about two months, from May 2nd to June 29th, 2003.

Iraq's Rocky Road to Democracy

Iraq's interim government was appointed by the United Nations on June 1, 2004, after consultation with the US-led administration and Iraqi leaders, and took over authority from US occupiers on June 30, 2004. Since then, Iraq has been in a transition period to restore Iraqi's sovereignty. The nation's first multi-party free election in more than 50 years was successfully carried out on January 31, 2005 to elect 275 members of a national assembly. The assembly, which has replaced the interim Iraqi government, debated a new national constitution. The current constitution of Iraq was approved by a ratification vote on 15 October 2005. In December 2005, elections for a full-term parliament were held leading to the formation of a full-fledged Iraqi government. Iraq's new unity government sworn in on May 20, 2006 with Shiites predominant on the list of Cabinet members for the government's new four-year term, reflecting the Muslim sect's strong showing in the December 15 parliamentary election and their large population in Iraq — an estimated 60 percent. Despite the failure to fill three ministry posts because of political disputes, a large majority of Iraqis declared it a "historic day for Iraq".

The situation in Iraq continues to pose many challenges for the Iraqi people and its new government. Attacks on US-led forces, Iraqi security forces, Iraqi officials and Iraqi civilians continue unabated. A "World Public Opinion" poll in January 2006[37] revealed that an extraordinary 77% of Sunni Iraqis still strongly support attacks on US-led forces, but only 9% of Shiite Iraqis strongly support such attack and so do 8% of Kurd Iraqis. Regarding the current situation in Iraq, the poll shows that "The majority of Iraqis overall view the recent parliamentary elections as valid, are optimistic that their country is going in the right direction and feel that the overthrow of Saddam Hussein has been worth the cost. Sunnis, on the other hand, overwhelmingly reject the validity of the elections, see the country going in the wrong direction, and regret the overthrow of Saddam". Iraq is badly in need of finding a way to integrate Iraq's Sunni population into the country's political process and to avoid a potential civil war. The main problem is to provide security for Iraqi civilians by reducing and controlling incidents of everyday deadly violence, explosions and attacks.

The path to Iraqi freedom and democracy has been rocky. Islamist terrorist groups have used Iraq as a training and recruitment ground for terrorists and have

[37] "*What the Iraqi Public Wants — A WorldPublicOpinion.org Poll*" Conducted by the Program On International Policy Attitudes (PIPA), January 31, 2006.

battled against the presence of US, Israeli and allied military forces in the Muslim world. A new wave of terrorism known also as "Iraqi insurgency" has grown in size and complexity and has continued to the present. Insurgents increased their attacks during key events such as the Iraqi interim government transfer of power, Ramadan and the January 2005 election. The primary targets of insurgents include Coalition Forces, Iraqi Security Forces, Iraqi interim government officials, and foreign diplomats and nationals of non-government organizations and contractors. Approximately 80% of all insurgent attacks occur in Sunni-dominated central Iraq, while the Kurdish north and the Shiite south remain relatively calm. Loyalists of the former-regime Sunni Arabs are thought to be responsible for more of the attacks against US forces. The disbanded Iraqi Army, including about 40 000 former members of the Republican Guard, are without any income but still armed and ready to kill, and they have become easy sources for recruiting militants from former regime loyalists and terrorist groups.

Islamist terrorist groups have claimed responsibility for insurgent attacks and advocated guerrilla war against the Coalition Forces. Foreign nationals from Syria, Saudi Arabia, Egypt, Jordan and Iran have infiltrated Iraqi borders to join in the insurgency with arms and other supplies continuously flowing into Iraq. Abu Musab al-Zarqawi (1966–2006) became one of the top Islamist terrorists, who organized insurgent explorations and attacks in Iraq. Zarqawi was a Jordanian terrorist who was convicted in absentia in Jordan and sentenced to death for plotting the attack on the Radisson SAS Hotel in Amman, Jordan, that killed Israeli and American tourists in 2001.

On October 21, 2004, Zarqawi officially announced his allegiance to al-Qaeda. Al-Jazeera (with main headquarter in Qatar), the largest and most controversial Arabic News Channel in the Middle East, broadcast an audiotape of bin Laden in December 2004, calling Zarqawi "the prince of al-Qaeda in Iraq" and asked "all our organization brethren to listen to him and obey him in his good deeds".[38] Zarqawi was then considered as holding significant power because of his heightened visibility as a leader of the insurgency against the US military and Iraqi government. The US government offered a $25 million reward for information leading to his capture, the same amount offered for the capture of Osama bin Laden. On June 7, 2006, Zarqawi was killed near the city of Baquba, Iraq, by a US air strike. On June 15, 2006, Egyptian Islamic Jihad militant Abu Ayyub al-Masri succeeded Zarqawi as head of al-Qaeda in Iraq and the Iraqi insurgency. Iraqi guerrilla warfare continues in the post-war Iraq, and suicide attacks and car bombs are near daily occurrences in Baghdad.

Even though no Persian Gulf nation openly supports the US invasion, they have assisted the operations of US and Coalition forces in Iraq by allowing over-flights

[38] Purported bin Laden tape endorses al-Zarqawi. Speaker also calls for boycott of Iraq's elections Monday, December 27, 2004 http://edition.cnn.com/2004/WORLD/meast/12/27/binladen.tape/.

and the stationing of thousands of sailors, troops and combat aircraft in Bahrain, Oman, and Saudi Arabia. Kuwait has hosted the vast majority of US and UK ground forces and was hit by a hostile missile from Iraq during US military operations. Qatar has hosted the US Central Command Center throughout the war and has been home to 1 400 US and British military personnel. Qatar and the United States also upgraded the al-Ubaid airbase in Qatar, which played a key role in the war and will replace Saudi Arabia's airbase as the future hub of US Persian Gulf operations.

This US war led to a "military victory" in less than a month, reflecting the absence of any state capable of challenging conventional US military power. The war and its intended consequence of building a new democratic Iraq under US guidance has changed the balance of power in the Persian Gulf region. It removed and eliminated the former Iraqi threat to neighboring states, especially Iran, and allowed the United States to become a guarantor of Persian Gulf security. The US effort is intended to increase the regional stability and opportunity for social and economic reform, development and cooperation with the rest of the world. A liberated democratic new state of Iraq is also anticipated to have far-reaching impacts on the peace process, help resolve the Arab–Israeli conflict, and promote peace and prosperity of the Arab world in particular and the Muslim world in general.

The effort to promote freedom and democracy, peace and stability in the Middle-East region has cost the US a very high price. A study by the Institute for Policy Studies and Foreign Policy published in Focus[39] reveals that US military casualties have been high in the recent Iraq war, especially in the "transition" period. As of March 29, 2007, 3 245 US soldiers, 134 British soldiers have died in Iraq. 24 314 US soldiers had been wounded. In addition, there have been an estimated 390 civilian contractors, missionaries, and civilian worker from US and other countries died in Iraq. For the time period from January 2005 to March 2007, fatalities of 5 089 Iraqi security force and 26 797 Iraqi civilians have been reported; the actual totals for Iraqi deaths are much higher than the numbers recorded.[40]

In terms of economic costs, the US congress has approved of $151.1 billion for covering the expense of the Iraq war, and anticipated an additional supplemental appropriation of $60 billion in 2005. In his 2004 State of the Union Speech, President Bush also said, "I will ask Congress for $350 million to support Palestinian political, economic and security reforms". As reported by Sean Gonsalves,[41] ac-

[39] A Failed "Transition": The Mounting Costs of the Iraq War, *A Study by the Institute for Policy Studies and Foreign Policy in Focus*, http://www.ips-dc.org/iraq/failedtransition/index.htm.

[40] *Iraq Coalition Casualty Count*, http://icasualties.org/oif/.

[41] Sean Gonsalves, *This is Your Bill for the War, 05/25/04*, http://www.informationclearinghouse.info/article6253.htm.

cording to Doug Henwood, the author of "After the New Economy", $4 000 is the amount that each US household will have to fork over in taxes to foot the Iraq occupation bill. Henwood says,

> "I feel a little callous about talking about the economic impact of the war in Iraq, which seems like an afterthought next to the human toll. But at a time when civilian budgets are being cut at every level, when clinics are closing and professors at our public universities have to pay for their own photocopying because there's allegedly not enough money, it's amazing how much we're spending".

Henwood pegs the military costs in Iraq to date at about $143 billion, with the tab rising to $4 billion to $5 billion a month. Reconstruction has cost about $20 billion so for, with another $50 billion to $100 billion still needed, Henwood reports. "If the occupation goes on for three years, which is what the military pundits say is likely, the total bill could come to $362 billion. Add to that an estimated 0.5 percent knocked off GDP growth because of high oil prices, and that's another $50 billion", he says. Add it all up, and the bill comes to nearly $4000 per household, not including interest. "I wonder how people would react if they got a bill from Washington for that amount", he says.

Indeed, American families have sacrificed lives of their sons and daughters in wars in Afghanistan and Iraq. The American people have shouldered not only the heavy financial and economic costs of supporting these wars, but have also carried out additional security and social costs associated with the 364 thousand reserve troops and National Guard soldiers who have been called to military service since the beginning of the wars in Iraq and Afghanistan. As President Bush said,

> "We are in Iraq to achieve a result: a country that is democratic, representative of all its people, at peace with its neighbors, and able to defend itself. And when that result is achieved, our men and women serving in Iraq will return home with the honor they have earned".[42]

The continuing deterioration in the Iraqi situation has caused great and growing concerns by Americans. The catastrophic fall in the polls for the President has caused the collapse of public support for the war in Iraq that could fatally weaken the Bush administration. The Iraq Study Group, also known as the Baker–Hamilton Commission, was appointed on March 15, 2006 for assessing the situation in Iraq and the US-led Iraqi War and making policy recommendations. On December 6, 2006, this bipartisan panel released a 142-page report — "The Iraq Study Group Report. The Way Forward, A New Approach". Among all the 79 recommendations, the Iraq Study Group has strongly urged a large pull back of American troops in Iraq and launching a diplomatic and political push to hold a "grave and deteriorating" crisis in Iraq.

---

[42] *Text of State of the Union, Washington*, February 2, 2005. http://www.washingtonpost.com/wp-dyn/politics/administration/state of the union.

President Bush rejected most recommendations of the Baker–Hamilton report, including the idea of negotiating with Iran and Syria and the idea of troop withdrawal from Iraq. In his evening address to the nation on January 10, 2007, President Bush adopted a new strategy that, he expects, will change America's course in Iraq and in the fight against terror. "... So America will change our strategy to help the Iraqis carry out their campaign to put down sectarian violence and bring security to the people of Baghdad. This will require increasing American force levels. So I have committed more than 20 000 additional American troops to Iraq. ..."[43]

The President also admitted:

> The challenge playing out across the broader Middle East is more than a military conflict. It is the decisive ideological struggle of our time. On one side are those who believe in freedom and moderation. On the other side are extremists who kill the innocent, and have declared their intention to destroy our life. In the long run, the most realistic way to protect the American people is to provide a hopeful alternative to the hateful ideology of the enemy, by advancing liberty across a troubled region. ..."[44]

"A hopeful alternative", however, has not been identified in the president's speech. Instead, the new strategy requires a new US troop surge in Iraq which could result in more war and violence in Iraq in the short run. This new strategy has gained aggressive support from some Republican Senators like John McCain, while congressional Democrats support various troop withdrawal proposals that would force a redeployment of US forces out of Iraq in 2008. President Bush says he will veto the bill if it contains the withdrawal deadlines, which have been approved by narrow margins and pretty much along party lines in both the House and Senate.

Iraq has been a battleground for more than four thousands years — from the Babylonian Empire (dating back to around 2400 BC) to the present day. From the historical background provided in this part, Part III of this book, one can see that Afghanistan and Iraq are not isolated states, but are in the heartland of the broader Muslim world. What happens in these two states concerns not only people in the Muslim world; it also impacts Muslim communities in every other corner of the world as well. Democracy and freedom in Afghanistan and Iraq may not root out the revolutionary Islamist force and stop it from spreading all over the world, but democracy and freedom can provide a new impetus along with opportunities for Muslims to revitalize their Islamic civilization. They can also help to generate better living standards for all Muslims and promote the establishment of peaceful and harmonic relationship with non-Islamic civilizations.

To achieve that result requires not only making unusual sacrifices but also adopting right approaches. The difficult experiences of the US in the present Iraq

[43] President's Address to the Nation, January 10, 2007.

[44] Ibid.

War clearly demonstrate that the conventional military methods cannot guarantee a victory in building a unified and democratic nation and in fighting guerrilla warfare. A comprehensive strategy is needed that takes into account a broad range of factors, including characteristics of Muslim populations and economies, Islamic religion and history as well as Muslim culture and tradition. This book has provided a rich array of statistics and materials that could help policy makers and ordinary criticizes gain a better understanding of the dynamics and complexity of the Muslim world. Some examples of such non-military approaches have been given in the previous Preface of this book, and more are possible.

Summary of Chapter 10

This chapter provides an overview of the modern challenges to the Muslim world staring with the early confrontation between the Arab world and Israel in 1948 and ending with the ongoing American invasion of Iraq in 2003.

The conflict between Israel and the Arab world is one major cause of contemporary struggles between the Muslim and Western worlds. Religious differences are not the main cause of this conflict. It is the claim to a piece of land called Palestine by both Israel and the Arab world that have frequently caused armed confrontations and civil revolts and conflict. The major Arab nations like Egypt, Syria, Jordan, Lebanon and Iraq have engaged in wars against Israel, and Muslim countries all over the world have supported the PLO (Palestine Liberation Organization) in their fight with Israel. The world's superpowers of the time, the Soviet Union, the United States, Britain and France, have all been involved. For over half a century this confrontation has achieved almost nothing. The situation of Palestinians today is worse than that of fifty years ago and the enduring violent Arab–Israel confrontation has intensified anti-Semitism across the Muslim world.

Troubles of the Muslim world are also reflected by the armed conflicts between Muslim countries and with their neighboring countries. Contemporary examples include the eight-year Iraq–Iran war in which more than one million people were killed and millions were made refugees. There was no winner at the end of this war and none of the disputed issues had been resolved. Iraq's invasion of Kuwait showed a split in the Muslim world with Jordan, Sudan and Libya supporting the Iraqi aggression and others against it. The US-led international coalition force pushed Iraqi occupiers out of Kuwait. In a Muslim-to-non Muslim conflict, Pakistan has engaged in a series of armed conflicts with the neighboring state of India for the disputed territory of Kashmir. Since both Pakistan and India have developed nuclear weapons, their confrontations pose the gravest threat to South Asia. Although intense mediation efforts by the USA and other global powers have brought the two sides to the table for peaceful negotiations, the disputes and conflicts between them have not been resolved.

The continuous global Islamic militant movement, starting with the jihad against the Soviet Union invasion and occupation of Afghanistan in 1979, has turned into international terrorism attacks against the USA and the Western world. Numerous large scale and well coordinated brutal terrorist attacks have occurred in both the Western and Muslim worlds, killing thousands of men, women and children. Osama bin Laden and his terrorist network "al-Qaeda" are responsible for murdering large numbers of civilians across the globe — non-Muslim and Muslim alike. In retaliation the US and Western allies launched air strikes on Afghanistan in 2001, shutting down all the terrorist training camps and overthrowing the Taliban government that had supported them. The US-led invasion of Iraq in 2003 was another major endeavor carried out under aegis of the "War on Terrorism". Military victories in these undertakings, however, represent only a preliminary success in the war on terror. Osama bin Laden is still at large and al-Qaeda remains capable of inflicting high-casualty terrorist attacks worldwide.

Summary of Part III

This part, Part III of this book, presents a retrospective of heritages of the Muslim world in three stages: (1) the creation of Islam and the Golden Age of Islamic empires, (2) the declining Muslim world and its colonization, and (3) contemporary challenges and struggles among the Muslim countries and with the outside world.

Islamic history brings to mind the glorious conquest, its swift expansion, and the superior Islamic civilization created by ancient Muslims in contrast to the colonial humiliation, constant confrontations and wars, and the persistent poverty suffered by generations of contemporary Muslims. This retrospection will help readers gain a better understanding of Muslim countries around the world: their past, present and possible future.

Combining this history with materials and analyses of the demographic transformations and economic interconnections of Muslim countries with the rest of the world, which we have presented in Parts I and II of this book, we may come to a vision that the Muslim world is now at a critical inflection point or at the cross road of the human history: (1) to join global communities for peace and prosperity and for revitalizing their ancient glories or (2) to continue fighting with each other and with the Western world and to ignore their huge internal population and economic problems. That is the choice for Muslims to make and for the world to help them make a right choice for the benefits of both Muslims and non-Muslims in the world.

References

9/11 Commission, Staff Statement #16, The National Commission on Terrorist Attacks Upon the United States, 16 June 2004, submitted for publication.

Adherents.com, Major religions of the world ranked by number of adherents, http://www.adherents.com/Religions.

Andrabi, T., Das, J., Khwaja, A.J., Zajonc, T., Religious School Enrollment in Pakistan: A Look at the Data, Faculty Research Working Papers Series, RWP05-024, John F. Kennedy School of Government, Harvard University, March 2005.

Bush G.W. (2003). Address to the nation, for immediate release. *Office of the Press Secretary* 17 March, http://www.whitehouse.gov/news/releases.

Canadian Society of Muslims, Muslim Population Statistics, http://muslim-canada.org/index.html.

New Columbia Encyclopedia. Columbia Univ. Press, 1975.

Columbia Encyclopedia. Columbia Univ. Press, 1993.

The UnjustMedia.Com, When Propaganda Backfires, Nigeria, http://www.theunjustmedia.com/Propaganda.

Daalder, I.H. (2004). The warning in Spain's election, 18 March, 2004, http://www.americanprogress.org.

Daily Times of Pakistan (2003). *Unique Hafiz-e-Quran Boy Fascinates Reception, staff report* 10 November, http://www.dailytimes.com.pk.

Davidson, L. (1998). *Islamic Fundamentalism*. Greenwood Press.

de Borchgrave A. (2003). Saudi mea culpa. *The Washington Times* 16 July.

Federal Research Division, SAUDI ARABIA—A Country Study, The Library of Congress: http://lcweb2.loc.gov/frd/cs/satoc.html.

Gonsalves, S., This is your bill for the war, 05/25/04, http://www.informationclearinghouse.info/article6253.htm.

Gowlett, J.A. (1984). Mental abilities of early man: A look at some hard evidence. In: Foley, R.A. (Ed.), *Hominid Evolution and Community Ecology*. New York: Academic Press.

EIA (2004). International Energy Oulook 2004, Energy Information Administration.

EIA (2005). International Energy Annual 2003, Energy Information Administration, the US Department of Energy.

EIA (July 2005). International Energy Outlook 2005, Energy Information Administration, the US Department of Energy.

ICG (The International Crisis Group), Pakistan: Madrasas, Extremism and the Military, Executive Summary and Recommendations ICG Asia Report No. 36, 29 July 2002.

Institute for Policy Studies and Foreign Policy in Focus, A Failed Transition: The Mounting Costs of the Iraq War, http://www.ips-dc.org/iraq/failedtransition/index.htm.

Iraq Coalition Casualty Count, http://icasualties.org/oif/.

IRIN news, "Pakistan: Debating Islam and Family Planning", UN Office for the Coordination of Humanitarian Affairs, Islamabad, 20 May 2005, news, http://www.irinnews.org/report.

Jansen, G.H. (1979). *Militant Islam*. Harper & Row Publishers.

Kozmetsky, G. and Piyu, Y. (2000). *Embracing the Global Demographic Transformation, 1950–2050*, an IC2 Institute Monograph. University of Texas.

Kozmetsky, G. and Piyu, Y. (2005). *The Economic Transformation of the United States, 1950–2000*. Purdue Univ. Press. p. 55.

Ladan, B. and Boroumand, R. (2002). Terror, Islam, and Democracy. *J. Democracy* **13.2**, 5–20.

LaFree, G. (1999). Declining violent crime rates in the 1990s: Predicting Crime booms and busts. *Annu. Rev. Soc.* **25**, 145–168.

Lewis, B. (2002). *What Went Wrong? Western Impact and Middle Eastern Response*. Oxford Univ. Press.

Madawi, A.-R. (2002). *A History of Saudi Arabia*. Cambridge Univ. Press.

Mahathir bin, M. (2003). Speech on the 10th Session of the Islamic Summit Conference at the Putrajaya Convention Centre on 16 October 2003, canibuscentral.com/forum/lofiversion/index.php/t28485.html.

Nazeer, A., Modern issues in Islamic education. Part II, posted in the website of the IRFI, http://www.irfi.org/articles/.

Nazeer, A., Why do people call us terrorists? Posted in the website of the IRFI (Islamic Research Foundation International, Inc.), http://www.irfi.org/articles/.

Nazeer, A., Modern issues in Islamic education, posted by Islamic Research Foundation International, Inc. in the website: http://www.irfi.org.

OECD/IEA (2002). World Energy Outlook 2002, the International Energy Agency.

Oliver, H.J. (2004). *The 'Wahhabi' Myth, Dispelling Prevalent Fallacies and the Fictitious Link With Bin Laden*. TROID Publications.

PIPA (2006). What the Iraqi Public Wants — A WorldPublicOpinion.org Poll, Conducted by the Program On International Policy Attitudes (PIPA), 31 January.

Peters, R. (1996). *Jihad in Classical and Modern Islam*. Princeton, N.J.: Marcus Wiener Publishers.

Ragab, N. (1995). The record set straight: Women in Islam have rights. (Duke University) 16 November 1995, http://www.jannah.org/sisters/noha.html.

Rostow, W.W. (1990). *Theorists of Economic Growth from David Hume to the Present*. Oxford Univ. Press.

Shahar, Y., Tracing bin Laden's Money, an ICT article, 21 September 2001, http://www.ict.org.il/articles.

Smith, A. (1993). In Sutherland, K. (Ed.), *An Inquiry into the Nature and Causes of the Wealth of Nations*. Oxford Univ. Press.

Stalinsky, S. (2002). MEMRI Special Report—Saudi Arabia, 20 December, 2002, No. 12, http://www.memri.org/release.

Syed Tauqir Hussain Shah (2004). Pakistan's Madrasahs: Consequences for Democracy and Free Society: Some Public Policy Options, Proposal for International Policy Fellowship-2004-OSI.

Text of State of the Union, Washington, 2 February 2005, http://www.washingtonpost.com/wp-dyn/politics/administration/state_of_the_union.

United Nations Population Division. World Urbanization Prospects, the 2001 Revision.

United Nations Population Division, 2004. World Population Prospects: The 2002 Revision, Vol. II: The Sex and Age Distribution of Population.

Wikipedia, Balfour Declaration, 1917, http://www.nationmaster.com/encyclopedia.

Wikipedia, Crusader, http://www.nationmaster.com/encyclopedia.

Wikipedia, Seljuk Turks, http://www.nationmaster.com/encyclopedia.

World Bank, The World Development Indicators, 2000–2004.

Worth R. (2001). The deep intellectual roots of Islamic terror. *The New York Times* 13 October.

Index